Sir W. Penn grew up in the 60s and 70s. Before Rock and Roll had really taken hold, he had met Jim Hendix and Syd Barrett, the original vocalists for the trippy group from England, Pink Floyd. He also met Mr. David Lee Roth back in 1964. Read further to unravel the mysteries of life and so much more!

I dedicate the writing of my life story to all the musicians, every music fan, and to every other being that ever exists, on this earth or otherwise.

Sir W. Penn

I WAS A 12-YEAR-OLD ROCK STAR...

Seer, Visionary, Inventor, Knower Of Truths, Lover

AUSTIN MACAULEY PUBLISHERS™

LONDON * CAMBRIDGE * NEW YORK * SHARJAH

Ordering Information
Quantity sales: Special discounts are available on quantity purchases by corporations, associations, and others. For details, contact the publisher at the address below.

Publisher's Cataloging-in-Publication data
Penn, Sir W.
I Was a 12-Year-Old Rock Star...

ISBN 9798889104230 (Paperback)
ISBN 9798889104247 (Hardback)
ISBN 9798889104254 (ePub e-book)

Library of Congress Control Number: 2024901850

www.austinmacauley.com/us

First Published 2024
Austin Macauley Publishers LLC
40 Wall Street, 33rd Floor, Suite 3302
New York, NY 10005
USA

mail-usa@austinmacauley.com
+1 (646) 5125767

Table of Contents

Prologue

To come to terms with my overall greatness and overwhelming superiority, we need to go back to the beginning of my family's existence on this continent. Not only will this allow you to more directly gain an appreciation for the complexity and totality of each and every single thing that I wish to offer you. You as well will gain a fuller perspective of the message that I wholeheartedly bring. It is one filled with promise, truth, and a vision for the future with a bright, fantastic, and brilliantly enriching world.

I proclaim to you here and now, when we face a certain reality, with the armaments of virtue, and a steeled passion for excellence, a new awakening will come to each and every one of us. A world brimming with a glorious vibrancy and a brilliant brightness shall embrace you warmly. There shall be presented unto each and every one of us, a future so full of promise that life will brim with a vibrant display of overwhelming satisfaction.

I speak to you now about a future with a fantastically rich and superbly wonderful world. When we face certain realities with the armaments of virtue, and a steeled passion for excellence, our vectors of fulfillment do truly align with the heavens.

One may begin to see our very existence itself as a vast and boundless, never ending, and beautifully bountiful dreamscape. Yes indeedy Ms. McReedy, I speak of a world that holds an eternity of tomorrows filled with a joyful sense of glee, and prosperity. I so sincerely do proclaim, once you have finished the entire offering before you, all that is left is your commitment to greatness.

Although your newfound understanding may cause you to question your very own existence, as long as we are one, as long as we are strong, as long as we persevere, victory shall be ours. Alas, so much of this glory, this profound ecstasy, consists of emotional and psychological wealth, rather than the foibles, fancies, or god-rotten lucre of so many foolish and jaded fantastical dreamers. You will, once you've uncovered the truths of who you really are, bask in the delight of such simple pleasures as a cool walk at night, a brisk bike ride in the morning, or even a secret and oh so slim dip, in a casual and quiet pool, of inviting and shimmering liquid.

Once one has had the opportunity to come to terms with my spiritual message, and then in ascending to your very own personal throne of a newfound ecstasy, life will become love. With a profound and spiritually grandiose awareness, the truths of our very existence shall beckon forth, revealing the sweetness and certain opportunities that life in and of itself, do so readily offer. A freedom and vitality shall adorn thee in its escalating exuberance, and a titillating sense of newfound wonder shall be yours to revel in.

If you will join in with me then, and pull in the corners, trim the edges, and modify any and all aspects of your very own persona, we will so readily begin. If after five years, a sense of total and utter satisfaction has been obtained, one may ask, "What is it then that I could work on even more so?"; "What have I possibly overlooked?" For those still searching for a personal sense of life's true meaning, go back over the book! It should be, other than any of the funny parts, a guide of what one should avoid through life. As long as one is adherent to certain principles, and keen on self-improvement, the years should so easily slip away into memories well preserved and so sweetly and deeply cherished.

To gain a deeper appreciation for who I truly am, a bit of family history is in order. In 1662, the origins of our family in this part of the world began. There were no states, no big cities, and only the small colonies. Some of these had been started by businesses types from England.

Since that may be the case here in America, that we've decided to go about things somewhat differently, we may consider that "we've won the war, but lost the battle." I mean do we truly have independence from the Royal Crown. All in all, this history of our culture exposes the mild business treachery, and coldblooded heartlessness that is indeed an un-separable part of our very human heritage.

Now back to the origins of my family on this side of the globe. My father was a man with an intelligence that was genetically enhanced. If your family roots, to such a great extent, hail from England, I feel that you too, no doubt, have an advantage when it comes to the prevalence of the main language still being utilized here in the U.S. I want to be honest about our strong family heritage on this continent.

I truly feel that if indeed your earliest ancestor does not go back at least to the 1860s you are most certainly a newcomer. Over back in England in the 1660s, there was unrest over the desire on the part of Ireland to be independent. The new plan of England's was to arrest, and ship out any of the miscreants that may now, or even at a later time, pose a problem. "Let them then plot their rebellion from the distant shores of America," is what was said.

Those English captors would set up a table in the town square, and as each man stepped forward, he had his Mac whacked off. These poor innocent fellows were told "there, now spell your name without it." As their hands trembled, barely able to hold the quill steadily, after such a hideously treacherous thing had been done unto them, they were required to complete this formal written transformation of identity. They then boarded the ship to the American Islands. This temporary slavery, which was to last for a ten-year period was known as *indentured servitu*de. It's been said back *in the day* "that they were easy on the white guys. They didn't work the white ones right to death." Yes, that was all so true. It is no exaggeration. "What doesn't kill you, makes you stronger," is indeed yet another old saying.

When I learned of the things perpetrated against those earlier folks in the Americas, a creepy feeling ran up and down my arm. With the plight of others so closely felt as my own, a sense of true appreciation maybe is all that it was. On second thought, what reached out to hurt me even more from that distant past was the fact that Barbados was actually the worst place to grow sugar cane. I actually took them a full fifty years to come to terms with that little factoid.

After the five years on Barbados had passed, five long years starting back in 1662, our forefather was given a reprieve when a farmer from Vermont bought his services for another term up north. We had been told in grade school if this type of fellow was nice enough, he would perhaps offer you maybe $2.73 or so, and an old horse just before it died. That would be to ride upon, straight out of Dodge and into your new life of freedom. Massoftwoshits, as I refer to it, was the place of our family's new life.

Within three generations my family had ironically become more English than Irish. Next a grand move would be in order. After an uncle had become a politician a symbolic move was undertaken. It was the 1823 decree of Andrew

Jackson that my family continued to adhere to with little exception. That particular ruling had made it so that no white man could cross the Mississippi without an official government permit to do business there.

Indeed then, such a grand movement was not beyond that major country dividing river, the Mississippi. My Great-Great grandad moved here to the Midwest in 1872. We all too quickly became Norwegian, German, and Polish, in that order. Within one generation, my very own grandfather was born. When he was only about 4 years old, the doctor came and, gave the harsh, cold diagnosis. Once that was performed, he would carefully leave the residence, and go, and sanitize himself. That was all that could be done when dealing with TB.

Great grandpa went from home to home in an attempt to get the two boys, and their older sister, safely away. Door after door, to home after home he and my grandfather finally moved. It was heartbreaking. Those families took the girl and the younger boy, but apparently our grandfather was not quite cute enough. He would end up staying at home after all. He got to sit in the death chair just outside of his mother's room in the hallway. That was a safe enough distance from the doorway. He could to talk to her just a little through the wall, or opened door that way. The memory of these visits would be all that remained after death's hand came harshly knocking.

The town shunned them now. Great grandpa was let go from work, and not allowed to return. The three children were sent to the orphanage. After growing up at that place, grandpa chose the more immediately gratifying work of farm labor. At sixteen, a real man could 'drop-out', then work hardcore on the orphanage farm. Once he was old enough, he joined the U.S. Navy. By the picture we have of him you can see that he apparently stole the army's goat as a prank.

The President was so overwhelmed by his bravado, so well awed by the sheer grandiose audacity of this impishly scheming act, that he decided to make the goat the official Navy mascot thereafter. I just recently learned from an uncle that all of his photos of Grandpa involved an army outfit. Was that an undercover disguise, used to pull of such a stunt? Perhaps he felt patriotic and re-upped with the other branch. Maybe he had failed to save enough cash to live on his own. Oh well!

After some deep recollection I remember now the actuality of it all. It was the way his handsome looking self was viewed in town. Any man that young and handsome should be risking his life for his fellow patriots it was felt by those enviously staring. I believe that he managed to return the goat to it's proper holding as well. According to mother who received the stories, he went through some barbed wire advancing and moving forward. All around lay the bodies of his brethren. His life expired within minutes of this final look up to heaven, and that dramatic retelling.

He, back in the day, just after his double military stint, was later married with two boys. His first wife took ill, and was gone so soon as well. Grandpa later managed to pick up a waitress and to take her as his wife. After re-marrying, things went well for a while. Grandpa had an old Indian motorcycle to prove it. He would also drive around with a small gun in his boot, although that was for the coyotes, and wolves, and any 'dog-oaties' as well. Since motorized cycles were a newer thing back then, it wouldn't be surprising to have one of these beasts rush you from the brush and try to bite at your leg.

If something was moving along on the open road at a good gait, why it just had to be dinner to them, right? Grandpa would pull out the gun, and BAM! No more confusion there, Captain Bucky, if I do say so myself. Just after father was born, the stock market crashed. Grandpa now out of work, drove around on his cycle until he came across an old rock rabble, weed eaten scrawny patch of dirt. He talked his way into having the family move into the hired hand's house.

Just a bunch of boards hammered together with nails was all that it was. No insulation. No central heating. I believe they had indoor plumbing in the kitchen, as far as that goes, though father did mention the Sears catalogues. There in the old outhouse you could look, and tear. Look, and tear. Wipe and look. Wipe and tear. Tear and look. Pops also said one day that he had to go so bad that he went running to the door. It was so close to the curtain call, if you know what I'm saying.

He had had his mouth wide open believing that would help him make it to the old outdoor john even faster. Just then, a fly flew in. Into his mouth I mean, not the john's. Well, the thing squirmed, and struggled. Then gulp! Yep, it went down without much more than a whimper and a buzz. So, this older farm residence other than the kitchen had not much else in the way of modern accommodations. There was an old radio, and a Brownie camera, and that was it. Dad said it was fun when it was cold in that old place, because they all would camp out together in the living room, to be close to the wood burning stove in the kitchen.

It wouldn't be until Father was finally in high school that he once again felt left out. Family rule number one on a farm: the smart one goes in and studies, the regular brother gets to stay out and do farm work. He claimed that after his younger brother and Grandpa would come in from the chores, all buddy-buddy, and yucking it up real good. Such a thing was not a repeat itself for the younger two at that first place.

There was a special day on that farm back then, or should I say almost was. It was about to be the 1st annual Pig Day Celebration. Offered to them 'on account', from the farmer, there were a few big hogs, and sows pulled off to the side as the family's very own. They were theirs to raise, theirs to love, and theirs to mate, if the pigs were old enough anyhow. The final payment was about to be made on those porkers. After all of the hardship, turmoil, and mostly dedication had been administered the party was all set.

Such a righteously well-earned and prominently victorious praising hour was so soon about to be felt. You can imagine the joy, the freedom and the hopes that glimmered in those harshest old times of yore. Certainly, a hoedown was in the works, and maybe a pie, and some ice-cream as well, you name it. All of that, plus more, was no doubt on the agenda. But wait. Just then, the farmer's wife pulled out a calculator. Which back then was indeed a stubby pencil, and a small scratch sheet of paper. (Think local public library.)

Wouldn't you know it? The rent was raised to be exactly what the payments had been before, to the penny. (So, you know she really did use a calculator.) Suffice it to say there would be no Pig Day. Soon afterward they were formally evicted. The time was up. It was back to the city to look for work. It wasn't long as Grandpa had a good work record, and considering he found a way to keep busy while so many others had been out of work to some extent, it was a matter of days before things came back together in town.

There was one not very so special day, back in those times as well. The next-door neighbors were moving. It was only a slightly better place, yet with the closeness of vicinity, the decision was made to go ahead and carry everything on over into the neighboring home. The same man owned both houses so it was an easy enough decision for that fellow as well. Most of the things had gotten moved over, and only a few items remained in the original rental. One of those last items was an old-school-type icebox.

These were things involving a huge ice cube being placed at the very top of the unit. As the ice would melt, it would drain down the snaky copper tubes located within the icebox walls. One may easily believe since those were merely tall chests that they wouldn't weigh so much. However, nothing was further from the truth. Though one point to make here is, with those old units one could really let all of the cold air out, when '*shopping*' for yummy treats with the door wide open.

Grandfather had come to the conclusion that the only way to get it moved over was to strap it to his back using a pants belt. The old neighbor next-door had just moved away, and the other neighbors were not that closely known to the family. With that realization well set in, Grandpa got that heavy sucker strapped on good and started to move forward. It would be night soon, and time was running short. He struggled mightily with that mini behemoth holding firm. Then so soon after, a dark harsh cold reality set in. It is known as the as *the life of us*. It was just more of the same.

Grandfather's toe caught on a corner of the sidewalk. It was jutting out upward slightly, due to the annual freezes that occur up here in the north. He came down hard with the icebox just on top of him. He somehow managed to get all of the remaining articles moved over but something was horribly wrong. He crashed onto the newly moved bed after he was finally finished. With no working telephone, and the hour growing ever later, the decision was made to hold off until the morning, as far as any medical treatment being sought.

The hip was broken. Not so much of a bad thing in today's world. Yet back then they didn't re-break hips. My grandfather would forever be in pain, and limping. At the very end at work, they took away Grandpa's job, giving that position to the janitor. You can guess what his duties were thereafter. A few years later, they broke the news to him gently. It truly hurt them to see the guy in such sad shape. Because even the janitor work had become too much of a task, he would be forced into an early retirement. Here and now though it was still the early 1940s.

My father soon entered the 9th grade back then in 1943. He had his mind on one aspect of life. He longed to be one of the cool guys. They were quite apparent, and well noticeable, standing about together before the start of school. Father mentioned that he thought about it, getting to know a few of these jazzy swingers, yet didn't want to come on too strong. Rather than to impose upon the group, he felt it better to hang back, and groove some kind of cool on his own. What was his final verdict then? He would take up a swinging instrument, and work things from that approach.

The music teacher that father was assigned to, was an old schoolmarm from the 1890s. You know the type, bun in back, no apple on the desk. She had pointy boney fingers, one of which she may point your way if you didn't watch it. She had her reasons. It wasn't just plain old meanness, not at all. There was a method to her madness, one might think. His entire goal leading into this confrontation was to be a boogie-woogie bass player. Her mission was to teach an appreciation of true music to her eager young students.

With a sense of serious attention, and an eye toward composition she insisted on certain standards being held and maintained. Father would simply need to satisfy the stern instructors wishes, do his very best to placate her demands, and all would work out just fine. After the old-school rehearsal had been displayed, he would really turn it on. That was merely a dream. So, soon enough it was his turn to perform for the class.

He wasn't going to spin it, stopping the wildly turning four-string within a moment's notice. Not just yet anyway. As there is time to become cool, there is as well, time to learn the more basic, and even the more instrumentally challenging rudiments of upright bass playing. Father's performance was coming off fabulously. He had the boys, and girls, eating out of his hands. Then it happened.

Teacher gave him the hook. The phrase comes from a shepherd's crook that was extended from behind a curtain back in the old Vaudeville days. If an act was failing horribly the hook would be extended and the foul performer pulled aside and well into the backstage area.

After the turn of the century, even up until the early 30s, stage shows or Vaudevillian action, was what people watched rather than television. This shepherd's tool, the same as that held by Little Bo Peep of nursery rhyme, was just what the doctor ordered.

Here, old Mrs. Crabbington, yes that very gal with the super tight bun in back, the one choking off blood to her heart apparently, said to father, "That will be quite enough young man, please take your bass, and return to your seat." He wrapped his arm around the neck of the bass like she was a drunken date at the prom. A lack of true evenness in the old schoolroom floor boards magnified the disgrace that his bass was being put through. He was so let down though. The comparison of being a star, to now a dud had overwhelmed him.

It was all just a setup, I say. The evil hand from the very depths of hell itself had reached up to wrench its gnarly grasp upon father's torn and fragile world. This a lesson so well learned, but far too late. In addition to getting the hook, Mrs. Crabbington relieved him of the classroom bass playing duties, and he would return home that evening naked of its pleasures, void of its glory, and stripped of the honor that both of those aspects bestowed upon him.

Back at the house he moped, and planned. Finally, it would come to him. "Okay this is how it works, Pa," he had offered, "you will take Mother to work earlier than she normally arrives. I've discussed this with her, and she is just perfectly fine with sitting, and looking at the paper or something, whatever she needs to do to keep herself busy is quite alright with her. It'll be just dandy," he eagerly added. "We've gone over it, and it's been decided," he pleadingly offered.

Those intrinsic, needful, and oh most necessary facets of an aspiring young man's life shouldn't be toyed with in such a way. These were more than just innocently exposed issues from the bottom of his heart. "Mother will sit in the back, out of the way, not disturbing any of the customers, nor taking up any of the potentially precious room for them, even if she has to stand," he continued. "You then after dropping her off will take me to the school."

"You'll then convince those in charge that the best thing for everyone is that I have my bass back, or you'll otherwise force their hand on the deal. We'll get my bass into the backseat of the car, it will be there all day while you're at work, then once you've returned home well safe, and soundly return my bass to its proper home, then it will be mine again, and everything will be fine again," he threw in as his last urgent emphasis on the appeal. It wouldn't be quite as simple as all that.

Grandpa explained to Father that it was actually the school's bass, so therefore it was up to them to offer it back for him to play. This was the one aspect of what he had imagined to be a life that he truly longed for, one with satisfaction and purpose. Other than being a pirate with an earring, as far as childhood visions go, this one issue being so realistically achievable, therefore would not so easily die by the cold bony hand of another. It was a life changing moment that could not have been foreseen by a freewheeling, fun-loving youngster from the Midwest.

The cold harshness of World War II came so quickly along right after. My dad's older brother that had just moved out on his own was of the age to enter service. The precise term for anyone not voluntarily joining up, was known as a 'Section 8'. That meant precisely that you were unfit for duty. Meaning either that you were born as a special needs individual, or worse, suffered from a mental illness. This older uncle of mine had a girlfriend as well. It was that things had not heated up enough, for them to tie the knot just before his departure into basic training.

The younger half-brother was right behind leaving for the service as well. The elder brother joined the Navy as was the family tradition, with the other choosing the army for his duty. One day the messenger appeared at the door with the news. The elder's ship had been sunk. By the time help had arrived, there was nothing left afloat but debris and an oil slick. The grave itself sits empty now, over in Arlington Cemetery. Life's cold hand of fate though, was not quite finished with our family's existence.

Uncle Charles bought it from the Germans crashing Normandy. It was a case of 'failure to report for duty'. What was the estimated time of death? It was approximately between 5:00am and about 8:00am. He, as a side note, had a starring role in the major motion picture 'Saving Private Ryan'. He would have been one of those fellows lying face down in the sand, just as the opening credits finished rolling. There would be no second chances when it came to getting the bass back for father after those family crucial, and life altering events.

Grandpas only comment was "that's it let's go back to the farm." It was all over from there. As I had mentioned, Father had told me that what he really wanted to be was a cool dude. Perhaps there's more than one way to row a boat, therefore. To be a pirate with treasure, wearing an earring, with maybe a sword was again, one of his first fantasies.

Soon enough a reality of maturation so readily soothed his troubled spirit. The whole works had been dreamt of, and then filed away so neatly. What pops actually got instead was eleven years in the service. I was told the Captain of US Naval vessels never would, in a really high, and excited voice say (think Curly Joe from the later Stooges years) "Oh look over there, let's pull over, and look for some treasure!" It just didn't work that way. Nye, a Captain's mission rarely involves such easily appreciable foibles.

My father was a man born with a mysteriously temporary growth over his newborn face. The *mask*, as it is called, is easily removed with no scar tissue remaining. The legends did say that anyone with such a condition would have special magical powers. Though perhaps they'd be saved from the eerie virtues, and the weighty burden such a power brings. Maybe this individual would turn out to be a normal-Joe, with no insight into the future whatsoever, no premonition of things to come, and no ability to see beyond the simple certainties of his simple life. A lucky man then, I'd say he even was.

Early 1960s

Dad was a man with two jobs, two wives and two families. With the extra expenses of his double duty, two jobs was the only way for it to work. That was the way it was back then before court ordered child support became so prevalent. How he avoided alimony is lost to the past. I take it she didn't have the heart to pursue such a thing. With his starting another family so quickly, then giving her yet another baby, things had become stretched to the limit.

So, yes, on a visit with the older kids I assume, things got carried away, and the next thing you know another baby is added to the picture. She was born just before I was. There were way too many children, and way too little in the way of income for any alimony payments to be available. His being still overseas in the Navy, at least until 1958 anyway, had put any ideas of good money coming in, well out of reach, for either of his families.

It was around this time that things began to take a turn. I'm not quite sure what the impetus for all of the extraordinary events truly was. Some things were good, some things bad, and some things so surreally paranormal that I've never even begun mentally to broach those subjects in everyday terms. During this time, my two older sisters began to make long stays at a cousin's house far away. They were away from us, away from the mystery, and safely away from any harm.

I myself would witness firsthand the demonic reach of hell itself, and how it would rise up, over, and over to scorch with its fiery grasp, not just my life, but that of those around me. Although, what I remember going back to 1961 is crystal clear, much of course, is lost to the foggy haze of toddler-ism. I do have a photographic memory, although mine is not as complete and whole as one may prefer. With things like, "Where are my keys," or "oh so sorry, forgot," popping up a little too often, mine is either out of whack, or was only involving the unusual to begin with.

It is the American television actress Peri Gilpin, or Roz from the sitcom 'Frazier' that claims to have this rare ability as well. So, yes, there are days when one is all alone simply because not a single other person recalls even one aspect of such stories I do honestly, and actually remember being a little over one year old. It was just after supper while I was still awake. Mother suggested we three kids pose for a picture. She chose the pajamas we would wear, citing the fact that they were all newly washed.

I was posed in the middle against the wall with a sister on each side holding an arm. I clearly recall the feel of the cloth, the scent of the detergent, and the mild yet loving embrace from my dear sweet siblings. Even I knew then how much it really meant to have a girl on each arm. The two had never been nicer to me. Since both parents were shutterbugs the developed pictures from the exposed film often did not come back for about a year or more.

There being way too much film waiting to be developed a backlog had grown. All so soon the flashbulbs would be eagerly capturing more than could actually be paid for. I would sit alone on the sofa early in the morning. Mother had developed a late-night TV addiction.

I let her know that I would be fine on my own. I would then around 7:00am, sneak the power button on from that very same TV set. I would as well go through old photos mounted in the books from so many years past. When new photos were added, a chance to go back in time would brilliantly present itself. Such was the case with those freshly washed pajamas, and even though the girls were blood relatives that still counted.

Another memory from those early days that comes back with regularity is somewhat traumatic. I was at the kitchen table with Mom and Dad. I was first learning to tell time from the kitchen clock. Father said that I needed to go to bed for a nap. No whining, no resisting. "Just go in there lie down, and go to sleep," he had said. He carried me from the kitchen table down the hall into my room, and lay me into the crib. "Remember now," he reminded me, "No whining, just lie there and go to sleep."

Just as he made his way out of the room, a huge, peanut-in-the-shell sized spider crept upward upon the wall, from down low and just behind the bed. I need to point out here that I do not have some strange type of attraction to the things. It is rather, they do toward me. The huge arachnid made its way across the wall getting closer to the headboard as it moved. This was a refugee from the cellar no doubt, and maybe noticed the others were being picked off, one by one.

Those from underneath the hot water heater were about half the size of my tiny little-baby tennis shoe. Our house, bran new and never lived in before, had been built atop, or near to what must have been a spider's nest. As this eight-legged monster made her way closer and closer toward the headboard, I began to worry. I was under orders, no whining, no begging, just close my eyes and go to sleep. I sincerely did try, at least a bit. Finally, though, the huge spider was behind me against the wall.

I felt its presence getting closer, and closer to the other side of the bed. Nearer, and nearer to my left shoulder it moved. I then closed my eyes, and prayed. Each night at bed time, Mother would help us to do our prayers. I was taught at a very young age all about that essential and necessary ritual. Here though was an emergency situation. It was to no avail. The thing crawled up and presented itself upon that very wall. It then made its way onto the bed, and closer, then closer to my face.

I held off crying out, because of what I had just been asked to do. Finally, after an excruciating timeframe lasting at least 2½ seconds, this oh so clever, yet quite needful and desperate arachnid, sat upon my shoulder. It finally then sat high up upon my cheek, very near my eye, yet just under it. I could take it no more. I was now being held hostage. "Aahhhh. Aaaahhh," I moaned, in a weak and feeble manner. Father had heard me, and begun to slowly make his way down the hall.

It took forever. He turned to look. As he did so he began to remind me of his demand to lie still, and sleep. Before he could finish, he set his eyes upon the brown furry beast. He froze. "Oh Father, how can you abandon me in my time of need?" I questioned in my mind.

I somehow could be that creative at such a young age, at least from time to time anyway. I apparently knew instinctively common English phrases, and even some well-known quotes from plays. Just then, I felt alone, and prone. Slowly, slowly he needed to act, so as to not disturb the rigid monster as he crept closer.

He had mentioned around this time the abandoned island out in the Pacific, north of The Philippines. He was required, as an act of procedure, to land upon said land mass, and to investigate any possibilities He must have been utilizing his best commando moves learned so well in the Navy.

From 1947 to 1958, his service was offered. His first gig was three, then each term afterward was a stint of two years, or vice versa, it's been a while since he mentioned those terms. It was relayed to me well back in the day, that the island father came upon was no doubt a Japanese outpost from WWII.

He was, after drawing his naval-issued side-arm, to secure that island along with an additional crew member or two. It was as creepy as could be, he had felt. Suddenly, Father claimed, from out of nowhere a sense of peace and calm securely overtook him. He could only describe the situation as being one involving an angel hovering just overhead, just over his shoulder. A gentle sense of peace and serenity had then claimed the moment.

Here and now though, and suddenly without warning, Father moved his hand in and snatched the threatening spider, whole and well intact, from off of my cheek. He went to the kitchen door, and dispensed with it. The next day when he came home, he showed me his hand telling me how it all went down. As it lay trapped within his grasp, and with the door open he moved to thrust it down. He pulled his hand back, but as soon as the muscles tensed, she dug in. "I slammed that thing down onto the sidewalk as hard as I could, and what do you know?" he asked.

"It just crawled away like it was nothing," he claimed. "She didn't even turn around to face me," he had added. The fang marks on father's hand were deep, and wide. From the new type of outdoor spider gracing our yard every summer afterward, I would say that she was more than pregnant, and knew exactly what she was doing. It was her life, in exchange for the safety of my face. That was all that she demanded from this daring, and harrowing exchange of ours!

It is the writing of this book that has caused that stranger day to return to me now. As our home was first built just before we took residency, bugs were not the only thing to have moved in before we did. We also had a small field mouse with a cartoon type entrance into our kitchen, from under the sink. What had been a very large knot hole was now well chewed away, and from time to time the little peeper would show himself, then pop back into his hidey hole. Father bought some wood, and went to work, all to no avail.

Since we had faced the spider crisis together, we decided to go downstairs to investigate. He had already let me know in hushed tones that the little critter still had domain in our cellar. It would crawl atop the steel pillar, and metal cross-brace that was holding up the foundation. He held me in his arms up close, as we surveyed the area. "See right around here it was, that he last appeared," he motioned. We were now positioned just under the kitchen area.

Suddenly, from out of the depths of darkness a shadow appeared. Father reached up, and we all freaked. All three of us did so. I could feel the intense sensations rocking through the very cement floor that we stood upon. You see right where he had reached up his hand, the mouse had frozen in its tracks. Then wow. The electricity flowed like a teasing gentle lightening. It was so, that the new trio we had formed went into a bit of a simultaneous shock together for a moment.

He would later claim, it wasn't only the hair on the back of *his* neck that stood up, every hair on that timid mouse's back was quickly at attention as well. One way or another we finally managed to get rid of the unwanted houseguest. Although, since I was such an animal lover, it was yet another thing that was so carefully gone over by my somewhat considerate father. Never to be spoken of, ever again in our home, not even once, we can all surmise fairly easily what that removal truly involved.

How much Mother knew about Dad's other family, early on anyway, with the extra kids, and all of that, I don't know. It was my dad's cousin that lived right down the street from Mother. That was how they had met, through his cousin. The four original kids were dropped off there one day. So, that everything was out in the open, they were moved over to my maternal grandparents' house. How long it took after that ceremony of connection before certain ghosts of the past emerged is hard to say.

We drove from home to my very own grandparent's house and two of those elder siblings were in the driveway. The oldest and the rawest of the bunch began his approach. As soon as we pulled up the drive, the younger, the bad boy, was already making a fist at me. He was the 'kiss goodbye' baby, if you will. Upon arriving at the rear door, the middle brother held up a guitar. Once I entered the kitchen, I saw that my half-sister was helping to dry the dishes.

She was a young woman of grace. To stand near her was a pleasure. Unlike the other two she was doting, loving, and a very caring individual. To this day I have yet to meet anyone with such a strongly willed, yet warmly generous quality. Grace I've found is a genetic gift for some. Even men can possess this unseen, yet so well felt quality. My very own boss, one of many, someone that I eventually began to call El Capitan, or Stratego, after the board game, had that special characteristic.

I recall one day how he came to help me load a truck. After a good half hour he apologized, claiming he needed to go back to his office to do paperwork. No, no I thought. It's work again. Oh it's work again. My arthritis immediately kicked in, and the toil of the task at hand, grew heavy and laborious with his very departure. Apparently, therefore grace comes with a goodness felt, and a moment shared. I would often catch one of the others standing before him in his office, beaming with a big grin, ensconced in a hallowed glow of common human joy.

My sisters once again, had returned home from another visit to our cousin's house. They were beginning to make me feel left out as was par for the course. I had a plan to get them in line. I would take one of the special toys that they had brought back with them. Over, and over she continued explaining that it was part of a much bigger set. It was that the two items before us were no doubt sympathy loans from those three girl cousins from out of town. The family budget would truly never warrant such opulent extravagance.

We had two doors on our bathroom. Since they wouldn't let me play, I had decided to take the special chair, and run, and run, over and over again. No matter how many times it took, even for the rest of my life that's what I would do. They had made me feel left out, and this was war. My older sister made a fuss. Before I could even begin my first run around, Mother entered the living room, and put a stop to it.

Within reason, now they would have to let me play along, even though I was a boy, and they both girls. Although, realistically, my being allowed into their little circle at any time may have depended on the day of the week, the toy in question, or even the mood of the elder sister. Because most of the toys we had were specifically girl's playthings, like miniature furniture, so cute and small, or even dolls too, it was a toss-up as to whether I even cared.

On such mundane play-days it wouldn't matter if they were being kind and generous, snubbing me with every preplanned sense of exclusiveness that they could possibly muster, or otherwise. My feelings are truly what was at issue here. Therefore, I say hoorah. Here and now victory was mine! I immediately felt a bit guilty about my thievery, and absconding with the goods and all, only to race around mischievously through both bathroom doors. Oh well, if that is what it took then, so be it.

With so many boys to carry on with the dream, Father maintained an interest in the music scene, yet now it was all for us. It was or the four of us to keep the torch lit. He knew a bar over in Chicago. If you were looking for the action in town eventually you'd end up at this joint. I was over there with him on only one occasion. That was at a coffeehouse. It was a real genuine beatnik place, where the girls wore all black, including the berets. This 'diner' was a dinosaur of the poets beat.

It was 1963, and the flames of an old dream flickered, and licked. I can't say for sure how long it lasted. I sincerely recall how Father had spoken to one of the Hispanic young girls. She was sweet and kind, and loving. We took a stroll after her shift along the railroad tracks. I was at peace with the world. I had found that a man could be friendly with even a young Hispanic waitress from a local coffeehouse. It was simply another of life's good lessons.

The time had come. My sisters and I would play sock hop in the spare room. The super old radio was plugged into the wall in the corner. A safe amount of furniture polish was laid down on the floor. We took off our shoes, and began to dance. I was asking my sisters to help me to dance. "Oh, we don't have time now we're too into it," the older one offered. "You just need to get groovy, and work it, dog," they were telling me. I turned my back to them and stepped in close to the player.

All at once, from out of nowhere, I busted a move. What I had somehow stumbled upon, while staying swiftly upright, was the one, the only, the "Moonwalk!" I certainly wouldn't realize that I and I alone, had the coolest dance move ever, not at least for many years. I want to say right here, sometimes very special people receive special ideas from a very, very, special place that somehow exists in its own world in its own universe, in its own time.

So, even though I have never displayed my secret dance move to anyone, it nonetheless would one day become the greatest thing since sliced cheese, and then some. Under such a circumstance, I can only laugh to myself at the very folly of our strange existence together, here on this earth, at this particular time. So, yes, due to the slickness of the floor, I had somehow come up with the most spectacular dance style ever performed anywhere.

Here we had all been sleeping in the same room. My two siblings slept on bunk-beds and myself in the baby-bed. There was a mattress that would be rolled up, and forced into the attic. That was generally used by my good brother, the middle one. The question had been put forth at the dinner table about the two sisters finally moving into that room. The parental units were not quite ready for a full-on and permanent shuffle. The older sister, as some sort of consolation, came up with the disco idea.

I wasn't sure who Mother spoke to on one strange and surreal day. It was easy enough to see that she felt someone in a different world could hear her. It's even as though, right now at this very moment, an evil force is waiting to carry my thoughts, the very words on this page presenting them to that otherworldly entity. Then while whipping up a demon's spell, it would draw me into its dank dark spaces. She, as we stood in the kitchen looked up, shouted, "Oh yeah is that the way it is," then grabbed a little league bat, and fractured the arch of my foot.

Since then, I have from time to time fashioned a theory about such occurrences. There indeed must be doors, and passageways to hell itself. These portals of energy are what can allow verbal soundings, spoken or otherwise into the minds of others. Is this the secret way that inventors come upon their next ideas? Is this the fashion of evil cursing that is utilized to drive people mad? Do criminals get their dastardly schemes in this unbelievable method?

Is there for each and every one of us, a potential and possible opening unto hell's door itself? Can we keep these pathways closed off, at least those that are more vile filled, and more treacherously perilous to us? What I have come to reason so far, is that some of us may be a little more sensitive to receivership from another world. Hear me now and hear me good. I speak of actual sounds, not of the easily audible sort, but rather involving a verbal thought process not of our own design.

One strong notion I would like to announce is to all those people that really did hear voices, it's all a trick to lure you into potential acts of criminality, or fool you into believing you've totally lost your mind! Yet if you fall for it, like one such young lady, you are sadly, and definitely more than a bit of each. The voices from beyond told this dear young woman of the recent past, to extract the unborn fetus from a neighbor. She was then to pass it off as her own.

Suffice it to say she acquiesced. I can find no more dramatic proof of the evil underworld, or 'insane dead', as I refer to them, being so harshly present in our everyday existence. Believe what you will. I know my theory is the only one to surely make some sense. How else could what appeared to be an average everyday next-door neighbor, become some crazed lunatic, harboring fantastical illusions of passing of the other girl's newborn as her very own. She had just realized that she herself was barren. That was the only opening the evil underworld needed in her case.

I was made more than commonly aware of one aspect of this type of phenomenon. It wasn't unit I was downtown and came across a haggard old lady. Again, I could sense the demon lurking with its presence well inside of her. You may have seen these types yourself, street people, with clothes perhaps from another decade, maybe a shopping cart, or just some bags. As I came nearer to her, the demon spoke. They went back and forth a bit, and it was all so soon over.

I had all that I needed for my research. I was now certain; a form of temporary possession could transpire. With the victim even sometimes fully aware of what is occurring. It was that she became angry, just after she spoke in a gruff gnarly voice, quite obviously not her indoor voice at all. She was saying something unintelligible in a deep and otherworldly tone. Her response was along the lines of 'ah you get outta here'. I since have only read of such things.

I've most definitely come to the conclusion that there are two types of afflicted souls here on this earth with us. There are those that are somehow tricked into committing nefarious acts, and those that know good and well that these evil beings do indeed exist, and that they should be wary of their presence. Somewhere out there perhaps even from hell itself, these wicked things attempt to take our joy, luring us into the engagement of heinously inhumane and unkind actions! It wasn't COVID-19 that caused me to be out of work, mind you.

You'll read all about it, with patience, near the end of things. The only question is, "Was I given a favor by being let go?" Would I have ever finished a book that I put down just 5 months after dropping over $4,000.00 in Vegas? No doubt, you have heard of or witnessed for yourself, such frightening inter-worldly behavior that I refer to.

Ask yourself, "Would they have kept these types, in days of yore, in dungeons if they weren't truly possessed by demon spirits?" If this state of being were not so completely shocking to the sane, would those suffering in such a dramatic way, have ever been taken from their very homes?

It was in old England and throughout other parts of Europe that such a necessity became the only and oh so required standard. When I go on about spirit possession it is not always of the type that is so veritably frightening, or all out overpowering. Such an occurrence of which I talk, plays out I believe, for some women suffering from P.M.S. What may be perceived as a mild case of crankiness, may actually be caused by interference from the bowels of hell itself.

My only question to date is where the line can be drawn between honest and original behavior, and the reactions of those meddled with by the demonically possessed. Using illogical castings, an intentionally negative sense of interference, and the desire to throw us for a loop, the maligned spirits of the evil underworld apparently have at us, at least when they can. Are some so desperately prone to such a cranial invasion that we should be compelled toward sympathetic tendencies? In regard to medical treatment, and our overall feelings about such troubling realities, do we over-medicate out of a sheer sense of horror and fear?

I believe you know exactly how I do truly feel about it all. We're all in this together people. Let's make it work! I have a keen theory about men crying from one eye during movies. That explanation plays so wonderfully into my understanding of things. Would such a happening, with only *one* tear, indicate the hovering presence of another being? I mean a female spirit to be exact. Are these types able to watch our lives like a movie themselves in some instances?

The insane dead, I call them again, at least the bad ones anyway. They are no doubt people who have sold their souls in exchange for the ability to enter this world. At Halloween we dress as the dead, or at least used to, before all of the fun costumes came around. The giving of candy to the beggars is an attempt to show them true human compassion so that they do everything to move out, and into the great beyond, searching for the proper portal into the one true heavenly realm of beings in the afterlife.

That would be an opening that will allow them to return on their journey toward the one and only light. Isn't that exactly just what we so ceremoniously hope they'll seek, even especially more so on such a '*Holiday*'? I say here and now that we need to keep the harsh and original factors of this 'Holiday' in mind when engaged in our daily activities. There, as per legend, are visitors from another world! Whether or not they are somewhat visible should be beside the point.

Can we then lump other types of extreme behavior into this group of troubled souls that I'm compiling? Yet another aspect of the demon world that I've perceived is through the act of being materialist, or outright greedy. With greed for *filthy lucre*, rather than to be satisfied with a common amount, we have those that somehow need more. I will go on about this subject more in the epilogue. I have to say, as old as I am, I believe I've found a new facet of my hypothesis.

I originally had considered that too much accumulation of food, material goods, and money tilted the balance of our very existence. Just what moves from the rich-man, then over to the beggar is hard to put a clear finger on. Mojo, and Karma have been used to try and identify this mystical and supernatural presence of which I speak, at least roughly so. What I would like to do, is to open the eyes of every person on this god-rotten planet to a clearer vision of how our thoughts and actions undeniably affect others, even those on the other side of the world, or even those from any other century!

1963

Along those lines, yet outside of the template I have proposed, is an example of such an affectation. Some truly spectacular things occurred back in 1963. Some were so unbelievably awesome, and some so terribly wrong. I was playing in the living room on the floor while Mother finished up the morning dishes. 'As The World Turns', the old soap opera came on at noon central time. Before Mother could finish up in the kitchen, and force me to lay down for a nap, the news broke in, with a special bulletin.

Walter Cronkite took over the announcing. It had been reported that the President had been shot, and was dead. Mother stopped her cleaning, and came in to see for herself. It was all too unreal, but there before our eyes was the harsh cold truth. Soon after, she asked if I was ready for my nap. I was dazed, and weakened from the emergency broadcast. I had no strength. There was no argument, and I quickly gave into the suggestion of lying down.

The nation would mourn together. In shock we were. All or at least many, moved through the following two weeks, in a state of trauma. The malaise would seem to creep back in, from time to time. I have found the farther back in time these horrible realities occurred the easier it had become to come to terms with the selfish and cold brutality that the world did often offer. Finally, hardly a sigh would be summoned, and all of the trials and tribulations of life's ins and outs would move on. With a sense of caution, no doubt, any other positive energy moved as well.

All of this happening, while in the backs of many minds was a terrifying roar of nightmarish proportions. Those cold shocks to the psyche are waiting for the next tragedy to rear up, and display itself in cold hard fashion unto us. The early sixties, for the most part, were a part of that post beatnik era with the hippie lifestyle yet to fully take hold. Some people weren't just ignorant. There weren't just those with an all-too-common sense of 'reality'. There were those that were outright everyday sinful.

Mother at this time was now over the edge. Her manic state continued to vex her. I was told to watch over her, even though I was only three years old. What father was saying was that to keep her out of the mental institution, she only needed some rest. That was going to be it, nothing more.

"Because I have to go to work, I cannot sit here, and watch over her so it's going to be up to you."

"All you have to do is to make sure she stays in her room, and she has agreed to be cooperative."

"Right?" he looked at her, and she nodded in agreement.

"Just make sure you don't let anybody in. No matter whom it is, no matter how much they knock, or ring the bell, do not answer that door. That's all I'm asking of you," with a serious tone Father had plead.

"Yeah sure," I said, "I can do that." Suddenly, there was a knock at the door. Was it just a test? A test of my will, and ability, or was it something really important? The woosh of the door opening was all that it took. Since he didn't have a quick reason for being there, I felt that I'd been had.

All too soon the bedroom door flung open. With a raging quickness Mother flew into the room. "Go," I urged him. He darted across the street. She attacked like a tiger running and chasing after him. In only her nightgown, she was ready to pounce. He was tackled hard, just on the grass of the local park. It looked like a serious hit. I could not bear to watch. Soon though, she was back in. She was upset that I failed, and so quickly back in bed. I believe she nodded right back off. We both slept for most of the rest of the day.

With my two sisters still at the cousin's house Father and I made our escape. We would be staying indefinitely at the foster home. Whatever it was, this alignment of realities it was somewhat frightening. Everything had come together now to create a sordid triangle of a type demonic possession. Yes, most assuredly, the X-Files had nothing on us. We could, over time, fill an entire file cabinet with the goings on, and unexplainable phenomenon experienced by our family on a truly regular basis.

Once Mother had stabilized, Father returned to our home leaving me behind with the foster mother. I don't recall much of those times other than the fact that I didn't have to get a haircut. There is a noticeable one-year gap in the duplicate photos, and the differing poses and snapshots. With not one but two shutterbugs in the family, there would indeed have been an available photo for every child, grandchild, and even great-great grandchildren, even into the next two or three centuries of heirs.

Mother did not want me to remember having hair, so there would be no photos whatsoever, not even a one of me from that year. Not until I had gotten another boner-haircut was I allowed such doting attention. (This lack of picture snapping left the younger of my sisters feeling quite unloved during that time period. It again had really nothing even remotely to do with her.) One other thing that I recall so very vividly about having hair, rather than a crew cut, was how Sissy would part my hair, being sure to pick the right groove to move over on. To this day, I still struggle, as she did, choosing the exact line to part.

She was a fun girl, and was willing to race me when I asked, and otherwise dote on me for moments while giving me the love that I so desperately needed. So, warm, so bubbly, so alive, she was. The perfect and most ideal sister a guy could want. She was pleasantly somewhere between a cousin, an aunt, and a babysitter, all rolled up in one. Being eleven years older, it was easy to love me as a baby, and she took time out of her busy day to humor me so.

Sissy ended up marrying a millionaire. He must have loved her just as I did. Therefore, if all humans could live up to the best of their abilities, especially when it comes to their strengths, and fine points, while always trying to hone or at least control those lesser characteristics, we can all better appreciate each other's value and truly what we bring to the table as individuals, or as a member of any one select group.

Soon enough, Christmas rolled around I would have my chance. I had developed a deep relationship with the foster mother's daughter, she a year older. It was comforting to have someone my own age to lean on. She was such a good friend. We were even in love. It was an innocent puppy dog love. I asked for her to come along when I was taken home for the holiday. In the back of my mind, even though I loved her, and my oldest sister was so kind and loving, this was my chance to get back in with my own family.

When the door opened to my parent's house on Christmas Eve, I turned to say goodbye, and really meant it. Father all too quickly asked, "How it could possibly work with me moving back, without even as much as a bed? I could sleep in the baby-bed, I'm not too tall," I claimed.

"You just need to bring it out, and set it up." Mother soon implored him, and he caved. Within minutes, the bed was being set up in the bedroom.

We three would share that room for a while. With my bed against one wall, and the bunk-beds against the other, it was actually nice and cozy. That way, the other bedroom could continue to be used as a guestroom for my good brother, the middle one, or even more so, as the disco for dancing such as we did from time to time. The guest bed was comprised of a simple mattress that was squeezed together as tightly as possible. It was then stuffed back up into the attic.

Since I was back living at home, by summer the girls would be over with the cousins to stay awhile. Mother had noticed an interesting occurrence that was happening just outside our front door. "It's like clockwork," she assured me. "Maybe not on the dot, but at around 8:13, this huge deer emerges from the woods."

"You'll see," she claimed. "Come on over by the door," she beckoned. "I swept up real good, and washed this rug in the washing machine," she added, while motioning me over.

I moved in closer and she had me sit on the floor with the main door open, so that I could watch for him through the screen. I looked up at the clock. It was about 8:12 pm. I began to boil with excitement. It wouldn't be long. Seconds, seconds ticked away, and then just one more. Soon enough there he was. As big as big could be. His enormous rack nearly spanned the width of the entire street. With those well mounted extensions, he must have been even seven feet tall altogether.

That deer seemed to be looking into the picture windows as he moved along. I did believe at that point that he was upset, and that we were encroaching on his home turf. Perhaps he was even born nearby, even right where he now stood. Before he could look angrily at me with any sort of animalistic disdain, or even a human-like sense of being disgruntled, I felt that I had had enough and moved quickly to my bed. The last thing one desires is for a huge wild animal to have you on his 'bad' list!

Being a hyper little dude sometimes, I would wake up at 4:00am, and be ready for action. I would certainly be back asleep by 5:30am on most occasions after becoming wide awake all too early. Here now, I was being given permission to turn on the TV as long as it was started on a very quiet volume, and was crept up slowly. "I generally get up on my own," Father stated. "So, I don't need you to come in, and get me up."

"I even wake up sometimes, seconds or minutes before the alarm goes off," he added.

I guess his body clock, he was saying, was attuned to that time after all of those years, but he still would set the alarm just in case. That, just in case item was an old-school Baby Ben, a big bell alarm clock that would possibly be thrown against the wall in certain comedic situations. Yes, it was that type of alarm clock that is so startling that one may consider, at first in many cases, to indeed have at it with the blaring little monster in such a grand and dramatic fashion.

With permission granted finally now, to go ahead and lie quietly by the set, and to wait patiently for Daddy to arise, all was good. Everything was falling into place. It was now 4:40am on my first official tryout, with Dad still asleep. With the TV set now on, and he about to wake at 5:10 it should be a breeze I had felt. It was two minutes later, and I already couldn't take it anymore, I was freaking out. "No, No I won't do it," I proclaimed. "It's just, let me see, a half an hour, that's all, that isn't long, it'll be in no time," I lied to myself.

I started to tremble a bit. Some strange force was entering not just my world, but my very being. Rising up in me, and taking over. I resisted. Suddenly, the answer came clear. It was all over. The wait was too much, but I had an out. I convinced myself that this would work for the best. From out of nowhere, my first hit song had presented itself. Certainly, it would be a legitimate reason for waking Father. Here it was then, "Wake me up before you go-go, and don't leave me hanging on the line for so long."

You see the clothes line was attached to the house just below the eastern facing window in my parent's bedroom. If I slid along that wall I could make my way over to Father's head, and begin to sing. I slapped him on the arm, and went into my new routine. Because that song truly was a genuine and actual hit from point one, he was kind and didn't rail into me too hard. It was more of a finger pointing incident with a gentle reminder.

Somehow the song made its way over to the band WHAM. I sat in front of the TV during its televised, live visual debut. I smiled, and rose. Such instant hits are hare today, goon tomorrow, as they say. (A reference to the talent show at a neighbor pal's grade school event.) Life is so very, very beautiful when you're a seer, a visionary, and a true poet. So, I was a music lover with no instrument. The TV though, was in slick competition. It would only be the second one of those devices to be owned by a member of our family. Father, it should be noted, was more of a reader.

Near our home it seemed that everyone had a piano. Two of my friends did, as well as the next-door neighbor. I asked if we could please get one. Father had to think about it. The next thing you know, I was to go to my friend's house two doors down, to audition. If I had enough natural talent, we would indeed be buying a piano, or at least, I'd be taking beginner lessons from one of these neighbor ladies. I was a bit nervous, though was only expected to display any innate potential to the evaluator.

I rang the bell, entered, and made my way to the living room. Seated on the bench was a flamboyant character with a big wave of hair. It was Liberace. He had me run through some things like stretching for reach and that. He checked my movement on the strikes, and before you knew it, it was over. The next day at the supper table it was announced. Although, I had the desire, and even some promise, because I was not an outright virtuoso in the rough, we would not be buying a piano.

I took it like a man. When your very own father was all set to be the biggest, boogie-woogie daddio this side of the Pecos, one learns to be cool. It had all, so easily and briskly, been torn away. During the end of the depression era, one found the easy ways to get buy on less. Alas, it was not to be. In most everyone's life, there are those moments when our hopes and desires are shunted, and stifled. We carry on. I had easily learned about being cool, and letting things drop.

Life took a turn for the worse from there. The reasoning behind my morning loneliness was more mundane than all of the drama surrounding it. The hard cold facts of Mother's TV addiction were apparent. I believe she may have been the very first addict that ever existed within our newly-graced, electronic lifestyles. When you stop to consider the times my family lived in, a greater appreciation of the seriousness of such a momentous occasion begins to perhaps develop for some.

Mother was so hooked on the tube, that later on, within about five years, she had spoiled the evening meal by featuring every intricate facet, each detailed plot move, and any terror filled scenes, of the horror movie, The Fly. She was still so totally wired after ironing and cleaning all day, it was so one could measure the electricity sparking excitedly from her brow, with an actual voltmeter. Every detail, with no spoiler alert offered, had to be descriptively gone over, even the very ending.

Oh, thanks so much for that hot little potato I had considered. She was so juiced, and wired from the night before, that the intensity level was palpable. "Oh, this movie is going to be good," I figured. It was. Not two years later we would watch it together, and it was every bit as exciting as she quite excitedly proclaimed. We had a roof top antenna, and could even get some channels from the other main city, about 45 miles up the road.

On a good day anyway, depending on the weather and the channel, it was clear enough to watch. I will add here, at my grandparent's place, the neighbors across the street had cable. That basically meant an antenna tower, triangular in shape and about 35 feet high, had been erected in their yard. That was back in the early 1970s. It was definitely not an HBO level experience for any of those early viewers. It simply pulled in stations from as far away as 50 miles.

With any and all sorts of photos nearby on a coffee table, now that I was going to be 4 years old, I was just okay with those starts of my day. Watching the tube was all that we did to some extant during the day anyway. Other than my being forced back into the bedroom for more sleep, there wasn't much real action to be had. Now that you've been so well informed of the impetus of my slight morning loneliness, you'll comprehend what soon follows as a theme though, more so, throughout most of my life. One song that I penned way back at the age of 12 was Excitable Boy. That little ditty was later performed in full, by Mr. Warren Zevon.

When my father's dad drove around on his circa 1923 Indian motorcycle in search of a farm to work, it was an act of desperation. In the midst of the great depression things were very much…well…depressed. That bike would eventually be sold and as Father had claimed all they really had was an old Brownie camera, a radio, and once in a great while a little ice-cream for dessert. They lived in the old hired hand's shack, as I mentioned, something that was no doubt built by the original farmer as his very own home.

So, luxuries like plug-in refrigerators, and television sets were not considered as necessities in those, rawer more self-supporting days. According to mom in her neighborhood back in the day a guy came along every day driving a horse, and wagon. In the summer they would chase, and chase him. That was mainly just for fun. All the while they would plead for a pop-sickle.

Back in those days Ice-Men did have those cool, cool treats. Those were just really a piece of ice that had perhaps broken free from its original block.

If it was hot enough, maybe 84 going on 90, he would stop. Dude would open the back of his setup, and give each of the kids that longed-for icy treat. If he felt it wasn't the right time, or if maybe he was running low on the cold stuff, he just kept right on going. Ice boxes, as they were called ran on a big block of ice, and the freezing cold water that dripped down from this huge cube. The copper tubing inside snaked and essed back and forth, and led to a drip pan at the bottom that had to be drained into the sink at least once, or twice a day.

This is where the dads got the 'don't open the refrigerator, and let all the cold out' from. Although, yes, that would really happen, even with the new electric models as they would turn on, and re-cool the interior of the storage facility. That was considered a waist of energy so the old rule still applied. "Shopping," my dad called it. "No shopping in the fridge with the door wide open," he commanded. I to this day, now that I am an adult, do my best to plan out any excursions into the fridge beforehand.

You at some point understanding of my connections to ancient history. Both grandfathers where from the 1800s. Both served in WWI. My mother's dad was a fourth-grade graduate. Because of the importance of farming in those days, a young man could drop out of school at any age, as long as he was to work on the farm anyway. Why, before the child labor laws were enacted, a minor of only 8 or 9 years old could even work in a factory.

My Mother's dad though had quit school by age 10. His father had passed away quite unexpectedly, and all of the boys had to work together to save the old place. Mother's dad was one to listen to the Cubs' games on the radio while sitting out on the enclosed porch. It was such that he and his wife, my grandmother said we'll think about it, as far as having a TV in the house, such a grand and lifestyle changing form of entertainment. Soon enough the answer came, it would be "yes, yes you may."

You can fully appreciate then, when considering those casual aspects of life in general back in those days, why a future cornerback for the Dallas Cowboys, Frank Clark, would stop over just to chat with Mother. In the years just before, apparently when Big Frank was making his rounds, he'd have Mother on his list of go-to girls. *"Visiting,"* it was known as back in those days. With only one's homework as an option, a person may consider that visiting was on many a student's agenda. It didn't hurt that Mother was a pom-pom girl for her school.

The early 60s, my youthful era was a time when 65 to 70 percent of married women stayed home and took care of the house. Gals back then were often making bread, canning tomatoes, making jellies, and jams potentially, or otherwise spending every available moment tending to things on the home-front. Though, that is, unless they were wiling away the hours in talk, and gossip while sipping from coffee mugs, or glued to the set watching their favorite Soap Operas, and such.

In the neighborhood where we lived were a great number of young kids. A good many were young teens, with most of the rest close to my age. The older girl just across the way was just close enough to my age to hang around with once in a while. She would stop over in the yard, and I being curious and fun-loving, would follow her anywhere. Being American Indians, she and her siblings, like myself, enjoyed the woods, and those last places in the area left untouched by developers.

We would venture off and explore, walking the deer trails in the area. One area at the end of an old abandoned apple orchard had a woodpecker tree. The farmer's field to the south was home to the local deer population, especially when he failed to plant all of the way to his border line. That would have been up to the edge of the roadway. All of the usual smaller suspects lived everywhere as well. Think skunks, possums, muskrats, beavers, voles, and yes, foxes, coyotes, and again what I term as 'dog-oaties'.

One day Mother called out to me. I was nowhere to be found. "You must never, ever take him from the yard," she insisted to Jewel Boy. We called her that because she liked to play like us, and was really Julie, the older girl from across the way. On at least one occasion, I sought her out on my own. You might say we ran away together. Mother needed something to threaten me with, and what was handy was a breadboard. I had secretly planned to stick my butt out at the last minute to break the thing, since her threat had been well planted beforehand.

It worked! I mean my plan, not hers. I kung-fu-ed that bread board into two pieces with my ass, faster than you can say ouch. It was that I truly loved this neighbor girl with all of my heart and couldn't resist the thought of our being together. I was grounded once again for it too. Maybe, it was the setup at home that drew me toward her. With two sisters, both now in school, there often wasn't much going on as far as any fun was concerned.

1964

Otherwise, I was often engaged in super fantastical, overwhelmingly mind-blowing, true to life experiences from the early '60s. On one of Father's cultural missions to Chicago he met a guitar player from New York. He was an aspiring musician that had gone out ahead of the band to scout things out, although he perhaps left open the option of moving on without them.

Frank eventually moved into town, and got a small place above a storefront just down from the police station. I suggested at one point that he play for free at some bars. The one that he worked his way into was a girlie-bar. Now even I knew what that meant, sort of, anyway. I asked how it was going. He replied, "I don't think that those gentlemen are actually there to hear music." He continued to make moves toward not only a future stardom but L.A. as well.

The times we lived in were strange, with L.S.D. still being legal as I have mentioned, one could not expect a common rationality from each and every individual that one may encounter on any given day. I especially could not count on any normality as a constant from Mother. Although, things did even out and return to normal, back then on any given day it was truly a crap shoot. On one particular day, we were talking about meeting Frank at the park.

There was this other fellow there. It may have been Frank's brother. That dude was a mechanic. We at least called him Frank's brother. He looked way more common and usual in that regard. Frank's sons seem to substantiate their relationship with this 'shorter' uncle, simply vis-à-vis their *normal* appearance. It's the hair as well. No person that I have ever known had two sons that both looked potentially, anyway, more like his very own brother. As long as your brother is married, and one isn't engaged in international trucking I guess that could work!

This dark-haired fellow would show up in dirty greasy overalls, and hang out a little. So, yeah, since both of Frank's sons actually remind me of him, he must have been the real deal. Mother decided to kill him that day. Frank's brother was indeed present, and surely would be able to gain control of this whacked-out situation! She lured dude off to the side, and pulled a knife. I saw the blade being held up to his face. Frank's brother, resisted, holding her wrist with all of his might.

The struggle continued. My only question then becomes, is the fact that I am sitting here writing about this reality, creating a portal in time. I refer to one that opens exposing the future from the actual past. If steely demons from hell were not here, yet able to hear my thoughts in a far-off distance, would they move in to create the effect necessary for such an episode to occur? Is such a person even possessed? Consider the barren neighbor that tried to extract the other baby from the womb. Are you ready now to climb on board?

I danced around in terror, hoping for the best. Finally, the blade was taken, and both emerged from the vehicle unscathed, at least there was no visible blood. The police were called, and we all ended up down at the 2th District, oddly right across the street from Frank's place. It was at least convenient for him anyway. After some disappointed and disgruntled questioning, we were allowed to leave. Frank moved to L.A. the following year, yet would still show up back here on occasion.

As an apology for her serious mental issues, Mother took me over to Frank's place. I was placed in a high-chair, and had promised not to try and escape. The two came back soon enough with some food. Later Frank showed me his method of writing. Every night at about 9:20 or so, he would do his best to squeeze some new lines out. If he was stuck for a rhyming word, he would draw a line across, and keep going. It was later when Father got the idea for the whah-pedal that he went through Frank's method again for me.

A few years later Mr. Zappa was still a struggling guitar player, so he apparently needed to drum up some publicity. After arriving on the west coast, he came up with an idea that was well ahead of his time. Just what was his master plan? He would somehow coax a woman, a willing volunteer, into reaching the total heights of physical ecstasy. All of this would occur while recording the entire event for posterity. He apparently announced the taping of the upcoming event a little too grandly.

Suffice it to say the cops not only broke the door down once, they did it again. I have to think these days most people would just laugh such an occurrence off and get on with their normal and usual day. Suffice it to say that while such a loudly proclaimed activity surely failed to bring about an outright landslide of notoriety, it did however help to set a definite trajectory into the '*platosphere*' of space and time, just enough to get Frank some breathing room.

The next visitor to town came from the same place, Chicago. Jimi was on his way to New York from Seattle. He decided to stop in for a bit, and then came over. He was to teach me a few things, even though what I had was a plastic fiddle. I had received that plastic violin from my grandmother earlier that year.

My sisters and I accompanied her to the local Five & Dime. She would claim each year that because we didn't live in town, she had needed to make up for that by making a special purchase for us. (UPDATE: I know this is out of time, and sync, but the Salvation Army has not one but 2 violins for sale. Yes indeed, they are less expensive junior models, nonetheless my money hand started to itch!)

It would be nothing special at all to get too excited about, and with a set dollar limit. When I saw the violin, I knew that was what I really wanted. She held it up, and said, "Oh this item is over the pre-stated limit."

"But that's what I really want. You said to choose something that we'd like. Well, that's it," I moaned. She considered the limit she had just mentioned, and lovingly relented. I had never been so well treated, or blessed in all my life. My heart was filled with joy.

When we got back to our grandparent's home I tore into the packaging, quickly grabbed the instrument, and sat down in the living room to play. I had been hoping all the while, that even though, made only of plastic, that it was somehow magically a 'real' violin. Alas it was not to be. Right then, my father and grandfather entered the room, and sat down. I explained that I wished and longed for the instrument to be real, but it was just a child's toy. "Nothing more than a prop for playtime," I sadly offered.

Grandfather stated that there was indeed an additional item that was necessary for even a lesser quality instrument like mine to actually create a sound. "Did you look throughout all of the packaging or just throw that out right away," he queried. Just then, I had recalled how my father had lectured me on that very thing, and to not be in such a rush. I was now feeling quite uncomfortable with having disregarded that advice, especially after coaxing Grandma into exceeding her dollar limit.

My grandfather walked over to the garbage can in the downstairs bedroom, and within seconds returned with a small densely wrapped item sitting now right beside me. "See, I think this should be it, let's see," he brightly stated. "Yes, yes, this is the thing you need to really play," he added.

He took the chunk, and rubbed it on the bow. Testing it out he really made it sing. What a relief. I was whole again, and filled with delight. I had forgotten to that day about his very own violin. Yes, the one that he had purchased it at the local barbershop along with some lessons back in the day. Alas this is not his life story. Suffice to say that we both sound a bit like screamingdeadcats!

Here and now though, back in 1964, before me in my very own bedroom was a bona fide bluesman Mr. Jimi Hendrix. He stated that I would need to adapt the lesson to fit it onto just four strings. So, Jimi, while standing in my bedroom played a little thing that he said he was working on. I hadn't thought of that day at all until my buddy, from the band I would form the next year, showed me the intro to that song. That was so many years later when we were actually in high school.

The original lesson didn't last long, but is still very vivid in my mind to this day. What he had said was "I don't know what this is just yet, but I've been working on this for a bit." It would turn out to be the beginning of PURPLE HAZE. That was the song that I would later learn a bit more of from my bro'. It was while I was playing that number back in high school that the memory of the original encounter came pouring back to me.

Hendrix stopped over again to bid adieu. He made his way to New York, then finally England, and the rest was history I feel tremendously fortunate to have been in the right place at the right time way back then, even though our brief encounters were minimal in action, my understanding of life is surely bracketed by all of those features of my younger life back in the early 60s.

It being a newer style of playing, things could crawl right out of the woodwork, and be so totally awesome. I mean just like that. You may know of *places* from the 50s that would allow one to cut a single, thus getting them on local radio if they were good enough. Those were actually vending machine type setups, many in local malt shops. Although, to create the next greatest song a decade or two later certainly took way more than a common nickel.

There was a territorial rights dispute in our area that still goes on to this day. On the one hand the major city had put through a narrow boulevard with flowering trees, and other plants down the center meridian. At the town's border an abrupt change occurred as the clump of trees just ahead made notice of. Just beyond the brush and mighty oaks the corn and cows would stand. In those years that he hadn't planted, the farmer allowed his cows and one bull, full range of the unplanted field.

It was as though all technology, modern thinking, and the very system of life itself had ceased at this line of demarcation. We loved to slip off into that nurturing cover of pure and natural earthiness. I had moved on from the breadboard spanking, and was good to go. I mean, I could now go anywhere that I wanted to. Whew! I mean within reason I now had my wings. It was basically, "If you can manage to walk all of the way back home on your own, and aren't getting into trouble otherwise, you're good!"

Those two older siblings of mine were playing without me again. This time it was the card game Go-Fish. The older one had found a way out of our new deal to play together by choosing a game just over my head. I pleaded with them to show me how.

"No, no," the older one said, "It's too hard, and you're not old enough to learn. Therefore, we're not going to bother to teach you." The other shook her head in a sense of preplanned agreement. I begged again. "Right after this game you could show me, please," I begged. Their next round was about to start.

Mother got up, and put her foot down once again. With an extra emphasis, and her right foot extended, she ordered, "teach him how." It hadn't quite dawned on the family yet that I was a total and utter genius. This was the start of my new persona. Right there, on the living room floor it began. No longer would I be relegated to simply watching. We had played Euchre the sailor's game occasionally since the time I was three years old, so perhaps it was more about feeling that I belonged and was loved, and not the case that I was suddenly so much smarter. Nonetheless, the new era of my 'me' had arrived.

Another notable occurrence that happened around this time, in the early fall as I recall, involved an additional celebrity. A limo pulled up, and I got inside. It was Sonny and Cher that had stopped over that day. We took a short spin then I bid them adieu. Ahh, life could be so good sometimes from out of nowhere. Things settled down quick enough and I was back to my simple ways of living, yet now I truly longed for adventure. I was a wild-man, a gonzo-bopper, a crazed warrior, I was a rock star!

I was back again playing with Jewel Boy, and sometimes her brothers. Since she was in school, I would go the winter without her. She and the younger brother showed me a hornet's nest. It was attached to an old trailer on the end of the block. We made a plan to get them. I would keep a lookout, and she and Kurt would take turns hefting big rocks over the fence.

Once either one had made contact, I would give the signal. I would run down the front of the houses, and she, and Kurt would take the alley way back home. Of course, they would need a jacket, or sweater to cover their heads with, to keep from getting stung.

The day had arrived. We walked over to see if it was a go. A sense of nervousness prevailed. I trusted them as they were older. He one year, and she even two years older. We made our way down to the fence. My mother's friend lived in that house. We didn't really know the folks with the trailer. The decision was made. We would go ahead, and try to dislodge the nest. If for any reason we needed to call it off at the last minute, it would be every man and Jewel Boy for himself, or herself.

He heaved, he heaved again. Those first two were just off a bit I had reported. Then her turn came. The first one was just off to the side, the second a direct hit. "Go, go, you got 'em," I shouted. I still remember the few buzzing around on the outside checking things out just before that massively intensive contact was made. I made my way down to the corner, and around toward my home. I quickly checked to determine if a chase was on.

None were after me just as I had calculated. We all hid in our homes for days. After nearly a week when it was finally safe, I went to see them. Although, neither was very specific, it was really not that cool at all. Apparently, the coats saved them for the most part, yet the older brother had to come to their defense, and may have gotten stung more than once. It was a lesson learned for them, and they would never ever again mess with living creatures such as those.

My good brother, the middle one that slept on only a mattress was back with us, for most of the summer anyway. We could sit in Dad's '49 Ford, and play. I suggested that we get the keys, and even take the thing for a joy ride. My good brother said, "No way, why brother, we'll never get the keys."

"If you know how to drive, we're gonna' do it," I assured him.

"Yeah, I can," he claimed a bit nervously.

"Just watch," I proudly stated. "Mother, Mother," I called to her from inside the car.

"We need the keys," I begged.

"No," shesaid, "Because you can't drive it."

"We want them just to make it more realistic," I exhorted. "And need the keys to do that." Here I was playing with someone ten years older, so that claim must have seemed to make sense. She quickly returned, wishing to be good to us, and fun, and everything, and handed us the keys. "Now don't start it," she warned. As soon as she was back inside with the door closed, bang!

We were off. We drove to the local discount department store pulling into the parking lot. It was a spacious area with plenty of room to maneuver. All that we needed to do now was turn around making a return trip, and we'd have pulled it off. There would be no taking away of this wild experience by anyone. Not Mom, not Father. No one could change what had just occurred. On the way back we took a lazy side street. Up, up, up the hill we climbed.

Once we had ascended to the heights of that block, it would be all downhill from there. We simply needed to coast to the bottom make one turn, and it would be home free. On our descent something strange began to happen. The car pulled left, and then some more. The big heavy vehicle continued its magnetic pull toward the opposite side of the road. Further, and further it was drawn on over, until bang.

We sideswiped a parked vehicle. It was just enough to startle us both, and cause enough damage so that the value of both vehicles had greatly diminished. Later on, so many, many years later when I was all of 18, I had the opportunity to drive. A buddy from school, one of those that I had recruited to start a band during my first year of school, had lived on the bottom of that very hill. At the crest was our grade school. His younger brother had gone in together with some friends, and purchased a car.

He asked if I wanted *to*, so I said, "Yes, I'd love to drive your new automobile." Getting to the top was so familiar. Climbing, climbing slowly, and assuredly. The drive down the hill however nearly turned tragic. Just as strange unseen forces had pulled the vehicle over on that fateful day so many years ago, here this 1968 Dodge was moving, and drawn to the other side of the road in an exacting, and duplicate fashion. Over, and over it pulled. Closer, and closer the car moved until it was on a collision course with a parked car.

It was a car that somehow had managed to be parked in the exact spot as the other had been, on that long ago forgotten day. Before we hit, my bud's little bro grabbed the wheel with all of his might, and jerked it downward. He had saved us all from tragic peril. With none of us three fully licensed he saved more than a major legal hassle as well. The only thing that I could logically ascertain was that the road had been graded for storm run-off.

As long as one duly accounted for the slope in the roadway things would be fine. It was especially one the way down that the sloping seemed to take on a greater sense of urgency. A simple maneuvering adjustment and nothing more is all that it should really have been. Nonetheless, that easy maneuver is one that if not undertaken properly, could cost us all so dearly. I vowed to remember that day forever, should the need ever arise down the road once more again.

Back at home now in 1964 with the damaged vehicle, my Mother was frantic. "I've called your father," she admonished, "And you had better stay right here." Just then, he appeared at the back door. "That's right, don't move," he ordered. He was completely disgusted, and disappointed with us. Then to learn that the car actually had damage just topped it off.

He looked at my good brother and said, "That's it, you'll never drive." I piped up, and told him, "It wasn't him; it was my idea."

"Then you either, neither one of you will ever drive as far as I'm concerned," he said, "And you," to my good brother, "It's his idea, and you're going to listen to him?"

"Yes, that's the way it was," my good brother admitted. We both bowed our heads, and began a suffering of remorse, and one of regret as well. That maligned sense of sorrow hung heavily in the air for days. Within an all too short of time, father reported that the old '49 had been sold.

He took a loss on the ordeal as well. What was meant to be a fun yet minor investment had turned into a nightmare for him. He explained that once the buyer saw the body damage the bargaining began. Where the buyer had the advantage, it was no doubt even a double advantage, with his being a repairman and all, only a painful sense of reality could set in. Father would, as a requirement for work, occasionally travel to Boston for computer updates. The plant needed to upgrade and move to the new punch-card system back in '64. The company was slowly but surely retiring Brown Betty, the room sized computer. As opposed to Big Blue the largest ever, and smartest ever computer, Brown Betty could not play chess against a human.

Nor could it do really much of anything at all. When the super brainy dudes would go into her room at the plant for a thrill, they'd juice the old girl up, and watch the mechanisms whirl, and spin. What father had seen was how wonderfully terrific it made them feel just to be with her for a spell. That was based on their super-dorky smiles as they were leaving her rarely used retirement chamber.

His newest idea offered up upon his return involved a gas pedal type mechanism. He discussed how it would mediate the sound as a 'post-guitar pre-amp' mechanism. In our basement at the time was an oscilloscope. If you've seen the early sixties Sci-Fi classic *The Outer Limits*, you know exactly what one can do. It offered no useful purpose that I was aware of, yet could dance around a bit with its eerie green light. (The '47 Crown Royale typewriter, as well a couple of post WWII oscillating mountable office fans came from the company rummage sale too.)

Today's guitar amplifiers, for the most part, come with built-in options negating the necessity for extra chords and such in so many situations. To be honest Mother has nothing left but the $40,000.00 from Father's life insurance policy, so how this tremendous idea was furthered I do not know. Oh, that old schoolmarm from the 1890s, and still teaching back in 1943. That gal really did a number on pops alright! Later on the overall concept of these pedal effects was transferred to versions without a foot pedal as well.

Those newer 'effects' mechanisms are known as stomp boxes and generally have two or three dials to adjust, and an on/off switch. After Hendrix moved from New York to England, he really got the hang of using these two new, early concepts, presented especially for him. The other, without the pedal, was called a fuzz-box. With a couple of British chaps, he began to record what many would say was his best work. I have his last three releases, and truly enjoy more than a few from each. He put together an African American trio near the end, and said something like, "I'm done specifically writing for the white guys now."

There was to be some type of event downtown. My good brother would make it down there on his own. Once we made our way on foot, into the downtown area, Dad said, "Stand right here like a soldier. Don't move don't talk to anybody. For no reason whatsoever are you to speak to any one person at all."

"Do you understand me?" he asked. As soon as he moved away, I checked out the situation. I simply couldn't help myself. Here was a cool looking guy with long blonde hair. His hair was even longer than the Beatles had back then.

I struck up a conversation right off. He told me that he was from out of town but was so excited to be here. Because Father knew that I couldn't be trusted, he had turned back to look. I was busted. He came back and introduced himself to David. It was indeed, Mr. David Lee Roth. Father mentioned that he had sons about the same age. How Dave actually met all of my bros, I can't quite recall. He did however continue to visit his aunt each summer thereafter, for any number of years even up to 1975, or so.

That summer back in '64 was monumental for an addition reason as well. After Father began to realize that I possessed such a wonderful memory, and been not only able to play Go-Fish, and Crazy 8s, but the game that I began to play with a bit of assistance, Euchre, as well. Father then decided to go ahead and teach me to play chess. At first, he concentrated on the moves, and my being able to independently act on my own. "The horse can jump," he told me. "It is the only piece that can leap over another man," he reminded me at first.

From there, after learning each of the other piece's basic moves, we worked on strategy, and playing a full game. Within weeks I had mastered each piece's ability. I believe he may have *allowed* me to win on at least one occasion. The main point was that I could recall the correct options, and was learning strategy. True learning, even at the young age of 2, or 3 years old, involves a patient sense of repetitiveness. Don't ever underestimate any of your *chillins'*, as far as a genuinely keen sense of learning, and an ability to comprehend.

Another aspect of my early learning involved the tea table my sisters had gotten for Christmas one year. I was allowed to sit on a box and participate. The eldest sister would ask mother for every penny in the house. What she loved to do is so very simple and basic, yet it allows for the teaching of multiplication to even 4-year-olds. So, it was that the eldest of us loved to stack pennies. Not in a mere random format, mind you. Her things were stacks of ten. She called up to Mother for more, one day. "We're so close, we have 73 now," the eldest called up from the lower chamber.

So, Sissy '*got off*' on having ten stacks of ten to count. Oh well, better luck next time! An additional special treat that I was allowed to take part in was to accompany my two sisters to the food store. We had a special short cut through that old apple orchard that we would take. The two both earned 10¢ a week helping with the dishes, and performing any other cleaning chores that they could handle. From my previous experience in that area, I had hatched the perfect plan. As we came upon the first of the apple trees, I laid it out for the two to throw in on.

It was all so very simple. I didn't know why we hadn't been doing it the whole time. My master plan involved a very clever aspect of shopping. We would go into the drug store sure, but merely to look. This was an old school, drugstore setup with stools, and a malt mixer. A young fellow with a crisp white hat, apron, tee-shirt, and white slacks would spin the mixer right in the glass. Next to that, near the register, was a window filled with penny candy.

Because of inflation those did now cost 2¢. Over in the back were hot-rod magazines, and comic books. Around the corner in the second aisle sat plastic put-together models. As long as one didn't smell the glue too much, you'd be okay. They called the setup quite quaintly, "The Quad." The fourth corner was still mostly farmland yet finally managed to become Citified.

I had been given a dime on this special day, yet was warned not to ever expect such kindness again. So, my plan was perfect. We would eat the apples, then while completely satisfied and wonderfully satiated, browse, and consider what we might possibly desire once the cache of yummy good apples had waned. My oldest sister was resolute. Although, being only a one-eighth Polish, neither of the two sisters back then was able to convey things verbally, in a clearly swift and well-pronounced fashion.

She claimed that these precious gems of the shortcut trail were somehow no good. "What do you mean no good?" I grumbled. My dreams of everlasting contentedness were being snatched right from my very heart.

The other sibling nodded in agreement. "Now what do you mean, no good," I further demanded.

"Here," the elder offered, "I'll let you try one, then you can see for yourself how they're '*no good*'. I selected the best one reachable and she plucked it down then offered it unto me.

"I'll show you; this is going to be good, and I'll like it," I insisted.

I took a healthy bite. "Now look," she scolded, pointing at the now exposed interior of the dirty rotten fruit. "See?" she questioned. I quickly spat out what I had been righteously chewing on, and threw the rest to the ground.

Okay, okay you were right, but what is that anyway, I wondered.

"I don't really know, but worms are one thing they can have, whether that's what that was, or if that's something else, I'm not sure," she explained.

I spat again to the ground quickly just in case any wormy remains had lingered. Damn Polish girl, how funny she could truly be when she so desired. Lesson learned. The thing had been, we always ate crab apples, and those had never had any brown yucky lines running through them. We wended our way upon the trail, then made it to the drug store and bought our stash. Good, good yummy flavorful candy never tasted so pleasing, nor was it ever so appetizingly satisfying.

I made it a point to save something for our walk back on the trail. As we passed that wretched tree I so ever triumphantly, and in a pleasingly grandiose fashion, popped a small candy in my mouth "Ehm, yummy," I thought as a sweet and precise footnote. So, much more delectably desirable those little candies had become. *Take note self, sometimes big sissy does know what's best for us*, I had thought.

We were going to the Cubs game. Father's younger brother would be on leave from the Navy. An additional aspect of day involved seeing the home run swatter Hank Aaron. He was with the Braves, a team that had recently left Boston. Tickets were 50 cents. I noticed one aspect of our arrival in the front row. African Americans were saving the entire front row, seemingly for any white fans.

I understood all too well, in that day and age, about race relations. It nonetheless made me a tad bit uncomfortable. Ever so quickly my joy had returned. It was Father that had taught us a lesson from his pops. It was a family rule. We would never pre-judge any person based on assumptions, or quickly derived, and potentially biased opinions. As well, with Mother's infrequent gentleman caller being none other than Frank Clark himself we maintained a staid sense of neutrality through those days of yore.

My older sister had been very excited as of late at the dinner table. It would be approximately 24 hours later, and the event would begin. This girl that rode the same bus to school with my sister, from down the block, had really gotten her pumped up for the whole ordeal. That friend at the school had been mentioning the next greatest thing to happen to just about anyone. The new musical group 'The Beatles' were coming to America.

That wasn't all. The landing itself would be televised, so that all of their eager fans could witness the very first steps of these Brits, actually being taken on American soil. The Beatles would indeed be playing a local show. The anticipation at that school my sisters attended grew more and more each day.

The younger brother of this classmate had gotten the '61 flue as well as myself. You see we had both suffered terribly from what the girls had brought home three years before. The older girls would have been in kindergarten that year. My friend had to be rushed to the hospital no doubt suffering from Ryes' Syndrome. It was discovered much later that children under the age of 2½ or so, should not be given aspirin to reduce a high fever. I myself was up to 104 degrees. We both now suffer from tinnitus and a loss of balance. (Update: My sister starts to rock back and forth nearly falling, when she is alone in a room just the same as I do.)

Finally, the day had come. There was only one catch. With father going off to his second job so quickly, we had been eating dinner quite early. By 4:00pm actually it had been. The landing based on the ETA would, no doubt, be conflicting with our meal. There it was though. Mother gave the word. We could, if necessary, rush up from the table leaving our food behind, while racing into the living room, and plopping down in front of the television set. As long as we used proper manners, and were excused anyway, we could.

It was more than determined that the likelihood of interruption was imminent. We listened closely. Mother told us to "now just sit there, and wait for it." There it was. The newsman reported.

We sprang from our chairs, and rushed forward. We sprawled with excitement upon the living room floor, as close to the set, as reasonably possible. That nearness to the boob tube, with us sprawled upon the floor, was a distance that would have already been so readily determined beforehand.

Such a calculation would have been well defined during the airing of shows such as TOM TERRIFIC, and THE MOUSKETEERS. Tom Terrific was a sketchy, crude cartoon figure with a funnel for a hat. Whenever he needed to come up with a super new idea, the thoughts would flow from outer space, then move right into the top of his special hat. Mickey Mouse was the mascot for the Mousketeers Club TV show.

The plane door opened and The Fab Four emerged with smiles. They moved out to a throng of uncontrollable school girls no less. We all were giddy. Not just myself. Not just my sisters. No, it was every single being it had seemed, for a quarter of the earth's surface around, was now on cloud nine. Those sweet young girls though, were more than frantic with glee. The overwhelming crescendo of youthful fervor would rise to an effervescently brilliant climax.

The excitement for me was innocent, and beautiful. Considering music was the main theme of the event, such an experience could only be a good thing. Just as I was getting another bolt of it, it happened. A young lady about twelve years of age had fainted. All of the girls themselves had been clenching and clawing at the chain link fence, erected to keep the lads safe. These young ladies could barely deal with whole reality of this 'Fab Four's' presence. The young gal that became overwhelmed, was now picked up, and carried off by local law enforcement.

She was merely the personification of each and every emotion shooting, spraying, spewing, erupting, and overflowing so beautifully, and now rolling across the screen, and into and through all of our hearts. It was a frenzied hysteria of joyful jubilation. I so quickly realized that this had to be the best job in the world, as far as being a musician. I somehow knew another fellow here in America, yet off in the distance, to the east even, actually had been feeling the same things, and coming to the same conclusion as myself. Wowza!

Here is how the questions may have come for the group.

Reporter: So, what is your job.

One of the Beatles: Well, we make girls scream, and faint, or otherwise go crazy.

Reporter: Is that a good paying job?

Any one of them: Why yes. It pays very handsomely, so far anyway.

Can any fellow imagine, or appreciate the totality of this awesome new awareness. One that had reached so far deep, and into me that it was awe inspiring. To think making young girls faint is a well-paying profession.

Some may know of that other fellow from the east that I had fathomed. The one that I knew was just out there somewhere. With him feeling it all so giddily overwhelming too, I mean. I laughed a hearty laugh at it all, as well. But it was none other than Gene Simmons from the Band Kiss, they, a group that would rise up within ten years with a steamy pulse of its own. I finally heard this man proclaim his version of how things played out on that tremendous day during an interview presented on TV by around 1980, or so.

Weeks after that New York landing, my older sister took us into the bedroom. We sat on the floor. She had something very important to tell us. Not only were the Beatles playing here in town, that very night, she had told us, there was something even more. "Oh," she sighed, "It would have been so nice to go."

The answer naturally would be, no was no. She had reconciled for some time that it was just not to be. "But guess what?" she added. "Just before the show they're going to stop here. They're supposed to anyway," she claimed.

"Ohhh, are you kidding?" I asked, as my younger sister, and I started to get excited, and giggled with glee. My older sister nodded her head with a certain assurance stating, "Yeah, they are, really, really supposed to, anyway. You know if they have time and are not too busy, at least two of them, anyway."

"So, who knows what else they may have to do just before the show, it could be anything, so maybe not, but they are supposed to, if they have time," she reassured us. I immediately got the idea to offer a tribute as a *show* of our appreciation.

I said, "Let's write a song, and then sing it to them before they leave." We began to reach for words for anything. I did so vocally. "Let's see, LOVE, LOVE. Come on help me," I pleaded. Suddenly, they started to bale on me even before we had given it a real shot. Once more I sang "LOVE, LOVE."

"Now you two come up with something that goes with it," I had requested in an urgent and needful tone. They shook their heads. It was of no use. They were just too, too excited to come up with anything. I said rather disappointedly, "You're going to ruin it, we need more than one word for it to be any good."

"No," the younger said very safely, "Let's not."

"Well, I'm still doing it," I protested. I just need a few more words. The older sister was like, "Please don't embarrass yourself, we tried, it didn't work, just say hi," she ordered in a mature and calm tone. Just then, the doorbell rang. We moved out cautiously from the bedroom easing our way down the hallway one small step at a time. Finally, I was in view as the other two stayed back a bit. "Hi," I said. It was John, and Paul, as plain as day, and in their stage attire.

They said hello, my sisters did as well. I then went into it. "I wanted to sing this song for you as a thank you," I informed them.

"LOVE, LOVE, LOVE," I shakily offered forth, in a trembling and nervous fashion. Oh well that's as far as I got. "We were working on it just now but they decided not to do it," I apologetically offered.

"Oh thanks," one said. No doubt it was Paul. With that they had left, and the thrill of a lifetime was over. So, soon we were off to bed never to mention such an occasion again.

As far as my true and overwhelming joy for music, it must be genetic. On some days, my father would play his Bell Amplifier, and Harmon Kardon tuner. For the most part it was about playing my birthday record. That was the one from Marty Robbins Father had purchased while Mother gave birth to me. Either that album was played, or it was the William Tell Overture album, with the Boston Pops performing those orchestral numbers. A new group to groove to therefore, would be just the thing for all of us. I have come to realize the music thing come from both sides.

Mother brought home a picture from her parent's home. The professional level photo shows an older fellow that had obviously been in the service. You could see that he had sold his military horse, moved to the U.S., and then used the remaining funds to buy instruments for his new town band. You could tell Great-Grandpa was a high-ranking officer by his cool white suit. He pulled some strings back in his homeland and managed to have de-certified uniforms sent over for his new gang as well, seemingly anyway!

He as well, taught them how to play if necessary. I now realize that I am a superhero from heaven brought here to continue with Great-Grandpa's work. So, what if his very own son, a dude that is my grandfather, sounds like I do. I mean again yes, like screaming dead cats when we play. We work it dog! It may actually come down to 'style' rather than sound when considering the appropriate placement of 'screamingdeadcats' and where those wailings may actually fit in the best.

My Indian friends were in the alley playing again soon after. I suggested that we go out to the woods. Previously, I have written that we had tracked a deer, and had seen where it had slept. It was startled, and ran off before we, the younger kids had a chance to see it. We would go off to the same area, but took a left turn instead, this time out. Half way down the trail, I convinced the brother Kurt who was six at the time to go on ahead as I needed to talk to his sister alone.

She was maybe only eight or so, nonetheless I was in love. When Kurt came back, and found that I was trying to *make out* with Jewelboy he became quite angry. He said let's go and moved on forward but made sure I was left behind a little. I said that I needed to make sure that I wasn't lost or anything because of the way I had gotten it from Mother the last time. With her now having broken a bread board over my butt, I just wanted to be careful. Kurt said, "Too bad, we're not waiting. But I will make sure that we're together at the end of the trail."

"Oh, why is that? What is it, what?" I asked.

"Of you'll see when we get there," he assured me. Once we arrived back out in the open air, he said, "Come on over right here little Willy, right here." He had been standing next the giant ant hill. Not that the ants were any larger than any others. The hill itself was a good foot or more high, indeed, and at least that far across as well.

He said, "Now you sit here right on top of that hill, and if I turn around, and see that you're not still sitting on it, you're really going to get it." With that he shook his fist at me. As he and Jewelboy turned to walk away, a deep fear filled my veins. I was petrified. Just then, the ants began to crawl on my legs, and even up my back. Mother appeared from out of nowhere. I had nearly begun to cry at this point, and the turmoil was unbearable.

She had taken the street, and those two had taken the alley back home so she was not quite aware of what had been going on. She waved her arm, and I called her over. Once she reached the area, I explained the orders I was under, *not to move*. She suggested that maybe I was once, and for all done with those two, and I readily agreed. "Maybe I am," I stated as I made sure no tears trickled down my cheeks. "But I like them," I added.

"Oh, you like them when they do things like this?" she asked.

"That was Kurt," I told her, and couldn't very well explain any justification for his actions without implicating myself. I merely needed for it to all blow over as quickly as it possibly could. It was actually two years before that, when I had first come to the grand realization that Jewelboy was actually a girl. I had somehow forgotten because of how adventurous, and fun that she was. But there she had been, coming home from her first communion.

She wore a beautiful white and blue dress, one with a lovely floral pattern. I had just experienced a whole new appreciation for my special friend. Not only was she so much fun to be with. Not only did I love to be with her. Now indeed I even loved her big-time as well. It was in such a deep and passionate fashion that I couldn't help myself. Here and now, because of my previous grounding, it looked like the final curtain had fallen on our nature loving relationship.

1965

The summer had begun to warm. Two houses over from where the stinging buzzers had been removed, they set up shop again. That home had sat vacant allowing the nasty buggers an easy option, as far as moving to newer digs. Next to the porch grew a bountiful treasure. In the woods similar growth was abundant but always green, and not too tasty in the slightest. Yet there up on the hill by the door where no one lived, grew the reddest and now tall, ready to eat rhubarb. A bowl of sugar was all that was needed to sweeten the deal.

My good friend's brother came walking along so merrily with a stalk in hand, and a hardy smile as well. He explained that not only was it about the last one there was, there was even a greater reason to put away any desirous thoughts altogether. It was that, so near the wonderful plant growth, and all abuzz mind you, was that brand-spanking-new hornet's nest. Or wasp's maybe. Does it matter at all when they look to be about two inches long, with stingers, and are perhaps not new to being disturbed in the general area?

A while had passed so I coaxed my friend into taking a closer look at any new growth. We just needed enough new stalk growth, plus someone brave and bold enough to pick it for us. The few stalks that had remained from the last foray were just nearing the perfect height. Back, and forth with a threatening presence were the stingers. That was all that we needed to see, for now anyway. It would seem that the family of pests from the trailer on the end of the block hadn't moved very far at all. If they possessed the gift of memory, 'twould not be good at all to hang around here for very long.

Later on, I was out at the other end of the block just hanging out not doing much. Who should ride up but my good brother, and his school chum. They had ridden all of the way from the old neighborhood. It was at least four miles, and they were now resting. My brother's friend had an old, I would say, 1963 Schwinn bicycle that had been modified. The parts were available at the local discount store on the main street. Old Highway 39 it was. That was the safe place my brother had taken us to turn the old '49 Ford around, midway through our joyride.

The friend's bike had a shiny golden body that still looked fairly new, and was obviously well taken care of. The new seat was long but not so narrow. Only brand-new bikes came with a sleek narrow banana seat. This one, although just a bit wide, was covered in a cream-colored upholstery. The handlebars too had been swapped out, for a high pair. High like the chopper motorcycles had. The friend expressed his desire to be in a big-time band.

He said quite honestly "Yes, right now I have a bass guitar, one day though, I'd like to be in a band." It wasn't long after the two stopped to rest that they were set to get back on their way. My good brother and Geddy Lee, who himself would go on later to form the Canadian band Rush, turned their bikes back around and headed back home. Not long after I remember meeting someone I called 'Geddy's cousin'.

She was about my age, although perhaps she was actually a young American Indian. Geddy is Jewish, but she reminded me so much of him. It was at the local café that I specifically recalled our meeting. That was the café that I had appeared in, after having donned a replica 'Lone Ranger' outfit. I ask myself if he was even there on that day with 'her'. It was only a brief meeting, just to say hi I guess, it's still a little fuzzy. Years later, I walked into a bar, and there she was.

It was not the first time that I had traveled back in my mind to that day at the cafe. I had spotted this young lady from across the street on more than one occasion. Here in this smaller location with only a few patrons inside the place, I had the chance to sit next to her. There was not much really going on. It was already getting late when I had first walked in. The bartender soon loudly announced 'Last Call'. Geddy's cousin turned, and so very sweetly planted one on me. It was not a romantic kiss at all, yet still with purpose, and an honestly simplistic meaning.

She looked me in the eye, and said, "Well, goodbye then." I was thinking, "No, no," I believe that I even uttered those words aloud. In accepting that the night was through we got up to leave. I never saw her again. To this day, I recall the innocent sincerity of our goodbye. Let it be known that I have more than just a common fondness for Native American girls. Some have my heart all of the way, yet none are here with me now, at least near enough to go for it with.

Within a year of meeting Geddy, I had heard the news. He was leaving town. He was actually moving very far away, all of the way to Canada. I feel that my good brother still has a very minor sense of bitterness because of the way that things worked out for Geddy, and yet not quite as well for himself. One day in 1973, I happened upon my good brother at an old location. It was not only that Dave had busked the crowd at the summer festival, doing his mime act while wearing his good humor gloves in that nearby location.

It was the year before I looked over to see none other than the 'good-one', my middle older brother. My dad slipped me a five, and I joyously turned it over to dude right away. He grinned at the opportunity and moved off to enjoy himself much more so, now that he had some breathing room in his pocket. We had gone years before that 'not talking' again! One can easily understand therefore that this was so very special for us in such a regard. I mean still 'not talking'!

Things rolled out fairly smoothly for me the rest of the year. It would seem that my older siblings had been well occupied with school homework, professional activities, or even more. I had my new friend from two doors down. His house held my audition for Liberace. Although, he was often busy being tended to at that young age, we were promised more freedom down the road. My next-door neighbor, the fellow that attended the other Catholic Grade School, would be around enough in the meantime.

In addition, I had conquered my fear of so many ants raiding my panties all at once. Sadly, that came with one caveat. Mother's only option for self-defense went against the grain of my deeply held feelings, if you can follow. So, she finally gave up trying to appease my worries and woes. After I proved to her that the dirty little buggers still came at me like a Megaton Blonde, (actual song from a small local act) she felt that she had no choice. She even herself, demonstrated how her last resort option worked.

"See," she said. "Do it just like that." With that she stomped the closest little bitch. Then, ever so quickly, she womped and mushed the next. Ants have this special rule concerning the dead. For reasons that seem to have to do with the old adage "waste not, want not," they drag the dead off to their underground lair. One can only surmise the type of funeral arrangements that are then 'not' made. It, I believe, is more like a cold storage approach. I guess they take after humans just a tad after all.

I still remember the day that I enrolled in school for first time. I had fallen asleep, even though I loathed having to lie in bed all alone. Within half hour or so, I usually nodded off. It was beforehand that I hated it so much. This day was special though, I just needed to doze, then wake up to the beginning of my well matured school days. I sat on the back porch to try and break through the after-nap haze. There wasn't much that actually took place soon after. I sat in a chair in the principal's office, while Mother did nearly all of the talking.

I got a brand-new rain coat for the occasion. An army green canvas special. It was the color of that particular issue that I liked so much. I had just received a pair of British army style shorts with so many pockets that they couldn't all be possibly filled, at least all at once anyway. They were just the thing to go out to the woods with, especially since I had been forbidden to engage in such an activity. I knew better than to ask, so was simply cool about it, doing my best to not come home with any evidence or tell-tale signs of such an adventure having taken place.

A new friend from my kindergarten class was aware of the Beatles having landed. His brother was around 8 years old at the time. I hatched a plan, involving Beatle wind-up guitars and a *show* that we would perform. He and his special honest approach called for a disclaimer. So, that we could not be considered as impostors he felt it necessary to clear up any potential confusion beforehand. I believe one should truly respect such innocent, yet well placed virtue. Talk about values. Whatever man, I just wanted to do my very first *live* performance.

It came off well. I believe we had at least a couple of the girls really into it big-time. If I recall correctly, a few as well, were a bit let down. I decided to walk home to my new buddy's house as he lived just down the way. I missed my bus, and had to walk home. It was a pleasure with the sun shining down, and the temperature still warm enough. With only one major street before the new subdivision where I lived, it would be a cinch. I was warned to be more careful down that stretch of road, and fully obliged.

I got home on the bus not long after that day. Father was home. In addition, a very special guest was in the hall checking out family photos. Eisenhower was a few years removed from office. He was balding and gray, and somewhat shorter than father. I had to believe afterwards that it was an undercover investigation being conducted not so much on behalf of The Prince of Wales, but because that prince was indeed, actually over on a brief visit the year before.

I did consider even back then, that no one was going to have Royalty over, without an official vetting of all and any necessary circumstances. Those nosey buggers down at headquarters, er, I mean over in Washington, wanted everything that they could possibly get their hands on, when it came to any potentially embarrassing chicanery, tom foolery, hijinks, shenanigans, or otherwise potentially embarrassing actions, or activities. We all knew to play it cool. It had seemed to come off without a hitch, as no further evidence of any high-end snooping did occur afterwards.

Old boy did give me a pep talk though, about being tough, saying, "Things aren't easy at all," and "that if one wanted something you had to go out and get it." After that brief peptalk, he was gone. I've never told anyone, yet who would have believed such an outlandish tale. I had to believe I was in some way being groomed for success, or at least prepped for that very thing. Perhaps I really, really was. If even in a small and minor way, I was inspired.

1966

It was near the end of school? My friend, a classmate as well from down the street by where the corn grew every other year, had let me in on something exciting. There was a deer family just behind the brush at the edge of the trail. That brush was 5 yards from the old ant hill. I believe someone had at them well before. Here it was actually more of a warning about babies that my pal was imparting to me. He took me over to the spot that was still seemingly safe.

Whispering he let me know that they were just out of view, back behind the leaves. The other thing he mentioned was that it was best to leave them alone. Not only do they need rest and quiet for the baby, he told me, the dad will jump out, and attack. I questioned the validity of his claim, yet he swore to it. One fellow had already found out. The hard way it was at that. "He is big, and bad, you can believe that, no one wants to mess around with any of them," he assured me.

Not long afterward, I couldn't help myself. Perhaps it was being told not to do something that was getting to me. I just had to see for myself. I got my buddy and we crept over to the safe line he had shown me previously. I let him know what I was up to. "Go ahead," I said, "I will give you a head start back home. As soon as you're in the clear, I'm going to shake this branch. I'll see if the dad really comes jumping out."

I waited, and waited. I called out. "Not yet," my pal replied. I gave it a few more seconds then grabbed, and shook just as I was told not to. I heard a rumble. Lo, and behold. Up leaped a huge deer high into the air. Without warning he was already in mid-air, placed just above the trail only a few feet away. Before he had landed, he pulled off some kind of a ballet move. With the type of execution only a well-studied prima could maneuver he had gone from facing east to now facing south in my direction.

This mind-blowing move was executed all the while miraculously and gracefully held aloft in midflight. He landed with all fours securely on the path, and ready to trample me in an instant. My mind went wild. I panicked, and moved as quickly as possible. At the edge of the trail were the road dead-ended was a drop-off. I recalled somehow what my older sister had said about bears. If one needs to, a person should curl up in a ball, and play dead.

It may not work, but it would be your only hope she had added. Near the top of the incline, I lost my footing, and tripped. Whether it would work with a deer I didn't know, but I instinctively curled up into the smallest most still and quiet ball of idiocy that I could manage. I prayed, "Oh God be with me now." After a few seconds, I realized that he was not thrashing me about with his horns or his hooves.

I mustered all of my courage, and peeked. He had waited politely at the base of the trail.

In the ground, he marked a line. Again, he showed me what he demanded with a ferocious motioning indicating, "cross this line and it's over." He imparted this message in a wordless, yet all too clear demonstration of well vocalized body language. Recall how I read the mind of the largest deer on record. At least from my childhood, the record still stands. This humongous beast had somehow felt each and every human inside of those homes were trespassing.

At least during *his* rounds, we somehow were. Again, I state, "He must have been born right in that spot!" I got up here so close to the start of the pavement that I could taste safety. He showed me once again the line of invasion. He then displayed more prominently his rack of discipline. *Alright*, I thought, and proceeded to walk backward away from the nightmarish scene. For a half a block I did so. *No, no*, I thought, *I'll give him at least a few more feet.*

That few feet became the end of the entire block. I looked once more to the farthest reaches that my eyes could perceive. I truly had never really moved my gaze much away from the pit of anguish down below. I was about to turn, and walk normally, but no. There was no need in taking any chances. I may as well just go ahead, and continue the backward approach for now, just in case. Even though he couldn't see me at all, even if he had decided to not charge up the hill, I could not shake an impending sense of doom.

I mean even though a race car could not have reached me from that point, in under two minutes, I still needed to play it safe. I moved around the first corner a tad recovered from his demonstrative manliness. "Why take any unnecessary chances now that I was nearly home free?" I had thought. Just a few more steps onward toward the alley way, and I would be safe! As soon as I had turned to move in a common manner the horrifying terror returned.

Maybe just a few more steps backward were all that I had needed to engage in. Wouldn't that remove the panic-stricken fear of dread, encased so deeply in the essential core of my quivering heart. Check just once more, and another time again, I had thought. Again, and again I needed to see for myself that he indeed was not rethinking his strategy. Now somehow, now unprovoked, was it deciding to make one last and final charge at me!

A full block, and a half away I was finally at my home. Just one more glance down the alley, I had felt. Alright, alright, I had considered, he's still not coming. I considered that I had better not mention a thing to anyone. Since I was the instigator in this fiendish plot of trespass to begin with, a victim's hat would not wear well. After about ten minutes of total and utter anxiety, I just felt the raw and utter need to go back outside and check down the alley once again.

You know, just in case that pesky deer was still hanging around scratching at the dirt and such. With the greatest sense of relief, I have ever felt in my life, I saw that the coast was clear. With the stark, total, and utter realization that he was once again, peacefully with his loving wife and child, I went back inside. That last time I was finally able to relax. Whew! Sometimes it is better to refer to some heavier tomes, or at least something substantial in writing at the library, rather going *all in*, all at once.

In the meantime I had cooked up this hair brained scheme. I got my buddy to go over to the house with the rhubarb, and *sting-e'ros*. You know, *enEspanol es Waspeses, oHornetas*, at least based on my one year, *o un an'o de Espan'ol*. The instructor was of Spanish descent himself. He would fill us in on Cuban vs. Main Homeland dialect, letting us know of any differences in the local lingo. Though, traveling backward in time now, to the year of rhubarbos, I am even now more so enlivened with a brazenly brash sense of boldness.

I said to my bro down the way, "see this rock? I'm going to smash that nest off of the house so that we can finally get some freaking rhubarb of our own." Keep in mind, I was a youngster and didn't use vulgarities at such a sweet, kind, gentle, and much younger age as that. Considering the fellow's parents were Baptist and Lutheran, in that order, I indeed was careful not to tread too heavily in any regard. His pops even felt that tattoos were somehow a sin against God, so one may easily imagine a sense of acumen, and social politeness would be highly recommended around any of their kind.

I had apparently failed to truly grasp the silence of my young Indian friends that resulted from our last foray into the unwise world of 'messin'. You learn after a while you don't mess with this, and you certainly don't mess with that. It only makes plain common sense. In lacking that bit of logic, I was set to move forward. My friend pleaded with me to resist the urge, yet it was all too late. Sometimes a man's got to do what a man's just got to do, or a really stupid kid needs to in this case.

Mother had warned me to stay away. It was to no avail. I gave my buddy a generous head start. Once I felt that he was safely near enough to his own front door I readied my ammo. Cocking back, setting my aim now keenly affixed to their creation I simply needed to release. If on target, success would be mine. Heaven forbid I should miss a little, merely angering the flying critters, especially if they remembered who I was. This was the moment of greatness that would surely place me upon the pinnacle of heroes, at least in a common and local sense of heroic lore anyhow.

A trove of yummy rhubarb hung in the balance. I was set, and fired. I turned as quickly as possible without regard to the outcome of my attack. I flew swiftly down the hill, and spilled out into the alley way. I ran like I had never run before. As I was nearing the back walk to my house, a horrible sensation settled in. Are you aware of the comical display offered up in cartoons that involve a bear, and some honey. If you have seen one of these, you'll note that the flying insects form the *shape* of said bear or other victim, just before making contact.

I heard them now just behind me, droning like a jet engine. I quickly surmised that a speedy football move would be necessary in order to shake them. I put my head down, and did my best to switch directions. It was a fatal mistake. They within a foot or two of my back were in total and strict formation. Imagine a flying shirt made up of hornets. Yeah, you've got it now. I moved past them but they all too easily changed direction, and began to settle on me.

Landing, and stinging. Stinging, and landing. I yelled, and instinctively moved into a neighbor's yard without a fence around it. With lightning-fast speed I needed to accelerate. The fellow that lived there had heard me, and came to my rescue. He pulled me inside, and as I lay on his kitchen floor, he pulled the buggers right off of me with his bare hands. He was stung repeatedly, and his wife now was in a panic. She rushed to the ladies' room, yet needed to quickly close the door on those that had entered.

She hesitantly returned to assist her mate.

Even while fearing for their own safety, one by one, they managed to dislodge the huge and vengeful monsters. He crushed, and stomped, slapped, and hit until none remained alive. When the dust had settled his wife was crying, he swore a bit at those few that had flown into the bathroom. So, soon then a hollow silence carried through. He walked me back home, and I slept. I had gone into shock, and was still dazed the next day after sleeping throughout the entire afternoon. My mom asked how I was, and if I could recall the tragic incident of the previous day.

Yes, I could. I managed to get some food down, then went back to sleep praying. Praying for the neighbor, praying for my own forgiveness, and I indeed was praying so that I could finally somehow put together a sense of right, and wrong. When I awoke on the third day, I had nearly fully recovered from the utter sense of madness that I had wrought upon myself. One minute there was peace, and then because of my foolish carelessness, total chaos reigned. Heaven help me.

I still wasn't supposed to ride the little girl's 24-inch hand me down, used bike that we had. I did it anyway and had gotten away with it more, and more. My neighbor was hanging out and I got on the bike. I would ride past our red picket fence, and he would lunge from his yard, and act all scary. It grew dark. About one or two more would be it, yet it was just getting crazy with the sun completely down. I came for a pass, and he moved toward me.

No doubt due to my near death, fever ridden flu experience as a baby, the one that left me with a sense of imbalance, I swerved too far to the right and impaled my chin ever so slightly on one point of the pickets. Mom didn't drive and Father was at his night job earning money for his other family. Mother would have to scrounge around for a ride. It didn't take long and we were on our way. My first stitches did not amount to anything substantial.

Wildly delirious fun was never so excruciating. It seemed so much worse at first than it actually, truthfully was. Later on, once I had recovered for the most part, except for the removal sequence, I was back to being my wild and crazy self. Those stitches came and went quickly and I was as good as new, for a while anyway. As sure as shootin' it would no doubt be a short ride before the next owie, or boo-boo all to quickly caused an additional timeout in my young, wild, and freely exciting young life.

Our new teacher was a nun. I recognized two of the girls from the public school kindergarten class. It was my very first day at the Catholic Grade School. We started on that first day by listening for our names. By about C, I had drifted off into my own world. (Check my many nicknames, 'Drifty' is one, it is definitely not because I'm a railroad tramp.) "Now?" she asked after perhaps going through the entire list she had been reading from before her. "Who did not hear their name called?"

I raised my hand and fessed up. I had known since I came out of my malaise at about the S's that I was maybe in trouble. "I called out your name and you were not listening, try to make sure that doesn't happen again," she scolded. I would become that very person 'Drifty' by my junior year in high school. That had more to do with it being my turn to go, rather than any hobo-train hopping type of experiences from those teen years.

Whew, I was just glad to move on to the ABCs. Our early studies also involved simple addition, and humungous flash cards hanging on rings upon a rack on wheels. As I've said before, and no doubt will again, it's all about memory. The less one has of that gift, the more rigorous studying that shall be required of an aspiring young individual. The way I have been blessed, you can believe that I truly *do* go back in time, to that first day, with her advanced cue cards and all.

Those would be dragged forth from their treasure trove in the far depths of our school library. She made it quite clear that some '3rd' grade work wasn't truly that at all. "Why, no it wasn't," I gladly agreed. It was 1st grade work for us super-smart kids in 1st. One day she brought in a tape recorder. They had around that time, shrunken down reel-to-reel tape players. Huge, old-school-movie projector types of tape players would no longer be the standard. They had modified the two reels, into tiny small, self-contained, portable mini rolls.

The original reel-to-reel, for those not in the know, was perhaps about 2½ ft. high, by 1½ wide. One would play out the recording then place the single reel into a box. The reel originally placed onto the machine, now empty, would be used to wind the next reel onto. Anyone over 50 may recall indeed, that those old movies could be brought in to the classroom, using the same concept of full reels wound onto the empties, as those educational cinemas played out.

We would now each read from the book while talking into the microphone. When done, she began the playback. Drat, I didn't know that I sounded like Charlie Brown from the Christmas cartoon. I would need to work on my pitch, range, and a greater sense of manliness. Oh well, I had time. With my first report card, however, I did experience a shameful reckoning. If one readily looks to the future, such an experience offers a chance for self-betterment. My most recent boss used the same approach.

Unless perfection is displayed there is always room for improvement. I felt fairly well about the whole episode, as far as the recording went. I still have that feeling of being slightly harmed though, when I come across that little 'saved item' from my younger days. I do mean my 1st grade report card. That is what is just a tad off somehow. A brilliant genius such as I am must be fully 'on' or a sense of sheer and utter disappointment does wait for me.

Although, one aspect of my downgrading back in first grade may have been all too easy to readily identify. I was seated next to a boy whose twin sister sat just in front of him. I still do indeed recall each and every aspect of this particular scolding his twin and I received. When you consider that I ran into a former classmate of ours, and went into the whole ordeal just yesterday, it isn't hard to understand. Back in 10/21, I recalled for her how it had all come down. The twin brother instinctively knew better than to talk. He at least knew to not go on about things.

It was already too late. His fraternal twin was way too revved up and rolling. She went into a slight bit of overdrive just before the hammer came down. Since I had, no doubt audibly, as well as visibly, just offered a return comment to her in response, we were both so very well busted. The medium width masking tape was already in tow, and all too ready to be applied. The Catholic Nun warned us to not attempt to remove that facilitator of such seriously applied strict discipline.

She as well had let us know that she would keep us so readily us in mind in the interim. I mean should either of us somehow so suddenly become more than a tad uncomfortable, or heaven forbid, experience a more than urgent need to suddenly communicate a verbal offering to another, our teacher would have been all too 'at-the-ready'. Ready to pounce upon us like a wild cat, no doubt! That, oh so 'non-veiled', threat was offered to keep us on our toes. Recess never came as such an invigorating relief!

Another interesting aspect of the first official year of education was our teacher's tale of New York City. She went to college there, and had the opportunity to meet a theologian. Over there, somewhere over there, on far east coast, on the fortieth floor of a very large building, I had imagined that this older fellow went about his studies debating issues contemplating realities, and making discoveries. When she spoke of him, she was in another world. It was as though the roof lifted, birds sang, butterflies fluttered, and angels strummed.

In a very special and blessed way, she truly would leave us, and go back east to a younger day. It was with an innocence and purity that she certainly would breathe in with admiration, and a solemn respect for this older 'beau'. Teacher has a boyfriend, is what I thought. She went on to tell us of their special romance, I mean 'platonic relationship', and how much she cherished, and adored this much older man.

They would get together at the coffee shop across from Central Park, and have rap sessions concerning all things supernatural, and Godly. If you know the American television show 'Seinfeld', where the cast got together for talk, and coffee, you're close. I considered that it was a very special thing for one to cherish such a relationship, even to the point of piety, or at least with such a special closeness to this man to extract such reverent feelings.

It's Christmas again. I had been back in the home for two years now. I was thinking that there would be more than the hand me down presents from that previous year so quickly forgotten. The year was special indeed. I received a toy cowboy, Johnny West, and an American Indian figure, though only one horse. In addition to those minor playthings, an official cowboy guitar was given. I do believe now that I had childhood arthritis. If you continue on, you will read about Christmas 1971. I'm as tough as they come, when things involve true grit. As far as guitar playing, it still hurts me to play to this day.

1967

It was a warm late spring evening. The news had just gotten over, and I needed to choose a show for some simple viewing. I was all alone, although my sisters were no doubt here or there. Upon arising from the sofa, I looked out the window to the empty street out in front. From out of the south comes a dad riding his daughter across the bike frame just in front of himself, while he himself was well seated on the saddle. It was a darker blue and white Schwinn special. Compared to the one that Geddy Lee had, I believe it was nearly identical, sans the Atlantic Mills-discount-department-store upgrade.

In a moment they drove back on by. Slim trickles of blood drained down the young lady's leg. Only one thing can cause such harm. I mean I would see the older kids from that clan double riding the younger kids on a regular basis. Oh well. This was a family of doers, I would say. I will be so very well blunt to clarify that this gentle sweet girl, 5 or 6 years of age, was running around like a wild monkey in a full lower leg cast, within weeks of her sudden and unexpected mishap. So, while having her lower limb get caught up in the spokes was most assuredly tragic, you can't keep a good girl down I would say. Not for very long anyway.

As I was quite honestly motivated by the Speeches of Dr. King to maybe become a preacher, what was happening out in the world hit home a bit harder that it would for most other youngsters there were of my age. "What next?" one might wonder. Then it came. Down the road just, just a four-year term later, Bobby, the younger brother of JFK was now running for the highest seat in government. Before the election took place, he too was taken from us.

It was the same as with his brother, though with no concrete evidence to support any overt or covert connection. The main suspect would be the only one brought forward to pay. He, a foreigner, had to have had a cartel of conspirators behind him. Now we had two additional icons of social popularity taken from us, with the third, a preacher, having no phony(?) suspect, or a real

73

and genuine individual offered up for persecution! Did they think the sacrificial foreigner-lamb would not be necessary in this case, because of skin color?

My older sister had a plastic toy saxophone. She would play air sax, wishing it still worked. Because it was nothing more than a feel-good toy, it was nearly sad for her. "Dream on, girl," I had considered. One day not to long after that gentle summer day that we lolled away lying on a blanket in the shade, I caught her trying to write a brand-new hit. She was using the little plastic sax as an inspirational prop.

She had a pen and paper laid out on the dresser. I quickly became excited, and wished to help. She refused to allow for it. She claimed that she *needed* that one. It needed to be just her work, and wanted it so dearly for it to be all her own. I recall the mist rising up from the newly paved road. It was one of two days that the fog hung like a thick quilt covering our young neighborhood. Those two forces combined made for a mysterious near gloom of an afternoon.

Just then, the register kicked in. In most homes with gas heat anyway, the register pulls air into the furnace while the vents push the freshly warmed air back out. I had it. "The heat is on, it's on the street," I joyously rang out. Years later, although it took a while to come back to me afterwards, I saw a young and cutesy woman wailing on an MTV video. So, yes, the fine young lady was so dramatically wailing away on a genuine, full functioning, *alto sax*.

It was love at first sight. Women like that make me feel so very well alive! You had to have a true appreciation for free TV I do proclaim. It was not long after the debut of that new sax number on the radio that it was visually presented as well, for our in-home delight. You see, back then on Friday and Saturday nights, every moment in song, at least those so readily available in the proper format, would be laid out in every one of the videos ever created up to that point. I mean even going back to the history of time itself. Within reason anyhow they would.

I even saw an ancient visual from the 1970s band Jethro Tull, and an older one from McCartney, and his wife as well, on one of those 'free TV' video shows. I don't mean to be cheap here, but I still refuse to pay for entertainment, unless it's music. Although, I do truly enjoy a good film from time to time, those occasions are rare. Indeed, my last new viewing occurred in about 2001 with the first Harry Potter release. So, anyway, there is nothing cuter than a sweet little honey railing on her cute little Alto-Sax.

Father had purchased the necessary materials for the work at hand. They were stacked about on the basement floor ready to install. He had mentioned his goal quite readily at the supper table. Not long prior to the display of stacked ceiling tiles having arrived, he spoke of a fantasy world with basement-bars, and battle-cars. No wait, that was the Canadian band Rush with my good brother's pal from school using a bit of my very own writing. It was the drummer Neil Peart that usually did the writing for that group. Perhaps he even finished a few of mine.

Here and now though, situated before us, was our very own dream come true. I still recall with a true sense of belonging, how we would start on one end of our cellar, then work our way back to the other. Family time was never merrier for a rambunctious 7-year-old such as I was. Father had known enough about electricity from his work as an electronics tech for a local company. Going to school in Boston was less often, but if necessary, Father would occasionally continue to travel for those updates. Here he was getting a break between night jobs and would have the time for the installation.

He had let me know that since the house was new, any line to a lightbulb could also supply an additional bulb, plus two outlets. He checked the wiring, and was very pleased to be ready. He would be running outlets down from the ceiling. Those boxes would not be covered overall, but would be neatly accessible for use. He also had plans to run switches down from those *dangling* bulbs, currently accessed with mere pull strings.

The *pesta resistance* would be the fresh new ceiling tiles placed around the new ceiling fixtures that he had chosen so well. Those lighting frames would work to sharply hold in place the new lights. As I was the apprentice, a true learning experience had arrived. So, as long as I wasn't in the way, or dropping things that he had asked for, I would learn from the master. All that he knew about wiring, plus essential basic construction would be exhibited.

In no time our ceiling was up, and we could turn the lights off, and on, without running in the darkness toward the stairs. When down in the cellar with my sisters previous to our updated remodeling, we had always been checking for any unseen spiders, centipedes, or mice, just before the oldest would grab the pull string on the overhanging light bulb.

Such a careful activity, as far as turning off the lights, had previously been performed in a tightly woven group with each individual taking a third of the area to scan over.

Once the all clear was called, the light would go out, and we'd race toward our salvation. Now we'd be able to casually strut across the floor without any other concerns whatsoever. Yes, with this convenient new lighting setup, no longer would we each freak a little, just before dashing so quickly up the well-managed upper chamber, and to the more natural above ground world. If you'd recall that '*big-mama*' from my baby cheek, you would then so easily imagine the hurried frenzy of our late-night missions!

It was once again summer. We would be going to Canada the long way. We took the car ferry over to Michigan. The one thing that I readily recall about that voyage itself, other than the feeling of being out in the middle of nowhere, was a young gal I met near the bar aboard ship. A band was playing, and the people reveled in the experience. I searched about, then finally spotted an open chair. Three grown adults were seated around the circular table before me. With the band going strong, they simply smiled.

From out of nowhere a very young lady walked up and sat down. She was perhaps 18 years old at the very most, though if the pals she was with were buying, she wouldn't have needed an ID at all to consume. I apologized for taking her seat, but she insistently grabbed my arm pulling me back toward her. Well, since she was so demanding I thought I could at least for the remainder of that number, hang in there.

The heat from her short-skirted leg began to penetrate through my very slacks. It was such an exciting feeling that took over nearly every sense that I could have ever experienced. I needed to be cool about it. Only true mind readers then could possibly fathom the total turn-on that was pulsing through my veins, so quaintly held within this minor social ordeal. She and all of her friends smiled and laughed at the prospects.

I couldn't just take advantage of someone's total and utter kindness just for a little leg action, could I? No, I had already made up my mind. No matter how much hotter that I myself, and that beautiful warm leg would actually get, I was going to head out, and away from her generous and kind graciousness. Finally, the song ended. I stood, and turned bestowing my sincere thanks upon her, and smiling.

She shot back the hardest sweetest grin. It was one that filled me with such an appreciation of love and life itself, so much so, that I obviously recall that blissful ecstasy of that very moment to this day. Whew…I believed then that I perhaps needed to go check out the little-kiddie area again! That zone was safely staffed with a nursery school type leader, and many, many playthings. Indeed! We eventually disembarked and drove over to Detroit.

It was the riot season in many larger American cities, and a curfew was in place in that larger city. After driving past Tiger Stadium, we stopped at a local café. There was not a soul on the streets, not even one person was out and about. Inside the café, a few diners were eating. Perhaps, they lived just upstairs in the apartments above. We asked for permission to be served, explaining we were from out of town. It was a Friday so we sat down and waited for our fish to arrive.

After that, it was over to the hotel. The following day we took what seemed like the longest, most lonely trip ever. I haven't been back since, but in those days once you got to about the middle of the state, nothing existed. There were not even birds or other animals around. For what must have been at least three hours, we moved through the most isolated stretch of large oak trees, and smaller underbrush this side of the Mississippi. Finally, after a stark sense of loneliness and isolation had settled in, we made it to the border.

The strange thing that I recall most vividly was being on the other side of Lake Erie, not that I had ever been on that either side, mind you. It was most likely the elevation. Up in that part of the world, you actually look down a hill to see the lake. It caused the entire experience to be more so, about the other country we were now moving through, rather than about any patriotic feelings of Americanism at all.

We finally crossed over to the Atlantic region stopping at an authentic castle the very next day. Later we would move back stateside, close to the falls. One memorable moment occurred when we donned raincoats. These were readily provided for us, so we then walked through a tunnel. While standing at the very edge of flowing water, we were thoroughly soaked by the misty cascade. After that close up view, we went up to the top of the highest building in the region.

Atop that lofty structure was a restaurant. It was quite the scene, yet the closer experiences outdid that mile-high café by a long shot or more. When you're Niagara wet, it means just a bit more otherwise. We so soon moved over a bit upstate, staying at a friend of Father's that he knew from the Navy. Upon leaving the area, we drove just outside of New York City. A good safe distance away on the freeway was as close as we would ever be to that huge metropolis.

Back at school that fall semester the older boys from the next grade up had decided to bait me. They sent their fastest guy in to hit me on the back. As this speedy roadrunner went running to the protection of the pack, I was left wondering just what was up. Once more, he snuck up from behind, only tapping me on the back enough to show his all too close presence. Just as the other time, he so quickly raced back to his much larger buddies for protection.

What would the little scrappy guy say then if it came to that? "Oh, I just bumped into him on accident then he wanted to fight everyone so we had to hit him back," is that what the evil plan was? After the third attempt they gave up and relented. Since it was morning recess, they were running out of time anyway. I still needed to be so very careful, and still on the lookout during lunchtime though. There is nothing easier to resist than an invitation to get beaten up by older the older fellows, I do no say!

Another well learned lesson at school involved my control, or rather lack thereof. It was before the morning bell had rung. Each of the buses had arrived and we were killing those last few minutes with whatever pastime suited our fancy. Each of those third graders that stood back was at least able to give me a good fight, if not outright take me just like that. I thought about it but declined the offer. I'm smart enough to know when I'm being baited into a losing situation.

I decided to chase after a few of the boys from my own grade that I had considered as being faster than I. It was during recess that those quicker fellows would run about. Another bus had arrived. After the door was pulled open, one of those faster boys emerged. We ran and chased, and I ran and chased. Before entering the building, I was apprehended. Sister Ann, an older gal had been given the assignment of morning monitor.

She grabbed my arm as I moved to enter. She demanded to know why I was chasing that other fellow. I honestly answered, "I don't know." Her next question has stayed with me for life. "If you don't know why you did something than who does," was her curious question. I still wish to portray my innocence, but what a mind-blowing concept. The thought that another being could affect my behavior was startling to say the least. My theory about the insane dead had begun to formalize!

It was a milder evening yet rainy. Father was still working his first night job. Just before my going to bed there was a knock at the door. Who should be standing there, but none other than Cleveland Dave himself? He was as wet as the rest of the outside world. Mother let him in. He talked about getting stuck in the drenching downpour. We went downstairs. The thought was to dry the suit that he had on, just enough anyway, for him to get back to his aunt's without feeling like a wet sponge.

There were not many options. The dryer was one, but to hang his clothes on the line inside would take too long. We had nothing for him in the meantime, and father would be home soon. The thought was to try the dryer, yet I cautioned him. It should only be five or ten minutes at the very most. Even then he would need to stop, and check it before it was too late, to see if the shrinking process had already begun.

Either a full twenty or more so thirty minutes, would surely do his terrific outfit in. It seemed to be a one-of-a-kind, tan corduroy setup. Very sharp looking it was indeed. At least it must have been to those with the opportunity to check it out fully before the rain had its say in the matter. I said goodnight, and went up to bed. Moments later, even too many moments later, father had walked in. Even though Dave was only a teen, he was still a young man in a state of undress.

That state of fashion now being modeled while the man of the house was away toiling and slaving for his families. Enough said. I felt that I needed to get up, just in case to defend the honor of both. There was father looking rather stern with mother looking on. He was speaking to Dave in a bit of a harsh tone. As I approached the scene, that was it. Father pointed to the door, and said, "Get out." There stood Dave, looking like a something from a comedy skit, or from a scene straight out of a Jerry Lewis movie.

It was no laughing matter at all. Not with the trousers shrunken nearly up to his knees, and with the top undone. The sleeves of his once excellent looking sport coat now allowed for more than a Frankenstein-ish look. Oh well. I did try to warn him. To this day the memory tends to move in, and haunt me. Was I not quite precise with the five- or ten-minute part, and the stopping to check and all? Dave quickly left, and I was back to bed, sleeping so soundly and soon enough.

Christmas had arrived once more. It would not only be a special day with a birthday party for Jesus it also marked another milestone in my incredible maturation process. If I remember correctly, it was that little bro received a 'Marvel the Mustang'. That was a spring loaded, plastic and steel, steed that would actually propel across the floor as you bounced gently upon its back! So, he himself had reached a milestone of maturity.

If there ever was a holiday to get things back on track, that was it! Save for that exploit of my own involving wasps, hornets, or the secrets hidden within the deep dark depths of the nearby woods, I was really once and for all, back at home now. I would not be staying over here; I would not go and visit over there. No, once and for all the shuffling hand ended, and issues resolved. Things seemed to be very casual, usual, and normal, at least at the start of the year they did.

Mother, in noticing my intelligence with card games and chess, bought the whole family the board game Monopoly. I truly felt loved in a special way, and genuinely a part of the family. Let's just say family and friends aren't always held in such close regard. With our newfound joy for board games the oldest sister immediately became the banker. She insinuated that through a steadfast focus of attention, and with her demonstrative efforts regarding change making, we should so quickly learn.

With property issuance, my younger sister and I perhaps one day down the road, after a careful and needful evaluation, could ourselves hope to be offered that position. My formula for teaching preschoolers involves among other things, the learning and playing of that very game. With two penny rolls, five dice, a set of poker chips, a cribbage board, and a deck of cards, children as young as 3 years of age could begin to truly learn. The sailor's game Euchre involves only the cards from the sevens on up. That makes it easier for 3-year-olds to deal with.

1968

It had been some time again since I had seen my half-brothers. My older sister informed me that we would be going to visit. Just her and I would comprise the group. When we arrived in the area the plan was to go to a special place. Once there the true plan was laid out. We would all do some L.S.D. Upon further review this was more than likely merely a one-fourth hit of Window Pane. Perhaps it was a milder batch especially made for beginners, as my clear recollection was that it wasn't all that great. Apparently, I was born trippy and don't need outside stimulants or any other effectors.

"Just be cool back at home," they had said before the ceremony began. "No problem," was my reply. We started out on the corner where the local bank was situated. There was a cement platform that one could stand upon. My oldest brother had me climb up. It was all timed out to be some type of dramatic experience.

Right after ingesting the hit of acid, he said, "Ready? Get up there." With my placement high up upon this pedestal he said these magical words "You shall now leave this world and your earthly parents, and become your true, higher and heavenly self." With that, I was mystically energized.

It could not have possibly been the microdot, as it had only been seconds since I swallowed it. Since I was just told that it may take up to an hour to really kick in, I knew that it was the 'spell' or prayer as it seemed to be, that had done the trick. So, we were there in that area of town to specifically run around like crazy, wild hooligans, and to activate the dose into our systems with that exercise. I somehow though, was now already as high as one can be. Even like a Peter Pan type, I had become.

My spirit soared. I felt an overwhelming greatness that sincerely was on, or from a higher plane. I descended back to ground level, and we began our mysterious trek. Like some sort of tripped-out Pippy Longstocking gang we ran amok. Because of the lecture from Father on not trespassing I wanted to be careful. "Will there be any of that?" I asked. The oldest laughed, just then we crossed past a yard with a fence.

He ran up, jumped over, and then back again. It was just for the fun of it. "Does that answer your question?" he wondered. He was already a grown man so that made it way more fun for us to hang out with him. We all laughed some more, then thought we had better be cool for now. The last thing that I recall was not losing it back at home, and not really being that much out of it at all. Oh well. Maybe once more, as I've mentioned, I was actually born trippy, and LSD has had little to no effect on me whatsoever.

I was in my room after school. Thoughts would sometimes seemingly come from out of nowhere. These epiphanies often were so very dramatic for me, although the thoughts were otherwise nothing more than humorous daydreams. It had set upon my mind that I was to rise to the glorious and royal mantle of king. I truly mean the king of the world. Since that was not a current office I realized as well, that I would need to be self-appointed.

Years later a comedian, I want to say Norm Crosby here, although it may have been another, right square in the middle of the TV set claims that he just realized the he himself, rather than I, was king of the world. He quaintly too, was of the self-appointed variety indeed. Indeed, more than one of us had that very special epiphany. Seeing as he was just in it for laughs, I let it go. I had seen enough news to realize that there was trouble in East Asia, and the world was such a very large place for one man to handle.

But of course, that's what the U.N. is for. Although, the world is large, and so many different languages exist, we have found ways to get around those aspects of togetherness in government dealings. I still had time to learn, I had considered. Many, many things would transpire before I was completely ready to rise to that self-proclaimed mantle of greatness. Yes, I had believed, I had the time. Things would merely need to work themselves out in just the right fashion in the interim. Are they, even here and now, working themselves out?

It was my older sister's birthday. Even though she was to have just a few friends over I was to remain outside until any of the actual fun things had been fully played out and utterly extinguished. I walked around outside in the neighborhood a bit. I knew at some point that if I was with my good friends, I would have had a total blast by that point. I considered my options and needed to kill at least an additional 40 minutes to an hour.

I went here, then there. It clouded up even more so on that early April day, more than it had ever before. You need to remember Father was still in his two wives, two jobs stage. As far as the darkness of the sky equating to the festivities being over, that was an illusion at best. Since that was the case, I made my way into the backyard and did my best to resist knocking. In knowing the inevitable answer would be "no we're not done having fun yet." I resisted.

When I could finally take it no more, I knocked expecting what was said. I asked, "About how much more?" I was truly and definitely relieved to understand that things were beginning to wind down, and entry would so soon be gained. I still recall the photo just after eating. Perhaps I will include it with any others deemed appropriate for the end of this book! I am unable to locate that particular picture so will add that it involves me with my fingers pulling my mouth wide open, just as cheese is called.

We had the local race riots after the other cities had already gotten well into theirs. For some, those were all but over. Perhaps ours being a smaller city, the locals held off a bit. They were being led by any number of supportive Catholics. Our local character was not a violent man, so did his best to lead peaceful walks, preferring to take the lead of MLK rather than to use any example from more hardcore sorts such as Malcolm X. We had finally learned years later in school, of the differences in philosophy regarding the two types of approaches being taken.

Just as then, it only takes one bad actor to change the attitudes of many. A classmate's father worked for the local Police Department. He let us know that some of the cops had been stationed on rooftops just itching for a chance to fire down on the crowd. As long as things were orderly, these citizens would not be fired upon. Those hard ass bastard cops would then have to go home again without shooting anyone. Certain things seem to work themselves out. Others may simply become strange and weird.

Well, those trigger-happy coppers finally got their chance. A wild crazy man, clinically insane, started attacking people from out of nowhere. It didn't take long for the police to begin firing. He was taken out, but others were injured as well. It was not a good day for our town at all. Those few cops, stuck between waiting, and wanting got their way, yet someone had to die in the meantime. My pal's dad changed teams not long after, becoming a local sheriff instead.

My younger brother was at the park across the street. He had patiently waited, and waited to ride the springy hippo, or other animal figure newly installed for our use. One of the thrills some of the neighbors had been engaging in involved pulling the handle of the ride, or the head itself as far back as possible. That would cause the thing to dramatically rock back and forth in a frighteningly dangerous action. Here and now Little Bro had waited long enough. He decided to try and stop the thing with his own bare hands, even though he was only 4 years old. He failed horribly.

He came home with a bleeding welt upon the corner of his forehead, and mother insisted he seek professional medical attention. As Father had given up his first night job to take care of other urgent and pressing needs for a while, he was indeed home at the time. We all piled into the station wagon to seek the nearest treatment facility. After a few miles of driving, we hit the police roadblock. Since it was a medical issue, we were allowed to pass through. As well, he mentioned the closest place that he knew of. Then he let us on by. My brother's wound was stitched up and we were back at home in no time.

Later on, after school had let out, I was bored so walked out to the field where the farmer sometimes grew corn. It was nothing but weeds that year, and the trails along the side invited an adventurous young lad such as I was, to travel forward and investigate. I took the farther trail and moved away from the main deer trail. It was near where the deer had slept in past years, once the grassy growth was tall enough. I came along an old pallet.

It was the same battered old bunch of boards from the heroine strap hiding days. It seemed to have been set up to sit on, and kill some time, though many years before. I quickly recalled how my brothers wanted me to hide that very rig. It was right here or just back across the field to the short row of trees that I had first considered it. The truth was that one of our favorite summer pastimes was catching grass snakes. These timid and gentle creatures were for the most part about a foot in length.

Not at all like those somewhat larger varieties found down in Muscle Shoals Alabama. (See 1973) As long as one froze just before snatching, a ready capture was just about guaranteed. Those slithering reptiles fit perfectly into an old coffee can. It was out on the farther edges of things that we mostly avoided. That is where I was off to. The only place around that I knew of, without any others ever hanging about. Then again, if people did indeed kill time around those very spots, that would be the opposite of what I was ordered to do that first time from years before. Hide that rig.

In my distraction, I looked afield to clear my mind. Here the afternoon sun would gently warm one's face, or be it too hot, a slight shift over would offer the cooling shade of the tree line. Ouch! That pallet that had been falling apart, slowly but surely, had been shifted over slightly upon the ground. I clumsily moved about. I then stepped on a protruding and rusty nail. I limped back to the main trail determined to shed no tears. My aching heel had other thoughts.

It had felt as though it went into the bone. That's what I must be feeling, the deepest pain that one could ever fathom. The visible caked on rust, covering the nail, only made it seem more horribly traumatic. I shrugged it off. Soon I found that limping needn't be such a terrible thing. Here it was allowing me to make my way so very quickly back toward home. Although, the intensity hardly eased, I found I'd be alright after all. In no time I had made it to the warmth and safety of the inside world.

In removing my sock, I felt not so much a betrayal of my very own body, but rather an utter surprise that little to no blood was present. I washed it off and found my foot to now be completely pain free, as long as I didn't step on it. At the supper table, I enquired of Mother what may happen to a person if indeed their body were to be pierced by a rusty object such as a nail or other metallic item.

She informed me that it wouldn't be a good experience at all, since one may incur a case of blood poisoning.

She added you would need to get a shot from the doctor. "Well," I confessed. "I did step on a nail, but it wasn't really too rusty, so I should be okay, as for needing a shot, and everything." She made a face that told me if I ended up dying, that she would just feel awful about it and completely and fully responsible as well. I knew from there we would both monitor my condition for any serious symptoms. After a few days, the slight, yet tortuous pricking at my heel had subsided. I would pull through alright. This rusty time anyway I'd be alright.

My sisters and I were to go swimming at the lake. We would be meeting someone there. My older sister told me to just wait, and see who it was. I became excited with the fantastical prospects. I vowed to be patient. Finally, I turned to look. It was Dave. I swam out a ways to the farther distance of the deeper waters. Something underneath the water's surface grabbed at my ankles, and pulled me under. It was the undertow.

Although, infrequent, and less severe than one would find in the ocean, there are definitely strong currents in the Sea of Michigan. While I was still trying to come to come to terms with what had just happened Dave had swum his way over, and pulled me up. I'm sure he saved my life that day. We moved in closer to the shore and I vowed to be careful. It would not be until our future movie venture downtown, that I would see Dave again.

Later on, in school the teacher had decided to put our desks together so that it was like each of us had a partner. My partner was a girl from our school bus. Her cousin rode with us as well and lived on the corner quite near her home. It didn't take long for me to fall in love. I did my best to concentrate on the lesson plan, which was easy as my new love was always there right beside me. Our innocence held us closely to something pure, new, and oh so innocently natural.

I cannot be certain as to the origins of what came out of my mouth, and even now am shocked with horror as to what exactly that was. I apparently have chosen to selectively block that comment out of my mind. It was that my new love's father had passed away suddenly…It was a hard thing for me being so young and so close to one of the survivors. Since our class sat in the back of church that year, it was easy to be buffered from the main brunt of the ceremony.

I prayed, and prayed, and then again. It was all over so very quickly. I bowed my head as the procession passed by, with my purest of intentions offered. I fail to remember what it was that hurt my dear sweet so much, but it had fallen to a level with our immaturity; so that it was a shear form of petty nonsense, or so I had felt. Then it just immerged, the fatal comment that caused her to weep. It came flying from out of nowhere, then right past my lips.

I pray even now that it was not something about her being so ugly, she caused her father to die. It was just like the older nun had asked in the past, "If you don't know from where your actions emerge, then who does control you?" Who indeed? It hurts me even now to think that I could have chosen something so low, and heartless. Even a comment that I myself would never have spewed forth otherwise, somehow seemed to emerge. When fully realizing the harshness of such an ugly and unloving offering, I recoil, aghast in shock and horror, I cringe.

I was called out into the hall with a broken heart. I could never make up for what I had said. There now was no way that I could even attempt to apologize. The very next day, after my ex was given a temporary seating assignment, I noticed that the new approach would involve a desk separation, forever marking the painful significance of my blurted remark with a starkly apparent asterisk. If it wasn't the devil himself, then indeed who?

Was it an evil demon fresh from the bowels of hell itself, that had at me on that strange and fateful day. That is what must have entered my mind causing those destructive words to spill forth. I once more had the opportunity to further create and develop my theory on, 'Evil-outside' influences, entering into this realm to have at us, spoiling any and all joy that's ours. Alas, due to budgetary constraints in her family that spring would be my last opportunity to try to console my former love. Once school would start the next year, my life would go on without her. At least for the time being it was.

1969

The newyear offered another low moment. A classmate's oldest brother had perished over in Nam. We would once again assemble as a school, for yet another funeral. This ceremony was even more so mournful, with the deceased being a former student taken from us in his prime. The one girl, now the oldest, my classmate's sister, would help in the lunch room handing out food with the two lunch ladies as well.

The older girls in 7th, and 8th grade were asked to help out in that way on a daily basis. The middle brother would be expelled for bouncing a rubber band off of the inside of his desk as the new teacher walked by. He had claimed it was an accident and wasn't really aiming at anything other than the back of his desk. He had improvised a slingshot device with a bobby pin which made that weapon an unauthorized object brought to school.

It was thought that the teacher had engaged in physical abuse in order to gain control of the situation, yet not much came of it. The school brought in additional teachers the next year and things were shuffled so that the nun that had approached me about making sure that all of my actions were my very own, had been given that class now to teach. Oh, where was she when I needed her, the semester before in third grade.

Because of all of the extra kids in our family, we had a general rule about receiving a bicycle for our birthday or otherwise. The first one had to be used, and a hand me down as well, if available. I kind of got skipped in the rotation due to my unauthorized use of the girl's bike. Spring had sprung, and that meant one thing. Because I was going to be 9 years old, I would be receiving, my one and only, officially brand-new bike for my birthday. Days before the big event we went to scope those out. Why Penny's instead of Sear's I still don't know.

You see, Sear's had the cooler purple bikes. The most special 'cooler' item that they had on this bike for sale, were termed as 'Ram-Horn' handle bars.

You can just imagine. There was also something called a Spyder bike. It was the same cool purple color, same slim body frame, yet not as cool as the 'Spyder Deluxe', having only normally shaped high handle bars. Schwinn had a nearly identical version with the same rad' sixties colors.

I had dreamed and dreamed, of anything close at all to any of those models. This day was coming in my nights. I indeed was waiting patiently for the daytime realization of all of those nocturnal dreams. Electric green was oh so neat also, though the purple it would be. We strolled on into the local J.C. Penny's department store, and there it was. It had the necessary cool purple body, but something was amiss. Instead of a racing wheel in the back, it had a dirt bike wheel.

This, as far as I was aware, was the very first all-terrain tire ever attached to the back of a bike. It therefore was a hybrid. It as well, had a mini gas tank that housed the shifter handle. The five speeds were a standard feature on most purple bikes, at least those that were 24". Only the rare Sear's 10 speed Spyder had more. My new machine was a bit clunky at first, but would have to suffice. With its wide banana seat, it lacked some of the style and flare of the other cycles, but it was mine, and the open road did await me.

The older guys had been moving on to simple three speeds, and finally ten speeds. I was just fine riding my very first bike alone. It didn't matter to me. There was one drawback. The front wheel having a thin racing tire, it was somewhat dangerous when confronting big, large stones. If those were more than 3 or 4 inches wide the wheel could get jammed in between a few, throwing the rider. Good thing the city had just placed a dump load of those large sized rocks at the end of my neighborhood. I could practice falling down! I soon grew quickly accustomed to my new wheels, and a summer's warmth settled in.

I was invited in by my next-door neighbor. He was setting up some type of wired communication device with the neighbor from two doors down. Those two didn't always hang together, but we were willing in those days to do whatever it would be, to enjoy life and have some fun. I walked over to the far window to check out the setup. It was some kind of contraption seemingly connected through the far basement window over to this taller boy's home. Indeed, they had just completed such an electronic connection of their homes.

With only one catch, you had to know Morse code. What I was now observing up close was the finality of a telegraph patch-in. This type of *playful* communication could have been engaged in, as well, by using old-school walkie-talkies. There is only one catch, the duo or group would have to time the efforts to sync-up rather than desperately calling out then waiting. I had just gotten a walkie-talkie myself from Santa Claus. That was the day that one could really count on to have others aboard. Yes, on Christmas morning everyone from CBers to ham radio operators would be tuned in to see what was up.

A few weeks later the same next-door neighbor was at the front door. He was three years older but we did stuff together from time to time. He called through the screen 'Little Willie, Little Willie'. There was only one other person that ever called me that, and that was Frank. Apparently, my good brother with the same name had visited enough, for any adjusting of my name to catch on. We already had a Little Billie down the way, so I had to accept it.

Even my mother called me Willie to differentiate between us both. I had told her though, previously, that that was it. I'm all grown up and, I'll be going to school, so therefore henceforth, I shall be known as plain Will. There are only so many things that you can fix in life. The rest you simply need to deal with. Yet here and now with my neighbor's spectacular invitation that was coming through the door, only a sense of gleeful joy was offered. John was three years older than I was, just like Buck.

We all went to different schools though. John to the Lutheran School out on the main drag, the neighbor to the other Catholic school in the opposite direction, and I and our family were members of the congregation miles to the west. So, we really hung out together because of the closeness of our homes, rather than through any other association. It was also a strange coincidence that Johnny's mother had a piano. Our other connection came from her driving me to kindergarten years before in her actual mini schoolbus.

"Little Willie," he called again, "does your Mother have any money?"

"Why?" I asked. "Because if she does, we are going to go downtown to see a movie, a Planet of the Apes Movie," he assured me. By this time mother had appeared, and shook her head yes. "John's coming too, so get your cash, and hurry," he instructed. I rushed to get ready and quickly pocketed the cash now being handed to me by Mother. We raced out to the bus and within a minute or so of boarding we were on our way.

That we would be going so far would be half the adventure. The bus would turn on Main Street moving past so many of the downtown attractions, so it was impossible to get lost. Soon after the bus did so, a fellow riding a three-wheeler Good Humor cycle was just up ahead. *"Man, that guy was brave,"* I thought to myself. That 'guy' just happened to be Dave. We disembarked at the major downtown movie house.

This would be exciting. The original had come out just before, with trading cards, and everything. My neighbor had purchased a few and brought those over for me to see. That was the extent of my understanding of the new series of films. The Monkees' TV show had cards as well, but there was something intriguing about this mysterious culture of ape people. That was especially so since my neighbor didn't go on and on about things. He especially saved every detail of this new movie for me.

What I wouldn't give for each and every one of those cards now. All of those and so many others, no doubt tossed away so casually so many, many years ago. It was the coolest experience being downtown and safe inside the theater on a warm sunny afternoon. My life could not have ever been better than when hanging with my good older buds away from home. I came to take it that a part of Dave's run involved knowing when people would exit the buildings.

We watched Return to the Planet of The Apes, and then we were so merrily back out on the street. There he stood. Dave was waiting to make a sale. John and I needed to bring the change from the movie back to our parents. All of it! My neighbor though, had just enough to buy something. A Fudgecicle would be just the thing. They had gone up to 15¢ since Dave had started for Good Humor. My *special* older buddy popped one out for Buck and we were off to the bus stop.

I was over at the local park soon after. Father had purchased a padlock for my bike to keep it locked when out and about. Lo and behold, the dude from down the street was eyeing it up, and a little too strongly for my taste as well. Didn't he notice me? I was the kid that he had conned into convincing his mother that his brand-new transistor radio had been sold to him by me, rather than shoplifted by him instead. She hadn't bought it for a second.

The roars of anger coming from a single mother like her, I had never heard before. The fear rose so deep inside of me I began to panic. He, I just know, was used to it. So, this was the game? Steal a radio from the local discount store, get caught by Mom with a new looking item. Then tell her you just bought it from another kid. As far as the money needed for such a legal transaction to have taken place, well he must have gotten that from doin' stuff, and things, and such.

She didn't buy it the first time around. With her being so super-pissed I nearly went into shock. I began to make my way to the door. She swept her hand across motioning one of us to get spanked, and or, out of her house. Shew…I finally made it out and hardly cared if he was getting it bad. The sweet, sweet smell of fresh air was all that mattered to me at that point. Yet here and now on that particular day, he was eyeing up my bike.

Because it was a six-inch padlock the spokes could be locked to the forks. That didn't mean Mr. Grand Theft Bicycle wasn't considering every feature of a possible get away. He looked, and looked, even after I presented myself, saying, "Hey."

Somehow, he still was mulling it over. I guess he could work real hard selling it. He then could even steal something else from the Atlantic Mills. I had to wonder though if he wasn't permanently barred from that location. He gave up on my bike after a while and moved on. I would need to have my eye on him or rather on my bike more so, going forward.

Boredom would often get the best of me. I strapped on my official western styled cap gun. I was getting a little old for such things so took it out for one last stroll. From out of nowhere I busted a move for the second time in my life. I suddenly recalled having moon-walked back when we played disco' in the other bedroom. I still had it. Imagine a little kid moon-walking past your house while wearing a big black revolver strapped to one leg. It was all too real.

I was yet bored again. You know where I ended up. This time I would walk as slowly as possible even daring to venture right up to the very spot that the old pallet had stabbed me. I decided revenge against it would be the only choice. I simply needed to make sure that while swinging, and tossing the thing deeper into the tree line, I was keenly aware not to let any of the rusty nails graze my person. Even though the sharpened ends had no poison for me the last time, they surely would indeed now, after so much rain and snow, and rain and snow, and snow and rain had dampened, and moistened things over, and over again.

I made my way so carefully toward the very spot, being certain that no stray slats had made their way onto the trail itself. I trembled lightly with the prospects of my mission then decided to switch things up. Rather than heaving old wooden pieces, I would simply turn anything with nails jutting upward, downside right. Then, in stepping on those parts with any reckless abandon, I could drive any exposed nails deep enough into the ground. That way, anyone that should happen along will be protected as well. I readily found the debris of culprits and had at them.

After each visible protruding element had been dealt with, I made my way back toward the city. Feeling not yet relieved of my boredom. I considered that a walk down the farther alleyway would do the trick. As long as that huge boxer dog wasn't out, I mean. It stood about 4½ feet tall, and had a rut grooved into the lawn all along the 5ft. chain link fence. Whew, I was safe for now. Nearing the end of this block I noticed an interesting and new looking item lying at the top of one neighbor's trashcan. It was chrome looking, and still brightly attractive.

After I made my way upon it, I did then observe it to be a new looking razor blade dispenser.

Who would possibly throw something out that had barely been used, I wondered. No doubt they didn't appreciate the injector system, and had had it with that newer concept. I picked it up out of curiosity then decided to give it a try. Without it being actually attached to a replaceable razor system, I struggled to remove one of the many brand-new blades.

I braced myself again, and pulled harder. The action lever engaged as a blade ejected. It moved gracefully and demonstratively directly across the palm of my hand. I tossed the thing aside placing my good hand over the fresh slice. It seemed hideously deep, and were stepping on a nail may cause a small drop to appear, this action had caused the blood to ooze ever so easily from my injured hand. I adjusted the placement of the covering hand, and walked as quickly as possible home. Once home I had it doctored and dressed nicely.

Of course, I downplayed the event as something much more innocent, but learned a steadfast lesson. Only appropriate moves and motions should be engaged in when handling sharp weapons of any type. Yet again I had needed something to do. Walking past the rotten apple trees sounded like just the thing. I am not sure what type of car these kids were driving right on those very deer trails. That's because this actual fully fledged vehicle had no body.

It was just the frame the front seat and the engine. It may have actually been a Volkswagen. You know, some kids get all of the fun. That opinion of others joyfulness was based on the gleefully widest smiles ever witnessed on unlicensed juveniles driving around on an official motorized vehicle. Yes, I do attest, that those under-16-year-olds that I personally caught driving underage along that old apple orchard had it made in the sun or the shade rather, I mean!

The new school year so quickly started without much pomp or circumstance. We had to wait on the opposite corner, well off to the side of our small city block. One day I swear I had seen a hummingbird. It seemed almost to be a hallucination. It mattered not. It was still a really cool site to behold. I'm still waiting to see my second. One day that year, on the ride home from school, I heard my classmate's brother talking about an accident. The cars came through the intersection then, *bam*. The one in particular was totaled. I asked what he had meant. In nearly legal terms he expressed that an auto was considered as such, if the repair cost exceeded the car's current value. It was later in the year that this very word was indeed the last one, on the page for our upcoming spelling test. I mean even yes, "Totally." I got up in my room then went into my newest routine. Totaled, the car was so wrecked it was totaled. It was totally totaled, to-to-totally, totaled. It was so damaged it was totaled, totally.

Much later when a friend from school moved to California's Orange County my 'new' term was used on TV in a show about high school kids. Something Valley, I believe it was, with the actress from the show that Kramer from Seinfeld got his start in, Fridays. I faintly remember that that was the competing show, going up against Saturday Night Live, though obviously not on the same night. 'Kramer' had a character that wore black socks and shorts, or swim trunks, poolside.

If you know the Tom Hanks persona that offers 'well helloo, aandd gooooddbyye', I believe that you would have a fairly good idea where the skit generally could move to. Think 'Saturday Night', a couple of guys hanging around on a street corner. These fellows try to pick up attractive female passersby…In any case it just doesn't work. Not for Hanks, nor for 'Kramer'. Though was that a coincidence, as far as my favorite word to over emphasize, being used as a part of our everyday lexicon? I think not, as far as it *totally* becoming a commonly used positive word, anyway.

Later that year, my next-door neighbor came knocking. This time he wanted to know if my mother had any drinking straws. "Wait, I'll check," I promised. From the kitchen I called out, "Yes, a few."

"How about popcorn?" he asked further.

"Let's see," I replied. After checking I walked to the door and asked "why?"

"Just get some of the popcorn, enough to fill your pockets, and here let me have one of the straws," he motioned, "Then get your bike, and meet me around front here," he slyly added.

We both poured out a small amount of the raw corn. I then raced to lock up the house, and get my bike. My neighbor said, "This is going to be real easy. Just put one kernel in your mouth, and then at the right time blow, here I'll show you," he motioned forward as we rode. "Here we are," he claimed with the seedling in his mouth, then *spoot*. He slammed the corn against the picture window of our victim. "So, let's go around again for another shot," he commanded.

We casually rode, enjoying the weather while readying ourselves for the next assault. It was the end house we were attacking perhaps only because an escape would be made so much quicker with only two houses standing at the end of the block. With the alley in the middle, we could always duck through that avenue of escape so quickly. We came around once more, and smack, smack. Both shots were dead on. Faint yet sharp, a splatting sound hit hard onto his picture window. But was he even home?

Once again upon the glass, and we'd move on. We went back to appreciating the warm fall air once more, and had nearly forgotten our little raid on the old man's house.

He lived alone, though for a while he had his mom move in. She had died, and now all he had was his three poodle dogs, and an occasional visit from his brother. His brother was a WWII veteran and had lost both legs in the war. I knew, because I spotted him working on his car as the school bus swung around one day. As well, I had those facts conveyed to me by my mother as well.

This old boy's car however had become a source of ridicule. It was a 1955 Olds, which was fine as cars go. That at all wasn't the problem. The mistake he had made was taking it to Earl Scheib's to get a new paint job. It would have cost him $59.99 back in those days. It seemed that everyone that knew about this special discounted offering though, claimed it would wash right off in the rain. So, not only did he live in the corner house facing the other direction with his three stinky dogs (it was said that they had the run of the basement, and he failed to tend to their messes), he now was ridiculed by anyone within earshot for having a crummy paint job. I asked around about it myself.

Really, I mean, because paint is something you'd believe could never wash off. At least not wash off under a simple rain shower. A friend's older brother said, "Earl Scheib's paint sadly will."

"Maybe not right away, but in a few years or so it certainly will be fading." I watched for his car as often as I could, and you know what? From a distance, anyway, it sure did look like it was starting to wash off alright. It was just enough at that point anyway to vaguely discern.

But here he was, and chasing us around. By now we had joined up with our other buddy. The old man got slick, and jammed it into park, and raced through the yards to get us. Up until then we had taken our time, and listened closely to out maneuver him. He was on us like a madman. "Just wait 'til I tell your dad, Buck," he growled rather angrily at my neighbor. Buck was actually the third in his family to have the same name. I'm going to 'out' Buck, and really good right now, as far as his true name anyway. I simply cannot resist offering the truth here.

You've certainly noted by now that I am protecting the privacy of most individuals from my long and illustrious life. It was easier to call him by his nickname since even his grandpa stayed with them for a while. All three were duly christened as 'Norman Milo'. You may very well imagine that he is still going by Buck to this day. The other 'Milo', Milo from Twilo was a fictional alien character from The Dick Van Dyke show. So, anyway, Buck was like, "Oh well go ahead do that," to the old man who was now about right upon us.

Old boy was in too much of a rage at that point though, and he rushed up, and punched my neighbor in the arm. Our other buddy said, "Hey now, that's a little too much."

The old man asked, "Oh is it?" I guess the frustration from the years of his not being able to enjoy the paint job on his car had been too much for him to take. It was all finally over, and everything quickly went back to normal. Buck thought he was lucky enough to have only received an arm punch. Suffice it to say we never again spit popcorn through a straw at any other thing, not ever again.

It was back then that Mother was a volunteer Girl Scout Leader. She had made arrangements for me to tag along with all of the girls in our troop to the movie theater. Since little Bro was only four at the time, it was decided that he couldn't hang, and would be back at the crib when he did indeed fall asleep. It was a tremendous experience because it was in the older neighborhood near the lakeshore. Our area was pretty much still farms when movies first came around.

Even the two theaters in the area sat across from the last big spreads on the north side. That last bit of acreage became car dealerships by the 1940s, if not sooner. You can imagine then, that it was a genuine movie palace from the '20s or so that we would venture off to. We were to see the film Chitty, Chitty Bang, Bang starring Dick Van Dyke. He was from the popular, and now canceled TV show named after him.

The new feature as well, starred a Miss Julie Andrews, by then ever so popular for her work in Mary Poppins. The car of a titled note, would merely tag along for the cinematic ride. I like to make two points here; I hated going to bed at 9:00pm back when I was six years old. You know, right at the start of Dick's old sitcom. The other thing was that I surely loved seeing Mary Poppins, and was pumped heading into the event.

1970

My sister came out of her room, and in one of those taunting voices claimed that *sh*e was ready to go out. It was her jeans that weren't so ready. They were quite obviously from the year before, and so tight-ass it was shocking. There was some apparent wear as well, though probably not of the intentional stress type that finally became popular about fifteen years later. I thought myself that they were not such a serious problem. Clean enough, yet a tad tight, and a might too short as well.

I believe she was simply teasing, yet no doubt had even entertained the idea of wearing those out. In being playful and wanting the expected feedback from mother, she proudly displayed what the veiled (or trousered) threat entailed. In her daughter of a foreigner's approach, mother intoned, "get those off, do you hear me? Right now!" In doing so, she emerged so quickly from the previously out of view position on the end of the sofa, and the chase was on.

Within seconds, I was toward the door, and the two were down the hall. I stopped short of reaching for the door knob, and from the scrambling considered that I may need to referee. Just before I had reached them, the entry into the room was made. With a thunderous crash the brawl had begun. What would I find once I peeked around the corner? The two of them were both, lying on the floor atop a rug. The rumbling sound of serious wrestling that I had heard was indeed something a bit more frightening. Here they were in the position that a horseman and second rider would be in.

With even with Mom's hands positioned atop the shoulders of my dear sister, horseback was all that I could conjure. Each one had a grin of embarrassment upon her face, and was now beginning to laugh. I surely felt a relief in seeing that they had been taught a bit of a rough lesson, as opposed to something so much harsher. Things were fine, and I could leave, knowing that on such a good and joyous note, a true sense of togetherness, and family unity would reign.

There was an anniversary to celebrate. It was that my maternal grandfather was an identical twin. It only made sense then that they double dated a pair of sisters. Weddings ensued, then the birth of children, with two of those relatives, cousins, actually looking more like brothers. Both left town, one to Ohio, the other, after tasting that San Diego ocean air during WWII, to California. I have never met the lookalike cousin of my uncle's, and my own dear uncle himself rarely showed up for such events.

The rest of us were glad enough to party on without them. After the church service we gathered at my great-aunt's home to begin the festivities. As the adults engaged in joyous conversation, I noted some punch had been poured, and decided to try some. Most know the thick and attractive circular bowls such a concoction is so readily available from. I however believed that one of the older kids from the 'senior' class would have had to have poured in a little something extra for anyone's punch to be hard. Here it was so good, and yummy.

I had another, and another, and yet another. I still wanted more. I asked my mom's aunt if she could possibly make some more. She said not a word. "Hmm," I pleaded again. I turned to see why she was so indisposed. In doing so, I saw two empty quarts of vodka sitting upon the floor. It all came crashing down onto me so suddenly. My brain digested every possibility. I had to find a graceful way out of this predicament.

"You can't make any more, oh well?" I had tried to ask politely with a tone of youthful innocence. This was my opening, I got out quick. I really can't say that I was buzzed at all what with the merriment of family visiting and the special occasion we gathered to honor. I sure as hell came down hard a few hours later. Hard and heavy it was for sure I'd say. Is it possible to have a hangover before even going to bed?

Later on, that year we were caught in the act at school of having engaged in some type of un-Christian acts of behavior. The principal, a Catholic Nun who after having taught the first grade to my eldest sister, had now returned, and with such a promotion, was poised to cause us good old-fashioned Catholic harm, or rather I'm certain that I mean rather, a Catholic form of *correction* instead. Yes, it was a true sense of correction that she brought down upon our naughty rotten world.

Our duty this first time around was cleverly cruel. I mean to say that I don't recall the good sister's harshness having come out at any time before this incident occurred. This time around though, the hammer came down, and we were the nails. She, after making the determination that we had crossed some line of goodness into the very darkest depths of hell, felt the need to publicly shame us in front of the others. She brought us out and had us sit on the floor against the wall from where the bubblers ran.

One was to be do no evil, so had to sit on his hands, the other would be hear no evil, so had to cover his ears, and so on. The idea as she had put it was for enough of the younger groups to witness this act of torture against us, and for us to be shamed into a wiser sense of goodness. As well, it was for those too sweet to have ever done even any one thing very sinful at all, to be shocked, and frightened into some hallowed stage of sainthood. I do truly believe we were good on the latter end of things, in any case.

I was bored again. With not much going on that day I decided, as I usually would, to take a walk into the woods. It always helped to get away from modern life, and into the fresh air of the neighboring countryside. On this particular day that is all that it would be. Nothing more than a little break from boredom. On my return home that would all change. I looked up into the sky to see something seemingly coming at me. Was it a bird? Not a large one, mind you I would ask. I was thinking along the lines of hummingbird. Was it a huge flying insect? It would have to be the biggest ever.

I couldn't quite make out what it possibly was from the outline of this quickly moving object. Suddenly, just like that it was upon me. I don't just mean nearby. It was on my shoulder, and had landed with such a plop as to be slightly humorous. Although, because of what it was, I wasn't laughing. I immediately knew that I should and would be, kind and gentle. As I turned, I continued walking, all the while this thing is draped across my shoulder.

I came to the realization that this may be the one, the only, Wasp Queen. Not just any queen, but the descendant of those that I had tormented so long ago. Considering the far-off distance that it had traveled, and the fields, and woods to the west, if she indeed was that very thing, they would have moved, and migrated away from our neighborhood, away from the homes of human beings, and away from…well…especially me.

Here she was now the queen herself, and we would forge, and shape a lasting peace together. With that consideration I felt more than obligated to comply with any single thing that she wanted. Ever so quickly a clever dare came to mind. As I looked down upon her in a calm state of repose, with her so perfectly relaxed, so gently, and yes indeed, precariously positioned, I thought this should do it. In my mind, I was thinking, "Okay here's the deal, if you're still there, you will come in to meet Mother. If you're gone however by that time, okay then, you will not."

After a block of walking, and my checking only once, as the sheer weight of the beast was all that was needed for me to realize she hadn't bailed, I was ready to ascend the front steps, then up to the porch, and in. I ever so carefully, once in the kitchen, turned to face Mom. As calm, and as cool as I could be, I asked then of Mother, "Would you like to meet my new friend?"

She turned and faced the shocking truth. In a stuttered voice, she offered, "alright then, go back outside."

The closest that I can compare her shakiness to was when Lucy, from *I Love Lucy*, was on TV with her dream of the big time finally realized she just froze up, and could only muster, "Ohhhhhiii-ii-iii, Ed." The talk show host was in the studio, and they had a remote camera inside the Ricardo's apartment on that episode. Anyway, I gently walked toward the door, made my way back outside, then moved toward the top of the hill in our front yard. Before I could descend the steps, and make my way down to the main walkway, the thing launched. Yes, she was off, off, and away.

Later on, something did occur that I should have been warned about well beforehand. If you'll recall my friend's father felt that it would go against God to have a tattoo applied to one's skin. It wasn't just his father was a Southern Baptist. Apparently, you would never talk about a dog's genitalia.

"Why in the world do you get to that point?" became the question afterward! I feel totally, totally the innocent one in that regard.

You see my pal was inside doing something or other, and I was left out with his tied-up dog until he was ready. In being not just one-eighth Polish, never having had one of my very own, I had not been fully informed of a dog's danger zones. With familial allergies and such and no budget money for yapping canines, one can easily see why our family would never go there. So, out of boredom, I thought that I should test again then, to get this part beagle mix to obey, I said "sit."

That one move came natural to him, with the next move one's own, as in petting. Since I wanted to run the commands, considering that I don't love dogs, at least in that way, I ordered him to stand. He refused. Again, I ordered, again he refused. At this point I had felt that he needed some coaxing. Now with his tail guarding the family jewels, if you know what I mean, I firmly placed my hand to the base of his '*area*' I then commanded him once more before beginning to lift. Within one millisecond, the mangy mutt snapped and had at me.

Before I could move myself beyond his well-controlled zone he had managed to bite my arm, my leg, and my finger. Drawing blood on the latter he exacted such a super-fast and painful exhibition that I went into an immediate and desperate sense of shock. Having enough of my wits about me I quickly moved to the front of the house. Making my way over, two doors down, at first seemed elemental. As I neared my home, I began to lose it. "No, no," I had said, "You're too old, don't do this, come on."

I broke down. Although I only needed another step or so to be in front of my own home, something gave. It was the combination of shock, together with three total bite marks that pushed me over the edge. Within two tears, or at least a few seconds I had regained my composure and started to recover. Whew. Yet it wasn't over, what with the throbbing ache. I so soon felt the world being lifted from my shoulders, and a sense of total and utter relief.

Before entering my home from the back, I checked to denote this son-of-a-witches presence, in his yard, or anywhere in between. I was safe. For now, anyway I was. Mother suggested that we go see the man who would later become a ladies' '*diet*' doctor. Since we had insurance and all, why not allow the doctor to offer an opinion. How we actually made it there with her not driving at all back then I do not recall. I will say that it was reassuring to know that as long as my friend's dog had gotten his shots, I'd be okay.

In a sad and even sorrowful kind of way, vengeance was mine. Because of his often being too wild and crazy, even though tied up, it was thought that it would be best for him to retire at my buddy's grandfather's place. While there, another dog put the death bite on him from behind the neck, and it was over. No doubt the other dog was actually a male coyote or two! You will read further about the sense of peace that I maintain to this day, with that pooch's passing!

1971

Father had made the decision. We would host Easter this year, and Daddy would need to finally complete his duties in the lower chamber. He brought home all of the lumber so things began. Once again fulfilling the apprentice position I was at the ready. He had created a table saw out of our old TV from the early sixties. Since the surface was not quite large, he would require the services of an assistant. My duty was to keep the sawn ends from falling to the floor. No problemo!

I was around enough, to gain an understanding of the overall concept. In today's world we have such wonderful products as water proof sealant for cellars and such. Back then perhaps a clever invention was more necessary. Father mentioned a troublesome window. His idea was to create a drain from beneath that window and lead any actual water to the floor drain in the laundry section. In theory, his plan seemed solid. He simply needed to somehow get the catch tray adhered to the wall while completely covering such aself-made drain with wall paneling.

It worked. The remainder of our job was cutting the 2x4s for the side braces. After he had showed me the concept of drilling into the very thick cement walls, he expressed that by design these bolts being used to hold the wall in place, would actually make a stronger wall, rather than one with drilled holes poking everywhere. His other must? He simply had to have side braces connecting the uprights here, and there.

That way, you could not only hang a picture by nailing into one of those cross supports, who knows how truly vital they would become later on in regards to holding things together in a handsome and uniform way. The last hammering was in place and only one thing remained. His brainchild was to cover the old '50s fridge with the flexible wall panels, allowing that to blend in, rather than to detract from the overall look. It worked. All that we needed was a tapper handle or something similar and a way to attach such a thing to the broken fridge handle. Only one additional aspect of the work remained, a basement bar would offer the finishing touch.

Father had sent in for the blueprints of a home-bar offered through a magazine. It was perfect for the space we had, and would fit around the pole. It is a fact in our neighborhood that everyone had two metal poles holding the top half of the house up. One by default would be hidden in the laundry room. The other now cleverly holds family photos taken at that very bar itself, or at least nearby. A cutaway would need to be made at the very edge of the bar top nicely fitting around that pole.

An opening that not only allowed for the bartender to take his place, but one that could offer an additional drop-down surface with which to blend Grass-Hoppers upon was attached. Since the outlet was right nearby, that was the finishing touch. Aside from the broken refrigerator handle, everything went fine for our premiere debut that Easter. As long as a person is handy the most recent refrigerators could be 'molded' around. We're currently on model #2, a slightly smaller unit that is now well fitted into place.

It was finally summertime once again. I swam regularly in the neighbor's pool with my pal from two doors down. Although, technically our neighbor in between was still in charge of his daily care, my bud could gain access to his home when necessary, such as the day Skip had bitten me the year before. He and I were simply not to be goofing around all day inside his place, making messes, eating food, or doing whatever else working moms didn't care for. (Recall mine was a 'stay-at-home'.)

Life was great for us otherwise anyway with our being just like a couple of froggish tadpoles. One day however, I was on my own. The neighbor from two doors down on the other side had apparently cooked up a plan. Let's just stop here for a moment to take a look back at history. This fellow was three years older. When I was just six, he knocked me down and I swallowed a loose tooth that would have gone at least another few days.

On another day not long after, his brother runs from out of the back door fully nude. His mom pulled him back inside by the ear. The coolest thing that we had done together was to catch Hugh-Gass garden spiders. Those were my very neighbor's. He was the fellow that took me downtown with our other bud to see a movie. The creepy crawler machine was this other fellow's. That gizmo allowed one to create small toy figures made of plastic. You can imagine how the two things come together.

So, yes, for a while we had a full, two-inch, plastic-coated spider. That well tamed beast was on full display in a coffee can in the second neighbor's backyard for quite some time. On this particular day however, something more sinister was in the works. This young man now about 6' tall, and all of 14, was up to no good. He waited until I moved past the garage in the alleyway. At this point, he aimed sharply. He then hit me shockingly in the neck with an uncooked popcorn kernel.

Well, I wasn't going to take that. I moved in quickly to reckon with him. He however had been standing there throughout this entire sequence with an unlined fishing reel. He stood his ground and gave fair warning. I hesitated not. He whipped, and whipped again. Once more he offered a verbal warning, yet now with an assured look in his eye. It was too late, I was already jackedup big and bad, and what with my temper, I was not quite done.

One more good-whoopin' did the trick. A tear began to well up ever so slightly in my eye, and I relented. "That's right," he commanded from behind, "You get going and stay away, or else."

I blew it off and went back to the rest of my day. Upon pulling my trousers down for some business the very next afternoon, a shocking realization took place. The cool purple pants from Sears had torn open. Those trousers were suspiciously of a lighter tone than those in the catalogue. They were tight-ass as well.

I wore them the week before school started back up and they tore out. I coincidentally had to go. The welts and bruises swept across my legs like green and purple evidence. Just then, Mother walked in from the outside. I popped the door ajar and called to her. "My so-called grape-purple pants ripped out," I called from the slightly opened door. From the lower level of my voice, as in a seated position, she hesitated not entering, and spoke through the crack. I beckoned her closer. She peaked enough to view those horrid markings. She quickly went into shock.

The tragedy was spelled out in those 2½ to 3-inch green-purplish welts. Each of those was at least a foot or two in length. Before I could even finish up, she was off to tend to business. Within minutes, she was back letting me know that it was now up to his folks to fully deal with. I told her that I really just wanted to be cool about it, considering I trespassed on their property. No, she said, it couldn't be cool with the horror she had witnessed so close up.

"Oh well, they'll all work it work," I had considered.

It was September once more. The new school year began as usual without much fanfare. One thing that we all had to appreciate most realistically was our brand-new teacher. She was hot spankin' new and fresh from college. A tall German blond not doubt, with perhaps some Norwegian thrown in for good measure. I recall the first thing that I took note of right off. Since my chair was dead last and next to the door, I couldn't help but notice the new softball bats lying at the bottom of the teacher's open closet.

I hefted one up and took an introductory stroke. Ahh…life was good, the weather still fine, and I was young. One other minor newness did greet me that year as well. It was my honey-bunny from kindergarten class, none other than Jeannie herself (the one you'd dream about with light brown hair). Let's just say she was never looking more attractive. She was just like a girl from a song anyway. With us being only 11-years-old there wasn't much on my mind in that regard mind you, other than the smooth, smooth feeling she gave off to me.

Indeed, that was from a safe distance from afar. She sat in the first window seat. I resided in the last door chair. That was safe enough for now! She being placed so far from myself had me wonder. Was it merely that she had been placed at the head of the class, kitty-corner from my seat, or was even the school concerned with an obviously rapid shoot of sudden maturity? It's been said that more than likely, fortified breakfast cereals had the most to do with our reaching an early puberty, even before the age of twelve.

It mattered not from where our blossoming features did surely sprout. My adoration was unstoppable and grew in shortened measures as each and every day passed. I still recall, with only the slightest amount of embarrassment, how back in second grade when most of the others were off at the symphony, we were given some minor tasks to engage in. Those were offered in order to while away the lonesome hours there in the classroom by our lonesome selves.

We had been instructed to keep busy with the additional learning items and were digging through those old learning materials located in the built-in book-case running underneath the windows. We both were exerting the upmost in stretching and straining to reach those items further back. Somehow as I lowered my head to lunge toward the rear of that lowest level, upon arising I had found my head had somehow gotten underneath her skirt.

I thought that I had caught a glimpse of the corner of something. Quickly, an animalistic surge puttered through me like a blind mouse in a multi-mazed cage. We quickly disengaged and all so seriously got back to our work. Now here where I sat, sat and admired, and that from afar, was something so very genuine and all too distinctive to me, that rang out in expansive peels of admiration. She had mainly a blonde mane, with gentle streaks of light brown.

Her overall shape and figure was Jennifer Aniston average. I was enchanted. With no car, or much money to speak of, we would not be going places together. Suffice it to say I admired from afar. Even today, I do recall that no one, not any other girl in the whole wide world, could captivate me with such a simple and innocent sense of slimness. This was not a skinny shape either, mind you. By the end of the school year, she was just as beautiful as any grown woman could ever be, even at that ripe young age of twelve.

It had been an otherwise uneventful year for me. Safe in the sanctity of dull suburban life, I was shielded from any of the outside harms that could take a young man down. Not just, down but even out. It did just that, to one fellow from down the way. I still remembered the day Jerry needed a friend. There was nothing he had stolen, no alibis for me to offer, nothing we needed but some gentle rocking on the swings. I recalled that he wasn't such a bad guy once you got to know him.

He also offered me his very own swear. F*ck-a-duck. "That's what I say," he went on, "Just f*ck-a-duck." A bit jaded at this point he was yeah, but we connected in a neighborly way, on that laziest of summer days. In hindsight, I do believe that I had felt that Jerry was actually maturing. He was killing time with his mom at work, yet doing it in such a calm and casual manner. Perhaps there was hope for a young man without a dad at all after all. At least there was on that bright day.

It was a later day off for us. The call came in to my buddy's house. A funeral was being held at our church and his brothers had declined the offer. I was in. Now, these extremely somber occasions called for a very serious and respectful approach. When it came time to ring the bell, an even more respectful method of movement was required. That's why I stopped my other buddy that lived down the street from going all hash on the rope. "No, no, no," I admonished him. "One must first call the people together. These intonations must have a three count in between. When calling the people together, with that proper tolling not being carried through properly, it would be a blasphemous action. We'll wait until we signify the spirit rising, to give it all that we've got. Indeed, we did just that."

The whole goal of an uninformed novice was to pull the rope down as far as possible. Upon reaching the climax and moving one's hands upward to the height of one's reach, the weight of the bell itself would pull you up, a good four to five feet from the floor, and into the air at that it would.

Such an effort could certainly be made within the tightly religious constructs of our duties. One merely needed to wait until the end of the ceremony to engage in such a wildly ambitious style of activity. It should be so that God himself would approve, as long as the intonations were being correctly struck. It was only our most privileged and hallowed honor to be partaking in this most scared of rituals. The most egregious behavior would then therefore involve blowing the respectful pulse, or cadence of said tolling.

Being lifted right off of the floor by such a strong and sturdy action was merely a perk we could enjoy, as long as we were willing to wait until those services were actually over. We returned to the tolling, although with the necessary cadence of ceremony. My feeling had always been that as long as I respected the service, did my best to adhere to protocol, and serve with a sense of reverent respect, there was nothing more that could possibly be executed by myself.

Other than rejoicing that the spirit had risen, I mean. We heartily rang and clanged with a most beautiful sense of joy and relief at that treasured moment. Those emotions were now so well realized within ourselves as well. We did surely do our duty to the very best of our ability, on that staid and solemn day. Too bad for us at school we had failed to be as easily taught when it came to hijinks, chicanery, and a lack of total and utter respect.

I cannot quite recall the exact act of perpetration enacted against any one individual on this latest occasion in question. Nor do I recall the school's honor itself being abraded or harmed in any way, shape, fashion, or form. Yet there we were lying face down against the mostly cleanly floor with our noses to be directly touching the very tiles themselves. We were not at all to be pointed off to the side with our mugs for any sense of relief whatsoever.

It wasn't for many years afterward, that talk of the school having had asbestos tiling was mentioned. In a sense of relief, I had to consider that for the most part, only ceiling tiles were actually constructed of such a cancer-causing material. In any case, I truly did believe at the time that we each had learned our lessons, and there would be no further need for deeds of correction to be performed by any of us afterward.

On yet another day off from school, my two pals and I just happened to be invited over to Jeannie's house. Now considering, it is one thing to find a young lady attractive, but to ever so quickly begin to play kissing games or 'under-the-blanket' was not a mere leap. You see we were immediately escorted down into the cellar where an old kitchen table was set up. In addition, two other girls had been invited as well.

Before you go too far on your own, I will explain that we not only did not get there, I sensed a lack of true and total admiration streaming from the psyche of my one and at the time, only true love.

She even, perhaps maybe, had eyes for my paper delivery comrade. You see, all three of us were set up in this way. We ruled the neighborhood. Not one home in the area received a paper otherwise, unless they went and bought it from a store.

Alas, dates can seem just a little awkward when riding a girl on the back of your bike. Unless of course they're into it which means it's so totally on baby! (Just a note: the inherent danger of riding on the back involves a shifting of balance from the pedal pusher, causing a swinging of the feet on the rider's part. Should the foot of a back seat rider enter the spoke area, beware! Refer to 1967, and that young neighbor girl) I, as a newsboy's helper always had some cash put away, while often spending the remainder on the candy of my choosing.

One evening I got truly carried away. For unknown reasons, I got the hardcore feel for yet another coconut, and almond bar, and another, and another. The wicked jones wouldn't leave me alone. It was much like the song about Mr. Brownstone. That was perhaps a tune hinting toward crack smoking, rather than a digestible longing. After the last fourth, and final yummy bar had been consumed on that fateful day, I lied upon my bed with my belly protruding out, like a pregnant woman.

What could possibly relieve me of this godforsaken, self-induced type of traumatic dilemma. Think, think, I wondered. It wasn't that I didn't have the funds for a cure, I was only praying to the empty room for which remedy to apply here. That was it, after a mental rolodex tour of so many commercials, I finally came upon the one. That Pep-up Bismark pink stuff, or what have you, should do the trick. I meandered out to the corner store with hopefully just enough cash to save my night.

Walking now with my belly still pushed out in agony, I ambled on along. The small personal size bottle of Pep-up was marked just low enough for my urgent needs. So, let's see, candy bars went from 5¢ in 1964, to then 10¢ in 1969. That second increase was due to the sugar crisis, something perhaps caused no doubt by a major hurricane, or even local and or political strife. They had even gone now, at this later date, to 15¢. So, $((4 \times 15 = 60) + 2.89)$ for a total of $3.49 completely wasted.

I mean to say, I quickly made my way back home, tore open the container, and drank all of the contents, each and every drop. My tummy grew wider, and stuck out now with even a greater pain than when first I had set out. My advice to any of the other fools who should stumble down this rocky road, work it off. That would so sincerely seem to be the only answer. Better yet, note duly that you exist within the confines of having an 'addictive' personality, and be more careful otherwise!

Out of additional boredom that year I began to measure myself. It was the oldest sister that seemed to be a bit preoccupied with the ins and outs the long, long tape. Since she wasn't currently making anything for her Home Economics course, such a determination as to her interest was the only assumption one could logically come to.

I took temporary ownership of the mustard yellow device, and carefully marked a spot on the door jamb. I could proudly proclaim that I was 5' 1½" tall. So, soon it would be that I would be taller than Mother, and both my sisters. Since they somehow had all stunted at exactly 5'2", it would only be a matter of time. I reveled at the thought.

It was now Halloween. I had tried on my uncle's uniform from 1943. I suppose that he was not yet fully grown as it actually fit. I had decided then, my last year of so much candy would be a big one. Dressed from my head, with Father's hat, to my ankles, with the pants and top from my smaller uncle, I would go out with a bang. After donning the whole ensemble, I went totally musical for just a wee bit. I mean with a Gene Kelly song and dance musical type of number.

I hadn't practiced much for the part, so cooled things down right away, as I had work to do. I determined it would be nothing less than a grand experience to ring doorbells, while hand delivering the evening paper to my grateful customers. Some seemed to think a grown man in the Navy shouldn't be begging for candy, but eventually relented. I was being paid then therefore, technically, to retrieve candy from these very people. How marvelous.

My decision had been made, not only was I to be taller than the trio at home, I would also become much more muscular. Only one thing was needed. A set of weights it would be then from Santa himself, no less. To be honest, the one in the Sears catalogue would surely suffice as well. I had the boyish joy of a lad who got his wish that December 24th.

I had made up my mind, and set the course steady. I would become a muscle-man, or at least become somewhat stronger than I was in any case. Anyone should know that one must be diligent and persevere when it comes to the well fathomed roadmaps toward glory. To build upon greatness, one must exemplify greatness. To take grander steps, one must insist upon grander efforts. I merely needed to man-up, and the world would be my oyster. I was well on my way.

1972

Before the warmth of spring had thawed the land, lifting the deeply folded blankets of snow from the barren earth's surface, something bright and cheerful had been offered to my class. The memory so quickly forgotten had little importance to our youthful selves. We had become accustomed to quizzes and testing, for so many years before, during our early years.

At one point in the second grade, we had been told that although the instructor reserves the right to employ the use of quiz grades in our overall score, it will not necessarily be the case at any given time. Perhaps, any one of those grade school teachers would let us know of any impending usage, or lack thereof, of these pop-quiz tests scores.

Sometimes they simply needed to know where we stood in any one regard, in order to determine a righteous path forward for the benefit, hopefully of us all. Here now we were reminded of that very special, out of the ordinary testing that we had just mustered through earlier in the year. That very conversation, was rolled out so carefully and gently, quickly emerging into something more.

It somehow became one fantastical, marvelous, wondrous, proclamation of a well-founded higher stature. It is so that I am certain a gracious honor had been bestowed upon each and every one of us. Even more so, in a somehow religiously pious fashion, we were majestically honored. The totality of it all was indeed very titillating. It was so invigorating, and of such an empowering depth.

It was that it should have catapulted every last soul within our sweet young innocent persons into the outer stratosphere of emotional perception. With a newfound realm of positively fantastical cranial delights, we should have led the world. You see what was presented to us on that gleeful afternoon was no mere crown jewel of scholastic achievement.

No, it was rather the actual remaking of our very identities. This presentation of new realities offered not just a new persona for each young person present, but a total rearrangement of our psyches, reaching even further beyond our vast imaginations. It then made its way into our very souls.

The gifting of these new personas unto us was from such a usual and everyday routine that it came as a laughable and pleasant surprise.

It was then that we were offered this tasty little tidbit. It was according to the test results that we were the most intelligent and highly rated group ever to have assembled in one single classroom in the history, of the entirety, of the totality, of the far-reaching expanses of the very universe itself. At least within the local stratosphere of things and such, we were now considered anyway.

The highest ranking offered, of which I was apart of, was considered to be at the College Junior level. My forte scholastically, you may have guessed, was in English Literature. The lowest of us, with little exception was of the level of a freshman in high school. What was to be done then with such an impressive collection of studious thinkers of the type that we did now so righteously identify as?

Should we drop everything and open a chemistry lab? Should we all decide to abandon our collective greatness while attending other schools of opportunity? Since we were all 11 or 12 years of age or so, I don't know that there was truly much that we may have moved over to, at least not so much on an immediate level in any case.

So, our whimsical fancy was no doubt placed into the deep recesses of our personas with a certain respect toward our futures. It was grand enough simply basking in the glory of that wonderful afternoon. What was finally decided upon, just after our collective yet humble awareness had been presented, was to ditch the grammar style reading books in favor of novels.

The new list included, Of Mice and Men, A Salesman Always Rings Twice, A Catcher in the Rye, That Was Then This Is Now. Those, plus a few additional writings were what we would eventually work through. It was so that by the end of eighth grade at that local private Catholic Grade School, we had graduated to a higher sense of being.

Later on, that spring my friend's old dog Skip came for a visit. He had been farmed out to his grandparent's home as you may recall, though I believe they had needed a break now themselves. Indeed, it was that both neighbors to the north had pool tables. That close buddy from two doors down, would practice all morning at the next-door lady's house, only to lure me into his home, to try and run the table on me.

Because of the dog's interference we decided to simply sit on the corner pieces they had set up in the nearby reading area. Things were fine at first, albeit with Skip the dog's wild sense of hyperactivity fully at play. That went quickly from wild to crazy in seconds. Think of a bad dog that runs away, only to return years later. Said canine would thusly come back home wilder, bolder, and here and now, way gayer!

Apparently, in the dog world, once you bite someone and they run, you own them. So, dude starts humping on my leg. I, still with a tad bit of timidity in regards to total and outright animal control, hesitated. My failure to own the situation presented a lacking of the type that this pooch could no doubt outright smell.

One may humorously imagine that I was at first reluctant to aggressively get him under control. I beckoned my pal to do so instead, on my pleading and victimized behalf. Might I say that, he as well was somewhat reticent in his masterful sense of what should have been the total control of his very own *former* pet. So, dog is right away 'back-at-it' on me.

This little bastard beagle-wannabe, runs from my bro but then comes right back to my leg. After two times of his sexual assaulting me, I started to raise a fist. Not to the dog mind you, that seemed all too futile. No, I seriously threatened dude. I gestured to him, he the failing former owner of this now gay dog. I meant it.

If he didn't maintain, and or reestablish his superiority I was going to start punching him, then all three of us could go down swinging and biting, and humping, in an all-out free-for-all, or more appropriately 'three-for-all'! It was after the third time that he grabbed and humped that this little bitch of a male dog even left a bit of a wet mark on my pants.

That assault-marking was situated just below the knee. I am telling you here and now, I was surely so close to actually punching my friend if he didn't do something to regain control at that point. He finally stood up and took authority. He, while doing his best to remove that sucker all the way from the lower chamber, suggested that I get up on top of the pool table.

Oh great, I had thought once atop the old quarter machine. That former professional level table had been rigged with a paper clip to dispense the balls without any money being inserted. So, there I was on my hands and knees, completely exposed from behind while Skip, the bisexual hound is running *laps* around the pool table. My first fears shall go unwritten.

Suffice it to say, I prayed like I never have before, for redemption, salvation, forgiveness for my sins, and for the hand of God himself, to enter forth from the very heavens above. Yes, for he the Almighty one himself, to intervene on my behalf I had pled, and prayed for. Hallelujah, within minutes, the sucker was finally up the stairs with the door now safely shut. I would be mostly okay thereafter.

This same neighbor, the fellow that lived two doors down, and I would be going off on an adventure. After having been a paperboy assistant for a couple of years I had a bit of money saved up. Mother offered that she, and father considered that I should probably start a bank account but would not be forced to. Believing that it was good advice, I indeed deposited most of my money into the newly opened account. Therefore, the only question now was, did I need to make a withdrawal, and if so, how much?

My buddy my own age, and I would be engaging in what could even be considered a rite of manhood. We were going on our own to the summer festival. Now this wasn't just some stages with musicians jamming out tunes while adults drank beer. No, no, no. This was everything you could've dreamed of, e all in one spot. They had multiple stages, carnival rides, and good food. We'd also be on our own as far as any escorts, thus making it an ideal situation. It was merely the traversing of the landscape on a Greyhound bus that offered any challenge at all!

I brought about thirteen Washingtons, aside from the bus money, not realizing at the time that a situation could arise that called for a little more dough in hand. I was on cloud nine, with my heart filled to the brim with a jubilant joy regardless. Admission back then was only about $2.50, so there would be plenty left over for anything else that I should so readily desire, or so I had thought. We passed a guy on our way toward the ticket booth. He was wearing Good Humor Ice-Cream driver gloves, with his face painted white.

It was Dave. As we passed, he went into his mime act. One may consider this a graduation of sorts for dude. They call it busking these days, though most of those fellows have guitars, and little to no make-up if any at all. One of the first things we chose to do upon admission was to go on a fabulously wild ride. It was just afterward when I realized that I should have brought some major boku-buckage, rather than a childish amount of chump change that I now feebly was fondling through the front of my pants.

With the few measly singles that I had, only a grand sense of personal enjoyment could be had. It was the fine young ladies so readily about, here, there, and everywhere that caused my disappointment. As far as any additional dollar amounts being close at hand, it was well before the age of ATMs and such easy access to funds. So, anyway, this first ride is the spinning centrifugal forced type, complete with the drop-out bottom. A few seconds after that special delight had geared up, I swear I saw some vomit fly past me. From exactly where the said heavings did flow from and emerge, I was not quite certain.

Perhaps that $13.00 in my pocket was enough after all, if you know what I mean! I smiled at the two fine looking young girls now exiting just behind us. Based on the slightly embarrassed demeanor, more so from one of these young sweeties than the other, I was fairly certain who had felt that uncontrollable queasiness. We rode out the rest of the afternoon stag then finally made our way back to the bus station.

Some news came in from the countryside. Skip the dog was no longer with us. Now, I'm not sure how this scene played out. I mean because dog was found dead in the morning lying on the ground. So, did he try to get all gay and stuff with a coyote, or was this bi-dog hitting on the wild beast's woman. The prognosis was simple.

He died from a death bite administered from behind the neck. I myself was torn. On one hand, a sense of all too sweet revenge beckoned forward. On the other, the one-time frisky little puppy barley bigger than an adults cupped hands was brutally attacked. Either way, it was no good for me. I would need to put it aside and move on with more of a human themed equation in mind.

This same buddy and I were bored one day. For unknown reasons we lashed our bikes together. At one point I yelled stop, but he didn't. He was out in front and just laughed. Finally, he tore my bike apart. I specifically mean that he trashed my ball bearings in the pedal case. Our neighbor from across the way who was always tinkering with something was out near his garage.

Unbelievably this little nine-year-old, not only knew how to remove the cover from the pedals, although we jiminy-rigged it with a screw driver and hammer, he miraculously also had a replacement set of bearings, complete in a case.

Back now in our own time, I had to come to terms with our family budget. As far as I could surmise, none of Father's other children ever received a second bike at all. It just wasn't a part of the family dynamic. Yet when it comes to rites of passage for a young and eager American lad, only one substitute comes so readily to mind. That handy, dandy sweet green, little pile of money is what I seek. That for me again, came from being an official paperboy's helper. I planned, and plotted. I was reserved and cautious. I used a sense of frugality and common commerce. I had finally decided.

I would use up nearly every last penny of my vast reserves to purchase my very own 10 speed bicycle. The discount store would offer just the right product, at just the nicest price. Only one thing did lie in the path of my mechanical conquest. It was 6:37pm, and all of my moola was in the now closed bank. My middle sister looked to Mother with a knowing grin.

"Oh no, not this time," Mother exclaimed. My sister's smile grew wider. The entire event took on an eerily strange sense of allowance and trust. It was decided then. We would take the J.C. Penny's card, and charge the bike. After the purchase, my sister would mount up on the rear of my new machine, and we would be off.

I assured my younger sister that Mom's card would be safe in my top shirt pocket for the challenging ride home. It was warm enough to not need any jacket at all on that too easily remembered evening. Upon arriving back at home and stowing the new machine, only one questioned remained. Can I have the credit card back? I put my hand to my chest.

The panic so quickly set in. Just as the decision to allow for such a fudging of usage played out in an almost silent knowing fashion, here too, words were not so necessary. The only thing that I recalled, as far as my mind being on anything other than riding, was waiting at the last major intersection, with my head down in racing format. *Oh shoot*, I had thought, *That had to be it.*

My mind at the time went to thoughts of the card being neatly in place, yet when I started back up, my thoughts went toward the stability of my sister's legs, and that young neighbor girl with the blood streaming down her fractured leg from years earlier. That must have been it. The very moment when the card no doubt fell from my pocket, was in gearing back up from that stoplight. Mother determined that I needn't go back to search for the plastic.

Considering it was just after 9:00pm, and she could report the card lost the very next morning, we decided to let it go. Once more I had managed to disappoint, discourage, and destroy any faith at all in my common every day abilities. Aahh, 'tis the life of Riley, I do indeed partake in.

More expensive foreign models have the replacement bearings stuck to the round mechanism one by one. Using a thick grease, they are lovingly applied, evenly apart, by serious pros. Whew, I thanked little dude so merrily, yet he reacted like so many mechanics and said it was nothing. (Just a note: the snobs at the local bike shop have sold out, and they now over there, will work on old bikes with mere *ball-bearing cases*)

Our family was all going away. It would be the last family trip we'd ever take together. After piling into the old red station wagon, we were good to go. Oh shit, Dad forgot the keys, and inside the now locked house. "Don't worry, it's all okay," he assured us. "Will you come with me, we'll take care of this," he confidently claimed and assured me. "You can all wait here, we'll be right back," he had promised the urgent group. He walked me down to the first cellar window. Not the one that I had cracked out with a baseball bat years earlier, rather the window just over a few feet.

Father quietly conveyed what we were about to do. In a hushed tone he confidently told me after he breaks the thing, and clears the glass, I would be carefully lowered down to floor level, at which point I should then rush upstairs letting him in. In two winks of a leprechauns smile I was in. After I blew my cool years earlier, and cracked the neighbor girl's basement window, Father had thought to keep a spare handy just in case. Here that was now before us, the well planned for emergency.

I loved my sweetie pie. That was the cute blonde whose window Father repaired. She had lived a few houses down. It was actually my oldest sister that got me so super-pissed. I begged and pleaded to come along. But just like that it was done and over. It was almost as though an evil demon would take over my body and release the ever so quickly built-up rage. Here though, in our own time, minutes before our vacation would begin, we worked quickly and steadfastly to work through our dilemma. With the rest of the family patiently waiting, we emerged victorious. Within seconds we were all back in the old Ford, and on our merry way.

Let me simply spell out, since this blonde attractive girl from down the way was not a super close friend, my older sis' thought it best for us to not engage in any longing enquiry involving willingness, or availability. I had merely felt that she had diminished my very existence with her fussy social etiquette and visitation rules. I was primed, yet my older sis' was not quite ready. The fact that this neighbor girl's mom was just behind her in the kitchen didn't help things.

When I was denied my chance to make my play, I reacted. After taking their garden hose from the near the cellar window, I smashed it quickly open. Damn, what the hell is wrong with me?

Weeks earlier before a destination for our vacation had been finalized and determined, we had discussed the overall agenda as a family. Since only one of us was a small child, Disney World was nixed. Instead, it would be out to the Old West, at least the middle section of that area. First, we needed to move through the Midwest before exploring the Dakotas. Since Mother had an uncle, who at one time ran a bee farm, we'd take it easy and stop there for a spell. There would be harsh territory ahead. It is what is known as the Badlands of South Dakota.

We prepared well, with a cooler filled with ice, and sodas for everyone. We ventured fourth toward the harsh unknown. South Dakota had been hit hard earlier in the year. There was massive flooding, and much damage that occurred from the all of the rains. That was in late May. From the tall grasses laying down, to the ground being well muddied and flattened, one could surmise that some of the roads that we had driven down, were at least 2 or 3 feet under if not an outright 4 feet. Thankful to have avoided such calamity, we merrily made our way onward. Soon enough we'd be arriving at our destination. Here though, the ride would be more than just that.

The Dakota Badlands are as barren as any desert could ever be. With one simple difference that is. Everything was black. I looked back at the ground we had covered. We had now been swallowed up by the vastness of this dark foreboding and barren wasteland. The long stretch, and lonely emptiness of the road ahead, and especially the dryness of this frightening and all engulfing terrain so easily took over our senses. The sodas brought along were consumed. Just as quickly we thirsted for more. "Water, water, water," I had plead, only it was not in jest.

No one individual would ever become facetious in such a drastically dire situation. We each were allowed one cube, as Mother had decided to ration them. With her warning that they were '*cooler*' cubes, the admission that thirst knows no difference whatsoever when it comes to the source of origin, was well agreed upon. All too soon the cubes had melted away, as though our very mouths were as hot as that roadway stretching out before us.

"It's just another twenty miles, oh twenty miles to freedom," Mother had proclaimed. With that gloriously welcomed revelation, the fear and weight of our venturing burden was lifted. Indeed, just like that we were free, and back to civilization, back to liquid refreshment, back to a hotel. The thing is, to those who may believe I've embellished a bit, this was ages before the creation of clunky, old-school cell phones, and I cannot recall at all seeing another car along that barren sun parched roadway whatsoever. No, nary a one was even about. That car didn't have air either!

We would take turns with the Atlas for the remainder of the trip, cueing each other in on relevant factoids gleamed from that hefty book of maps. No other tidbits, or miles of info could've compared to arriving safely out of that northern desert. We soon enough made our way over to Colorado. I'm not certain what I see when I look out of the airplane window when flying by, but it looks a lot like Mars, or something similarly barren, vast, and so keenly void of life. Along the way, here on this trip, we stopped at a minor attraction or two. We as well skipped that dry, barren, and parched-earth section of Colorado in a smart and intelligent fashion.

The first lure outside of the Dakotas offered specifically for tourists involved pictures with a donkey for a few bucks. The next one offered a genuine stage coach ride. We climbed into that old-school taxi to begin the trip. Let me tell you a person could likely get seasick on one of those even in a dry barren dessert. Though it was the terrain that was genuine, that was more so than what came next. We were held up by some desperados before we could pull into the station. We had nothing of value so they let us go.

Next up was the purchase of some Coor's cans. I asked if I may please have some, since "it's like a souvenir thing, you know," I added. "One mustn't go to Colorado without doing it right," I tossed in for good measure.

Father passed a can he had some sips off of. Yum, yum it tasted much better than the Hamm's from 1964, I had considered. This was much smoother. Here I was now, a man with this rite of passage enacted, fulfilled, and justifiably engaged in. No doubt the cool, cool Rocky Mountain springs had much more to do with my graduation from childhood, than the actual type of liquid consumed. The only question was would I be buzzed? A little, yes indeed, just a tad bit or so.

After leaving the hotel in Boulder, we traveled upon one of those slim mountain roads. I mean the type that had you wondering if you should pull over to let the car going the other way on past. All that was visible on my side of the car were steep inclines with a side salad of horrifyingly well-imagined scenarios involving a tumultuously tumbling death.

Such an imagined demise did definitely, harrowingly, and most assuredly wait for any unfortunates who should miscalculate. They then would be getting to so quickly find out, what did indeed wait just below. Soon enough before we perished, tumbling down into that engulfing vector of steepness so close, a flatland high up and to the side of things fell open up ahead. A sign reading horse-rides was displayed.

My sisters had briefed me on the finer attributes of riding. Other than the small ponies that made me cry when I was 4, I hadn't quite had the proper opportunity to employ such special training. What they had said was basically "pull right for right, and pull left, to go left." Well, those being girls, and a one-fourth Polish at that, you can only imagine.

One aspect of such a move involves going so freaking fast that the horse won't turn in time unless you guide him a tad aggressively. Here at this mountaintop flatland, before this genuine cowboy running the joint was able to bring our horses around all saddled up, he needed to bring some order to the corral. This one apparently older fellow, a very special medium brown dark tan horse, was trying to get a ride on some of the other horses. Colorado cowboy-dude was throwing big dirt boulders at this confused animal. He aimed for the gut as hard as possible.

Are there gay horses? Anyway, he finally got old horny Joe under control, and we mounted up. My older sister's horse was a young stallion. It bolted for the hill just after our photo shoot. I tried to steer mine, and paid the price. I am certain that my older sister made no effort whatsoever with her dark brown pony. Her most necessary agenda no doubt merely involve hanging on for dear life.

A horse will go where it needs to generally, without much persuasion. It's when it is new to an area that they no doubt need a bit more guidance. One only needs to use the reigns to turn them around or if there is a Y in the trail otherwise. You especially don't want to try and steer an older set-in-his-ways type of 'moseyer'. They will only stop in their tracks and lock up as mine did that day. Due to the fact that you're nothing but a green horn to them, you don't deserve any respect. You may now imagine how that actually works.

Awhile after, I mean that 'way-younger' stallion was gone baby, ranch-dude got that racehorse under control. He then came back for me. After pleading and pulling, coaxing, and cajoling, the old-man-of-a-ride I was on, finally decided to give me some due breakage. Once more we were off. With the runner now under control we rendezvoused at the base of a small hill. After ascending the small slope, we turned right into some cover. At that point I felt just like Mr. Clint Eastwood himself.

My younger sister's horse took a poop right in front of my horse's face yet he took no umbrage from that fact, and kept right on moving, bringing up the rear. Riding a horse, even only once again, is still on my bucket list. I don't mean just outside of Boulder. Anywhere I can manage my longing will be just fine. With the urban sprawl around here, the nearest place is about thirty miles to the north. It'll still be there when I need it. I hope anyway.

With the old west adventure of a lifetime under our belts, it was time to move up to Yellowstone. I was bored while sitting in the middle so decided to employ the use of my brand-new souvenir pocket knife. It came with a can opener. Although, the soda I had just consumed was easily opened with a simple pop and pull method, I was in the need of some tool usage.

The challenge I had created for myself involved cutting through the top of the can, one snap at a time. We came upon a road sign reading 'The Grand Canyon of Yellowstone Next Left'. A new element of my challenge had been presented. Could I manage to break through the entire top before our destination was reached just up ahead.

Click, clack, pop. I soon wondered if I was getting on anyone's nerves. Furiously, aggressively I tore the metal apart. To set the record straight, soda cans were made of a heavy-duty metal back then, not aluminum. That chintzy-seeming product, at least in comparison, was still a year or two on the horizon. If you consider a soup can, you'd be close enough for Rock'n'roll, right there, Captain Bucky if I do say so myself.

Real men with great big meaty fists could squeeze those into a crushed sense of thinness, with little effort. That occurred on the school bus one day when an eighth-grade student performed that feat with a hardy and gladdened smile. Alas, I was never able to accomplish such an act before those sturdy hardcore cans went out of style. I am still amazed at that fellow's power, ability and shear manual baseline strength.

Here though, we went quickly around a bend. Just ahead I spied a left. After my calling that fact out, Father grabbed the wheel, and pulled down hard. It was fool's gold. Someone's private drive it seemed. As we twirled about, a truck with a camper trailer emerged from a tunnel and at a fairly good clip indeed. Dad punched it and we scooted forward. The truck bore down, a collision was imminent. He clipped the very corner of our tail light. After we parked in the drive, the other fellow pulled over. The men emerged and gathered in the rear.

It was determined that it was a minimal happening. Father opened the trunk, and pulled out a beer. "So, is that it?" (Hinting of a probable intoxication) this old man asked.

"Well, no, we just got out of bed," Father replied. "I am certainly going to have one now, would you like one?" he inquired.

After popping the cap, he mentioned the 'Next Left' sign, saying, "I certainly don't think it's this one." The two exchanged information, and we were back on our way.

We noted another tourist notification. This would be the oldest known tree to exist in any accessible area. It was dead when we arrived. Only about 16 feet long, it lay on its side in a lifeless state of preservation. It was gleaming with a shine that had to be considered glass-like. As hard and cold as icy steel could be, this wonder of the park had managed through rain, and storm, through snow, and sleet to resist every last thing the earth could throw its way.

I believe it to be over 40 million years old. I may have to dig up the pictures to be sure. Soon enough, at the ground of this ancient artifact, right before our very eyes, amassed a squadron of prairie dogs. They were as tame as house pets. We got permission to pull a box of cereal from the trunk. "Peanut Butter Crunch should do the trick," it was considered. We retrieved the opened box then began to feed them from our hands. After it was decided they had had enough, I couldn't resist performing a test.

The question was, did they know by smell that you had a treat, or was the learned behavior merely based on the extension of the hand. I held mine out with nothing in it. One came close and with the gentleness of a little lamb, it bit down on my finger. It was slightly shocking yet no blood was drawn. Whew, no further research was required in order to determine the behavioral aspects of small brown scavengers from the Yellowstone Park area.

Soon enough we saw yet another sign for a major attraction. The highest drivable road in the world it was, and only a short number of miles ahead. "Why not, one only lives once?" We had considered. We then ventured higher, and higher, and ever higher. Finally, a road sign warned us "Last Intersection on This HWY." We were drawing nearer to a climax of height. I looked outside, and upon the ground was snow. In the second week of August believe it or not, there was genuine not yet melted snow. It was lying upon the ground on either side of the road. We pulled over to see for certain.

I quickly scooped a good amount together. It was icy cold, and so very hard to the touch. I pulled back to throw, but first a quick picture was called for. Soon enough we were back in the old '67 station wagon, and continuing to climb. A distressing fact suddenly came to light. The trees no longer had leaves. I turned to look back, yet we had gone too far. Everywhere around us, the early death of mature saplings, and other would-be flora laid a bare testimonial to the harshness of the present conditions. A true sadness brought itself forward, draped across the landscape like a reaper of the mount. None of these young innocent ones was more than four or five feet tall.

"The tree line," Father noted, and we chugged along rather slowly, as even the auto found it hard to function in this nearly barren wasteland. Higher, and higher, and once more then again, we made our way to the farthest reaches of any welcoming land. At the top, and now out of the car we were heavy, and slow. Any exertion was dangerous. Plodding along we made it to the gift shop. Once inside, we noted an oxygen machine with a fresh supply of oral paper cones. A few breaths each, was all that was required, and we ambled back on down the winding easy roadway, to a warm meal and finally a good night's rest.

We soon enough hit Old Faithful. Nearby we saw green smudge pots, which are like boiling holes of sulfur, and drove past black animals with spiraled horns. These tame and gentle creatures lolled beside the road. Hundreds grazed on the left. So, many more lounged lazily upon the right. As well were those apparently waiting for nightfall.

Yes, a few were indeed trapped right in the middle of things. No biggie, not for them, in due time if they needed to cross, they eventually would. That unusual aspect of Colorado made it an adventure to remember. Let me be honest here. I may have mixed some of our adventure together in a failed recollection of chronology. Nonetheless, I never need to embellish!

It was all over after that for family trips. Never again would we get into that car. It was traded in or an LTD four door. In two more years, my sister would be married, and we would no longer squeeze ourselves into that smaller vehicle either. I would be a teen the following year after our trip. That meant the parental units would henceforth leave us home alone, while enjoying places like Hawaii and such.

School had started up again as usual. With newly sharpened pencils, fresh and clean sheets of paper and a virgin sense of what could be for the future, a brand-new year of dreams and possibilities had begun. This year however offered something entirely different from those previous walks down autumn's finely leafed lanes. A girl, one year older, had a yen for some hot Irish stew if you know what I'm saying.

Her family was Italian. She had an older sister in my younger sister's grade, and two younger brothers, both younger than I was. I found out through the grapevine, if you can dig…baby, or actually it was my very own younger-older sister, that this slightly older honey was just a bit more than enthralled with dreams of true togetherness and passion. After I had saved all of my paper route money for six weeks, just as we had done together, to buy my very own 10speed bicycle, my younger sister and I went out shopping.

This time however, we would both take the bus home, rather than double riding. Just as Gimbel's bought out Schuster's so goes the legends of old. It was that Sears bought out K-Mart. If you are well acquainted with that now failed endeavor you understand how the shopping game goes. So, we sidled up to the glass jewelry case and began to search. The actual gem encrusted solid silver ring that I decided upon had brilliant dark blue stones. There were eleven in total if I can remember correctly.

Even my own sister was mildly impressed with my selection. At least ten or twelve additional customers had been standing there throughout the entire event. When we finally had been approached, I gleefully pulled out $11.00 to cover the $10.48 charge. My heart filled with anticipation. That was a bright and beautiful Saturday morning. When Monday pulled around, it had been set in advance. I asked my good young sweetie to come around to the far side of the church.

It was just outside the door leading down to the church basement. That is where, on occasion, the yummy smell of donuts would waft up and through the nostrils, in a sweet and intoxicatingly overbearing fashion. Even here and now, as I sit typing, the call to purchase those chocolate frosted treats overwhelms me. On that fine morn however, a circular ring was not at all edible.

I had the dark blue dandy just in my pocket. Upon removing the overwrap, and displaying this gorgeous number unto her, my sweet, sweet lover-girl was overcome. She smacked one on me that registered bold big 10s on the Richter-Scale of passion. I was somehow magically lifted from ground level, and elevated above that surface by at least 4 feet.

As school was about to start, we made our way back around to the entrance. I still recall with my heart aflutter, not being able to feel my feet, just beneath me, as we moved so close to the door. It was there that a statue of St. Stephen the admirer was propped up, upon a stand surrounded by a planter. Just as I passed, a sense of normalcy was attained. I was relieved.

The air had dried. The leaves turned brown. Warm sunny afternoons would all too quickly come to bask us in the glow of a seasonal welcoming. Finally, one evening the doorbell rang. The candy had been set out the lights slightly dimmed, and the last-minute announcement of my solitude offered up to me. I would be alone, and in charge of dispensing the goodies. It was ta ta and hasta luega from the rest of the family.

Within seconds guests had arrived. One, the closest to arrive, was grandly adorned in full spider regalia. She had learned to move the legs by wiggling her back to and fro. The next, her elder sister was…oh it's faint, a Raggedy Ann. Then the brother was well noted, with he being a scarecrow. Each was a Hollywood quality outfit of made from the highest standards. Their father, dressed as he himself, asked to use the phone.

Well, I wasn't so sure, but after noting the hurt, not only on his face but in his tone, I quickly relented. "Honey we're in," was all he stated, and then quickly had hung up as the group made their way to the door. It would take a while to remember but it finally came together. It was Little Kimmy, and her entourage. No doubt 'big brother' had funded the event. I was filled with a faint glow, and lingering glee for the remainder of that special holiday. It would be in just the next year or so that I would see my lovely little darling once again.

She wore a black blazer at our next meeting, and her bro was there as well. How could I have gone all of those years seeing her on occasion, and not recall each of those treasured episodes. It wasn't until I moved in to the old foster home that I finally did recall our earlier get-togethers. I had a dream that instead of the sidewalk that her dear father had laid, there was another room on that old place just where that cement walkway actually moves past the window. Two 1880s show-girls were sitting there casually. Both knowingly smiled at me. It was so clearly distinct, and in color as well. Everything right down to their beautiful garments was so unbelievably vivid. I awoke and turned to see the wall staring back at me.

It was later in the fall of 1972. I was to go visit my half-brothers perhaps for one last time since the older one was now well past the age of consent. The next brother was of age as well, with the youngest soon to be 18. It would be for an indefinite time, and even though school was in progress, I would not be attending classes for a short break. Who could possibly say then, what this visit would entail. The avenues began to widen, and expand beyond even ordinarily believable proportions. It wasn't long before I would morph into my Rock Star self.

Considering that I was not in class all day, and the fact that this side of the family was not too big on television, one may allow for the fact that a cranial opening had presented itself. A grand expanse needed to be filled. A valley floor was there to explore. An abyss, endless in its offerings, and ever increasing in size had opened wide.

The doors of time themselves would fling themselves open unto me, and pour forth the grand and opulent riches from deep within its fold. The vastness was breathtaking. The detailed clarity of that cranial exploration being truly awe inspiring, offered delight. A sea of ideas flowed forth from unknown places, and all of this extending from my very own mind.

It started with just some paper, and a pen. It was something to occupy my time until the next really cool thing came up. I ripped off a couple of mediocre standards. The elder one laughed. "You expect me to consider this quality material?" he asked.

I replied hurt and wounded, "Well it's better than some. Perhaps a producer would be interested," I added.

Within hours a new level of quality began to emerge. *Hah, this one's not bad*, I thought to myself, and continued on.

For days I forged ahead with these wonderfully curious streams of rhymes dancing like fireflies in a constant wave of tremendous brilliance. They fluttered merrily, gaily cavorting, and moving with a grandiose energy of spectacular delights, from within the playful cavities of my eager inner-mind. With each passing day the sheer quantity and professional level of writing would somehow magically multiply itself, flowing freely and unto the very page before me. Inventions as well, were displayed unto me!

Soon my grand and marvelous abilities were so briskly relevant, an entirely professional approach to lyricism had begun. There would be normal partying, yet a new concept to the proceedings involved V.I.P. status visitors. The first two were young blonds. They had both stepped out of their television roles to drop in to say hello.

I truly believe they were around 13, or 14 years old at the time. The door opened; I was on the second floor of the home wondering what was up. Nearby, once upon a time my plastic fiddle rested safely in a nearby crawl space. From below, the footsteps sounded rather light. The eager steps approached me as I moved out to greet them.

It was two girls, both from the same show. How splendid, how marvelous, I was truly delighted. Something from within me stirred. I reached out, to embrace, to clutch, to draw them closer. To have them all for myself, was all that I had desired. They somehow sensed my longing passion, and began to retreat. Giggly and laughing they raced back the other way.

"Oh please, come back," I barely mustered, and made a halfhearted move toward the pair. "Well, goodbye, my loves," I remember feeling. I was alright enough, yet while sinking into a sense of tempered disappointment. After all, they were now so safe, and with I casually accepting this mild loss.

I was in the main living area of the old home as one more beauty walked past the window. She had the fairest skin in all of the land, yet her other features did so readily compete. After entering I set my eyes upon her in the flesh. It was as though I had become elevated from the floor at least three feet. She had a head of flowing light-colored gold. Those lengths were as fine and shimmering as the rest of her wonderful self.

There was a feeling of buoyancy and delight inside me. It was something that I hadn't experienced since my first real kiss. I was able to bring such passion, and hunger to a heightened fruition within my luridly capacitated mind. It was so that I so quickly came to realize I was one of the unfortunate individuals known as 'minutemen'.

This latest blond on the list of visitors stopped in to pick up my older bro, and the two departed. The very next day a small petite Italian girl, the traveling companion of the previous houseguest knocked upon the door. I was taller than she, and that excited me. This was my very first experience being that close to a woman, while looking down in a ravenous masculine way.

"Is your brother here?" she asked with a tad bit of urgency in her voice. Her eyes were large and welcoming.

I turned to hide any nuance of the fleeting fancy I had so quickly stifled within myself. "Yeah, he's in there," I allowed, and pointed beyond the entryway.

I had no idea what they would all do together at night, nor in the day as it was, but indeed there was a fourth wheel along as well. He hailed from Texas originally, although one may greatly wonder how this group of three had come together as one. The very next day they stopped by to bid adieu. _The Three_ were driving what appeared to be my brother's Volkswagen.

I rushed out to say goodbye and wish them well. Just like that they were gone. No doubt _The Three_ had been given instructions to leave the car at the airport before boarding their plane. I would never see the trio again. Not in person anyway that is!

I was up at the old foster room near the front. I had spied Dave coming up the walk with an unusual looking device. He set it down when just inside. After plugging in this animation-cell viewing editor's machine he hit the switch. What was displayed before us was a whimsical fancy of a fantastical nature. It was a demo seemingly of brand-new characters. They were little blue elfin creatures playing upon a hill.

I vaguely recall very large polka dot mushrooms figures appearing before these early Smurfs began to play leapfrog! Am I indeed then, the one, the only, the all too, true to life 'Brainy' Smurf? I believe that the artist needed to engage in fruitful labor so had put the project aside. Nowadays, anyone between 30, and 70 years old pretty much knows who the Smurfs are. Let's see, one dad, an array of various children, I think that I've seen enough!

An old brick building once abandoned was now a rehearsal studio. We made our way west toward the coastline. Just before the splashing waves would reach the shore, we turned right. This older structure from the 1800s had been redone a bit on the interior. Rooms, larger than most master bedrooms had been created. What really got me was the drummer who stopped in. He was an English fellow from the band Genesis.

Many folks these days know Phil Collins and Peter Gabriel, the original vocalist from the group, from their solo projects. Just as I was taller than the short brunette with rich brown eyes, I was tall enough, compared to Phil, for that fact to give me a jolt. I claimed that he was my new big buddy, and that we needed to go and have one. He smiled and laughed, and we made our way onward. Both of those former Genesis members would go on to individual acclaim while using some of my songs!

Another day brought yet another visitor. She was a tall slender gal from a few TV shows that I had noticed. My oldest bro and I seemed to have the same taste in women. I was learning that factoid so very, very quickly. Jane had some time to kill while a readiness and plans were made. I went in to sit with her, but seeing that she took up so much of the bed, I knelt before her with glee. I soon was pouncing but only to steal a kiss. She quickly rebuffed my advances so I had to think fast.

I grabbed some paper and a writing implement. After asking if she wanted her future read, I began to quickly jot some things down. Since the implement was not in red, I had to hope for the best. What I zoomed in on was not just one, but two letter Ds. One stood out boldly from the other.

"From what I have here, your future holds something to do with the letter D," I assured her. It was hard to say for certain at the time, exactly what such an experience may eventually entail for this oh so young, yet experienced actress.

Brother had heard of my attempt at the stealing of a quick one from our newest lady friend. He was enraged. I only felt that he should have warned me if he had called dibs on that first bit of action with our slim, tall friend. Let's just say my oldest brother is also the shortest. I mean, how does that leave me hanging, in the meantime? He struck me once but I was unfazed. Was this all just a show for his new lady friend? Had he not been so busy primping, and prepping he might have tipped me off so very quietly to his prioritized intentions.

Just then, a knock on the door interrupted his hard core, mean, and sharp sense of discipline. It was my parents with a Mr. Ps to the rescue. That was pizza, and not just any you mind. It was the best in the neighborhood. That was just the thing we needed. We nibbled a bit, and I believe the tall thin one then departed back to L.A.

Here one may wonder, "Could that have been the future that I had predicted with those letter Ds so quickly jotted out of nervousness?" Consider so easily that within about four years' time, there would be not only one show with a capital D at the beginning, rather somewhat mystically, there were even two of those more popular primetime dramas!

After my request that Phil Collins, the drummer from the English band Genesis, was merely laughed at, I believe older bro got an idea. He brings me in to a room. In laying down a just delivered box upon the bed, he drew it open. Pulling from the parcel, a Hollywood quality fake mustache, he proclaims, "here you'll need this to go downtown."

As per my instructions I cheerfully marched to the downtown district. It was that same area that Dave would start out with, during his Good Humor Ice-Cream days. I distinctly recall the bartender's willing and eager grin as I turned away to sit at a table. I had to believe from my quickly reasoned theory, nighttime drinking was way less intoxicating.

Frank Zappa stopped in one evening early on. It had been eight years since he had a place across from the old Second District police station. It was nice to that he was doing well. He pulled out a guitar, and showed me a little thing that he was working on. It involved many notes on the bottom of the neck. The high strings were being quickly ripped at.

I like to try and reproduce the sound myself once in a while. It not only takes me back, but sounds really cool too. I did finally recognize it on a song from Frank one day. Perhaps there were even a few offshoots from the approach that he managed to work into his repertoire as well.

I was onto yet another brainstorm. It was just after I had listened to some Pink Floyd music. I had believed at the time, because it was an instrumental number that was offered, that I imagined to the point of this new entertainment format being created. It was somewhat and loosely based on the whacky shenanigans of The Monkees. At least once during every show the cameras would roll, and the music would play.

They of course had albums, and singles out as tie-ins. Here though, there was such a degree of instrumentation in that particular number, that any depiction of sight and motion could only be held bounded to the ground by an intentional simplifying of imagined events. What I had back then, though only in my mind, was the first of the '*music videos*'.

Let us be clear, and open about this new genre. It was actually done in minor fashion by such bands as Jethro Tull, and even Paul McCartney, to name a few. It was now my thought that we should take a further look, at those yet to be explored deeper possibilities. I truly had little to nothing to do with the actual creation of MTV. It was however, and most notably, handed over to Michael Nesmith, the one that we called the 'Smart Monkee' in our house. I remember vaguely that moniker had something to do with an article in the TV Guide, if not even an additional write up as well.

Seemingly from a dream world, yet right in front of me and in the flesh, three members of Pink Floyd had shown up at the door. I had concerns from the get-go after spotting the drum set so carefully erected in front of the picture window of the entryway. The session didn't last long, no doubt due to the lacking of proper, and high-end drumming mechanisms.

The trio began to exit with a sense of controlled disappointment. I rushed out to the vehicle to wish them off. I of course brought along a few sheets of song lyrics that had been streaming endlessly from deep within my cranium. I offered that it wasn't much, but I thought that they may wish to give them a look. One politely reached out to accept my offering. It was set!

Any memory that trio of the four total would have retained about our brief encounter may entail the color and type of vehicle the group moved off with. No doubt, they like The Three, left that special transport machine at an airport, to be retrieved at a later time. After their latest release, Dark Side of The Moon, Pink Floyd managed to create music using some of my words. Debates potentially ensued as far as approach. I still feel somewhat responsible for the band's much later, yet eventual demise.

Much worse, a tragically horrid phantasm finally crept in. On one early after bedtime night, a worried and troubled thought crossed my path. What if the struggle to compose for an outside band member became such, that the 'way-cool' stuff that may have actually been produced, never quite got deep enough into those far-reaching cranial spaces, to be royally birthed upon this fair land of ours, the planet earth! For those not in the know, the stuff can be considered the very first 'space-music'.

The American TV show Lost in Space was running concurrent with much of the group's earlier works. If actually researching the genre, think 'movie-soundtrack', if you will. An additional approach may be to google, or otherwise search 'THE PROGRESSIVE MUSIC SCENE'.

Those imports cost a pretty penny back in the day, but I'll try to toss you a few if I can. So, let's see, Goblin is an Italian band, a band that used some of my lyrics that hails from England, is one in a million, or the musical act Marillion. Let me think now, Mars Volta, I believe is another.

It was actually my bass player that made sure to record every single radio broadcast of such types that he could. (Of Note: if you are reading this, it means that I will try to get the band back together. I have recently learned from dude's neighbor of his departure from this land! May we all move forward then now, and always, with a steady sense of confident awareness, and a sharpened appreciation for joyous glee and celebration!)

My good brother wrote the instrumental opening for a number on the very next release of Pink Floyd's as well. Please note here that none of us has ever breathed a word about any of our main connections until now. I as well, have at least one song-worthy group of notes performed on an acoustic guitar that I managed to compose. I guess it runs in the family.

Recall if you will, Father's lessons from Jason Argos I's other grandfather, and how he moved those on down the line. (P.S. Go ahead and try.) I mean those of you with the opportunity, to create a 'dueling-guitars-rhythm' type of groove. Also consider checking Dueling Banjos, the country number. Another good one to check is Devil Went Down to Georgia. Wait, I swear that's one of mine, yet…oh, I'm getting old! Okay, I'm back, whew, The Charlie Daniels Band performed that, one, of my hits.

The new day was mine. I entered the room to behold a gracefully inclined young lovely. Everything about her was average. I mean a Jennifer Aniston average. Sometimes that is all that it takes for a man to feel the wonder of life, the joy of connection, and the attraction that turns so readily to a lustful need. Her hair, her height, her size, every detail would be finally equitable with that very actress.

You see I, and I alone, discovered Ms. Aniston one day during a photo shoot. She emerged from a pool wearing a lilac, lemon yellow, and green bathing suit. That scene is embedded in my mind like a crusty jewel yet to be worked free from its hardcore rocky surroundings. Remember, I 'did' have a photographic memory!

It was a Sunday evening, a day like no other day. The show Ms. Aniston appeared on, was In Living Color. The one well noted difference I now had before me for comparison's sake, was that I could feel, rub, no, caress more so, the lovely young beauty so deeply and passionately close to me. Yet I will never know firsthand, of the deepest comparison of all.

Unless a woman wants to let me fall to my knees, rubbing my face back and forth, back and forth, on the tummy, on the legs, and anywhere else that comes to mind, comparisons will be impossible. Until such a day so readily presents itself a final judgment cannot be made. That sweet young lovely there directly before me in this instance was about 20 years of age.

She maintained the innocence of a pure and sweet young teeny bopper, yet held a maturity that allowed me to wonder if she wasn't actually just a local stripper. It mattered not that she was merely average. The very sight of her legs alone was worth a twenty-dollar tip. It was that every square inch was just as comforting as the last. Her tummy, her arms, her shoulders, the gentle cheeks, all of those body parts were of the finest and smoothest quality imaginable. I smoked some weed, and fell asleep, I mean once I had drawn myself reluctantly from the bed, I ventured back to my own and quickly passed out.

It was back to the drawing board. My next big idea again came from a vision. This thought, rather than vague and fleeting, was presented to me with the upmost in crystal clarity. It shone through to me as bright as a summer's new day. Although, unbelievably true, the gist of the concept appeared from nowhere, and was out of my mouth in a flash. They were little silver records. I held up my hands to show the approximate diameter. Only one would not play them with a needle as was used back in the day. "No, you'd need a laser!" I confidently exclaimed.

It was a year or two before this that a film had come out displaying a red laser beam alarm system. Yet another film was well noted of course, by the infamous and daring question of James Bond's, played by no less than Mr. Sean Connery. In that picture the evil Q had Bond strapped to a laboratory table while a cutting laser which moved across the scene, was gaining so ever dangerously close to the inseam of Mr. Bond's trousers. "Well, Q, do you want me to talk or die?" Bond asks, to which Q responds, "Why, but of course Mr. Bond, I want you to die."

A California team, so soon after my loose proposal, had the concept of laser playback to investigate for about three-plus months, before giving up on the idea. It was important to finalize and bring to market such new products quickly. Those early mechanical engineering searches became public knowledge within a short time.

Once a ripened fruit now in the public domain, it could be harvested by those frisky Japanese as a part of our post WWII relations. Well, they got their hands on it, and within months, about a year after the California team had given up, the very first laser music player was now available. That indeed was a $480.00 laser, <u>vinyl album</u>, old-school-type of turntable.

One catch though, it would be about 4½ years later that the actual 'little silver records' would join in, with some of those even being boldly, of another color. I had felt all along, the concept of *send* and *receive* needing to exist on the same side, and in such a small compact unit, was the insurmountable hurdle that those in California initially faced. Nonetheless, actual physical contact was no longer necessary in such the delicate fashion that the older, more mature aficionados had been using for all of those previous years.

Nor would any overly eager young teen girls ever again flip 45s in perhaps an aggressive and abusive manner. No, the dawning of a new era had arrived. One drawback exists with those little silver records. For undiscovered reasons, they begin to lose a sense of cleanness and clarity, after somewhere in between 20 and 100 years.

I had yet another visitor. She was yet another blond. She was ready, and waiting for me right where I would doze. I was beginning to realize that I perhaps was a bit of disappointment to these women. I am not so sure again that I realized what a minuteman was back then, although I had a deep sensation that I was learning the hard way, about that very thing. This latest lover was around 30. Let's just say that I was not the first to wipe my feet upon the welcome mat. In too short a time, it was all too well over with.

Without much fanfare, nor sweet goodbyes, she had left me. I of course passed right out again. Since that time I have arranged a floor show to display for my lovers, if you will. This floor routine may or may not include the pommel horse. (ha-ha) Such a drawn-out attempt should at least include twenty minutes of anything, and everything to be performed as a warm-up to the actual down and dirty deed.

In stage one, a man would call home. "Tonight's the night my dear, I want to eat out," he'll impart. She then, if she decides to, will place some clothes in the washer. Now, I've only heard this on a second-hand basis, but her opening act involves sitting atop the washer, and or dryer, I cannot recall which, so would recommend trying both. That being merely a naughty little prelude, it is only the opening act for some.

I read of one gal's claims in that regard. So, when finally arriving at the restaurant, and without too much fanfare, the man would, while holding his drink up to his mouth, proclaim, "You know I really did want to *eat out* tonight."

Let me rephrase things. If you catch a bite at home before leaving, the dryer thing may work. It may not make much sense for some to finally go into your laundry room, after returning from an evening of dining out.

The rest of such a meal should be played adlib without too much overt and extraneous romancing. Once having arrived back at home the third stage of action will begin. You then, as a man, having predetermined your floor show, would begin the festivities. That being a necessary aspect of the overall success you will achieve. Mine goes something like this: 20 minutes on the overall body, with or without a massage. Then 20 minutes down there. I have since modified this section of my show. In my early days I may have felt that a simple act of oral copulation may have been more than sufficient.

Depending on your very own size, I believe taking a whittling knife to those 'big-joes', they have, or Steely-Dans, as their called, would offer a less intrusive opening presentation. Sadly, such conversation is often avoided out of embarrassment. I say whatever it takes, one must duly consider. We all have different temperature settings in that regard, so it may be vital to consider one's partner, over one's own selfish and desirous passions.

One thing that I have read about involves the fact that the female flexes to one's size, down there. That way, a fellow would know if some other huge family van was temporarily parked in the garage. It may be a firm necessity to trust your woman. Yet it is what it is. I would stop myself from rushing to judgment so quickly. One may wish to borrow his neighbor's grinder, rather than going at one of those ridiculously over-sized toys. I mean, right, anyone? The type of grinder which will work on coal shovels, or other tools should work quite well on those big-joe sized devices.

Once, with your lady's help, if you prefer, you've brought some justice to the situation you can begin Act I of the finale. Here for those ignorant of all things *satchel*, the last thing that a man would want is to spoil his lady, either in this wrongly executed fashion, or by the hand of another man. If indeed you are using the mechanical method, a system of taps is necessary to avoid missing your target. Based on your history of expiration these taps should be timed out for an eventual simultaneous climax. The timing can be tweaked for any de-escalation of arousal on her part in between acts.

An adjustment to meet at the finish line together should be equally configured for a sense of endurance. With a fortified lasting power, provided by perhaps the consumption of alcoholic beverages beforehand, an extra minute or so can be added in for good measure. In the least, the goal of coming together for this special engagement should offer fun and games, and a spry sense of frolicking for the remainder of your youthful lives.

One early morn back then, the eldest called me into one of the rooms. He and the other two had obviously been at it for days. He quickly showed me what he had. They did not know how to do basing with coke so they had come up with a somewhat lame method of dealing with the additives and impurities involved with smoking that illicit substance.

They had placed a half pound rock inside of a coffee can. With just a very small amount of lighter fluid applied, the coke was lit. While using the coffee can cover to control the opening I was told to go ahead, and take a really big hit. I did so while placing the cover on the can to douse the flame. I blew out my hit, and became myself. I would never recommend this to anyone so don't get me wrong. I turned, and began to pace.

Somehow, I was now a fully mature adult, and needed to wisely consider things. All wiped out, the others dangled feet, and lounged about while I, at a full attention, paced back and forth. Well, so much for that. I believe they had had enough of this risky type of experimentation, and rescued the remaining product afterward, to ingest in the usual fashion. That would come by chopping and snorting. I however, was not involved with the drug any further at that point.

Cleveland Dave stopped over. He informed me that we had a bit of a mission to attend to. We walked along the warehouse district streets. At night only the nearby traffic from the busy streets bore witness to human activity. Grain-train rats three feet long, a few mice and cockroaches and Dave and I were about the only living things around.

We eventually made our way over to the brand-new rehearsal studio. Once inside, we made our way down to the end of the hall. Upon entering the room, it was apparent that an audition had been arranged. There was the drummer, a larger fellow with long dark hair, his little bro on guitar, and a borrowed bass player from the general area.

Although, the group mainly knew only one number there was something quite clearly distinct about the sound being offered. The drums, even on that well scrounged set was adequate, the bass, being played by this large local fellow, was steady. Yet the guitar itself brought a separate note of clarity. It was magically as though angels themselves hovered over and above the very essence of this 15-year-old strumming phenomenon.

They went through that song and did so again. When things were wrapping up, I talked to the young guitar player about lead playing and sustain. He took his instrument and pushed upward on a string. His finger fell off the mark after a brief attempt. It was quite obvious to me that this expert from California had been focusing on his overwhelming forte, rather than no doubt, what he had felt the other dude in his eventual band would play.

I right there motioned for the six-string and showed him what I meant. I reassured him, "yes, that what he had attempted was one type of lead playing, but how about this?" I offered, while faking it. In moving my fingers quickly up and down, and then my hand up and down the neck, I displayed a frenzied style of quick movement so readily used in rock music ever since. The Van Halen brothers had just auditioned for me and Dave.

As far as Michael Anthony, the eventual bass player for the band hooking up at a later time, I would say that it was a natural thing. You may not have realized it yet, but my eldest brother had been creating what is now so readily termed as '*networking*', these days. With his actions going all of the way back to 1964, one couldn't argue! So, yes Sammy Hagar, he formerly of the rock band Montrose, took some classes at the same University that Anthony Michael attended, in a state that John Ritter lived in! His dad, Tex was a Country and Western star.

My time visiting came to an end all too soon. I was back at home and back in school, yet continued to have strange and unusual guests stopping by. About my first full day back, upon arriving at home I found the soft-rock duo Tears for Fears awaiting my arrival. Now certainly these two youngsters had not even been into a recording studio at that point. Nonetheless, they would return home, keeping in touch with each other, only to come out with '*our*' big hit so many years later.

Another unexpected guest was my brother's musical buddy's girlfriend. You must recall here that my good brother had had aspirations of going big with Geddy Lee who was about to form Rush. His friend, a guitar player and he, waited in the car while the young lady came up to the door. Suffice it say that I chose to make the most of that '*one-minute*' that we were indeed together in my bed. I wished to make it so very, very special. Within seconds, it was all over. She politely excused herself, and I passed right back out yet again.

I can be so truly frank here as the last that I knew of it, the two had hit the skids with their relationship. The other friend of my good brother's, the dude with the pony-tail and Doberman puppies that he would train, had rented out yet another old tavern. This latest rendition he had opened happened to be a block and half from my home back in 1993. I as usual was broke as hell, and could barely afford even one. When she, the young beautiful princess stepped in all alone, one may imagine right where a guy's brain would travel to.

Alas, out of the fear of rejection, or was it more out of a keen sense of outright reality, whichever dominated, in the two evenings that this quick nighttime stranger and I were together again, it was apparent that too much time had gone and went from our first encounter. To consider from afar in such a case, would be as far as it had gotten. We had simply occupied the same general space for moments.

One super strange thing did happen just after those barren occurrences. I had a dream that there was a door smack in the center of the wall behind the bar. Beyond that was some type of inexpensive indoor volleyball playroom. I still recall peeking in, and then waking up just afterwards. Oh well. I do believe an inexpensive fiberglass 'shed' over a volley ball court would be just what the doctor ordered, especially in the rainy upper Midwest.

The very next day back then, after that sweetest of redheads that I've ever known stopped in for a minute, a large car with a group of girls pulled up. I so very naturally got in while they did the rest. A joint, or marijuana cigarette was lit and passed around. The one seated close to me, the youngest, unzipped me and took care of business. It was all over so quickly. I still feel that I wasn't such a wonderful host for any of them.

Within days of all of this, one of the young blonds from my wild times at bro's house, stopped in to say bye. I had assumed that they were migrating to California, perhaps though, that did not come for some time. Indeed, this young sweet thing was even on TV for a while back then, about five years after our having met. It was during the commercials for those dramatic presentations that I finally had happened to recall our super quick get-together back in the day. Wow.

1973

A new kid on the school bus was taking his time getting off. That was a mistake. My pals and I moved to the front of the bus. I sat down in front of him then went into my rant. I said, "You're going to stay on this bus, and go to the other school. That's the school you'll be going to from now on, and because of that, you'll have to find a way to get adopted by one of those public-school families. Now we're going to get off, just make sure you go that public school today, and be sure to get adopted by that other family from that other area as well."

He freaked. Though we had thought everything was cool when he indeed exited just behind us, walking right into the school as we did, that wasn't quite the case. Maybe it was our principal that was the one that freaked out more so, rather than that sweet, poor, unfortunate lad himself. She was that same Catholic Nun that had taught first grade to my older sister and her classmates. Yes, you know all too well of her!

She paraded us out to the hallway, all the while scolding us for intimidating such an innocent young boy. "To your knees," she commanded.

Just outside of the first-grade classroom. What would occur next was either a sideshow antic, simple parlor trick, or a bona fide miracle. As she railed into us with all of the might, and strength that a 5-foot nun could muster, she squeezed or heads.

Then with all of her human power, she lifted each one of us up from off of the floor. I was at least a good eight to ten inches in elevation myself. We each weighed between 134 and 150lbs. "That did the trick," I whispered as we returned to our classroom. We would respect young sweet boys forever after!

Later on that year, it was a warm March day, the early spring thaw brought life to our minds, and a soothing relief to our bones. It, as well, put a joyous bounce in our step. During morning recess, we had made our way to the edge of the stream outback. Even though we had been given a loosely worded mandate about this no-go zone, the few of us in the group that chose to be defiant, ambled up toward the edge of the curve in the streamlet just before us.

There was an old farmer's bridge constructed of cement at the midpoint of our playground that we were specifically not to venture across. Though just behind the backstop of our softball diamond, lay a world of white laden wonder. A mysterious domain of yet to be explored territory did beckon us forth. As the call was irresistible, at least to myself anyway, I asked should we dare move forward.

"Oh yeah, lets," was the reply. I took one long step in an effort to brace myself onto the edges of the bubbling rivulet before me. After determining that my reach was at the farthest extent, I moved so very quickly to shift my weight onto my right, and now thoroughly committed foot. All at once, I was in nearly up to my waist. What was just seconds before an innocent movement of melting snowfall suddenly became a wicked monster-stream of a dangerously rushing depth. It was surely ready to take me downstream, and devour me whole.

I turned toward my men with arm outstretched to be pulled out and saved. It would appear that they had all, each and every one of them, recoiled in horror at the fate that I had just invited upon myself. Only the one, my good chum from down the way, the one that had shown me the farmers beautiful corn back in 1967, was brave enough to stand his ground. You may recall that he as well had warned me of a new father's antlered ire. "Well, come on," I beckoned. "Pull me out," with that I was yanked from a certain wetness that would have covered me from head to toe. As it was, I was a bit more than half way there.

Once inside, I surmised that I should tough it out for the rest of the day since only one leg was completely soaked. I had felt around to note the water was sponging up my backside a little more than I cared for, but I would be alright. Facing the hour or two that would be needed to actually even start the drying process, I so quickly questioned my ability in that regard.

With the shivers so overwhelmingly taking over, I had a change of heart. I reported to my teacher who relayed my fate to our principal. She called me out of class then down the hall, around the corner, and onto the phone. Mother said that she would call Father at work and let him know. "Maybe a half hour or so then," she assured me.

From there I was led a few feet into the library. Off to the side on the left was a nurse's cot. As the librarian was also a Catholic Nun, she doubled as the school nurse. "Off with those," I was instructed.

"I'll be right back with something, a blanket for you to cover up in," she offered.

I heard, and I obeyed. Here I would be, in my school's library, and perhaps to some degree in front of a nun, completely nude. The thought was very comforting. She was being very calm, and, as a matter of fact about the whole ordeal, so why should I not be as well?

When she returned, she carried a very, very large size military-style wool blanket, and a paper bag that she set down on the floor. She held the covering aloft to block her view, and the exchange was made very casually. She pointed to the bag, and said, "Here, put the wet things in here."

Once your father has arrived and you're into the dry things he's brought, you can go ahead and join the others in church.

It was, I had perceived, an opportunity for her to exhibit her motherly side, and I relished in the nurturing glory of each appreciable moment. Father took an early lunch from work and was there in no time. I quickly dressed in the boy's room then hurried off to church. A few quick prayers for the whole scene, and I was quickly loving the warmth and comfort of that warm early spring day.

I made sure to be quite careful when things involved water for the remainder of that school year. Other than a few rainstorms I remained on dry land avoiding any pools, puddles, or especially so, any streaming rivulets, or outright gorging rivers whatsoever. I need to be so dramatically frank when I talk of the rushing waters in these parts. Most of the smaller streams have been turned into sewers. Those in turn wash off toward the Sea of Michigan. When it rains however, there is only one option for the water to wash to.

These inches deep streams can turn to torrents at a moment's notice, even reaching depths of 6 to 8 feet in no time. One of those lazy rivers runs past, just out back here. Well, to the west of my place here, the young boys were unaware of such a sudden outburst and how so much of a rushing liquid could come all at once. One slip and that could be it. With that tidal wave of raw power able to take them down to the sea in minutes. Two perished, a while ago, with the third able to pull back just in time.

Summer so soon arrived, and I was back on my own. I had my older neighbors, the classmates from down the block, and an old chum from years gone by, to hang out with on any given day. An old-school chum from years before had called from out of nowhere. He explained that he thought we might do something together. He finally came clean.

His mom, and dad talked it out, and it had been decided that he would attend the Catholic Grade School for that last year. I still remember his sister handing out food in the kitchen at school for hot lunch. The eldest brother was my oldest sister's age. The other brother my other sister's age, was sometimes distracted. Making jokes, being funny, or sometimes becoming the victim of his own pranks. He was in seventh grade when things snapped apart.

The mainly harmless fellow was the one that had created a rubber band launcher utilizing a bobby pin, or was it the other way around? Recall his expedient expulsion. It was the next year that my old pal was allowed to attend the local public school as well. Apparently, there were some hard feelings about the rubber band incident that lingered deeply even for the whole family. If I recall correctly, my sister claimed that the brother's encounter with that new teacher bordered on child abuse.

Now this family after being relocated due to the airport expansion had a good home. The dad continued to work at an auto manufacturer, and had a brand-new economy car parked in the drive. I believe the only daughter was in college, or married by then no doubt. The now eldest boy was doing well in high school, and even there was Curly the youngest, so joyful, merry, and innocent was he.

They had moved to that fabulous home, just blocks from my house down the way on the main drag. The thing that was so special was the extra living room or front room, as they are often termed in this area. My old pal though, had lived a more common life just years before. It was in a small home the same size as my family resided in at the time. Those are termed 'Cracker Box Palaces', as in my song performed by Mr. George Harrison.

The last time we were together, outside of our school hours, he had taken me to see his old neighborhood. You see his entire street by then consisted of only empty holes, along with some trees that once lined the street, now just a dirt road. Construction in reverse you may consider it. We moved along until we came to one particular depression. "There it is," he proclaimed. "That's it, or was. You can see what's become of it," he continued.

"So, you have your pit memorized?" I asked.

"There were so many days with it all together," he added. With that wistful type of memory, he held his hands up in appreciation of what once was.

Being in that spot had reminded me of another fellow from class. He had told me that he had gotten bored one day. So, without a bicycle he decided to move on out onto the runway. That other fellow from class had told us all about his wild adventure in school, on the Monday just afterward. I gather he was just being a daredevil, yet somehow, he managed to just miss being hit with a retracting airplane wheel.

That was based on his fabulous claims to the incident. That supposedly was just by a few good feet, as far as his being whacked. He had told us that at the last second possible he closed his eyes, threw his shaking body forward as much as he possibly could, and prayed to God to save him. Let us just say that he may have peed his pants as well!

So, now my old pal with the best house on the main drag would like to do so something once again. He showed up with two cucumbers. I smiled broadly not just at the sight of him, but at the thought that he'd bring a gift. He assured my they were not pilfered from some hopeful family's garden. He then offered a tutorial on how to skin it with your teeth. He assured me it was a cinch, as long as I had no serious dental problems.

We made our way down the road, and finally ended up at the farther park, the one nearer our daredevil buddy's house. This former classmate from earlier times was not quite the ladies' man, more so the social type. Yet indeed this was his turf. Guys, gals, he knew them all. He related to me, after offering some introductory talk that his brother had recently fallen in with the wrong crowd at the public school.

It was serious. He could barely bring him himself to say it, but dude stole a car, and was serving time in the boy's home. His mother talked, and fretted, thought, and planned, then paced and considered. "That was that," she declared, the same dire fate would not happen to the dear sweet younger child. I apparently got a pass because of our previous relationship. As long as any of our things are well below car theft, we'll be just fine he had told me. "I'm not that way, are you?" he queried.

"Well, not at all, no way," I assured him, and we were back to goofing off, and hanging out.

Day two of our being back together was beautiful, sunny and mild, and the perfect day for a bike ride. I mean if you had one that is. We went back again to the old neighborhood, the small business area that had now been claimed by profound imminence, or rather imminent domain, as it were. We had the old farmer's pumpkin patch on the beginning of this ground the twenty foot-wide, above ground sewer in the back, a hotel-bowling alley, fast-food joint, the donut shop, and across the street the other hotel.

When it's summertime, and one is so relaxed so as to let one's guard down, rude awakenings can be oh so startling. Certain types may simply give you the bum's rush, as such was the encounter that we did have. After moving up onto the sidewalk, we meandered around the bend. Ah, so casual so calm, so what? A uniformed officer had jumped up from out of nowhere.

"Alright hold it right there," he ordered, after moving himself before us to hinder any possible escape. "That's right, stop 'em right there, you," he demanded. "Did you young men realize that it's against the law to drive on the sidewalk?" he quizzed us. We both gave up a slightly puzzled "no."

"That's right, especially at your age," he admonished. "Though how old are you?" he said, as he pulled out the arrest book.

At this point I began to realize that we had just been pulled over, for riding bicycles, on the sidewalk. He issued a type of informal ticket, and ordered us to acquire Bike Licenses, reporting to a station house of our choosing, with the evidence of our acquisition, or else! Overnight my pal cooked up the perfect adventure.

We would ride all of the way downtown to City Hall no less, and get our bikes registered. "After all, that cop can't order us around anymore, he's done his *job*. Yeah right *"job,"* I ask myself here and now. I wondered how his station buddies would feel about all of his hard work, when they talk about their very own busts, and their more hard-core standard types of arrests.

"If you think we can do it," was my reply, to the idea of riding six miles to City Hall. It was all downhill from his place. It would be no stress, no straining for us. It was actually quite a good ride, save for one detail. When we got to the river just before downtown, we stopped. It was disgusting. I had never been that far on a bicycle, and never more disappointed in nature.

The thing of it was, once things really got rolling around here in the 20s and early 30s the river was a life source. There was ice skating in the winter, the occasional sailor or two, and a swim club. Jumping, swimming, diving, learning, it was the thing to do in all of that fresh water that was moving down from upstream.

So, where do your toilets drain to, when you flush? Ours, the whole time, were going into the river. Well, before our adventure though, they had created a separation plant. By law, the *stuff*, or dried human poop, can only be applied to fields, lawns, or golf courses, as a natural form of fertilizer. By the way, I came up with a really cool t-shirt slogan. Based on the reality of what did happen, or what would probably happen at some point during the 1988 Super Bowl. This game it was proudly announced in the weekly paper, would not only be played in Pasadena at the Rose Bowl, they would be applying our dried-out *stuff*, a good ten days or so before kick-off.

I came up with this catchy slogan just for the occasion: "I did my part for the big game in '88, did you *do* yours?" Of course, there would be the figure of a haggard old gent sitting on the pot, looking straight at you. Bear with me here, I had imagined at some point that one of the players in that actual game would arise from the ground, pulling stuck-on mud and grass from his face mask. I would proudly then proclaim, "I really, really did *'doo'* my part for the big game." Hardy-har-har!

My pal and I eventually arrived at our local district station proudly sporting our new bicycle decals, or official license tags. They took our names and removed us from the naughty list. Now where were we? We decided to stop at the closer park the next time around. A younger fellow, about two years younger to be exact was playing, and goofing off. I turned mean, yet I don't know why. I told him his bike needed a ghost ride down the slide. Now, ghost-rides were given readily in my day, so why should it be any different for him?

No, my mind was made up, this was happening alright. He begged, and pleaded, "No don't please, you'll bend the rims." It was all to no avail; his nice new shiny cool bike was on its way up the staircase. This boy was heart-broken. I mean I almost cared, about he, and his little Dutch boy haircut. He quickly went into a deep lament on how that was just the wrong thing to do. I let him know for whining, that round two was coming up, yet relented, and let him off easy.

We did a little of this, and a little of that, and came around the very same corner from earlier. "Don't look now, but I think we're being followed," my pal quietly threw to me. We made our way to the edge of the woods, and crouched down.

"I think this just may have something to do with the Dutch boy incident," he whispered. "Let's leave the bikes here, and scope around," he gestured. Well, we were gone just a little too long. My pal noticed our tires were flat, he also knew that you could remove the valves, and that's what ole' boy had done.

As we were surmising our next step, the foster father jumped out. Though menacingly emerged was more like it, with he around 250lbs he *muscled* his way over, and confronted us. We gave up our home phone numbers, and could be expecting a call later, at just the right time. In case we had any funny ideas, he could have actually followed both of us home, and probably did. He showed up, and went through the whole episode, about how this poor boy, without any real father of his own to speak of, was tormented by this gang of two hooligans, and how that should not at all have happened.

We were feeling horrible and red-faced at my house. I retired to my room to avoid any further turmoil. Within about an hour my younger half-brother's foster father had gone. No wonder the whole affair seemed so natural at first, this near stranger would become a good friend later on along with my dad's other visitation—accident baby. I still remember her so lovingly clinging to me when my youngest sister and I had first met. All of four years old, I was. With her being about five at the time we got along fine. Oh well, you get what you get, as long as you don't take more than you deserve. Dan the Dutch boy we'll call him, is married now with no children, at least none of his own that I'm aware of at this time.

That year our main TV went out. It just so happened, that one of father's hobbies was not only bringing old air conditioners home but television sets as well. One ended up in the basement over in the corner with an extension from the roof antenna attached. It was my go-to place for Monday Night Football, and any other show that was vetoed upstairs. Those others were mostly The Dean Martin Show, and the comedian Flip Wilson's show.

It was storming one night outside more than ever before. We stayed nice and snug in the cellar, until we tired of it all, then moved on up to bed. I want to make a serious and valid point here. Centipedes may get funny and crawl under your armpit while you're lying on the floor, then racing toward the corner beneath the safety of the older set when you would least expect it. Just a heads-up for some, I mean.

It was that place in the cellar that I recall being in for a very special occasion. With Father's cousin over, we would watch the original moon landing back in 1969. It was certainly not our first choice in accommodations for such a momentous event, yet when all of your color TVs are either being used or on the fritz, you work with what you've got. That was one small step for John Glenn, and about 13 steps for us to venture down into the lower chamber. Suffice it to say the basement bugs were being very normal and friendly on that day.

From out of nowhere a surprise visitor had arrived. Upon entering our home from school, I was made aware of a special meeting to be held in our cellar. I had not been prepped for such an out of the box proposal, so was not quite ready with a normal response. Let's go back in time to the actual beginning of my first meeting with this younger fellow.

Mother had been quite understanding when it came to all of Father's extra chillin's. Even this most recent entry into the world of 'all of us' was now accepted. He was a young blond boy back then of about 15 months. My good brother was up that morning first. He told me to get back inside and watch the baby.

He held up the smoke he had just lit, and beckoned me back inside with a stern and quiet order. Some outside force, the same one seemingly, that always shows up to make me react in the most reprehensible of ways possible, entered the room. I felt the force of its power. It rushed into my brain with the urgency of an ambulance. Like that, I rushed toward the baby and pushed. He was simply playing on his own, moving in circles and humming. He was now upon the floor, and moving to tears.

I raced to the door for big brother. He got up, and entered. I as quickly, raced into the bedroom of my parents to announce my failure. We had gone through all of the basics, again and again. I had promised truthfully, to my best ability, to obey and adhere to the proclamations of order fun, and togetherness. I once again was the biggest loser the family could ever know of.

Little bro was quickly packed up and gone. Here and now, with the 'roommate', or foster father, as I had dubbed him, spilling the beans, a new wrinkle had arisen. Father, apparently had stated that he was still the same perpetually busy individual that he always was, but with me as ambassador, all doors would be open. I totally lost it without the heads-up warning.

I immediately cried out in a pathetic childlike voice. No…no…no. My own brain was not even functioning or involved. It was my mouth, and my mouth alone that was in the _on_ position. I, after Father waved me off, with the whisk of his hand, ran upstairs like a rotten little spoiled brat. I fell to my bed in a sense of lost and sullen curiosity. It went from pain to pondering, from mental turmoil, to emotional tragedy. What had just happened?

I could only rue that I hadn't been given that heads-up. The earlier encounter could only dance upon the outskirts of my now fettered mind. Did an evil force rise up to deny my very own brother, a piece of his sincerely longed for and deservedly desired existence? I'm sure that it had. One can only pray with a total and utter sense of faith, over so many of these emotionally traumatic experiences. We would indeed not be 'friendly' brothers for at least a few more years!

My pal from two doors down and I had been making some extra money picking strawberries and raspberries on a farm nearby. We would ride through the alley ways often, then down through the trail, and out onto the neighboring roadway. This time we got a sight. After watching the evening broadcasts in the lower chamber because of the weather, I was up and at 'em and ready to pick.

There had been a tongue-twister or dust devil as they are called, because of the very small size of those tornado *wannabees*, that had passed through the night before. This one though, was a might bigger than a tongue. There, before our very eyes, were the tattered remains of an entire garage, now leveled before us, into nothing more than a seeming pile of toothpicks!

There wasn't one piece of anything still standing. The entire structure had been flattened and dismantled with only those, spindly toothpick like shards of any wood remaining. Nearly mind boggling was the additional sight we did behold. In addition to the remains of what once stood as a newer and sturdier structure, one that nearly *seemed* to have been taken apart, bit by bit, piece by piece, meticulously, and with an abundance of care, seemingly by hand, only one other thing spoke the truth harsh about the previous night's realities. A few feet away stood the other neighbor's garage.

It itself was somehow untouched, and unscathed, save for one defining aspect. It had a 2X4 jammed through the closer wall, at about the exact halfway point of that single piece of wood. Please let me note, what was left of that 8ft. piece of wood, would have barely measured four, or five feet! That one remnant of the previous night's storm told the entire tale of nature's potential fury. Wow!

I was bored while in this particular friend's garage one day. I took the basketball we had been shooting and placed his mother's old swimsuit upon the orb. They were snug but fit rather well. Suffice it to say, if your father is a strict Southern Baptist, and mom a devout Lutheran, another fellow may not be able to have a quick chuckle at another's expense.

I simply had felt that since the item had lain upon the floor of the garage for at least two years that meant his mom's swimming days were well over. He however had learned a looser type of respect that gave dominion over one's articles to the righteous owner alone. Anyone else messing around would be in big trouble therefore. Oh well.

His dad was back to tinkering with cars again around that time as well. I recall the 1963 Buick, or Dodge he had for a while, and even another vehicle or two being worked on back when that neighbor's father worked at the local Texaco Gas Station. This newest model was a dream. It was a '39 Bulldog complete with the bulldog hood ornament.

The most special aspect that I recall of these old pick-ups was being there having been made on a contract by Dodge. The other unusual feature involved the option to start it up without the key. One can readily imagine that we didn't actually drive it around at all. It was that the option component had seemingly broken so that anyone at any given time could just get in and drive away.

I later had what may be considered the opportunity of a lifetime that summer as well. That neighbor-friend's older brother was now 16-years-old. He begged out of going down to visit the grandparents. This meant there would be room for a different guest to travel down south that time around. I gladly accepted.

The elders lived just outside of Muscle Shoals in Alabama. We started out at around 7:00am. Having stopped for a bite just inside Illinois, we needed to make good time on the rest of the journey to arrive by the dinner hour. After maneuvering through the red clay of the south we neared the Shoals. Those, for rock fans, are sung about in the song <u>Alabama</u> by Lynyrd Skynyrd. What I do recall is those steep cliffs, or shoals being so unusual, and jutting from out of nowhere.

We crossed the bridge overlooking that deeply descending aspect of the area, and continued to make good time, arriving about 6:15pm. It was an honor to be seated at the family table. There was merely one aspect of the meal that caused a bit of wonder. It must have been the beans in the leftover salad, because each time I placed another forkful in my mouth then took a drink of milk, this horribly curious taste came over me. Overwhelming my senses, the chalky aftertaste was hard to ignore.

Oh well, we hung out a bit then lay upon the floor at the foot of the grandparents' bed. I maintained a strict sense of concentration then was out for the night. In the morning we took turns mowing the lawn. A time saving component of that yard-work involved most of the side yard consisting of peanut plants.

Soon afterward we walked down to the swimming hole. It was being dredged and was empty of any liquid whatsoever. It was okay because a small store was located on a corner down the hill from the home. I had plenty of paperboy money, so picked up not one, but even two bottles of Orange Squirt. Yum, yum, that day is still so sweetly locked into my memory.

We casually made our way back up the hill, and noted that Grandma was baking freshly picked goobers in the oven. A white duck lived in a sink hole just across the street and would come out in the afternoon to sun itself. Apparently, that triggered a memory of grandpas, and he laid it on us. The old vehicle from a few years back had needed some maintenance.

Grandpa had been ill with the flu for a bit, so felt it was about time to take care of business finally. He believed the car work had waited long enough. He pushed the vehicle out onto the lonely old road so as to have a nice dry surface to lie upon. After he adjusted this, and tinkered with that, he was about ready to call it a day.

He simply needed to give the mobile the old heave-ho and back into its parking space. The streets had a shallow ditch about six inches across rather than a curb with a gutter. The beast got hung up a time or two on that depression. My buddy's grandpa had worn himself out performing the mechanical details, and was now struggling. Just one more good push ought to do it, he had felt. He eased the machine back out onto the street enough to really put everything he had into it with this one last shot.

It was one, two, three, then using each and every bit of energy he had left in that old retired body of his, he gave it his all. Oh shoot, something gave alright. Having had the flu, he now found himself with a sh*tload in his britches. He went inside, and Grandma had about only one thing to say. "Oh no, no, no, no, you take care of your own britches," she told him. Then she moved quickly away from the basement steps. You can imagine grandpa still blushing red just a touch, from the reconciliation of that impending chore.

That night we were offered the chance to sleep on the sofa bed. I was quite appreciative even though I had felt they were holding out on us that first night. Apparently, I do stuff in my sleep, because just after I dozed, I was socked in the arm. I awoke, looked over, and hit him back lightly. I mean as long as I don't become gay somehow in my sleep, he deserved that bit of payback. Nothing more was done or said for the rest of the night. In the morning we would head out to have some fun.

First, we went to the old blackberry patch. Some type of giant bees, or what have you, were dining on those huge juicy delights. After about the third one lifted off a branch that I was working on, I finally saw what they truly were. Big, big June bugs were having a special feast party. Since that was so much of a warmer climate, June bugs are seemingly everywhere in sight, and even around in August. We just needed to avoid selecting any overly wet, or way too juicy berries, as those would have been most definitely, the ones that had been chewed on by the bugs.

We ended up moving toward the old neighborhood. Nothing stood any longer but a broken-down chicken coop/greenhouse type of a structure. We were headed there. Once we had left the main city locality a strong sense of peace came over the scene. We moved along on empty graceful roads basked in a private tranquility.

I finally asked the men in front if that was an eight-foot stick, or just a long grass snake on the lonely old road up ahead. Grandpa wasn't sure, so we made our way down the long dirt pathway toward that straight and narrow object. Once we reached this long thin unidentifiable thingy, we exited the vehicle. Grandpa touched it with his shoe. The lengthy legless one, turned tail and ran up into the grasses on the side of the road.

I could only be glad we weren't speeding along. We could have rolled right over in the car after a mushy squish-out. I could only imagine any and all of those brother, sister, and children snakes crawling all over our injured bodies. They would have crawled through our hair. They no doubt would have slithered over our broken limbs. As well I believe they would have slimed us with their smelly peeing bodies, before finally leaving us the hell alone. There could be no worse fear in regards to roadway mishaps in such a fashion then any of those that involve snake pee!

Well, better safe than sorry, as they say. We ventured over to go inside the glass house. It was a monstrous structure with many broken pains, yet with enough integrity left in it to feel safe. My buddy's grandpa pulled out an old sock, and displayed the contents. It was an official police revolver purchased at the barber shop. We would each take a practice shot for fun. Just as the first man fired, I looked over and saw a good-sized toad.

"Here's a proposition," I offered, "We shall each take a shot at the beast, if one of us connects, why then he dies. Should each of us not hit the mark, then of course he lives." It was on baby.

After each of us tried our best (maybe), I rushed over to pick the sucker up. Take a note, any of you who failed to realize beforehand, number one, you don't pick up a toad you've just been shooting at, number two, even though it may well indeed take a year or more, warts will eventually begin to grow on the part of your body that got tinkled on. Trust me. The older gentlemen giggled and laughed and admonished me for my stupidity. "Doh," as Homer Simpson would say.

From there we moved on over to the Dairy farm. There was a distinct reason that the bean salad tasted so gnarly. It was unpasteurized milk from a nearby farm that had been served to us upon our arrival. We walked to see the farmer hanging out near the barn-door opening. In order to be helpful, I unscrewed the top of one of the huge mason jars then handed it to the dairyman. What I had failed to noticed was the farmer's nice clean hands and how he was actually the one doing the unsealing of these freshly cleaned glass items.

To think my hand had not only toad all over it, but toad pee as well. I got a big angry 'doh' from each of the elders, each one a little sterner than the last. The dairyman rinsed just the top in a mostly sanitary barn sink. He had them quickly tapped and filled and we were on our way. A good thing Grandma picked up some regular milk on her trip into town for us boys.

One exceptional occurrence from those olden times of my early teen years, that is still very disheartening to this day, involved the thief from just down the street. Yes, the same one that was eying up my bicycle one day, although my machine indeed, was duly padlocked and well secured. The same fellow whose new favorite swear involved ducks, was dead! This other older fellow, the guy with the pet monkey had found him drowned in the swamp across the highway.

He had said, as they waded through the water "hey look, a log with a shirt on it." Upon further review they shockingly came to realize the harsh reality.

He had gone missing for days, and the autopsy could not truly offer an explanation. If one is religious, I find, death is not so hard to deal with. I therefore pushed out any further consideration of the subject, and did my best to recover from such tragic news. Here he was now though, as cold as the water they had found him in. The police were quickly brought in to investigate. It was told to us that the first attempt to retrieve the body had failed.

It was in such a state of decomposition that whatever body part that they grabbed at, had so quickly fallen off. They then brought in a specialty device and pulled him out by the one thing that doesn't decay so easily. The head-hair! I recalled how I never had any inclination to travel across the main drag to that far-off area. That feeling, or lack thereof, was now doubled. With the other people watching as they dragged, they dragged away any last feelings from my heart and mind as well. Live hard, die hard, I guess. I didn't want to think about it, so did my best to block it all out.

My heart grew heavy whenever the cold reality trespassed back across my cranium. That old farm was far enough away in that area so as to not offer such a frightening ordeal, yet I knew I could never venture forth into those deep and haunting woods. Not even once. Not on my own anyway I wouldn't. What truly had happened was now lost to time. Here we have a common thief whose mother can't come close to even dealing with half of it, and a faraway strange place with a lagoon, or swampy area, and who knows what else. To be quite honest, in these parts all one needs to do is dig far enough down, and you'll strike water.

Those deep holes generally go from being rock quarries, to becoming swimming holes for the local kids. Quite a few of the younger neighborhood individuals would walk around with B.B. guns, or bow and arrow sets, often wearing official rubber hunting boots. We all wore those back in the day before snow-mobile boots become popular. I had never witnessed any shooting or takedowns, so who knows where these potentially imaginary deeds were actually performed.

I had to believe, now that we were older, that such a far off and hidden area was their new spot for kicking it. Back when I had last had hung for just a short while with dude, his delight was such that I had no choice but to forgive him for his lusting after my cross-training 5-speed racer/mountain bike. Here and now, he had paid though. He had paid the price, and dearly. Yet for what misdeed was this final payment extracted at the time of his actual demise? I'll never truly know.

The summer had waned without much more action. My pal that thought it was safe to be together again and I got together. I guess because we were now to be in school together my bad influence couldn't be blamed on the local public school system. We went over to the farther park. There were two flatbed trailers still remaining from the dredging of the pond. I turned the handle on one just a bit, not really understanding its purpose.

The exact and precise reason for these cranks is to lower the flatbeds down onto the cab of some sort of truck. Then with those trailers finally secured, they would be driven away. This time it was an officer that arrived at our door. After a stern lecture to my parents about potential costs, and charges, he let us all know that we'd be let off with merely a warning. It was the cost to lift that flatbed back up that was the troubling aspect.

It was now a Saturday. My old school chum suggested once more that we hang out at the farther park a bit. I am not so certain what exactly was at play, but I ask you now, how you would have reacted to the following scene. The squirrels were playing and romping on a calm fall noontime part of the day. Without warning one of these scamps rushed over and jumped up on the wheel of my bicycle. He paused and lingered for an unnatural amount of time, seemingly saying hello.

Then, after going back to play and romp with one of his own, he returned. This time he decided to get a bit closer than before. From out of nowhere the thing started to crawl up my leg. Stopping then just a hair above my knee, he embraces my leg, giving it a noticeable amount of squeeze. It hugged dearly, hesitated, then casually moved on down. I froze, though before I could truly come to terms with the whole event, then I began to giggle.

Just like that, he was off and running with one of his own again. I did suspect that at least one other person, specifically the park worker, had fed him peanuts. That would explain his keen interest in my leg perhaps. Although, it truly is way more leg shaped, rather than like a goober. I was certainly honored in some strange type of natural way, yet still wonder if that was some type of sign for me to pick up on.

I got up on yet another Saturday to go hang out with this old Catholic school buddy who'd been calling lately I merrily jaunted out and onto the main road. Before long I noticed a massively huge dump right in the middle of the sidewalk. It was, no doubt, the work of the local St. Bernard. He stood nearly 5 ft tall, but was rarely up and about during normal daylight hours. I had however seen his handiwork before. I made a mental note of the situation then continued on with my noon time walk.

The day held little so we made our way to Kathy Z's house. She lived a hop skip, and a jump from that park, up and over the hill. She was always good about a last-minute bell-ring, and would come on out with a ready smile. We otherwise kicked it around wherever we could in the area, and folks seemed to appreciate the unexpected visits. Jim, who lived just over from Kathy had been tinkering in his garage. Nothing much was up with him either, unless of course one knew advanced rocket science, or whatever it was that caused him pause just before we ambled on up and in.

After a good long day of this type of friendly fall weather, my bud, and I were ready to pack it in. The fresh dry air enveloped me in a shroud of comfort and bliss. The sun was shining and the big, white, hooded sweatshirt I wore had been quite adequate for the day's warmer temps. I all too soon made my way up the back porch, and in the doorway. Within seconds Mother began to lose it! She stepped closer with her hand covering her nose and mouth.

That meant either vomit, or…or dogsh*t. As soon as she made it close enough to see beyond the kitchen table, that was it. She totally lost it, then physically shoved me out the door. "Hey, what are you doing?" I enquired.

"Well, get yourself out there and see," she demanded. Before I had even gotten fully out, I could tell what was up, or should I say smell? She shut the door quickly and I was abandoned. Shamefully alone I was now and dealing with this tragic misery. Upon moving away from the door so very quickly, the evidence was clear. I stopped any efforts to remove more of the stuff, and demanded to know how such a thing may have come about in the first place.

Each and every step moving from the yard out to the alleyway evidenced an ignorance of my own device. Though more so, one of an innocent sense of casual Saturday afternoon bliss. I knew from point one there had to be more of the same down the way. Even to the point of those being even embarrassingly large protruding mounds of evidential clarity. The upcoming visual severities would prove me correct.

With my head in the clouds and anticipatory thoughts of the late afternoon dining, I somehow drifted off. I didn't always eat any lunch at all, and my hunger caused me to fantasize about the forthcoming meal. Now hadn't I told myself, "remember *that* on the way home?"

"Remember the bigger-than-human-size pile of a canine's excrement," is exactly what I had thought to myself. Did I not then, as I approached the offending mass, remind myself once more, to avoid that bigger than any human's, 'Hugh-Gass' pile of dung?

Here though, in retracing my steps, with each loping movement I took, with my coming closer to the original mass, those huge glops that had fallen from my shoe became more and more troublingly large. I finally had rounded the corner and the trail was hot again.

Upon standing next to the somewhat leveled out, and now well-trodden upon mound, a sense of shame and embarrassment took over. I looked well down the way to question what had happened after I had recalled the hazard. Oh well, the day had not been so filled with glee and sunshine after all. Though perhaps it was just that *something* wanted to tag along for the ride! That largest of all St. Bernards in town, was most certainly the actual culprit.

It was finally cold enough for ice. The distant park not only had the pond dredged, it was filled back up, frozen, and now time for some ice skating. I grabbed my skates with the laces already tied together, and made my way out the door, and down the main street. It was only about 3 miles away, and it having been some time, I was even excited about the whole ordeal.

It was a Friday evening, and things were pumped. The older kids, still in high school, were filled with glee, and the entire occasion became a regular party. We went inside to get warm. Some of these older gents had gathered inside the boy's room. Not much was taking place other than some joking, and laughing, finally now, on everybody's part.

One fellow called me over closer. Closer he implored. He then grabbed me by the bottom of the skate, and flipped me completely upside down over the partition, and into the stall next-door. They all roared so heartily, and it would have been a good one, save for one catch. The tip of my skate kicked the toilet bowl, cracking it completely in half, sending at least a gallon or two of befouled but fresh toilet water all over the floor. I mean it is befouled based on its temporary container, isn't it? We all shrieked in horror and ran, one by one, as the decimation became fully apparent. So, now I was a wanted man for that as well.

I'm doing my best to keep this next thing as chronologically correct as I possibly can without checking into intimate details on-line at the library. The tall and short of it involves my lack of finer admiration for one singular and individual National Football League quarterback. Namely this man is the one, the only, former Dallas Cowboy by the name of Roger Staubach. I don't care how well he did so many years later. I merely wanted him to suck so bad that Coach Landry pulled him from the game.

I may not have liked the team in general, yet if Staubach got pulled, I would be filled with glee. Therefore, I became the biggest Craig Morton fan. Morton was the respectable backup. If Roger the Dodger needed some discipline, Landry I'm sure, loved it coming from Morton, just I had come to truly appreciate. I would root, toot, and even become giddy with delight, based on the better play of Morton, playing in Staubach's stead.

I remember one game in particular. Saturday games were still somewhat of a new thing. What better way to waste the late afternoon of a cold and windy weekend day than to spend it huddled inside with the warmth of the heated central air flowing, and the supposed better teams of that year at odds. On the particular day in question, those opposing groups consisted of the Big D. and the San Francisco 49rs.

My guy John Brodie from San Fran could truly go into desperation mode in the second half of games. Just like the elder Manning, a very large man that played for Houston, this well experienced missile-man, Mr. Brodie, would begin to heave 40 to 60 yard passes well down field. As long as even one connected with a receiver, the team had a further chance.

All too often 'Arch the Starch' himself, as I call him, would be just a little off with his towering bombs. Here on this day though Mr. Brodie was on target enough to keep his team in the game. Well, you know what happened next. "Boom, there goes the boom," as P.O.D. likes to sing.

Yes indeedy Ms. McReedy. Now here comes Craig. As long as the 49rs won, I didn't care how well the Cowboys overall had performed. As long as my man Mr. Morton was making dude look like the unskilled rookie-type youngster that he even was, I was on cloud nine. This game had it all. It went down to the final minutes.

You'll have to research the results yourself as I already had everything I wanted in that regard. The only two other truly wishful experiences I had back then involved wanting Jim Plunkette with the Patriots to throw one with his left hand. Just to screw with everybody's mind. That's right, I say. I wanted him to toy with their very beings. He had come out of college as a highly touted rookie. Things got rough for him immediately upon getting down for the hike.

Suffice it to say those college days of glory were oh so over, in the wink of a turtle's eye. The other fantasy evolved for me within a few short years. The story on Terry Bradshaw was that he was from Louisiana. I wondered how his business minded grandfather had gotten all the way down to New Orleans, or so, yet that certainly was a major port area back in the day.

It was the blond hair of Mr. Bradshaw that drew my interest. Could he himself possibly be a bit Norwegian such as we are in our family? My mind reeled keenly. I only had one dream. For Mr. Bradshaw, yes even with him beginning to lose hair at that young, young age, the crowning glory of his Professional Football League days would've involved his growing two ponytails, then joining the Minnesota Vikings as a free-agent. Imagine his getting down in the stance with those blond fronds dangling from beneath his football hat! I still am thrilled with a tremendous amount of delight, when I cranially go there on my own.

Hanging with my old pal, now back in school with me offered a little more than adventure. If you'll recall Mr. Friendly knew everybody. One fellow that we had come upon one day had a very unusual name. Immediately I broke into song using the syllables of his surname for emphasis. "One two, three four DuLemor'." (Or something close to that.) "Oh Doctor, Doctor, Doctor, Mr. M.D. I said Doctor. Oh, the cure is what I need." The kid was just twelve years old so with this song being an oldies number it failed to have quite the effect that I though it should. He was more like, "Ahh yeah, I guess, but get over its guy, already."

It would turn out that this fellow had a sister our age. She had a petite yet quite exotic look. It was something hard to put your finger on. Like maybe a strange combination of Italian, and Greek. With her other sister being even two years older even more mystery entered the picture. Think belly dance for some reason. The family name was actually French. So, I'm going West French Indies, with even some Spanish from Spain.

Think even Moroccoian maracas. The girl my age was slender, and trim, refined, and pretty. She had an air of maturity, but yet with such a distinct sweetness, and at our age only 14 and just now entering 9th grade, something elusively beautiful, and graceful was what she imbued, even from the

159

innocence of her very being. Her older sister was a more advanced, slightly larger version of the same.

After I laid eyes on her, I felt just a bit weird for giving her brother the whole song rendition back when we had first met. Oh well none of that mattered now. It was a new year, and I as a first-year student had way too many girls to think about, to dwell on even one of those fine young beauties for too long.

That pal from grade school was starting his first year in the suburbs. His mom had second thoughts, and the only solution for her was to pack up, and get her sweet, sweet boy as far away as she could from guys such as I had become. I was there for him in the interim, but too many kids smoked weed in public school for his mother's taste, I guess.

At school one day we were surprised by the news that a major sports star had come in to see us. The only thing was, that he had agreed to read from one of our school books as we read along. This man from New York was a former Catholic school student himself. He went on to attend UCLA, and was then drafted by a nearby team. Who may have pulled the strings to get him to come on in I really can't say. I had the idea, instead of allowing a professional sports player read to us, that we would go on strike.

That was such a huge mistake. It was much too late for a huddle as he sauntered in and parked his 7'2" inch frame, comfortably into the teacher's chair. Soon after he started to read, a book hit the floor. Then it was another, and another. The strike had begun. After all, we just wanted to hang out, and perhaps pose a few questions, maybe talk about strategies, or even game time thoughts that may run through a pro's mind. We certainly did not want to engage in average everyday school book stuff.

He took our actions so seriously his disappointment was nearly palpable. My heart dropped from my chest, so I arose to come forward and apologize. He accepted that reluctantly, letting us know that he was never more insulted in his entire life. I offered that since he had no teaching degree, we thought that we could get him to relent.

In hindsight, such a statement was not doubt only bad icing on a cake of cold harshness, the disrespect offered to a former fellow Catholic Grade School student was now so glaringly and obviously as heartless and vile of a welcome that any could ever truly offer. He good naturedly promised to finish the reading, and most of us accepted his willingness to continue on, with a dual sense of regret and wonder.

Kareem Abdul Jabbar decided to go along with the exact same story line, as a guest on the television show The Facts of Life. I was back in horror, upon viewing that scene from the 1979 broadcast of the sitcom about two African American foster children adopted by a white single father. I duly cringed once again at my utter and totally tasteless actions from that all too real, and seemingly forgotten, original day. Doh!

It was a mostly normal Sunday afternoon one middle December day. Out on the east coast a blizzard was moving through Buffalo, NY. It just so happened that a game was in process, and was the locally televised AFL game of that day. It was crazy enough in the first half, but when they announced that there was no end in sight, and that it actually may be even a bit worse in the second half, I got ready to rock baby.

The predictions for the weather held out to a tee. Buffalo mainly handed off to O.J. who gained 200 yards for the day. The quarterback for Buffalo, Joe Furgeson was 3 for 5, with a total of 70 yards passing for his total stat line. What I recall with such a glorious joy and sense of merriment is the way the line judges and refs had to shovel up to 4 inches of snow for every two carries by O.J.

That effort was just to measure for the first down. Most of the 3rd and 4th quarters went like that. It was a constant shoveling and a constant thumbs-up for the first down, every two carries by O.J. I do believe the final tally came to about 14 inches of snow for the day. I am still waiting for another fun, crazy snow-game like that one was.

1974

It was spring. The icy blast of winter had dissipated and the warmer winds from the south had finally come our way. Anyhow Mother had mentioned that the neighbor, and the boy with the very first laser turntable to ever exist in our town, had been over. They were checking, and measuring, going over things. Looking, and searching, trying to find any one aspect of our finished basement sections, and especially those visible workings in the unfinished part to execute on their own.

She mentioned that it seemed like minutes, and they were gone. Weeks later the neighbor boy called, thanking her so much for the opportunity to examine Father's construction in the lower chamber. Also, it was offered as a matter of fact, they were all done with his basement work too. Another investigative inspection, therefore, would not be required after all.

It was now May. Things had started to warm up rather nicely. My chum from school brought cigarettes to school again. I had told him no way. We're on the team. He was number 13, and I was 33, after Kareem. The old uniforms stored away in a box from years before had gotten musty, and started to deteriorate. The decision was made to have a bake sale. A few of us brought our paper route money, and pigged out a bit. It was a pure delight to be so close to actually having a team, as the previous year it had all fallen through for us.

Another aspect of our clutching, and tearing our way back into the league was the name we were given. We found out that one of the joys of our school having left the Saturday League was that a team that hated their name could petition to steal ours away. So, after having sweatshirts made up with the moniker of Jayhawks, we had it dropped on us that we indeed were the Mooses. Jim and Bruce's Mooses we had become. After we finally became more well-established, Jim actually dumped us, going back to his walk-on assistant-track-coaching job, at the local technical high school.

The fact was this athletically minded individual had smuggled out from the local high school, the Army R.O.T.C. weight training handbook. He had heard how I had received a weight set for Christmas years earlier. Truth be told, I believe the next manual to be issued to those young aspiring commitments may have been titled 'Special Forces, only the Best Can Make It'. Within months, I became a lean, mean, human flexing machine. Just check the team photo to come to terms with such a keen advancement in that regard.

Oh well, we didn't need Jim anyway as an assistant coach. Bruce's still rhymed with Mooses, I always will consider. One practice though, got a bit out of hand in particular after the split. Bruce felt he was being dissed by my man. I came up and demanded, "What the hell, what are you doing?"

Dude got up off of my bro then jumped on me, twisting, and wrestling me to the floor. So, quickly then, he had encased me in a desperate head-lock. He just stood up right away and asked, "Well, are you ready to practice or what?" Yeah, whatever dude!

One thing we did manage to engage in together with both coaches was attending an actual NBA game. You may know of these Berry fellows, now retired from the game. That would be Rik and Jon. Rick Berry Senior was the bigger pro. Our team was up by one with seconds to go. Rick Senior dribbles up toward the midline.

He stops just short, and with three seconds on the clock launches a shot of desperation. That was well before the three point rule went into effect. It mattered little since the Warriors won by a single point. Wow! I just laughed. The others were upset, yet I felt that we had just witnessed one of the most spectacular events in sporting history. It still gets to me like that.

Here now, NBA Basketball playoff time had arrived. Things had gotten a bit dull with me and my other bud keeping a low profile and all. He did mention once that they were still after me for the toilet, yet no one was talking. It seemed to be a natural thing for us to be more than careful. Basketball on television would be just the thing. Save for one dire, desperate, and needful aspect.

Earlier in the year Don Nelson the sixth-man sub from the Boston Celtics had intentionally poked Kareem in the eye. This appeared to be not only a flagrant foul, but a dirty way for the Celtics to advance farther toward the Championship than otherwise attainable. Kareem was going in for a rebound, or deflected pass when 'Nellie Boy' ran over and gouged him but good.

I am sure that I recall seeing a nail file in Nellie's hand just before he reentered the game. We should have called him *'pretty boy'* at that point. The only thing was Don Nelson was a pudgy pear-shaped small forward that wasn't quite that handsome. He was however a true scrambler and Kareem eventually forgave him.

Though, that was not before that 7'2" center turned and punched the upright, with all of his might. That bit of uncontrolled and animalistic response was so quickly regretted. That he went from total and utter anguish in his eye, to an even more broken spirit, while showing an unbelievable suffering with his now shattered hand, was the low point of that year for so many. Seconds elapsed.

Finally, long drawn-out minutes of sheer agony, and undeniable pain then ensued. They quickly walked him off the court to the backstage area. The morning paper finalized the drama as *"out indefinitely, playoffs in jeopardy"*. I cannot recall anything further about the remainder of the year, though I believe they squeaked in, then moved quickly back out of any further play.

(Future side note): Don Nelson would be my enemy for life. The worst move that the team ever made was making him head coach. I became sickened every time the camera panned over to the bench. I would close my eyes, and wish it all away. They toyed with greatness even until after my son was born in 1982.

With Nellie Boy at the helm, nothing less than the outright title would suffice for my desperate needs. Philly stood in our way once more, and that sad chapter in the team's efforts was finally closed. I still recall having the game on that year. My one true love, and our son Jason Argos I, had moved back in with her mother and father. One more loss therefore, of any type, would truly mean little to me.

Dude with the paper route comes over. With him was the fellow that I replaced. I, unknowingly at the time, had ruined his strike. These amigos only had one thing in mind, wine. Some homey says, "all that we have to do is hang out at the bar, since the liquor store is just across the street, bam, we're in like Flynn."

"So, these *people* are just dying to buy alcohol for a bunch of desperate kids?" I asked.

"Well, we'll tip him a couple of bucks, and besides we're almost old enough," he claimed. He indeed was at least a year older, a casualty of the midterm graduation experiment from 1966–67. Once that was abandoned, if one could not pass the test, one had to repeat second grade, or rather half of it all over again.

The bass player from the band I started after the Beatles landed here in America was one of those that struggled early on as well. He was one of those that failed to make the grade, and had to repeat, though now a full year of second grade rather than the half year he had already gone through. He somehow was so devastated from that entire ordeal that he actually flunked once more again!

I was not at all too keen on the idea of engaging in young teen drunkenness on that particular evening, but went along with the plan anyway. It went amazingly smooth. Within minutes they were handing me the hooch, as I was to take the deer trails back as a precaution. I received the goods and as they nervously scanned the roadway for interference, moved quickly toward the open field just ahead.

I swiftly moved deep, then deeper into cover. It would have helped if the deer from my early years actually had been keeping the trails up. They apparently had all receded across the street into the thicker brush of safety. I decided to cut to the chase and made a beeline for the end of the road just ahead.

That unfinished roadway was still lying incomplete due to the border war that would never truly be ended. I began to take long and strident steps to reach the clearing quicker. All at once from out of nowhere the most chilling experience one can ever have, when all alone anyway, had thrust itself upon me. Even if this was just two blocks from my home, total and utter shock and fright are still the same.

A startling honking from beneath my feet sounded the wildest escalation of frantic chaos echoing deeply into my quickly weakened heart. I nearly peed, but it all went down so fast. From out of nowhere with a dramatic burst of frenetic energy, a pheasant, one that I had nearly stepped on, one that was intentionally quiet up until that point, sprung forth with the energy of a thousand screaming meemies.

All too quickly, within two seconds, it was so far away I could have laughed. *Well, maybe the guys will*, I had thought, *If I tell it just right*. This Boone's Farm, or Annie Green Springs as it were, went down all too smoothly. Perhaps the pheasant's thundering was a sign. A sign, that at least I myself shouldn't be engaging in such drunken activities. No, I surely didn't enjoy it. I sat for the remainder of that night on the back porch, trying to sober up. Yuk!

Summer was now upon us. I had left the rigors of Catholic Grade School behind. Whatever it was that Mother feared, as far as my attending the local public school, lie just ahead. In the meantime, I not only had a job, I was still hanging on as a paper boy's assistant. This same character, the actual delivery boy, whom I believed was even up to a year, and half older, had managed to work his way into running the corner gas station right across from the local tavern. It turns out the manager, a man from down south had been sitting in that very pub, watching, waiting, keeping his careful eye on things, so very easily from across the way.

On one dead evening he sprang up from out of nowhere. While I was over visiting my pal at this gas station during the slower evening hours, he had raced onto the premises. I ran out back to the apple orchard. It was all to no avail. Within seconds he was on me, and asking me to give it up. I did so and we both went back for a little meeting with my bud.

First off, the issue was that one of us was on the clock, while the other was just hanging around. The man politely asked that I not linger, and to not come around unless some detail of vital import needed to be discussed. I agreed and went home. Before the week was over I was hired on as the other night-weekend attendant.

Imagine Tommy Chong if you will. That would have been Bruce the factory worker. Gary's dad had two stations, one for himself, and the other for Gary. That left our southern buddy pretty much on his own, aside from the new hire, my older friend. My help in this case was just what the doctor ordered. Whatever other pleasures a young man could partake in during the glorious summer months would certainly be worth a look.

I walked up to the small strip mall at the beginning of our neighborhood. There was my next-door neighbor in his $3,000.00 Volkswagen Beetle. It was a light blue with installed speakers. He asked me to get in while playing Frankenstein by The Edgar Winter Group. He restarted the tape so that I could catch it all. After the good part, which was actually a different version from the radio shortened depiction, he started 'er up.

He liked to keep the car clean, as I would often see him with chrome vacuum cleaner parts headed toward his vehicle. I was honored to be a guest in his home after not having spoken for a while. As soon as we were on our way his comrade pulled out a corncob and torched it up. "How about you?" he enquired.

"Why certainly," I answered, "It's not my first time." Within three or four hits, I was feeling good. I mean because it took that many, as this was low grade imported stuff from Mexico. So, it wasn't quite Panama Red or Brown Columbian at all.

My neighbor took me on a tour of his delights, as far as I could gather these had become regular haunts of his. First it was onto the playground of the neighboring community's grade school. I found out, ever so dramatically, that a very small car fits perfectly under the monkey bars of a schoolyard. Living just on the boarder offered us a quick escape, if need be, as well. His buddy from down the block needed to take care of some business so we dropped him off.

We headed toward farm country just after. Living on the border offered anyone who needed a quick and ready escape into the finer delights of country living, a warm surprise. I still recall the sweet, sweet smell that ascended up from the landscape each and every night, a few hours after sundown. It was a combination of dew and wild plant life. Being in love can cause one, to even so totally appreciate weeds!

I had been out there in that area to the south before. It was on my bicycle, riding out to the outdoor flea market. This area was beyond the county line. My neighbor after crossing over, so quickly drove down a road with an urban legend attached. I felt okay, and put that story out of my mind the best that I could. We drove on, and on a bit, until coming to a dead-end barricade. I still to this day do not know the truth of this detour, not even one little bit. After pausing I noted a ladies under garment had been draped over the striped wood before me. About a 38C, I would gather.

"Do you see that?" I asked nervously.

"Yes," he indicated, putting the vehicle into reverse and tearing out of there. He made good speed back to the main part of the road, yet now we still had to pass the *scary story* spot. I tried, and tried to block out each and every possibility. I tried to control my thoughts about any recent conquest. There was still that horrible bridge that we had to cross a second time, and whether or not the girl who had lost her undergarment was actually a friend.

Just maybe her virginity as well, is what was now gone. Maybe she was a girl that had picked up in a local bar. He did love the big city bars of the town to the north. He would tell me the truth if he really wanted to, I considered. The older legend from the nearby bridge as it were, involved a human head dangling from a telephone wire. Soon enough though, we were safe and sound and back into our own county.

One of that next-door neighbor's friends knocked upon the door. He really just wanted to get buzzed, yet apparently was a new acquaintance, and didn't feel comfortable knocking on my buddy's door on his own. It smelled like Christmas trees, standing on the porch. An installed fan was up on high, and pumping. We were allowed in. We then made our way into the lower chamber. There above the sofa was a pull chain, attached to the fan. The whirling apparatus itself was embedded in the very cement of the cellar wall.

My neighbor brought over some old-school metallic vacuum cleaner tubes. "Are you going to be doing some cleaning?" I enquired.

"Well, you can if you'd like, as a matter of fact…no, just kidding," he joked. These are bong parts. "We didn't just make this whole space, complete with a bar and accessories," he added. "My buddy and I also made this," he had offered. "I just have to get all of the pieces together," he claimed. This whole time I had simply thought he liked a clean vehicle. Well, how clever he had truly been.

On Sundays at my corner gas station, I had been servicing one regular, of particular note. He would go over to Chicago at least every other week to see his mom. He also drove a somewhat older vehicle so I would check his oil. If need be, I would plunge a spout into one of the old-school oil cans. He insisted on pouring it in himself. I believed he enjoyed being self-sufficient, as from one of his arms, just beyond the elbow joint, sprung a tiny little misshapen hand. It was mainly nonfunctional.

It was after about the third time that he had stopped in, that things turned bad. On that later weeknight, two strange fellows strolled on in. Of note was the fact that they were wearing what were termed *pimp-jackets* back in those days. These were long woolen coats that became fashionable during the early to mid-70s. They did not speak quite clearly, but were going on about their car, and needing change for the pay-phone.

As soon as I hit the register, the guns came out. One took me into the back room while the other grabbed all of the bills from the till. The fellow with me saw that only mechanic rags were lying here and there, so offered an alternative to tying me up. I'm not going to do that, but if you get up too soon, and see us still here, we're going to have to shoot.

I agreed that neither of us wanted that, and he rushed back to the front of the station. I asked myself what would be a reasonable amount of time to wait, and how long would be considered unnecessary. After about two, or three minutes I rose than moved to phone the police. Underneath the counter we kept a money bag with all of the bills yet to be deposited.

At night, we would place that in the safe located near the floor in the back room. It had been pushed far enough to the back of the shelving to go unnoticed. Good, about all that they got was perhaps $200.00 from my pocket, and the cheap crappy radio with the broken antenna.

Mother was now concerned about my safety and claimed that I could not work weeknights any longer after 8:00pm. My late-night availability was considered an essential part of my job duties, so within a week I was let go. Alas, my first stint at real genuine labor had ended on a sour note. I had felt that the likelihood that those criminal-type characters, or anyone else for that matter, would return to pull a stunt like that was minimal at best.

School would be starting soon, and my focus would be on my new classmates at the public junior high, and courses such as algebra, wood shop, and metal. The only question was, "Did that man open up his big mouth up in Chi-town about some kid running a gas station all on his own?" No doubt he did. Probably after stopping at a local pub, and going on about it. Hard to say though, indeed it is, so hard, so hard to really say.

Another aspect of life that worried Mother involved live performances. Out of curiosity, I had queried her on the aspects of my having attended a fabulous rock show. The evening news had broadcast the event with even a live shot of the festivities. The band was none other than Pink Floyd. The performance was held outdoors at the local ballpark.

Her response, "No way, knowing you, who knows what kind of trouble you would have found for yourself." It would indeed be an additional year or so, before I did actually make it to that plateau of teen gleefulness. I mean as far as concerts go anyway. The actual *outdoor-stadium* show I did finally attend would be at least three-plus years off, and down the road. Yes, indeed, it would be so safely far removed from that gleeful on-air news about such a musically fabulous night.

Near the rotting apple trees on the way to the drugstore someone had created an underground fort. My workmate and his neighbor, the fellow whose paperboy strike I had spoiled, wished to go in and investigate. We crawled through the opening. The roof of plywood was trussed with an 8x8. Piles of dirt from digging the fort had been placed atop the wooden structure. Inside, it was pitch black. We felt around and located some old car seats to sit on. Was this the private sanctuary of those kids that had their own body-less, Volkswagen-type car?

After chatting for a few minutes, a burst of laughter emerged from the dark corners of the man-cave. I at first nearly went into shock. With our having believed that we were all alone, only a nightmare it seemed could allow for another being to exist in that subterranean shelter. Yet that was what made it so funny to them. After scaring us for being in their fort, they seemed like pretty cool guys. We however would take no further chances with their hospitality. Not any whatsoever!

Soon enough some of my new classmates were all over me. Not in a Hollywood movie star way, mind you. It's not like I was total rock star cute and lovable, or anything. Sometimes one just needs to be in a brand-new setting, and all the fine young ladies, in seeing that you're not attached, decide to give it a shot. The first had her friend ask me.

They were both average looking girls, with one having huggably-thin, and shapely legs. The other sweet young lady, a big blond, possessed a sense of gentle kindness. Yes, that is still how I recall her even to this day. I do even really mean that the texture of her voice was enough to put raging coyotes to sleep, or how about roaring lions? That honestly sounds a tad more like it.

I was taken aback a bit, and still being in shock said no. I thought that they would be my morning friends, and nothing more. In hindsight, I would have gone with either. With all of the rubbing and touching, I believe that I would have gone to town in a Cadillac on those gentle young honeys. Yet mind you, I had had sex with grown women, and felt it was best for one and all, if I left my hands off of these precious young sweets.

Of course, I was certainly into such sorts of things, don't get me wrong. It's just that a person needs to start life over again, after living to such grand heights previously at such a very young age. The way the thin one of the two had moved away before the end of the year, I had felt that I had missed the perfect opportunity. I mean you don't need to really break up with someone that's only 14 years old and now living in another city, right? The smooth thought of those trim young legs can still evoke a mild sense of longing in my quickly aging brain.

As far as the other's voice, think of bedtime stories. I don't just mean those filled with compassion, fun, or adventure. I mean the type of which would lull one into such a soft sense of relaxation, that only heaven's loving arms could await, with a sweet, and wanting anticipation. Now that's smooth baby!

About three weeks after school started that year, another average looking girl approached me. This time the fine young lady was out on her own. Just as soon as I became comfortable with my locker placement it happened. I was marching back and forth to my classes, and getting my books for the next classes, and had that all down pat. From out of nowhere, the girl from nearby looks me right in the shoulder, or chin or something, it was somewhat close to my eyes.

Having used up any spare energy that she possessed just to pop the question, she had none left to look deeply into my medium brown-golden-speckled peepers. I would like to add here, with Father having had green eyes, a small amount of that color became spread throughout both of my irises, though with a more golden hue than most. Any one individual however, would need to be right up close, and staring intently into my hypnotic love chambers, to actually notice.

I hadn't detected such an unusual coloration in my lookers myself until I was at least 35 or so. If anyone insists in a needful fashion, I mean, I guess that I could let them 'Go For The Gold'. Then in getting up nice and close, and that all to just truly peer so deeply into the visual vibrancy of multi-colored ecstasy that are my eyes, one would certainly become mesmerized.

With what she was about to ask me, you may well understand a slight bit of shyness on her behalf. Just like that, in a whirlwind of excitement, and with a gleam of undeniable joy she hit me with it. "Would you go out with me?" she said.

I was taken aback. It was all happening so very quickly. I said the only thing a guy could, when confronted with difficult choices. "Uhm, no," I replied. That was that. It was all over so quickly.

Her locker was one down from mine. She had big, big beautiful hair. It was about down to her beltline. Imagine getting mixed up in all of that. The very idea of it to this day gets me a little excited. We quickly both got over it and tried our best to look the other way when at our lockers thereafter. I once again had wished that I could be smoother with girls. I mean going out with each one, and then breaking up as quickly as necessary to engage with the next fine honey, sounds like a plan, right?

We would each then, after being so 'almost-romantically' close, head to our prospective first classes, while getting farther, and farther away from each other. Even safely away, it would truthfully then be, now that I knew of her romantic desires anyhow. Safely away I say, away! I would ever so quickly be away enough to gradually take in, indeed, what had just transpired, or what had failed to ignite in any such case.

This girl was okay looking, and everything, and with her real big hair one could imagine whiling away many a weekend afternoon getting so up close and familiar with that long, long do. Other than for that brief moment, one that rebounds, resounds, and plays itself all over for me, I had been really just getting my books in the morning. You know how that may work. You're putting your coat away, thinking about first hour maybe. Unless Cupid struck first in your direction, serious business is fresh at hand, not becoming lost in a sea of gorgeous, flowing, light brown locks at all.

During fourth hour we had Social Studies. There was a girl in that class that things were brewing up for. I did not realize any extra attention at first, although that hand was carefully laid out before me all too quickly. She was Rosita. Her family had fled Cuba back in 1961. Her uncle, she had said, used all of the last of his good money, to send them to America. Due to the new rules of government no one could have good money anymore.

So, her uncle used the very last of his, to safely move them to Florida where they could begin a new life on the continent. She maintained a familial bitterness toward the new regime that one could tell was handed down to her by the attitude of the elders. Those were folks whose harsh feelings so easily lasted through, to the next generation in such a way.

Here on the floor just above, it was that a fellow with a bit of bad luck and a lack of some aggressive studying was still only a 7th grader. He'd be smoking a quick Kool King, in the boys' room, across from Miss Newman's class. He was the bass player from my would-be band. That had happened to be his homeroom, a coincidence that left me feeling worried. He claimed to me that Miss Newman had no interest whatsoever in just barging in at any given time, so we were cool in that regard.

She happened to be my sixth hour English teacher, so I indeed needed to hear such a statement of confidence in order to relax, considering she became upset when the girl next to me loved whispering small comments in my welcoming ear from time to time. Wow, I had felt. Easy, easy, easy, there teach. She was as tough as a stale cafeteria dinner roll.

Let's wrap up the year in one final paragraph. I love women. Most men do. I love girls. They are so sweet and pure, so young and innocent. It is not even necessary for them to have been Girl Scouts at all. They inherently offer a special something. Seemingly by God's hand. I also love young boys. They beckon from the past my own boyish charms, my dreaming fantasies, my future world before me. The men are my brothers. Together, we forge a movement of unity and strength.

That movement becomes a force of pureness. That pureness, in drawing from the innocence of life itself, is manifested in the Holy Spirit. So, you so easily see now. We are drawn together naturally, as one. When we are able to unify, multiply, magnify, and verily verify, that we are all present in the spirit, we grow then in our strength and a steadfast union.

1975

It was a Friday. The spring dance would be held. I decided to go and check it out. Rosita smuggled a beer out of her parent's home to share with a friend. She apparently downed most of the brew, as she was not intimidated socially in any way. I would say she was downright and so totally buzzed. I had asked her to go oral on me previous to that night.

She was so in love that she claimed she would, even agreeing to perform that action, out loud, in front of the other girls in Social Studies class. I had told her weeks before where we would do it. There was a staircase for the maintenance crew to enter the basement. "Right at the top of the stairs," I had mentioned, "At the start of lunch we'll do it." She eagerly and gleefully assured me that she would be there. When the time arrived, I drew close to the door.

My heart began to pound furiously in my chest. I sensed that she wasn't indeed actually behind that very door with the small rectangular window. I nonetheless hesitated before walking closer. We didn't speak at much after that for a while. Now here she had wanted to dance. I obliged.

How do you tell a young girl that you would *bang* the hell out of her, all night, over and over, but you really don't desire to be in a close relationship? It would only take one man to help. That would have been her one true soulmate, if those are truly out there and for real. Oh well, we were young and life was good. This other fellow, her one true love, would come along eventually to sweep her off her feet. Soon enough he truly would, I had to believe.

Blackie's cousin was with a sweet young girl I knew from around. We decided to get some air. From what I overheard, and I mean that they were standing right next to me, he was breaking up with her. It must have only lasted for days. Here was my chance. Maybe not quite immediately, considering I was just dancing with a girl that loved me. I mean, out of respect for her, I at least ought to wait until Monday, right?

174

My brain was buzzing with bees. Looking back, I can see that it was just not meant to be. Right at that moment, even in front of my friend, I swear I was so close. It was all too awkward. No, sometimes you just have to let some of the fish go. Alas, she continued to be my sweet cute friend. You will read all too quickly how I became damaged goods before the end of the next school year.

It was a warm late spring day. I casually moved toward the 'boys' entrance of our Junior High. Upon entering, and oddly all alone for once, I espied not one, but two trespassers. It was my young blond nephew, and my good brother. Let me specify for you, why this needed to work a certain way. It truly did not work so well back in 7thgrade, when I left school for about ten days.

It seemed to be so setup for me to begin so seriously making out with my previous year's teacher, instead of Dave going after her the way he did for me. You'll recall they threw out the reading books, and brought in teen type novels back in our private school for the start of our 7th grade year. Since Dave couldn't be expelled for doing it to Ms. Landsfield right on the floor, just in front of the chalkboard, their little plan to have me expelled didn't work.

I was still quite leery however about having any contact with even one of those half siblings from the other neighborhood, let alone skipping the remainder of the school day. I mean simply because a four-year-old, my nephew had tagged along, that shouldn't mean that I suddenly make my own rules, and do whatever I want. No, I defiantly insisted once, and again, and again. No way, I added in for effect. With that I dismissed them from my thoughts, and proceeded on to sixth hour English class, with no further consideration of the outside world whatsoever. Whew!

The teacher was known to be somewhat of a bastard. We had been talking, and puffing not seeing him approach us. There was no getting out of it, even though the cigs had been flicked to the ground seconds before his arrival. His old-man bastard testimony would be quite sufficient. When I arrived at school on the second to last day with an *old girl*, the kids all laughed.

My own mother, who was needed there to reinstate me, had a smile on her face as well. It was the last day of school. I decided that, even though I had refused to go with my brother and nephew, when they had just hidden behind the doorway inside the school, to skip out on that very last day of school on my own. The school couldn't do *jack* anymore after that point. Not on that very last day.

So, I would take advantage of the situation so very cleverly. I merely needed to walk away casually on such a beautiful, fine, last day of school. After making a brief appearance in homeroom the outside world was all mine. As long as I returned by noon, when we were to receive the actual diplomas, everything would play out fantastically. I walked down to the local park, and who should be there?

My bass player from the band I started back in 1964. I laughed. He pulled out some smoke and the celebration of graduating from Junior High had begun. Dude himself would have been moving on as well, had he only passed that required test back in half second grade. To be offered credit for an entire year, and avoid taking the entire 2nd grade over from the top, that one requirement stood for all. At least 18 to 24% did not make the cut! We let the tallest of us from the 8th grade basketball team off easy when it came to flunking. Since dude was so desperately sensitive when the issue came up, it was more a case of 'whatever guy' that we'd be thinking.

We however knew enough about the circumstances involved, to be snidely sympathetic toward he, and the other fellow who seemed tall enough to be a grown man. Those would be no. 10 and 13 from our Catholic Grade School team respectively. As I have mentioned, our other paperboy neighbor was apparently too devastated after such a karate chop to the psyche, that he even had failed yet another year also.

My good bud from down the way, the fellow with the other paper route in the area told me, "Even though it's true, and it was, oh-so-obvious, dude just can't deal with it." He meant, "I guess we'll just let it go, since he cannot come to terms with the awful truth." The bass player indeed only 8 months younger, yet two years behind me scholastically, needed to go home and practice on that fine, fine sunny morn. It then therefore, right at that bright shining moment, became the beginning of the *summer of love*, part II.

I merrily returned to the local school a few blocks down. Straight to the auditorium, I moved. A broad smile of pleasure soon reached into my mind. As I took my seat a sense of overwhelming joy set in. One must consider here that we had an unusual arrangement with the 7th, 8th and 9thgrades in one Junior High. There were way too many of us back then for any other option. I still rejoice though, when I recall those maturing moments. We were let loose at lunch on that fine summer day, to demonstratively begin our new sense of freedom. The sun never shone so beautifully upon my sweet, *innocent*, and young face.

I was invited over to the home of Blackie's cousin, Brownie. He said let's go upstairs above the garage to the chauffeur's apartment. It had been updated, and painted. His sister had been living there just to be independent, I had supposed. I believe I had caught a glimpse of her in the past, but this was different. She was in a state of undress while holding a sheet over her body.

I had seen all that I needed to. My mind raced a thousand thoughts per second, and they were all about her. I knew that I wanted her so bad, that all I could was to imagine her close to me. Her arms, her cheeks her lips, I needed all of those things right next to me. I so deeply and dearly craved her being near me that I became obsessed. I waited until we descended the staircase, and stood just outside the door. I whispered closely, "let me make out with your sister."

It didn't go over very well. He immediately became enraged, and almost hit me. I could not come to terms with his reaction. "Hey, if you wanted to make out with either of my sisters you are more than welcome," I calmly offered. This was an attempt to get to him to chill on the whole ordeal.

So, what gives? He thought about it hard and long then ordered me to stand facing the garage as some type of punishment. Pacing quickly, he made a plan. "For now, you can leave, but you need to come back later, to confess what you've done, and to my father," he insisted. I swiftly obeyed.

My brain wasn't functioning that day very well. I mean I was actually older by four months. Who does he think he is? As far as the dad part, what does he suppose we'll achieve by involving him in my fantasy love affair? I mean I had better not think of her at all anymore. If that was what he needed, he's got it, Jack Daddy. Especially with pops coming home all too soon, I mean.

I indeed returned to the scene of the crime. Brownie was waiting. He had me press my nose to the wall of the garage again until daddio arrived. Thankfully it was not a long wait. He gave a strange look as though I were talking Russian. I got enough of it out before my voice began to crack. "Okay, alright," he assured me in a gentle tone. I got out of Dodge and never looked back.

Brownie, and our buddy *Joe*, the one from the album that *Frank* came out with years later had stopped over. Enough time had passed since the sister fiasco, so water under the bridge does flow out to the sea I would say. At least in these parts it does. People would find that local factoid out the hard way when digging a quarry. It's only a matter of time before striking it rich, as you should recall. That is if you value water in such a way. Many other places around the world, no doubt have their own special holes too.

Here on this day, we made our way to the Nature Preserve. It was a beautiful place with trails and the *pond*. The swampy area wasn't much good for farming at all so the old owner allowed for those quarry men to dig. Some dirty buggers had fed ours with carp. In addition, any and all wildlife befitting such an environment had easily settled in. It's been mostly just geese as of late.

In some years a seeming thousand or more would bask in and around those safely sound waters before moving on down south. This is the same swamp-swimming hole that they pulled the older neighbor out of, by the hair. My younger sister knew people who stood around mesmerized by the entire tragedy of the situation. She is the one to have claimed at the time that body parts were dissecting during the initial attempts.

As the deceased had gone undetected for too long, it had become such a sorry nightmare. A clever recovery expert came up with the winning option. Here though, enough time had passed, or mostly had, so that we could concentrate on the positive actions of the day, and immerse ourselves in glorious summer delights.

We moved up from the water to a nice spot on the hill. There we sat, and rolled some doobies. We found what looked like some home grown. Let me start by clarifying that two types of weeds exist on this earth. What we dried looked to be close to some cheap Mexican, but what was really nothing more than hemp. It smoked just like hemp too.

I realized all too late that the beautiful sunny spot we had chosen to sit upon was actually a poison ivy patch with the hemp mixed in. Ouch. Huge blisters appeared on my wrist. They would throb with a tingling pain before subsiding. The next night we decided to stick closer to home. The Sunless Wonder, as I had called him, showed.

This younger fellow not only had bright blond hair; his sensitive skin precluded him from exposing himself during the day. His older bro' had been in a few of my classes including gym. We would stand in short lines based on our last names. Dude's brother was in mine, along with a Mr. M. who later became a politician. It was nice to have been so close to greatness once again.

We hung near that area closer to the center of things for a few weeks. The Pabst Brothers came along one night. They were so piss-assed drunk on that early-bedtime-evening. They swore that they would never touch the green stuff, and we all stood our ground. We did so in a silent, respectful manner, considering. To this day I regret ever having touched a drop. So, yes, I do have those buzzed up moments from time to time myself.

Coming home one evening that year, a new acquaintance called out to me. They said his sister was the toughest girl in the whole school so a young lady really needed to be careful of what she said in front of her. I do believe she was also the one that had a problem with the others hiking their bra straps up too high in the locker room, or having had those heights previously determined in privacy.

Any of those types were required to lower the flag by sundown, if you know what I'm saying. Again, yes, she was the brassiere boss, or height monitor in that regard, I truly do believe. So, anyway, my younger sister had purchased a used green Schwinn bicycle from her friend's brother. My Treasure Island special was out of commission so I had loaned the Schwinn for the interim.

My very first pair of spectacles from sixth grade had broken so I was temporarily going without. Back in those days a created miracle for us four-eyed folks not only cost big bucks, it took more than a few days to manufacture. As I heard my name being called out, and a slim figure standing in front of the P.D.Q. convenience store, I squinted to focus.

I waved back without knowing for certain who my good buddy was. The next thing you know I'm up on the bumper of a parked car, and my not so friendly friend is busting out laughing. To make it worse, I had hit the bumper so hard it bent the fork on the bicycle back until it wedged the tire up against the frame.

Fine, so I've got someone that I couldn't make out, chuckling and clucking, and now I have to hold the front of the bike up in the air just to make it another block and a half home! The next day, I came upon a brilliant idea. I would Frankenstein all of the Schwinn parts onto my machine, creating something that was at least somewhat respectable. Half way through my well-conceived plan, the Schwinn's owner caught me in the act.

"Ooooohh," she wondered, "Where did you get all of those grays?"

"They no doubt grew in overnight when I was coming to terms with this tragedy," I explained. "But look," I cheerfully offered, "I'm making the best of the situation, and this new creation is for you."

"Oh, you'll love it once it's done," I promised. The next night at the supper table I got the lowdown. Not only did she not desire to even remotely consider that monstrosity I had created, she let me know in no uncertain terms I would be paying her, for her now defective beauty.

Father chimed in, that $14.00 would be a fair price, and I would be allowed the kindness of a payment plan. He had calculated the supposed value, even utilizing depreciation to factor in the fair market cost to me. So, it was that I forked over $3.00 a week until the last payment of $2.00 was gleefully accepted by my little, older sis. Whew, I never wanted to go through such agony again!

We went back out to the swimming hole. This time the crazy farm boys happened along. They were pulling an old '64 Ford with a tractor. There had been a '39 pickup that still started next to the raspberries, so seeing who the culprits were should've come as no surprise. On the edge of swamp with a natural source of water, just off the side of the old farmer's road, were 10-foot-tall raspberry spikes.

We had smoked a doob then we went to work. By the time we were done we had created a maze of yummy, yummy goodness. With our bellies full and a grin on our faces we said goodnight. Sadly, that year marked the grandest in height and sheer bounty, for those sweet, sweet freebies. That old pickup truck had been towed away from that spot by that time, and only the 49 Olds, and 65 Chevy remained. Both of those lay just across the way and on the farmer's side of things.

I did find out years later that the land was being hijacked by these buzzards as well. That fact was so clearly displayed when the monastery land was sold, and those farm-boy's place as well. Since the new houses stopped well beyond the old corn field it was quite obvious that those rascally fellows had been farming beyond their border. Old corn cobs can still be found on the now weed eaten ground.

The Feds also filled in the stream and put in some type of inexpensive underground piping. Those farmers even rode around that barrier along the tree line, just to plow those last few yards of acreage. Here though, we wanted to keep it cool. The hillbilly brothers asked us to hop in so we did. While the two rode up ahead, we all took the thrill ride of your mama's nightmares.

Most every trail they took was for deer only, so you can imagine the destruction was not just on the car itself. We finally, after bobbing back and forth, from laughter to worry, came to rest upon the hill. "This looks like a good spot," the driver said and unhitched the auto. "See you guys around," he added, and the two drove off. Well, I sincerely hoped that we didn't as it dawned on me that these might be the two that killed my neighbor.

I mean if he caught them engaged in one of their shenanigans it wouldn't have surprised me if that's what they did. There was the '49Dodge, and the '65Chevy all parted out, and parked on the edge of 'their' cornfield as I have mentioned. You don't ever get away at all with those kinds of things, not at all. In the afterlife a person will pay, one way or another they'll pay. I would like to point out some of my beliefs for you at this time.

It will be nearly 100% psychological in so many respects when our past sins come to haunt. If the afterlife is 99% thought, and not 100% a physically real world, one can so readily imagine not being able to escape from one's past. In time they say, all things do work themselves out. I wish though, that we could more easily appreciate our psychological connections to the 'other' worlds that we know good and well, do really, truly exist out there somewhere.

The girls my buddies knew now needed some company so the three of us hooked up. Sue had a pool, so that would be cool. It's nice to be loved. Your heart rises above the mundane existence of all of those forgotten yesterdays, taking up new heights where the angels sing. Being young, there was some nervousness involved with our connection, at least on my part. Not to brag, but I had had sex with teenage girls, and grown women before this. The last thing that I wanted was to rush too quickly, or disappoint. At the tender ages of 14–15, one may need to ride the fence a bit where such pertinent matters are concerned.

Some of the time involved Sue and myself in a bedroom on the bed, yet fully clothed. I won't say that she was willing to let me have it in any particular way, but was no doubt as nervous as I was, considering. Well, it didn't amount to much more than kissing, although I would have taken that train home every night to the Orient.

I am not talking about lips, cheeks, head-hair or anything as innocent as that either. The relationship fizzled for any number of reasons, and I was okay with that. Three years later when she pulled up to the local park with her new beau, sitting inside his hot-rod, I finally felt the burn though. A cold and icy breeze blew through me, just like that.

It was now the first day of school at the big high school. In our area, as I have mentioned, the last three years of school had been separated from the next three just below. That was more because of the sheer number of students at that age, than for any other reason at all. Because I had gone to the Catholic Grade School for eight years, I still did not know too many people.

I found that my new classmates were most friendly, and welcoming. At any given time on any given day, I could walk up to any group and just start partying with them. Unless they thought you were just a total *narc*, it wasn't a problem. That they had no idea who you were was somewhat meaningless. I simply could not help myself when at school. I was like a kid in a candy store. This would lead to my overwhelming downfall.

I had smoked in the summer of 1974, more than just a bit, and had even partied starting in the spring of the previous school year. Why I even bought a one-fourth pound of weed with a buddy of mine over the summer. I had no connections to dispense with the goods, and ended up smoking all of the merchandise. That little aspect of the year in question may have pushed me beyond recovery. I want to make things clear right here. I was a bogus Joneser now. I would spot a small group of my new schoolmates having fun then casually make my way over.

Then some bastard f*ckers from some newspaper had sent spies in to investigate. Their quote was "one can pickup anything near the flagpole. Anything from *hair-on* to speed." We simply needed to be on our toes was all that came of it. My sad, poor decisions still became my downfall. I freakin' smoked every single day. I hardly ever had my own. Everyone was super cool about it though.

A dude's brother now had some acid. If you recall this would not be my first foray into the world of psychedelia. I had no qualms whatsoever as far as reliving the experience. I was a party dog then and loved the fun. He looked around, I looked at the flagpole. We were far enough away so the exchange was made. I again was born trippy, so either all of the stuff that I have tried as an adult was crap, or I was just too freaking high beforehand, to even trip the supposed way one is meant to.

In addition to now smoking on a daily basis it was felt that these dudes that had sold the quarter lb. to us during the warmer months owed us something. They did however mention right off that they had dipped into our bag to the tune of 6 or 7 grams, maybe! My bro told me to extract some payback from one of the gentlemen in question. I approached him to let him know of the situation so that negotiations could proceed.

He acted in a hurry, and moved quickly off to class. It was only a coincidence that I happened to see him skipping later at the local burger joint. I let him know it was dude that was pressing, and it would be him eventually that he'd be facing. He said, "All right, all right, but I only have one thing." He reached into his pocket and pulled out a small amount of some kind of new thing.

It was *angel dust*. For those who aren't up to date on all of the old-school narcotics, angel dust was nothing more than stolen or otherwise pilfered animal tranquilizers sprayed onto mint leaves. The concoction was to be smoked just like weed, yet had an inebriating kick that may catch one off guard. I brought it down to the hangout and displayed the booty. It was two grams of what looked like some real crappy homegrown. My buddy told me to go ahead.

I don't know if he was just being careful, but it seemed like he was more than wary. After three puffs my head started to swim. From lifting weights my lungs had enlarged and I could take in more smoke than most would really care to. Because I had doubted the strength of this concoction, I was sure it would be a disappointment.

I was wrong. I became wiggly, and wobbly, but felt stupendous. I mean I could hardly tell, or even care. I do most certainly recall that aspect of my reaction. Within half hour, 45 minutes I was mostly back to normal. My pal didn't really want his, so I got to keep that for the next day. I continued hanging out and smoking with the older kids at school, although I eased up some, not wishing to be a leech. Here and there I actually had my own stuff. I even thought to seek out some of those friendlier types for payback. Alas, I was so buzzed I didn't think I could even find a one of them.

Since both Brownie and Joe had gone through the same test and done the first half of 2nd grade over again thing, I was all alone, save for those kind strangers. Neither of my two new buds would be at school with me that first year. Both failed to pass muster, so were therefore still students at the Junior High. I was feeling a bit out there considering that I was now at my third school in as many years. I mean I was in some type of limbo where your happiest times are spent with friends, and the bare-boned drudgery of life is spent in school.

Yes, we were indeed a bunch of stupid fools to some extent. The truth is that only about 8 to 12% of individuals so totally ruin their lives before outright adulthood. So, some of us were being daredevils and getting away with it, and then the rest so sadly come to mind. It is that way with any vice, be it cigarette smoking or gambling. We already know all too well about alcohol and its victims. Some or most of these 'losers' are considered to be the addictive types. Alas, we never know until it's too late, do we?

I decided to skip 8th hour study hall, and take an early bus down to see my *other* buddies. Certain things in life don't always turn out the way that they were planned. This would especially be the case when a certain someone is seated by the window and watching you walk in to your former school. Now Mr. Seaberg knew me from having pulled the fire alarm during first half of 5th hour lunch, just the year before.

The thought of all of those well-prepared meals going to waste did honestly get to me. Alas, I felt horrible for those youngsters whose lunch trays had been eaten off of, or outright dumped into the trash cans. I mean, it was he himself that stated numerous unfortunates had had their scrumptious goodies dumped into the garbage, with some of those yummier items more so consumed by some bad actors. Those lunch dumpings, being acts that could not have occurred without my prankish misdeed, I took it to heart and felt even more guilty.

Naughty, naughty-hooligans aside, it was my bad apple to chow down on, when the memory did revisit. I feel that now that I am over 60 years of age that I am finally free of bad decisions that may potentially harm us at all. I now can only function in one fantastically positive, superbly uplifting, and heroically well-balanced approach to overall life. Whew, it's about time!

As I looked out the windows from the inside of my old-school entrance, a true sense of peace had come over me. I breathed in deeply the air that I would probably never taste again. From around the corner here comes Seaberg. He himself takes a breath to become poised for the encounter. Somehow as he approached, all of the strict superiority he no doubt intended to bring upon my world seemed to drain from his very being.

He took another calming breath then began his polite address. His concerns were for the bad influence a guy like me would bring to his warm and loving Freshmen. The high school remember, was only those last three years. Before I could go into any response of self-defense, he quickly mentioned that the biggest factor was that 9th graders were much too mature to be positioned so close to the sweet young innocents that comprised the 7th, and 8th grades.

No, he went on, we have a remedy for that. "I've been in touch with those that joyfully see eye to eye on this matter," he added. "It may not be next year, but soon enough, the unruly miscreants of that older age will be packed in with the rest of you hoodlums at the high school," he proudly proclaimed. "I am quite certain of it," he confidently ended it with.

He turned to leave with a sense of satisfaction that even I draw from to this day. Wow! With him taking a walk around the halls even further, I seemingly had permission to wait for the bell inside. What a day it was. Eddie the drummer from the Catholic Grade School, was now a public school student. I was there for the formal announcement! My band was back together after more than ten years of my forming it.

Indeed, it was without their one true leader that they had come back together. Nonetheless it was almost like a dream come true. They had reformed after all that time quite naturally in a way, depending on how you look at it. There was a fellow down the way that was trying to get something going on his own.

When his parents would go away, he would hold a jam party. We came to understand at some point that his true goal was strictly a personal one. Yet he was cool about how things went during that particular bash. So, here it was. "Tonight, dude's house, no prob'," I was quickly informed. He's cool, so I can come! As for the playing of the drums? Yes, it was most certainly the guy from church on Sunday, with his family, or ours, so often taking the front pew.

We knew the father at our supper table from the day he stood up and spoke to the whole congregation. After the new priest offered for such an opportunity, asking if anyone, anyone at all had a comment, dude stood up. It was his rough gravelly voice that we truly remembered for years! It was that, and the fact that on most Sundays again, it was either his family or ours, that would sit front and center.

There was at least one-fourth barrel if not a half, to start things out. In an open jam each drummer would play on the same set, but if you were tipped off about the setup, one would have considered bringing their own bass, or guitar. The festivities kicked off, and the music began. When all was said and sung, my band was back together, sadly though again, without me. One other thing of note did occur upstairs in one of the bedrooms on that evening.

The truth be told, the upper Midwest has been known as a desert of good high-quality voices when it comes to rock bands. Sure, we've had a few emerge since then, none though, are known as having the most beautiful or distinct vocals at all. Styx from Chicago, being one of the few exceptions of note, was therefore in my opinion, a very lucky group. When a female voice upstairs was heard getting ready, one can imagine therefore, a tad of excitement was felt.

The other guitar player was the younger brother of the two I had approached down the way a few miles from home. Indeed, even his older bro tried to get himself in on the action, alas the only band that I recall having three guitar players was the rock group WishBone Ash. That memory was based on a video from TV with the song I Thought I Had aGirl. It still remains to me one of the greatest songs of the early 70s. Things were coming together and I was invited to the brother's home to sit in on a practice.

It was sweet. Every aspect was beautifully performed, from the hard driving bass to the sweet sting of the lead. It was there all together to enjoy. I wondered how well I could sing, but somehow become embarrassed even though no one was around. I put any further ideas of horning in on the whole ordeal away for the time being.

1976

At the start of that sophomore year, I had started to more regularly hang out at night with friends. There was Brownie, Joe and sometimes his brother, and a kid that had met my older brothers down at his dad's bar in the old neighborhood. As well as those few, my younger half-sister (the accident visitation baby if you will, who was about a year older) who happened to be dating Joe's brother, another girl whose sister was a friend of my older sis', and on occasion Ann who encouraged the words to the Van Halen song Panama.

I sang it to her from out of nowhere one day like this, "Pan-anna-ma, Pan-anna-ma-ah-ah-ah-ah." Somehow, when I would go into one of my writing modes, it made the others feel uncomfortable. Oh well. One gal with big bright red hair was so huggable I went for it. She was somehow insulted a bit, and put off. I really meant it. She was just a tad overweight, yet with it in all of the right places, I needed to restrain myself. To this day I can still imagine myself rubbing my hands all over her gorgeous red-hot bod'.

One day Joe's brother thought that he could have a private conversation about my oldest brother right in front of my face. He was talking about musicians and songs and such. The bar owner's son shushed him twice. Then after dude says, "it was nothing, I was just visiting some older guy down the way in the old part of town," I said, "Oh him, I know him." I began to reel off my own work.

Joe's brother repeated, "No, no, no I don't know that one, that one either," at which point the bar owner's son said, "Alright, not even one of those has been recorded by any band at all, so, shhhhhhhhh, you need to keep it cool." It wasn't long after it had come out that my older brother was one of dude's friends, that my good brother showed up. He had some type of secret message for me, yet even though he was the good one, I felt something was fishy, and didn't trust him.

He beckoned me over several times. The way he was off to the side at the edge of the woods, I felt that anything he had to say he could say in front of the new gang, which was actually quite an experienced group. If you'll recall I refused to skip to hang out with my nephew and him. What was it that he needed to tell me? He soon gave up and went back home. Soon enough the other two showed up. These were the two that gave me trouble from day one.

That was at my own grandma's house, rather than at our dad's cousin's house just down the street. Here they were carrying gifts of kindness or so it seemed. Yet they had convinced everyone to harass me, and to be against me. Even passing me the doobie, they continued to berate me in such unkind and unfriendly terms.

I do not understand what it was all about, but my eldest brother knew I was a total genius, and he knew that I was a total rock star, so why would he wish to wreck my new friendships, and the brotherhood that I was developing on my own? I could after some thoughtful introspection think of only one answer.

He too could see into the future, and he was doing everything possible to change the course of my life, rather lamely at that, I have to proclaim. I'm an adult yet think back at all of the failings of myself and others. Alas today is a whole new day. I stand before you (well, sitting at my tax desk) now as a new being. I am strong. I am capable. I am wise.

I shall not be hindered any longer in my endeavor to enlighten the minds of any and all who can perceive of my honorable, and altruistic messages. It was about two weeks later that my eldest brother told the members of the band that Father and I had put together, that they sucked and would never make it. The guys were good about it, and let him spew and go on about their chances before he walked off.

He said not a word to me. Well, the band hadn't even had a chance to practice more than one time or so, up to that point. Nonetheless, he was dead on when it came to that bit of truth. I still think about getting us back together. Maybe not all at once, yet if four of us can play keyboard too, in addition to our basses, and guitars, we could perhaps make it work.

With my old bass player no longer with us, and he having left Joe's ex behind as his very own widow, I need to ready myself for an eventual talk. The female vocalist Colleen, from the jam party upstairs, was more than adequate. She would indeed go on to enter with the group into the Battle of the Bands, and is on one of their best songs recorded from around 1978–79. Things in life happen, some good, some bad, and Colleen moved out to the country.

Even, yet other things, would happen some more. The group would be at one point searching for the next greatest voice ever, once more, and once again. That most certainly would not be me. Nor sadly would it be anyone else alive in this world today. Not anyone from the vocal desert around here known as the Midwest anyway.

It was a Sunday. Upon loading into the family car, it was decided that we would stop at the local pancake house for some brunch. Upon entering the establishment who should we see waiting to be seated? It was the family from two doors down, the family that kept their fishing rods separate from the reels when not in use. Mother struck up a mild conversation about how things were going. Finally, expecting to hear about college, and dorm living, or words to that effect when she asked about the tall thin brother, things went sour. He's no longer with us, came the answer.

He committed suicide, a while back, his mom had added. It will be a year next month, she offered. My stomach dropped. I nearly became physically ill just a bit. I pulled back only slightly; I then turned my head. I felt too uncomfortable to be any part of it. I did my best to push it all away. It came back up once more inside me during the meal, but I was able to keep trucking. Even now the memory of that moment, coming to terms with someone's suicide is unpleasant.

I mean it was, even though my welts were inches wide from that unreeled fishing pole. I could never wish upon someone such a sorrowfully tragic fate. The lonely emptiness enshrouding my heart was somehow real. Yet it was that reality of someone else's life that allowed me to let it ripple, wane, and then to so surely die away. With its fading into one of yesterday's quiet memories, I am once more relieved.

It was the coldest winter that winter could ever get. It often dipped below 20°, even 0°, here and there it did anyway. As long as one dressed warmly with t-shirts, long sleeved shirts, and sweaters or sweatshirts underneath, and a good heavy coat, the bitter chill was abated. Something had come over me though. I was wired but was either completely straight, or trying to catch a buzz off of some cheap Mexican.

It went on for days. Finally, I laid in bed listening to whatever eight tracks I had. The player was a new gift for Christmas. Headphones as well were included so I could keep going all night. After a while I switched to the radio. It was a Jeff Beck tune that really got me. I arose wide eyed and bushy tailed not having slept for three full days now. The Beck tune was still pumping through my veins. I saw my sister's mother in-law on the bus, and was sure to say hi.

Normally I was more laid back, and even shy, but who cared I was jacked, and loving it. The day went normally. I had arranged to pick up a quarter pound on consignment from Little Man. I met him in the men's room and we did the exchange. I had worn bib overalls to more easily transport the goods back home. It looked a bit like I was Junior Sample from the TV comedy show Hee-Haw.

Upon finally making it through the day the stash was hidden, and all would be fine. Or so I thought. That night I was losing the ability to deal with things in a normal and casual fashion. I left the house, and just kept walking. I found a pen on the ground at one point, and squeezed out the ink all over one thumb. I walked up to a public grade school, and peered inside. There was a small demon figure on the teacher's desk. Probably a gift from a loved one with some private meaning attached. I momentarily freaked on it. I mean my brain got shot through with bolts of excited electricity. An immediate impulse of manic fear was deeply felt.

I walked quickly away and shrugged it off, asking myself what if any serious meaning the episode held. I walked, and walked, for hours. I cannot recall how I got there but I ended up in the interior of a Police Department interrogation room. They tried to get as much information as possible to assist me in getting home, or with anything else that I truly needed. I only had one response for each question that they threw at me. "You know, you know. You know," is all that I had for them.

Finally, two more officers from the hall after apparently hearing my approach entered the room. It became like a game. "You know, you know," again was all I said. When the room was jam packed with up to ten or twelve of them, I started to panic a bit, and you may well understand why. The shock of being outnumbered had snapped me out of the malaise enough to cause fear, yet I thought why stop now, I can't change it for the last two.

Motorcycle cops they were with tough looking jackets, and body sizes to match. They had my father's P-coat, purchased second-hand from my mom's WWII hero brother. There it was then, the opening I needed. When they saw the embroidered name on the inside of the coat, I told them, "No, that was my uncle's coat, we're the Penns."

They called my parents who were somewhat worried, and the nightmare had ended. When we all got back home, I was completely out of it, even more so than when the evening had begun. I was called to a private family meeting at the kitchen table. It was the police, father then had mentioned, that offered an alternative. That involved taking me to the local psyche ward.

The desk sergeant felt that it would be better if the folks brought me in, rather than the uniformed police officers. It would have been looked at as a more serious occurrence, potentially involving leather straps that are nearly just as serious as metal chains. Being brought in under custody I mean, may have allowed for those in charge to assume that I was a 'dangerous' sort.

I agreed with the uncomfortable solution, but needed to go into the basement to hide the weed I had smuggled home, in a better spot. My movement into the lower chamber only created further suspicion. Now I was not only held, a captive of psychiatry, but within days the parental units had found my stash.

Once I had stabilized, I was allowed to return back home. I had been made aware, upon arriving there, that the weed had been found and the all of the contraband then duly flushed. I had little option but to accept defeat, with both disappointment, and relief. I mentioned that I had gotten the score on a front, and now owed the dude. "Who knows how he's going to react, with my being back in school, and everything?" was how I certainly put it.

Within days the answer came. Rather than have me further traumatized by the entire fiasco I would be given the $40.00 that it cost for a quarter lb. of Mexican. Fairly inexpensive stuff in comparison to today's market I would say. I mean I imagine so; I would certainly have no true idea how those things did work. My assumption would have been surmised based on some casual reading in an explicit article from High Times Magazine, something purchased quite legally mind you at a nearby convenience store.

My parents did never come to terms with the fact that dude was 'Dan-Dan The Little Man', or just plain 'Little Man', as he became known to the others at school. He truthfully stood at about 5'2", and dated what may have been the smallest Irish girl in school as well. She was all of 4'11" if that. I'm certain while it lasted it was a great, and grand opportunity to have some social contact with the opposite sex, and get to know a person a little closer than what was otherwise so readily available.

As far as the recoupment of losses, Little Man held a party, and thanked me readily for catching him back the way I that did. I here and now, can only reveal the entirety of truths since he is sadly no longer with us. They found him unconscious and OD'd on the living room chair one early morning. No doubt the hard partying and his smaller body size had everything to do with that sudden end to his very young life. I still feel my very hand so deeply, well into, the entire fatality of things for him. A part of my heart and mind goes sour at the thought of it.

Within weeks of my first bout, I had experienced another binge of insomnia. I was quickly shipped back out to the County Grounds. Upon my next arrival home after a miraculous and hasty recovery, I set up another score. My parents felt that I should be escorted, back, and forth to visit with this friend. Once back in lockup, I quickly opened a clothes cabinet and torched up. The coat Father had purchased for my Christmas gift had a secret entrance to the lining.

This green Official Naval issue command jacket would do well for my stash. It managed to go undetected with the remainder of the nickel bag slyly hidden inside. That item of contraband was so named based on the actual cost of $5.00. They did bust me though, without any police action involved, for the other un-smoked half of the doob' that I had so quietly torched.

One fun thing that was offered at the loony bin was art class. I was allowed to make a super-bowled love pipe. It could have held a nickel bag, or two. That was 1/3 of an ounce, or 2/3. From out of the bowl, one on each side, were extra wide stems. It was by law that I was not allowed to take it home. The fact that I could express my very own self in that way was indeed a therapeutic activity.

So, this gal, the art therapy instructor was the nicest one there. I let her know in no uncertain terms that I was interested. She finally ended up married to the nicest man that worked there as well. That summer, I was required to see a therapist of my very own. It was a bummer because it was so far away. I remember their saying that I would be sensitive to light. I believe that is from the song by Ronnie James Dio.

It was over all too quickly and then back to the books once September rolled around. I remember hearing the band <u>Heart</u> for the very first time that summer. It was otherwise just about hanging out and groovin' to it. We would loll upon the grass of the nearby park with only music for our minds. As long as I was willing to walk the four miles to the counselor it looked like things would be alright, at least for a while they really were.

The rock band Kansas was playing down at the old live theater. On a lark, just after supper I asked Father if he would put up the *buckage*, and drop me off as well. He grinned a loving grin that only a true music lover could offer at the time, then popped a fifty out of his wallet, and asked, "Now, when?"

"Why yes then, as soon as I can get my coat, and brush my teeth quickly, anyways," I excitedly replied.

I pasted up, threw my warmer jacket on and we were off. He exited off from the expressway, and pulled in front. "There are two girls I know," I exclaimed in a very pleasant voice. He smiled once more in that special way and I nearly laughed aloud as I opened the door then thanked him. Kim and Carol were two of the more attractive girls from school. Each lived just off of the main street on the way to school.

We had triple dated with Joe, Blackie's cousin, their other girlfriend Sue, and myself. The other friend was a big girl with wonderful soft flesh. Huggable so, she was, with her perfectly average, yet taller body. Emm-emm. I get good feelings just thinking about her. "No car, no problem," I still say, if only all of the girls did still say that too, now that they're over 16 and all I mean.

I had from time to time considered asking either of these other two sweeties out, yet could never get myself beyond that stage of our love. The part I mean with me simply contemplating. Here indeed was another opportunity, and they gave me skips so we could sit together. They acted surprisingly warm, and I was truly near-Vanna with the entirety of how things had played out so splendidly, wondrously, and so very well filled, with a common gayety, merriment, and such a joyous sense of mirth.

I mean that several groups of friends, and acquaintances were scattered about the area, and even Blackie's cousin, and another buddy showed up just like that. Dude had some doobage so we went along the river's edge that offered a place not only out of the wind, but apart from any intruding eyeballs. We went in and I sat down with a girl on each arm. I will include a picture of myself showing the only other time that I honestly felt such a higher and royal honor.

I mean for certain that the loving glow of two fine ladies in the handsome company of an appreciative young man is warmer than any man who's not had the privilege, could ever even consider. Now, one needs to amplify that special love due to it being the band Kansas that was to perform. They being a group with decent vocals, heavy enough guitar, cool-cool keyboards, and to boot, a violin player, made this a kickin' experience.

I had to use the bathroom, and ran into Blackie's cousin while in there. He had more doobage going so we hit it some more. Now for those who were not privy to such engagements, this was common practice back in the day, and not anything one would engage in lightly these days, especially at the summer festival. Down there they have dudes looking all cool for one reason, and one reason alone.

That's to bust your sorry ass like a bomb being dropped right on your dippy little head. I've heard from several blokes about that very thing, I'll tell ya'. David Lee Roth's song <u>Goin' Crazy</u> is about people being busted for swimming down there! Now had a rolled-up marijuana cigarette, and handcuffs, and you're about home I'd say!

So, here is where the whole thing falls apart. My heart said, "Go back to the girls," but my now super buzzed head told me "To sit with my homies." Upon further review maybe dude was just so totally jealous, having gone out with both of those two beauts, that he merely lured me away from them with a warm invite, seeing how they had an extra seat and all.

In the back of my mind, I somehow knew what I had done. I did not find out until the next day at school from Carol, that the two were never more insulted or put off, in their lives before. All that I could do was apologize, and rue that moment's bad judgement. Here I have finally come to terms with the facts at hand. None of us had a car. I was soon to be 17, Brownie would be, by summer's end, Kay and Carol, both 16, had no jobs at all. I, an old good friend from days gone by, coincidently run into the pair, and am filled with a sense of grace, goodness, glee, and outright gayety.

My overwhelmingly positive emotional state came from one source. My having run into school chums outside of our regular studies is what made me so pleased, and satisfied on that special day. As an alternative to my selfish actions, I may have done my best to 'invite' my lady friends in on the action. I knew for myself good and well that Brownie could not hold such an insistence on his own, for exes as they both were, it would have made for an uncomfortable situation.

I bailed on them not once but twice, then therefore. I did so at the entrance as they saved my spot, and then again in the men's room. In going back in time, only cranially mind you, any number of possibilities may present themselves. Men, if you are young enough, tell your sons the truth. A lady will always hold more of a prominence, especially after all is said and done, then any homey, bro', buddy, pal, or any other friend ever could. One merely needs to keep things situated and separated the right way is all.

Togetherness is everything. I had that already, at point one. Friends don't bail on other friends. (duh) One especially shouldn't if two of those are of the female variety. In holding on to that one true thing, friends are friends, the end result will always be fruitful. You can add things like (I honestly *stopped myself* both that night, and the next morning) "certain possibilities may play themselves out, as long as you can hang back and let them develop."

Not necessarily on their own mind you, but patience is a true virtue. To be honest, I did, and still do, love both of those girls as people. Yet, when being honest, they would win a contest against Brownie on any given day, I mean it. As long anyway, as the two weren't holding a place in line, while Brownie pulls around the corner with some good stuff.

1977

That new year didn't fair me any better than the last. Perhaps it was something about the cold, cold air. Though, aren't people supposed to sleep more in the bitter freezing days of winter's blast? I have noticed from time to time that in the fall with all of the warmth from this area now blown away, I've curled up on the sofa, and nodded off. Upon awakening I've recovered, and am ready for what the weather brings. No doubt this transformation is due to my Norwegian genes. I saw a man on TV from the north of the Norwegian region. He showed how they dug holes in the snow, and buried some food for preservation. Just watching that PBS special made me sleepy.

One of our new pals from the area had a job. He claimed that they were actually looking for help. I considered the thought of having some pocket cash on more of a regular basis. I asked again, then had a quick interview set up. Other than the paper route, which was actually not my own, I had only worked at that corner gas station as far as real work was concerned. I eagerly accepted nonetheless, and started soon after.

My first week there, I was tripping. I got off at least some based on an incident there. A tiny spray of bubbling hot cooking oil bounced onto my forearm. I hesitated then stared. Finally, and quickly wiping away the hot oil allowed for something. I knew that I was grooving at that point.

There were standards to be met, and orders to carry out nonetheless. One responsibility that I shared involved making the chocolate and vanilla creams. I so quickly lost my urge for those formerly yummy treats. You see, cream here refers to whipped cow fat. Without the pounds of sugar added, that is so honestly is all that it is, that would fill the creamy donuts. Yuk! I otherwise could handle the duties, and even felt some satisfaction from my work. Alas, I was not created to work on this earth in the food industry. Please remind me, if need be, the next time I apply! I quit there before the second month.

I hadn't changed my habits at all since my insomnia took control a year before. It was happening again. I was put away, and would remain until the spring. Since they had done everything possible to return me to my home during the previous term, they weren't going to make the same mistake again. A full course of treatment had been ordered. By that April, I was back at home but taking the long bus ride every day to the school they ran for all of us. My lost junior year could only be found in one place. That would be the local children's psyche' facility.

For the Easter Holiday, my friend from down the way, the one that almost died when our sisters had brought home the flu back in 1960, asked if I'd like to visit has brother's cattle ranch. It was about 95 miles west. According to him the air was so clean out at his brother's place, one would become nearly ill upon returning from an extended stay. That queasy feeling came from the foul air that we even then, on a daily basis, had been breathing in. I eagerly and joyously obliged and packed for the trip.

His mom took us out in the 1962 Cadillac. There is nothing better than a nice long car ride out in the country with somewhere to actually go. We neared our destination. As we closed in on his brother's place my pal had a word of warning. Right across the street there were, potentially anyway, rattlesnakes. They're known as timber rattlers.

With one wrong move one may lash out. He assured us to not worry, and claimed, "That's what boots are for." Just as we pulled around before the drive, a large stag standing upon the turnaround noticed our presence, and moved on up the bluff. Well, that's what hooves are for too, I imagined, as this rather large male made his way through the brush and up the rocky terrain.

The first day started early. I had to fork a pile of hay that had fallen from a wagon. It was more like scraps, but I was fine. Any work is work when it's a ranch. I picked, and scraped, and picked, and picked. That wasn't enough. The elder brother came out and let me know just that. I let him know I sure did see the blades that were being reluctant, and went right back to work. After another 15 minutes I had felt it was finally now futile, and crossed my fingers.

Winner, winner, pasta dinner. I was good. I went into the house, and noted the elder's wife was busy at the kitchen table. She was a part-time school teacher, but well adept at all things homemade. She was, I could see, making flat noodles from scratch. "Stroganoff," she gladly imparted, "will be tonight's meal." I can still taste those yummy soft, smooth noodles now. They were so fresh and tender, and so eagerly yet elegantly, welcomed by the tongue. Yum-yum.

We ventured back outside. The business partner had just arrived with a load of baby pigs. Neither of these former college buddies wanted anything to do with them. We just needed to get all of the pigs together on the same vehicle for transport. They were apparently trying to make as much money as possible on the side, utilizing any resources available. These little rascals would make us work for every penny. They were wild and running frantically.

The partner let me know to just punch them in the gut "like this one needs right here," he motioned, before laying into the baby porker good time. "Don't worry, they'll get the message, but won't really feel it," he assured me. I tried to hit a couple of them hard, but just didn't have it in me. Once they saw daylight, thankfully, they ran right past. It was coming right off of the first truck that a few were just a little confused wanting to go right back on. Whew thank goodness that was over quickly enough.

While there, my friend with the way older brother goes into a story from long ago. Supposedly his brother and the business partner along with another buddy from college hatch this plan to go and buy a quarter lb. in Mexico. Because of the exchange rate you'd end up with free weed after finding another student to go in on it with you. They made the buy like it was ice-cream on the corner. Once back in Texas the driver made a lane change without using his directional. You guessed it, Captain Bucky. They were busted.

So, these three were all put in one of the toughest jails in the U.S. They had to call their parents for bail money, and on top of that this sounds kind of wild, they were issued what was termed 'butt-plugs'. My pal seemed quite serious, we other two just groaned. This action was apparently, so that none of the long-term gays, or guys rather, could intrude upon their short stay. Remind me to use my directional when passing through that town, hey! Right?

At the country dinner table, we got the news. There was a one-day teaching job in town, and the two lovebirds would take a little break by staying overnight. We were to be like men, all grown up, mature, and to not ruin anything while the lovebirds were away. No problem we let them know, and offered an oath of allegiance. First thing the next day, my buddy asks if I can lift 100lbs. He then pointed to the grain sack he was filling, letting me know that another scoop or two would get it there.

I hefted it up with no struggle, and began to move toward the fence line. He walked along with me, offering this caveat "okay the hefting part is just fine, only you have to lift it up 4 and one half feet over the barbed wire then dump it into their trough without spilling any. I was so close to getting there, no wonder he mentioned specifically about spillage. The feat was nearly impossible." He checked later saying upon seeing me, "Well you did spill just that little bit, as long as my brother isn't here, we should be okay."

"Hopefully," he added, "The cattle can get around to finding that spot, and all will be good."

"My exact thoughts as well," I cheerily replied, and the day went back to chores, or did it?

My friend's brother was in charge of another place. This older biker dude was their monetary sponsor. He preferred to be in Florida for the most part so we needed to go feed his chickens, and make sure everything was doing well. We pulled up and parked. Over in the yard across from the drive were some feathered friends running about, and clucking. They were rascally sorts, and ran in all directions as we drew nearer. Something otherwise caught our attention.

The ugly chickens were jealous of the older prettier gal, and had set upon her furiously. One took a last second poke at the top of her head just before they all scattered. Her beautiful brain was exposed, yet she was only capable of lovely thoughts on her own. We just couldn't figure it. Didn't they know that they were all just a bunch of dumb chickens? The smaller gals were maybe half breeds or something, yet without any rooster at all.

Why the unneeded beauty contest was being held was of no sense to me. We thought for a while. Putting the big pretty gal inside a small tool shed nearby seemed to be good solution. We searched for bags of chicken food but to no avail. It was then back to headquarters, and a phone call. His brother didn't call us a bunch of dumb clucks, I don't think, but informed my buddy that chickens have their own style of euthanasia.

We were also at the wrong farm. It was the place that the baby pigs had come from that we needed to tend to. We had to go to the more rundown house then, to feed those chickens. My pal felt that those hens could wait, but it didn't mean we couldn't check the old place out first. Or did it? We piled into the rundown pickup truck, and headed over.

Just as we crossed into the drive it was, "oh, oh, I think we've got a flat," which came from the driver's seat. We piled out, and sure enough indeed, one tire had no air. The cool crisp calm of the night was clean and invigorating. Initially it wasn't the worst thing we could possibly have faced. We had a spare alright but no jack. After putting our heads together for no more than an hour, a jack materialized and we were back on our way.

The next day things were brighter in the midst of the noonday sun. We opened the door to the coop, and low and behold, there the pretty little ground birds nesting. They had one boyfriend to keep the fertile eggs to a minimum. We just had to find the bags of feed, dump some of that out, and we'd be on our way, lickety-split. We searched, and searched, to and fro, all to no avail.

"How about this," I offered, "Here this looks right, it says Royster on the side of the bag, so that must be rooster food, right?" At that point we were 100% sure we had hit pay dirt. Let me impart here that we had better weed out there in the country as it was not just simple Mexican. The bag of Royster food was cut open, and the goodies inside dispensed. We were higher than kites, and feeling victory.

Later on, my friend's brother and wife returned from their little second honeymoon. The man of the house was stern but steady. We had to go do some "chicken-pickin'." It turns out that the Royster Fertilizer Company doesn't really make chicken food after all, and the harmful effects of their having ingested so much of it, would be of an unknown quotient. He gave us several burlap sacks, and sent us out to do our duty. I was just fine with it.

That was because I had what might have been considered disco style army boots. They had 3-inch heels, yet were styled after commando boots. I was ready to make amends, and then some. These were no hybrid skinny birds. No, they were like super-athletic birds all hopped up on steroids, or maybe it was just fertilizer. We noted that the male was attacking us, or nearly so, each time that we tried to grab one of his gals.

I had my two buds distract him enough, and grabbed a big fat hen firmly but gently holding down her wings. It was into the bag, then again. We had corralled nearly every one of the things, but the lower the count had gotten, the more ferocious, and fierce old big boy was getting. He had three wives left, and wasn't giving them up for anything. I mentioned that we really needed to give it our best effort or we'd be dragging it back to the shack, with our tails between our legs.

We gave it one last valiant go ahead. I asked for those two to distract the raging cock so I could lunge at an available hen. Yet it was all to no avail. Mayhem with farm fowl was certainly not our specialty. No one wants to mess with a hyper wild-man who's simply protecting his last three honey cluckers. We returned to home base a bit sheepish. These birds needed to be quarantined. So, up into the barn's attic they went until further notice.

My friend's mom had arrived and would stay the night. We'd all go back together in the morning. She had the air going for at least the last half of the ride home. I was dropped off in front of my home, and sure enough, it smelled rotten. There was a mix of hot asphalt, and overall pollution that was unmistakable. While I had to return to school at the psyche ward, my pals were out of school for an extended period because of the teacher's strike. So, they went right back to the 'easy' country living we had so joyously shared. I truly couldn't wait for summer.

It was a Wednesday. I picked up the evening paper, and began to page through the front-page section. Something of a grand proportion was being offered in a multiple issue story. The subject was Drug Induced Psychosis. My brain immediately began to question my very own state. I readily dismissed the thought, and began to read.

The main human subject of the article on day one had done something that could easily be looked at as a source of his woes. He had used angel dust for about ten to fourteen days straight. That stuff, as I have mentioned, was again, basically animal tranquilizers sprayed onto mint leaves. The rebounding human mind apparently can't take such sedation.

This episode in his high school life took him down into the very depths of hell itself. It was the demons that I do believe in, or the insane dead as I call them, that entered his mind in search of his eternal soul. Remember, they do exist, and the only way for them to enter this earth is through the human mind. At the end of his binge, he took the life of his dear mother. In painful shock, astounded horror, and a sorrowful sense of grief, I came to terms with what had transpired to this sorrowful fellow.

Again, though, I dismissed the possibility that I was as well, one of those individuals. Those poor unfortunates were termed as otherwise normal, even successful people who would not have exhibited any symptoms of mental illness whatsoever, if it were not for one thing, the steady and frequent use of _non-prescribed_ medications.

The article went on for days. Each one identifying what would have been considered an average every day person. I had finally realized fully that I was no doubt one of them. I suppose that it was my pride, and an uncontrollable desire to feel high, that allowed me to dismiss the findings as specific to others, yet probably not at all involving me. That was my lie. At least upon the first reading of that series, I had failed to connect the dots. It would be years before I was able to fully face the truth. Those times would be filled with abject failure, and a stunting loneliness as you will so quickly come to see.

Life went on as usual for me the rest of that year. My Polish buddy, yes, the one whose dad owned a bar in the old neighborhood had finally gotten his very own driver's license. He threw out the fake I.D. he had procured from some deep, dark mysterious outlet. Though, probably from my eldest brother is where he got his hands on such a thing. He had a red station wagon, again I wouldn't doubt if there was some connection there as well.

We both had discovered something wild and enjoyable the previous winter when practicing driving with his new machine. I know it's silly, and we were grown men, or least he was or almost was, but when the snow plows had failed to do an adequate job, and he took the turn a little too tight, one of us would call out, 'BAJA' in a really high voice which would result in the both of us laughing, and giggling like a couple of silly school girls.

Now we had matured. With the days of wanton silliness behind us it was time to get real. He picked me up to engage in some additional practicing. Spring had warmed the air to a delight. Only weeks of school lay ahead. The road was ours and we were young. As we neared our destination, he informed me that because the area was known as a party spot, he thought that he might get in a little practice.

Well, getting pulled over is what he meant without coming right out with a blazing banner. Being able to simply drive, in a calm manner and sober state, is a skill that becomes well developed with practice. You can easily imagine that 'buzzed' driving requires careful practice as well. As we pulled in to park, he added, "Because all of the action is over there, and I don't really want to deal with any of that, we'll park here and see how it goes."

"How does that sound?" he asked.

"Sounds good to me," I quickly answered. I could tell at this point that although he wanted to master being pulled over, there was no ready reason to actually tempt fate so closely, and unto us. In such the pleading and desperate fashion, we were in, there was no reason to push it, right?

The thing was, if we safely hung back, and even quietly approached the frisky area, we would have an advantage in that respect. "Or should we just call it a day, and casually walk back to the car," we had considered as well. Resisting any draw toward all of the excitement and engaging in anything else that we really wanted to do, would be a ready option. After all, we were free, and a young life was ours.

Fate had something else in mind. We heard some scrambling, and running, then two men drew closer. He at first noticed it was just a couple of bros. I suddenly realized it was my next-door neighbor, and the other fellow from down the block. They both recognized him from school as well. It went like, "Okay we have a second let's rest a bit." As we began to calculate our movements, upon determining the available route, we were filled in with the stunning details.

The cops decided to have a raid on that particular evening, and what really set 'em off was the way one guy got away in full hand cuffs. Behind his back, it was, no less. Then everybody was busted, informally though, of course. From what I recall there was hair pulling window smashing, that from a full bottle of PBR no doubt. A sense of wildness, anarchy, panicking, mayhem, fright, shock, and chaos had all so keenly and quickly settled into that area.

The fellow from down the way offered confidently, "I don't know about the guy in the handcuffs, but we're getting out of here."

"And I mean back to our cars, and in them driving," he added. My friend mentioned that we were in the other lot, so we couldn't exactly get back the same way. We decided to split up. They made their way down the cliff to the beach, and we moved back west to safety.

No sooner than when we crouched down to assess the situation did we see bare arms, and a short blue dress shirt. Finally, a cap and night stick came into view. I slowed my breathing, and we waited until he had safely made it beyond our intersection of escape. It was all downhill from there, literally, until just before where the lot was situated. We breathed a sigh of relief, and drove on.

Back at school a couple of the younger lads had suddenly gotten bored. From out of nowhere they began tearing my military-style fall jacket from my very body. Bit by bit, piece by piece, they found a way to remove it from my torso all the while giggling, and laughing like little silly schoolchildren. Okay, we were so totally and completely buzzed, that even I was laughing out loud, but still. This was a bit of a cooler day, and this was only lunch time. They're really lucky that I laughed a lot too.

I had felt all along that my condition had been misdiagnosed by the medical team out at the County Grounds. This was the same general facility that the young nurse who had been recruited to play on General Hospital had been employed. I was going back but needed to get tough, and hold my ground. I had thought about it off and on, and what such a bold move could eventually open the door to.

I felt sure that the drugs being given to me, simply so that I would not lie awake for up to three days, were somehow harmful to me. I had braced myself for any type of resistance. Just after this doctor from the Middle East injected me with a three-month supply, I let him know. "This is it, you'll never see me again," my firm statement was laid out before him.

He smiled, and offered adieu. Seeing that I was not involved in any court ordered action he had no other choice. I got up and walked out, relieved that the nightmare was over. I informed Father of my staid determination. He offered a slight smile with a side of confidence. In nine short months, I would be 18. I was on my own as far as my mental health was concerned. The final verdict would wait.

My good buddy Joe had a school project coming up. He was to create an animation by hand, or otherwise create an actual short movie, about 10 to 12 minutes in length. I so quickly recalled my oldest sister and her efforts along those lines. She would lie upon her bedroom floor, with her face pulled close, and a hand bracing for each delicate movement. She, back in the day, chose the easier method of project fulfillment.

That option, because of the times, was actually one of the most difficult things a young high school student could ever engage in. The procedure involved drawing, in fine line magic marker, an animation film. Each particular cell had to be meticulously created separately on its own. If you understand fully the concept of animation, you so readily comprehend the execution required. You see, to create the smooth sensation of movement, each subsequent image must be only slightly different from the previous.

If one fails with such an approach, a sense of jumpy hyper action would so surely ensue. Only SouthPark the animated series intentionally jerks things around like that. With such a needful requirement in mind, and an actual camera available otherwise, it had all been prearranged. We would film at my buddy's father's place, the one with the hobby farm.

I would ride the donkey while wearing a sombrero that hung from his father's living room wall. A genuine item purchased on one of his dad's trips abroad. I mounted old Jerry, as filming progressed. We needed two antagonists and my two pals quickly obliged. In no time the footage was complete. Only, hanging the sombrero back up after all of those years in place was another story.

With just the slightest bad move it fell from its nail again, and again. Finally, the hardest part of that day of filming had come to a completion. The hat stayed up and we tip-toed across the floor, and on and out the door. In no time at all the film had come back. With a giddy sense of excitement, and no doubt a gleeful sense of accomplishment for the others, our debut playback day had arrived. It became nearly like a professional endeavor for us all, as my buddy cued up the projector.

The light went on and the starring playback of my character's role had so quickly begun. A little too quickly to say the least! Before the light could be turned off, and the rolling of the projector halted, I so frightfully began a comedic duet with Jerry the donkey. I first got on so slowly. Only laughter was an option for that scene. Then after riding him just a bit forward, and flashing a criminally-mustachioed grin, my image began to burn, turning into fire before my very eyes.

Right then and there the last visage of my cinematic greatness melted away into nothingness. Right before my very eyes forever, and ever, and ever, I would die away a faded star. The speed of the projector was actually running too slowly rather than too quickly. It was so that the heat from the lamp had caused the film to melt. Nonetheless, it seemed an omen or yet so worse, a curse.

I got a call from my Farmer Bro. It was set, he had told me, if you got the money we are going. He meant indeed to Chicago Stadium, not a football field for the Bears, but an indoor arena were the Bulls played. Only we were not that much into sports. No, a free-bird must make careful choices when it comes to throwing down his hard-earned cash. $28.00, 28 stinkin' bucks I thought, why it will be my pleasure. You have to go back to my junior year in high school to appreciate what we anticipated.

It was not just the history handed down from the elders but the fact that we spent Easter vacation together while the cattle rancher, I'll call him respectfully had played hoochie-koo with his part-time teacher-wife, in town. He was the brother of that pal whose father worked at the J.C. Penny automotive shop. I call the other 'Farmer Bro'. As his dad who owned Clem & Leena's flower shop, bought the little hobby farm, complete with a hillbilly swimming pool, down the street from where my girl lived. You should recall the rest about those two pals of mine.

So, dude, my old neighbor (or almost neighbor) had his car, a 1971 Dodge Super Bee, if I recall correctly, Bro had his car and we were set. But wait, it had snowed. It was a late fall, early winter storm that covered the earth, and so much more. It was like three quilts, and a blanket of snow. With the drifts, the drop-off, especially on the right of the long, long drive, was clearly undetectable.

To the left the *Ellie May Special,* or outdoor pool, had offered every necessary-guidance, and an outline of demarcation. Nonetheless, just afterward, dudes fell well off track, and were up to Plymouth Logos and beyond, in beautiful, brand-new, glorious, yet so very restrictive, virgin-white freshly laden snow. Bro was asked to go back up to the house to get something, anything that could be of some or any useful, fruitful help.

"Oh no," he said, "I don't need to, here let's see." He was well out of his car, and soon had popped the trunk. We meanwhile had been shoveling frantically in order set the chains of motion into phase II. "Here it is," dude confidently exclaimed. It was a flat set of boards about 16 by 12 inches. My old neighbor, with a noticeable whimper in his voice, had pled "are you sure?"

"Yes," nearly laughing, my farm buddy exclaimed, his surety reached us jubilantly in the night.

"Though, did you ever actually need to use them yourself," I enquired.

"Come on, place these just so," his authority demanded in the evening sparkle.

"Well, how neighbor?" came the question from me.

"Wait here, like that, then, if I need to, I'll just push a little with my car, nicely on the bumper, if you can get it out enough anyway," came the reply from our man.

There was some trepidation having to do with the not so vintage high-quality 10-year-old car. That was so much I believed, more so over the whole affair rather than any one aspect of our dilemma. Now on the second try we made it, and were all on our way. The excitement began to rise as we made our way closer, and closer to town. We noted overpasses, and brick buildings, and sensed the escalation in emotion for us all.

Not quite all that is. As we neared another overpass the driver next to us, muscled us onto the emergency strip that would end in twenty short yards. Let us stop for a moment to consider the act of muscling. One knows good and well when they're being unduly muscled at about 60 MPG. Unless of course you have no concerns whatsoever for any potentially expensive body damage. We faced the cement support wall, while the other car now fiercely challenged. At 55 MPH we stared ahead at impending consequences. I refused to panic. Closer and closer we came, nearer to a certain death.

There was just one catch. We had to ride at first with two wheels on the emergency sidewalk of the tunnel. It was a hard shocker to say the least. Only movies with dramatic and wildly executed car stunts could compare. Finally, *Lane Boy* moved ahead, and with a firm grip of the wheel, my bro pulled hard, and fast. We had made it, and were experiencing the overwhelming joy of the tunnel's embrace. Enough room was available for us to move past that cement wall, and back into said hungry tunnel. A sigh of needed relief, we breathed in welcomingly.

Emerging soon to park for the show, victory was ours. It was an enjoyable experience, with the seats we had, while Neil played songs from his new album. Even though none of us had picked it up, our true appreciation was present. After the show was over it was a whole separate story. We began driving southeast all the way to Indiana. What I say here and now is that such a taller tale should be left for another campfire, a different get together, a separate round, and another day all together.

1978

Lasers discs had arrived. What I had pictured in my mind was now becoming a common reality. A new radio station had sprung up promising to only play CDs as they were titled. It was actually that specific format that all of us were drawn to. We were not yet working full-time, and living at home. All of us audiophiles were into it to the extent that we immediately went in *big-time* for this radio station, and even hard-core. It hardly mattered as far as the logistics, as long as the right bands were being played.

So, we had not one, but three stations now to choose from. We had the original rock station, the one that played foreign bands that my rocking buddies loved so well, the new rock station, and the other new rock station that sadly went down hard, due to the heavy competition. There was even a fourth. It was the local college station playing everything the others chose not to. Those were mainly no-name groups, or alternative bands, as some were noted as being.

Alas, it was that WZKP, the station from 1977 that was the one that had actually had its days numbered. There just wasn't enough of an audience for the advertising to cover the costs. With the discovery then that C.D.s may begin to disintegrate even as early as twenty years after manufacture, their mantle of greatness begins to take a bit of a hit. Take it from me, there will never be anything as bold and beautiful as a clean, crisp, and ever so clearly playing, vinyl record.

There has been a column in the Sunday paper with musical equipment reviews. The man himself brings these stereophonic devices into his home for consideration. What he has offered for those e-tuners is the opportunity to purchase what is referred to as the T-Tube. This device brings back some of the warmth of these downloaded musical numbers, so as to nearly replicate the original deeply harmonic and resonant sound of 'real' music.

My sweet young friend sat at the same table as myself during 8th hour study hall my senior year. She was the same girl that Blackie's cousin seemed to be breaking up with at the school dance back in 1975. For a fleeting moment I toyed with the idea of asking her out, again. I mean it was just the thought of it and merely that.

With her having been exposed by dear friend Brownie as a girl that would even approach a boy, and yes, with even a possible turndown looming, I had felt back then that a certain cooling off period was in order. I never got back around to asking her out for our very first date before the school-year ended. Here once more, we were simply friends. Alas, her sweet, sweet goodness shines on for another. I can be good about it. Here I couldn't help but go back in time to when I actually had a proposal on the docket.

Not only was my reputation shattered at that point, and with her being such a good young girl, I decided to leave her out of my dreams. She hadn't changed a day since we first met. How she knew to come to the grade school playground back in 1975 I'll never now. The only thing that I could possibly fathom in my mind was attempting to lay myself at her feet, and begging her to save me! Allowing her the chance to help with my salvation was the only sure option available.

She did have a brother though, so no doubt Blackie's cousin had invited this young one, back in the old days, and his big sister felt the need to escort this 13 year old fellow away from home. She had slender arms and legs, and smooth beautiful skin. I mean it was of such a wonderful quality, a guy would know instantly of any serious pleasures to be derived from close intimate contact with said epidermal quality. No, was the answer again back then. Sometimes a man just knows when to keep his paws off of the honey jar.

It was once again warm enough to try the outdoor filming of my buddy's class project. I was brought down easy about my lead and starring role not being reprised for this next film. I was fine, and actually appreciative to have the opportunity to play the role of an extra character, or sidekick. We went out for what was termed a probable dress rehearsal. If anything, we had felt that at least we'd be getting some work done that weekend. This time around it was a no-donkeys affair.

I was immediately informed after disembarking from the automobile that our newest project would be a good old-fashioned *western*. We all did our best to disguise the mostly modern winter coats that we had donned. We went through a verbal dry-run, and then the actual feat, without any film being used. It was then decided. We were so damn good as actors, even with the last-minute outfits, because of the genuine firearms, it would become a 'Made in Hollywood' type of affair.

It seemed to come off beautifully. There was only one situation to address. I had flinched not once, but twice during my death scene. "Wasn't that going a little overboard?" I was asked.

"Well, considering that we all die on our side, and that it is presumed that you guys have more than one gun, I only found it natural to be hit by gunfire…twice," I had concluded. I ended it all within the throes of death itself, before giving up my last breath and then very well lying there still, void of any existence on this sin ravaged earth. Yes, I say, I did lie there without even one last breath within me to force the taste of man's failure down my throat once again. It was too late for any further debate, and I was once again a star.

It was so soon now April of my senior year. On a lark I applied for a gas station job at the local Treasure Island auto shop. They were a discount store that was part of chain, until K-Mart and Target finally put them out of business. I was interviewed immediately and hired on the spot. At school they allowed me to skip 8th hour study hall. The shop was just a few blocks down the road. I was now on cloud nine.

Soon after, I stopped in at the local pancake joint. This gorgeous blond who had graduated the year before waited on me. Man. She was smokin' hot. I mean she was a good long step over Jennifer Aniston, with a cuter face, and slighter more rounded figure. Just the thought of her now gets my heart pumpin'. I ordered cherry crepes. A bit on the sweet side, and a little much for a fellow that had learned to skip lunch altogether, but having her finally take my cash as well on that day, made it the spring of my content. Alas, I would never see her again. Not ever.

About a week later, a security guard that was hired to keep kids from skipping out tried to stop me. I told him that I was in a hurry to get to work and did not have my official pass on me. One was supposed to use the main entrance if that was the case, but it was so far out of the way, that it was too much of an inconvenience for me. So, this small, skinny little black man tries to use all of his force and might, to push me back into the school.

It wasn't happening. He then grabs my shirt, tearing into my skin with his extra-long finger nails, and tearing my garment as well. He wasn't man enough. I repeated that I needed to get to work, and didn't have time for the whole ordeal, all of the while walking him backward further, and further toward the sidewalk. He finally relented and relaxed his grip, though not until he drew blood.

Apparently, a vice principal had been watching, as that was indeed his last day of work for the school district. I still bow my head in shame just a bit. Only faith can get one through those tougher times. I prayed for him, for his forgiveness, yet more so, for his very own career going forward. I still feel bad about it, but you can't go back in time to change things like that.

One can only vow to change himself, in order to avoid such issues and complications further down the road. Just a note, while driving past the back of the school, years later, I did notice chains and padlocks on the door just behind the one that I had preferred to use. The school as well, closed the lunch, so that no student was allowed to leave during the day without prior permission involving a note from a parent.

To put the hammer down even further, the new local police station was erected on campus. You could say that we ruined it for the youngsters to come along later. Joe's younger brother was one of those young boys that would unfairly pay the price for our well demanded freedoms. Alas, we do need to very well learn from our mistakes!

The grass grew quickly once again. I decided that I should put my foot down about the young man's lack of participation in such hard-core activities as shoveling a foot and a half of snow, or getting down on one's knees and clipping the grass with a grass scissors along the fence line after a full and complete mow. This was it, I proclaimed so silently to myself. I felt that the situation needed attention. I intended to make the order there and then.

Younger brother had come of age. He would finally now take over all yard chores, to indeed even make up for some lost time. The shoveling could well wait until winter, when it actually did start to snow. It was that he had encountered a thing or two in the recent past. It was nothing so permanent, or disabling that he could not now, after a full recovery, begin to pull his share around the house. One of the injuries involved his underage consumption of alcohol after which he roller-skated into a huge sewer hole.

It was one that was opened up for some minor construction work. The other malady derived I believe from the same sport but was a blow to the elbow, if not even more so, to the ego of himself. The orders had been handed down and there would be no relenting on my behalf, after all I was the one to have taken care of things, for the most part, since I was only 9 years old.

That very next week when I arrived at home, I found a very disturbing bit of circumstances indeed. It was Mother with the mower and not the young boy at all. "I feel the youngster should do very well, and on his own, without a lesson," I proclaimed.

"Well, I'm not giving a lesson," she replied, "I'm just doing it myself."

"What the hell?" I demanded. "So, I can go almost 10 years, and just like that you let him off the hook on the first day?"

"Well, he has those allergies, and…" she defended.

"I was the one with allergies, or don't you even love me at all to notice?" I went on.

"That's it, it's almost done so don't worry about it," she offered in a voice only a caring mother could give. She was good enough about it being her responsibility and not my own any longer. To have ended it, for the most part anyway, was going to be alright at that.

A live show in the local baseball stadium is all that. It was Steve Welsch, fresh from a short stint with Fleetwood Mac, also Foreigner, Nazareth, and Jefferson Starship. When Grace Slick from the Starship walked out on stage, she offered, "Hey, all of you local lobsters." Many, or most, hadn't applied any sunscreen at all, not in time anyway!

I asked the girl, a slightly buxom gal, just next to me, if I could use some of hers. After the last song I said to her, "There's no need to leave so quickly," in a smooth attempt to sound suave and debonair. Because of my lack of a mobile I got stuck at that point, and turned a bit embarrassed. Ahh, the outdoor music experience, with so many people, and such loud amplification, is really such a thrill. That joyful magic still remains for me in its own special way.

It was soon late May of that senior year. I and a couple of the guys had it all planned. We would ride our bikes to school, then, while skipping out of eighth hour, go directly to the lake. That's right, to the party spot. Though, maybe just a bit to the south where it was still much safer. It had been a while since the older kids had hung around, so we didn't anticipate much police action if any at all.

When I arrived at school a grand sense of love, and joy overtook me. All that I had to do was lock up the machine, and to make my way through the day. Well, most of it anyway. It was all business during most of the afterschool ride with a sweet adrenaline surge building. Let me please define any difference.

With sweet adrenaline, it's more like a sugar rush, yet it comes from the drawing closer to something special.

We decided to make camp temporarily at the height of the cliff, underneath the giant oak. It was the young dude from out of town that rode along. With his older twin brothers being more business-like and total straights, it was he, I, and Blackie's cousin on this trip. We relaxed in the shade, and felt the beauty of our surroundings. It was more than peaceful; it was more than tranquil it was more than wonderful.

Here it was quite honestly beyond words, so I should probably end this sentence right away. From out of nowhere seemingly when I had my back turned, the sky took on an ominous glow. I had never experienced anything like it before. I moved to rub my eyes, yet hesitated. I felt the requisite urgency to more clarify, and identify what exactly it was that had birthed itself upon a third of the early evening sky.

It seemed to be a once in a lifetime happening. It was the perfect and lovely combination of sunset, clouds, and the reflection upon the water's waves themselves. What had showed itself, as if from out of nowhere, was magical. The clouds, you see, where somehow reflecting the sunset, while the waves played, and danced upon that shimmering surface of the sky as well.

This was a triage of connection, offering an elegance of optical delight, twinkling, pulsing, throbbing, and moving. What made it so, were the distinct colors in that scheme, perhaps, even though salmon are more so ocean fish, their colors on that day sure hit town in a spectacular fashion, as if to make a bold type of statement.

In this dramatically beautiful scenic bit of splendor, those special hues starred in a showing of sheer and utter delight. Though to be precise, each of the water's elongated triangular waves set a template. Upon that template was reflected the light from the west. That reflection in turn bounced upon the clouds, twinkling and glowing dramatically. Though what made it so nearly unbelievable was that each rectangle had a different color.

Not to confuse you, it was like a Celtic pattern, of sideways triangles. I mean to be more specific, like sideways diamonds from playing cards these twinkling shapes had become intertwined, and magically connected. With that complexity of fusion, every other pulsating figure was either salmon pink, or green. Each of these mysterious shapes was held somehow together by a blended hue, offering the sensation of completeness that was so dramatically enchanting.

Soon enough the beer had arrived. The main carrier was like a big Viking fellow, though perhaps just German. We noted the light buoyancy, and eager cheer in his voice. The group was hefting along a half barrel. One more push, and the article was positioned. We called down that we would join them. I quickly asked the first, "Do you see that?" Then the next, and again I needed to hear it from another of them. I wasn't hallucinating after all.

A great sense of school hood joy welled up a bit inside me, as my feet wobbled sinking into the sand. Others were now joining us. Their clamoring voices filled with glee, as they made their way along the path. I needed to keep it a secret that some of us were tripping on acid. I had determined it would be best, considering the pronouncement before us of such a heavenly display. I so quickly poured myself a quick beer and blended into the electric fray.

It was so far from home for many of us, and with no moon to shine, things began to tone down well before 10:00. I had considered that it was time to wend my way on out of the maze, and on toward the road. It wasn't easy. At one point as I left the joyous and breezily mild cacophony of my childhood behind, an eerie sense of loneliness, and solitude overtook me. I was somewhere between desperation, and glee. I worked my way along the path carefully, slowly, and so quickly became engulfed in total darkness. At one point I was forced to begin feeling for things by touch.

Some leaves, the trail below composed of lannon-stone, it was almost anything that I had felt and even touched, just to keep moving and not suddenly freaked out about things. I soon recognized the light voices of the young ladies from the other park. I stopped to chat. They were without escort, and especially without wheels. "Oh, don't worry about us," one confidently offered.

"I don't just mean about a ride, isn't it dark and scary to you?" I asked them.

"Oh, thanks a lot, now byee, seeya," the same one insisted. That was LittleMan's ex-girlfriend. I offered my adieu, and was off.

The very next week, after the evening sky of a lifetime, Memorial Day weekend had arrived. I being an ignorant loser, and not mature enough to pull together enough common sense to become a well-adjusted and sober individual, had scored some more acid. There has never been, and perhaps never will be more adequately wonderful weather. The skies were always blue, and the mean temperatures about 78⁰.

I partied like the wild mad dog that I was. The only complication was that I was scheduled to work, at the gas station. Although, the auto shop itself would not be open on that special holiday, just in case any revelers needed to gas up, I was to be at the ready, pump in hand. I, after going all night, got out of bed without nodding off for even a minute.

I cannot explain the lack of concern, or even the absence of minor caring that I held in my mind on that day. I blew off work. I went back over to dude's house, the one whose parents both worked. He lived just a few doors down from my bass player. We hung out all day and continued the freestyle summer ecstasy that so easily was settling in. What I regret the most was having been careless enough to deserve the reaction that I got once I did show up for my next day at the Magic Island gas hut.

To clock in, it was required that an employee enter the main building. Once inside and down a flight of stairs, it was into the break room/punch-in area. Before I could get near the clock, one of the mechanics who was standing guard held up his hands to stop me. From out of the break room emerged my co-worker. He was to have worked until noon with me taking over for the remainder of that holiday. He had a date with his girl all set up.

It no doubt involved hugging, kissing, squeezing, and loving and touching each other. He was in between crying, and punching me. I mean I have never, not before and not since, witnessed a grown man in such emotional turmoil or distress. At least two of the mechanics, and the shop manager held him back. I was so lucky he then notified me. "Yes, that's it, you're done," the manager chimed in. Dude was waiting to jump me as far as I could tell, but those guys had come to my rescue. Whew!

I was offered the opportunity of a lifetime. I could trade my bicycle for a 1962 Harley 250cc. I just needed to learn how to shift, and brake, in order to get that fine jewel home. This fellow happened to live next to the railroad tracks. In addition to those trails since it was Saturday, I could use the parking lot of the business right next-door to get the feel for two wheels. This taller sophomore started it up for me. I got on.

I shifted from first into second. I looked down to notice that the stones comprising this large lot were of the type that always made me fall when I was on my dirt/racing-type 24-incher. Seeing that fact, I became more than distracted. I was in fear. When I looked back up, I was about to hit a parked truck dead center on the hub of the rear wheel. I panicked then braced myself for impact. I gently laid the bike down and then came in flying forward, with all of my momentum.

That action tattooed my forehead with blue-green paint. That artwork lasted about a week or so. As per our deal, if I needed to call off the transaction I was allowed to. I ordered him to return my bicycle and gave him back the now damaged cycle. Within seconds after taking a car jack to the front forks, he had it back in good riding condition. With a sense of relief, I mounted Old Blue the Gimbel's special import, and rode off.

The very next week not much was going on. I took Old Blue, which was actually a brand-new bike to the local park. Seeing as no one was around I laid the new blue number down on the ground and placed some tree branches and weeds over it. Awhile later an acquaintance walked up. I believe that he was both afraid of me, and embarrassed that he had just hidden my men's 10 Speed.

I never got it back! Although, I should have trailed him, something about a person that has just denied seeing your property sets you back a little. I still don't feel comfortable about any of it. Alas, I didn't have it in me at the time to jump out and have at him. I should have been more prowling and stealthier in that regard.

It was during this time Mother made the announcement. My younger brother would be attending the local Catholic high school. There can never be more of an insult to an older sibling than being considered a total loser, yet only because of the local public school system. Somehow attending a school so far away would be just what the doctor ordered for the youngster.

It took an hour to get home on the bus, and surely no miscreant losers would influence that sweet young boy with their smarmy and troublesome ways. What with a focus on good decent Christian living, how could that approach possibly fail? She had no idea that I had already taken little bro down to meet my buddies at the local hangout, fully initiating him into our underworld activities.

He had mentioned later that evening that he thought that he could hear snakes. That's just your blood going past your ears I assured him. With that we both passed out. That was 1975, here it was 1978. I do not believe I had mentioned to anyone at all that one of my comrades from the public school had been expelled from that very institution. No, they didn't play around at that school when it came to negative influences at such a *high* level of education. Suffice it to say little bro didn't make it more than two years. Then he as well, was done.

He had been warned about his choice of unsavory associates by the very vice principal of that institution. He, in addition, was warned about his needing to toe the line for the interim of his school term there. He would later lie upon his bed in a state of depression for years. Finally, one day he arose from it all, and got his GED.

Blackie's cousin had a party. His mom sat with us in the beautiful shade of the old tall trees in his yard. It was a mild and pleasant evening. Just beyond his yard next-door the people had a small vineyard. It was the beginning of the nicer area in that part of town. His place was one of the oldest homes. It had a chauffer's apartment above the garage. Yes, the same one his sister was living in when he went cooky nutty on me that day so long ago.

I tried not to think about it, but many, many guys go goo-goo gaga over their buddy's sister. She wasn't just the nicest person ever that one could meet. She was also a little more than Jennifer Aniston average. Enough, so that love at first sight, was a guarantee. As long as she wasn't invited, I'd be okay. It was easy enough to forget about her after a few days, weeks, or maybe months had transpired.

Thankfully she was either married or on a date. I didn't bother to ask. Now if the sister is younger than your friend, you've no problem amigo. Just play it cool, and hatch a plan. Your pal will probably laugh at you. You'll get over it. My buddy's mother was being supportive, but in her special loving way. Never one to nag, she could lay it on the line in such a suggestively gentle way that it would leave you questioning yourself.

"Get out of that park, you've got to get out of that park," she advised. "You hear me, you've got to get out of that park," she furthered. I heard so much more, though questioned myself as to how to go about it. She meant "quit being a juvenile and grow up." Make some career plans, think about the future. It troubled me, but I loved it just the same.

I felt it was so much more about that very subject, serious career planning, rather than not hanging out and smoking weed all the time. I could not commit to school at that time and really wanted to work. Just what was it that could move me forward in the right direction? I truly didn't know. I recalled how my own brother had tried to get me to stop hanging at that park. Now it was

Brownie's mom. Did they know something that I didn't? God help me now. I now hold the advice for others!

Halloween was here. What to do, oh what to do? Since at least a few of the gang were still in school, I ventured down to the local park. What do you think I saw? It was a ghostly figure in a clean white sheet, although the head of this spirit was not human. It was that of a jack-o-lantern. It was even more so frightening and mysterious from a good distance.

This wondrously ghoulish scene had morphed itself in hideous fashion, seemingly from the depths of some horror movie plot. Or much worse, it had come from the sacred and hallowed confines of our most dreaded nightmares. Although, it would truly seem upon further review that someone had purchased the very largest pumpkin available, and then maybe, just maybe, had carved a head-sized hole into the bottom of said record sized orb. I carefully approached, now certain that the figure was indeed mostly human. The thing would not speak. I begged and pleaded, yet the phantom would not relent.

Finally, I held up a fist, claiming that since the frightening creature was a danger to I, and any others, I would need to fairly well protect myself by smashing him down, and even tearing the pumpkin head off, from his sheeted and well shrouded body. He finally relented. It was one of the younger fellows from down the way that I had gotten to know very well. He was even one of those very young men that tore the jacket from my very body only years before. A lucky fellow he now was at that once more!

1979

It was a hot-rod afternoon, on a lazy weekend Saturday. My bro with '72 Super Bee stopped over to see if I was game. The projected destination was to be the medium sized lake northwest of his father's home. Yes, he was the one with the hillbilly swimming pool in the front yard, and the tame enough donkey, to shoot films for school with. I was game and never so thrilled. Having no vehicle, I couldn't imagine when I would have another chance. We were off.

He pulled off the freeway once we had crossed the county line. Right there, just to the other side of a barricade, were three attractive girls. With three of us all together, it only made sense for him to offer this proposition: "Okay," he said, and "If those three are there on the way back home, we'll stop. If not then, oh well, although perhaps the next time we happen by, if they're here again…?"

The lake had welcoming attractions such as small two-seater paddle boats, actual sand, and an upper & lower section for Channel type competition swimmers. The sun was out and we loved every minute of it. I mean every single lazy weekend minute of it. So, why was it then that we left so early? I had a real good feeling, and a very special hunch, but I didn't want to jinx it by saying even one small word. I simply smiled and got things ready, and we were off. It was such an enjoyable country ride. Dude with the Super Bee is like, "I decided to take the side road back." The other chimed in, "why?"

"Oh, I don't know," the first replied, "Just because." We all knew the reason, and were feeling good about it.

All so soon, with a pleasant shade being offered, and the gentleness of a peaceful mid-afternoon, we were upon them once again. Bright colored clothing shouted out from the short distance. Feminine legs reached out to greet us from behind the swaying branches. It was them! We pulled over, and emerged to chat. I failed to recall old family friends as the two younger of the sisters were in full costume at our last get together. They also had morphed somehow themselves as well.

Imagine the Viking woman at the end of the opera wearing a horned helm, and an iron-metallic halter-top. Okay now, I think you're half way there. Now de-age her down to a sinful and unlawful age but keep the metal bra on, and multiply by two. There now, you're probably close. They were smiling, and honored. We mentioned that we had noticed them on the way to the lake, and you know, just wanted to stop, and say hi, or to see what was up or anything. I threw in, "Were you all really here the whole time waiting for us?"

My girl offered, "well no we actually went back home and got bored again, then decided to come back out."

"Do you come here often," was just waiting in the background of at least one of our minds. So, soon came the reply, "maybe yah, with not much to do around here, it gets that way, so then even yes, we most certainly do." We got a telephone number and were on our way. Later that night I got a call. There was something we needed to take care of, and just the three of us.

"For now, just keep it under your hat," I was told, "Because who knows how this is going play out." We met at a park outside of the normal action, the place from the toilet bowl incident. Since our country buddy was not around, he sat out this bit of brotherly-business undertaking. It was just yards away from where I had broken my foot on the basketball upright. The taller one with the Cadillac, and as well the use of his sister's '65 Convertible, seemed to have had it all figured out.

We would draw straws for first picks. I lost the first round. My bro picked the older Viking girl. My other buddy gathered the last two sticks positioning those just so in his hand. I quickly noted mine was askew, unless he was being sneaky, he somehow had been lax in the careful positioning of said *girl-stick*. That would mean he specifically wanted me to choose the short one which he positioned so that it appeared to be the longest.

I smelled it out and pulled with the strange sensation of a raging bison whose heart was now tearing so beastly through my pulsating ribcage. Aha, I held it tightly and triumphantly. I offered that since I was taking what had appeared to be the younger blond, it would all work out. You know I said, "Because the taller girl with brown hair looked older, and with his being about 6'2" it would be a match made in heaven." He agreed, and the dates were on.

The first one involved us ending back at their house. When Daddy walked in, he wore a big smile. Apparently, he recognized two of us from days gone by. So, there was a meet, and greet, a bit of polite chatter, and then we made our way back to town. The second time things got switched a bit. My buddy brought his '62 Cadillac but was set up with Robin, my lady's friend from school.

I got a call from my girl too soon afterward, requesting that for the sake of togetherness, we switch. Well, now I really felt unloved. So, I thought to myself that since it was the kiss for Robin, as I was told, that wasn't quite up to par, I myself wasn't going to touch her. No, she would have to be all over me, and like a mad dog as well.

I certainly mean like the most ravenous love hungry, swanky-assed, goober-schmoochy, horn-poodle, that any man has ever faced alone. Although, certainly in 99% of the cases such an experience would occur while indeed quite alone with such a rambunctious lady friend. Sure, she was good looking enough or I would not have said yes. Tall and slender she was, even taller than my girl's older sister.

Pretty in the face and all, but no deal dog. There would be no takers for this last-minute switcheroo, I'll tell you that my Captain Bucky. I still hadn't recalled at all, the genuine reason for my affections. Not the time she was a preemie, not when she had pulled the brand-new doll from beneath the mattress, the one modeling a stiff, bent hairdo. No, it was something more in addition to our having met before. I'll call it love. Secretly, I will never love another woman again.

No one can stand up to the sensitive softness of my sweet, sweet, young, lovely maiden. I still feel that I will be alone forever without her. Again, a call, this time it became about us. Do those others really matter now, I was thinking. The answer was no. Now that I had a vehicle of my own those others certainly weren't in my thoughts. My bass playing pal had inherited his father's car. It was a rundown '62 Buick Electra. Why would I accuse it of such grand, utter failure?

For the driver's side power window to activate it required reaching into the mechanism case of the switch itself, and connecting two wires. If done properly with the window all of the way up it did lower. If repeated with the window completely down, whaalaa. It was raised. Not too much, I had thought, after all, it's only a window.

Joe's brother was getting married. His mother had just passed away. She had smoked Kool Kings for too long of a period. The slow but well assured demise did not linger long. It was ironic in a way that the wedding was so soon afterward. The thought of smoking my own Kool Milds left a sad and bitter taste on my mind. Perhaps I should switch, even back to Newports, I had considered.

That would maybe be enough of a change, though mostly for me in that regard. I had gotten a hotel room next to the wedding hall. My girl was still so young, yet thoughts of deep romance I could not escape. I realized what premature ejaculation was by the spot on my trousers. Though, that actually was the spot so easily facing forward with a 'shout gets it out' exclamation.

I played it off, and whistled Dixie. Ignoring the alarming signification, I forced the issue away from one and all. We walked through the lobby past the fountain. We made our way up to our room and ended up just cuddling, so such a spot or deeper encounter would indeed have to wait for at least for 2½ more years.

I later managed to get a temp job weighing up scrap from stamping machines. Mainly washers, and such, though with some of those paper-thin units cast from solid gold. It gave me a feeling of prestige. Though, I was transferred there from machine operation. I just couldn't cut it. Here it was Saturday now, and I was going out to see my girl. For the first time it would be just her and I.

I got into my vehicle donned my crash helmet (just kidding) and was off and away. It was not to be. The stars were not yet aligned. A mile away from her very home, the right front tire went flat. Luckily, I was strangely feet away from an old-school filling station. I called Father and he came to the rescue.

The frickin' new 'old' car wouldn't start when back at work the following week. Mother had just begun to drive and drove back and forth in front of me with a full line of cars behind her in a desperate search for my presence. With the battery acting up, the horn wouldn't blow either. After her second crossing, I was sure that she had bailed, and given up completely.

I waited five more minutes then pulled the hood up and jiggled the battery connection. Crossing my fingers, I tried once more before beginning the three-mile journey back home. Just like that, as though none of it had ever happened, the thing was running, and I was back to being my old joyous self. Coming around the turn at the corner gas station was a completely different experience.

The entire wheel came off. At least that is, that the lower connection had actually become disjointed. It was the steepness of the incline as well as the sharpness of the curve that caused the sudden separation. As well, the weight of this mighty beast itself played fully into the folly that is my life. In shock, I did my best to maintain control. I was on the way to cash my check so was only yards from victory. Any goodness being in my life at that point would have been all too welcomed.

I actually managed to maneuver the hulking monster all the way back home. Em, perhaps I had gotten lazy after just a few weeks of driving. Mother stuck her head under the front end of the behemoth declaring that a simple bolt or something had fallen out. I may have wished to garner a ride or two from the woman, but mechanical advice is where I drew the line. I begged to differ then called the junkyard. There would be no more misery, and no more young girlfriend, at least for now.

I got a treat from my one pal, the fellow that had the flu back in 1961 with me. He called to let me know something spectacular was about to happen. When he pulled up, I saw just what he meant. He was driving a 1939 Oldsmobile. For the sake of it, he had me ride in the back. I immediately knew why. There was something special about the height of the rear seating.

I truly felt a bit like Spats Malone. This rear seat felt almost as though a park bench had been covered in a cushiony brown fabric. The angle of one's legs was dramatically positioned so that a person was somehow above everyone else on the road. He himself enjoyed the idea of being the #1 to my boss character. With I now thoroughly pleased with every single thing about the whole affair, it was a grand enactment of appreciative joy that we did engage in.

1980

With two daily papers coming to the home, there as an ample opportunity to become well informed with not only local happenings but some of the events transpiring on a national level. The legislation being talked about lately had only to do with one concept, cheap foreign labor. President Carter would have none of it.

It seems that one company and one company alone had brought about the discussion to change things. It was a fairly new and upcoming business that was growing, and becoming more popular. Their business model entailed a very disturbing detail to some who had very valid concerns when it came to furthering this type of business.

The overall aim it seemed was to find the dirt-poorest people from around the globe, and to have them fashion products to the highest of American standards. We had learned about these single-minded individuals back in grade school. The main concern of these types was cost. If the lowest cost materials could not be found then the lowest paid workers must be utilized.

This business seemed to have perfected the recipe of cheapness, and was well on its way to prosperity. The fact that they began as an American held business with all of the labor being performed overseas twisted the dynamics just enough. Those evil, un-American, soulless bastards were known as Nike. Soon enough, way too many American companies took note, and wished to employ this same selfish 'it's the bottom line that matters' philosophy.

There was just one thing holding them back. American business law did not allow for such a thing. Nike it seemed had bypassed this economical hindrance, by having only the *investors* as Americans, with the businesses themselves all located offshore. So, many other cheap-ass son-of-within bastards now longed to make this skewed equation work for them as well. They began to lobby government to change the game.

It was President Carter's promise not to go along with that. Then something awful happened. I blame for the most part these blind-eyed money-grubbing, dollar clenching, bitch-fluffs. As low down and despicable as any one business model could ever be, it was so much more than a monetary election that took place that November.

Americans were captured in Iraq. There was a hostage crisis. My very own neighbor was one of those being held. It was a time of turmoil for one, and all. A secret raid, 'Commando style' had been devised. The U.S. Military would charge in and bull-rush the enemy, causing such a stir, while catching them off guard.

The mission failed. A helicopter was shot down, and American casualties resulted. The hostages remained in captivity, and the President fell into disfavor with too many of the upcoming voters. A victory and success here would have altered history forever. Not only that of our own, but of the entire world itself.

As it turned out Ronald Reagan the worst President that ever held the highest office in the land would be elected. It was November 1980. The stage had been set for the slow destruction of this nation. The talk had been going on for months with the Republicans putting forth the legislation, and the Democratic President guaranteeing veto.

I was home one day from work. The daytime Soap Opera General Hospital was on, as it usually was in our home. This time however there was a new character, one that struck me as being awfully familiar. It was Blackie. Indeed, he was the very fellow I had met about four years earlier. The day Brownie had failed to talk his family into bringing me out to the drag strip with them came flooding back into my memory.

It wasn't at first mind you, no there was just something about this character that hit me in a strange way. With his striking and unusual name being 'Blackie', I at first, could only smile.

He played a young teen looking to start a new life in Port Charles, the city that the show was cast in. I finally recalled it was my buddy's mother that was Greek. She was American enough, and everything, yet the way she liked to talk was distinct.

She had a friendly enough approach, although within minutes, one might realize they were actually being lectured by the best of them. Her speech had a friendly lilt, that was little different from her demeanor when she was talking recipes, shopping, or anything else she could put a positive spin on. It was at the end of it all that she would slowly give herself away with the last few words. They could still be sweetly offered, yet all at once quite so obvious.

Here though, the protection from extremism had been removed. One could only sit back, and wait. The clock ticked upon the wall. The second-hand was clicking off the final ticks of this nation's well-built dominance, and superiority. The nation we had forged together as a people, would suffer an economically derived, and slowly churned out death.

Ours was a country that had vitality. A nation built on strength, and cleverness, with only a shameful arrogance from those we call the 'Money-People'. Our strong dominance had come from the mighty middle class and from those unique aspects that our nation alone could stand proudly behind. Here now we would take a step backward.

A step so far back that my Uncle-the-Governor would be rollin'. Not doobies mind you either. No, we the descendants of an Irish slave don't cotton to bullshit mother-fluffers puffin' with gruff, as dollar signs and other selfish stuff, occupy each and every corner of their minds.

To fully understand the collapsing change about to take place, one must consider the evolution of industry, and the move from farming, and agriculture to a prominence of manufacturing, and automation. It was back in 1908 or so, that true change did occur. That year, for the most part, marked the leaving behind of an ever-changing landscape of motion, and movement to one of labor, and stability.

All of the Native American tribes had been settled on Reservations. No new territory existed, at least on the mainland. Cities would grow, and jobs would be created. The old west had been concurred. The revival shows were staged, and now even some of those were beginning to become dated and hokey.

Through the ups, and downs over the next seventy plus years, through two world wars, we climbed. Even further yet, through two additional, politically motivated battles of mostly foreign interests, we meandered. For all of this time the middle class would grow, and prosper. This newfound identity was the fresh face of the American landscape.

Where before, this group had consisted of shopkeepers, and small businessmen, it was now open to any who had the chance to work in these newer well-paying fields. It was a cultural and financial evolution of sorts that had taken place within the boundaries of the greatest nation in the world.

With this well-formed collective came a great ability, the ability to save for the future and the keen ability to spend like never before. It was a case of a peoples having their cake, and eating it too. The realities of grandness in the here and now were prevalent, as well as the fantasy of what could be down the road. Not only what could be in the future for oneself up ahead, but what could be even greater, for the generations yet to come. Immigrants who longed for such prosperity poured through the floodgates.

Along with two crossover Democrats from the south, (one from Kentucky, and if memory serves me correctly, the other from Missouri), the sought-after legislation passed. That rule change allowed for original American operations to relocate anywhere, in any other country. Businesses could now close up shop, and take all of their jobs overseas.

The America as I knew it, had been destroyed, it was now lost forever. It had completely vanished from the landscape, save for the cinematic memories of one with a photographic mind. Now, forever lost was such a grand stability, to all of those yet to come. It was especially true to those who could never fathom such a necessary experience to begin with.

I recall holding up the newspaper to my face. I felt the cold betrayal of my fellow countrymen like never before. My first thought after, was to wonder if we would let these young men still in school know all about it. You see the news articles for months had proclaimed this was a nonnegotiable action. It was claimed that only damage could be had from it.

They spoke of a widening class divide. Way too many rich, with way too many poor would come of such a law changer, and it was said that such a law change would surely over time, shrink the vital middle class. Women it was being said would have to work just for a family to make ends meet. That meant one thing.

Over time, more and more white women would enter the work force and compete for our jobs. Yes, you heard me. Women would be taking jobs away from men. Yet that endeavor is again, traced to that one action, so coldly embraced by bullsh*t, fluffed in the head, selfish bastards. Those job searching ladies would compete with me, those gals would do the same with you.

They would especially compete with all of the young men still sitting in those classrooms across our nation that hadn't quite anticipated such an overwhelming competition in the workforce presented by such needful women. With most of those gents likely not even having the slightest awareness that the game of life just got tougher, they perhaps would not be so ready for such a new challenge of life here in America.

That's why my first question was, are we going to let them know, are we going to make them aware of these facts. Not just any guys, but all of the guys that could maybe have taken for granted their place in society, especially I mean, those at the bottom. This new way of doing things was going to surely shuffle the order of the totem. It is no doubt how we ended up with unemployment for certain demographics at even up to 35% during low periods and economic slumps.

My friend from high school called. He mentioned his dad's company was looking for help. I could come in as a temp, a mere formality he had intimated, because high-quality people like me would be hired in a New York second with the contract bought out from the service. I merely needed to pass muster.

With a good word from him, pops would work his magic. I went there, and felt fatigued. The work involved moving paint roller extension parts into place so that the compressor could push them together. From there I would hand off those assembled units to the spot welder for final completion.

I had yet to be formally diagnosed with arthritis, though no doubt my aching joints played a role in my decision. I told my pal from school, no thanks, his disappointment was so readily apparent that I immediately felt bad. He would get over it. After all, there must be hundreds of eager workers who are just dying to work for a Union Company. Apparently, I was wrong about those aspects of that business. A strange feeling came over me from the time I got home. It would haunt me the entire weekend. I called him back on Monday late in the afternoon expressing my regrets.

"Well, you really are sorry," he nearly chuckled, "I mean because that was only a test, I would have hooked you up in the good department, which I already told you I could do, and now it's too late," he added. "I mean for all intense purposes, that job is gone, at least for now," he continued. "You can go back to the temp service, and let them know you'd like to return, but it's really out of my hands," was his final statement. "Well, thanks anyway," I lowly offered. I realized when I got home how much I really wanted the job, but here and now it even was 'too late'.

I found out why he was protecting me by that Thursday. The only other open position available, involved sniffing glue, with my partner being what we put in polite terms in those days, a slow learner. I soon came to realize that no one would know if he began to suffer from brain damage due to any close contact with the adhesives. I needed to perform at the top of my game, and to pray for a transfer. The women we worked with were for the most part, beautiful people. Only this 'dude', my workmate, liked women from the other departments better. As long as it was cool, I guess we'd be alright.

All of our gals stood at machines with what could only be described as wrapping paper tubes inserted. Once in place they'd grab the air gun and staple the end of the fur roll onto the end of the tube. Placing one foot onto the spin mechanism caused the tube to spin around. If then, it all went as planned they would end up with a three-foot paint roller.

After curing in the *hothouse*, the tubes were cut into smaller sections then shipped out to stores. It was my duty to bring huge, heavy, metal racks filled with fresh tubes along with boxes of fur. The one last yet vitally important effort, was to finally and with a Kool-Aid pitcher, pour in more glue.

Good news had arrived. My neighbor from down the street was dumping her '68 Impala. I jumped all over that offer. For a mere $250.00 I could stop getting rides from the buddy that got me into his father's company, and even start picking up my girl again, and taking her out. This neighbor girl's dad was a mechanic working for the Air National Guard along with Joe's father.

That meant the car had been tuned up, and was running as good as it possibly could. "All good things must come to an end," the saying goes. Just how far I could take it was anybody's guess. I called my own sweet girl and we were back in business.

As far as those women went, it was the nicest job I ever had. There was indeed a reason dude like those other ladies. They worked in an isolated location, so one would not be detected as *chatting-up* those two cuties. In our department one of the girls was related to my brother in laws aunt. It was only a restaurant her auntie had though, awarded to her in the divorce.

So, it was nothing more than a coincidence when the Feds put her in jail, threatening to sic the IRS on her. She replied, "I already said you could bug the table where Joe Balogne sits, I won't tell honest," she had implored them. They let her sit and smell the jailhouse roses if you will, for a while anyhow, just to bring home the point. All three, the father and the sons, went to jail.

Another gal at work was young and friendly. One day she asked, "Should you really be wearing those *old grandpa t-shirts*?" That's what I called them because of my neighbor's grandpa Milo Senior. *Wife beaters,* I think they were known as, in New York. I lifted my arm to pour more glue, then wondered, can't she wait until she gets home to her husband to talk 'sex-talk'?

I put my index finger under my armpit making sure some hair was sticking out. "Is this what you mean?" I asked, wiggling my finger up and down to look similar to a certain body part. She feigned anger, and nearly turned red, yet then honestly gave up a "yeaahhh."

"Well, no," I replied, "I'm just fine, just fine and dandy with that part of my day."

Janey from Alabama also worked at the paint roller plant. She claimed where they lived as kids, they had a shortcut nearby. On any given day, the giant grasssnakes such as I had seen down near Mussel Shoals, would drop down from a tree branch saying in a voice ala Sulu from the late 1960s show Star Trek, "Helllooo." Her brother would just laugh and giggle while she became paralyzed in fear. Even the slightest mention of the 's' word could set her off. She would frantically shake her arms back, and forth while closing her eyes, and freaking out. Though, while also praying to God, no doubt as well.

One of the gals was fine and slender. Nearly perfectly average, she was a French girl with a friendly attitude, and an easy-going demeanor. Even though I was involved in a telephone relationship at the time, with my '62 Electra having been junked, at least at first, I couldn't keep my mind off of this French woman. Yes, I finally purchased that other vehicle, and even had made a promise to my girl that I would never two-time her. Feelings would rumble from deep within. I needed to keep my mind on my job so packed away those nasty thoughts into a suitcase bound for nowhere.

I took my sweet young girlfriend to the bar, where I got shot at a few years earlier. It was all a misunderstanding back at the time. I was more than a wag and jokester. Perhaps I had failed back then to read the signs of my own existence. My one buddy, whose dad owned a bar in the general area, was not a gossip. I was horn-dog dirty. The gal running things at this new place had just been raped. I tried to come on strong, though in a humorous way.

She pulled out the revolver and put a bullet into the heavy wooden door. We quickly left. So, dude says, "that's what I meant by just be cool." Because the old man, her exe's father, needed the business, she was willing to let bygones be bygones. She wasn't just bending over backward mind you either. She was also letting my girl in with no ID.

This bud with the '39 Olds suggests that we dude it all out for Halloween. I don't mean just any old costume. He meant we should even take the Old Beauty out for a night on the town. We just needed suits, and or hats to match this special occasion. He brought the true-to-life machine-gun case that he had. My girl and I met him there at our new hangout. It went as planned with me having donned my Frank Sinatra 'Special'. For those youngsters unaware of such an item, it was Father's church hat from about 1953.

The undeniable, all too genuine, way over the top machine-gun case was quite unmistakably real. It unbelievably included an access hole cut away for emergency use. That was how you knew about that, ever so serious function of such an item. The thing had obviously not been fired in such a manner, as any such occurrence would have left a tell-tale hole in the barrel-end of such a handsome gun cover. It was quite impressive, and now that I had more than made up with the Bonnie lass, she was nicer than ever to all of us.

I, back at work now because my honey-bunny was too young to do it (I mean the bad way, or the good, perhaps even), I was checking out the French girl again. I should have refrained, even if it meant bringing a bible to work to pray over, rather than those luscious buns of hers. It would get to me a little, but I could keep it out of mind for the most part. Those days were over.

Just as I promised, I phoned my sweetie-pie at lunchtime and broke the news. What a fool I was. I had mentioned here that she would never have anything to worry about because I would never two-time her. "You can start worrying," I coldly put it. Here was someone I had known since shortly after her birth, and I was hurting the person I truly loved, but being honest about it. That moment still drops my heart from my very chest. Ouch!

Things went as planned. The French girl had 9-foot pot plants growing in the spare bedroom. It was only ditch-weed, but all too cool. We smoked a little then went out for a while. Because it was a Thursday, after we did it, I got up to go home. Her body chemicals were draped all over me. My brain said goodbye, yet my body was screaming to get back in there. I had never felt anything like that. I quickly assumed it was only body chemistry, and tried to shrug it off. It was nearly impossible. Good thing I had some of my own weed. I still remember that night like it was yesterday.

Cheers the TV sitcom was on when I got home. The theme song so quickly played. It would all so soon be over. I mean we went out again the next night. We engaged in another round of romping in the hay. My heart was then torn even further. By Sunday I had made up my mind. I couldn't be emotionally in love with one person, and so deeply physically satisfied with another.

Torn between two lovers was a song that I didn't want to sing. I got my girl out to the bar, and came clean. Regardless of her decision to take me back or not, I would be able to move on without the heartache. I swore to her that it was only about the sex, and not about any relationship whatsoever. We made up.

Back at work it would not be so easy. The French girl took me out to the bar for lunch. In so many ways what she said was "I don't care about that other girl I want you back." I almost cried. My brain was being twisted like a pretzel. I said it was off, then left. She almost lunged at me to embrace me, seduce me, caress me, physically care for and love me, but I moved too fast. I was in my car and smoking hits as fast as I possibly could. Once back at work, I did my best to concentrate on only my job duties, and not at all on her fabulous well-shaped body. What a fool I had been the whole time.

My sweetie and I, over the coming months began to form such a deep bond that to this day I still miss her. The fact that her grouchy dying ex is a cold-hearted brainwashing son-of-a-witch, doesn't help at all. If I go over again before he's dead he'll probably call the cops on me again. If I wait too long, my girl may move in with one of her brothers, further pushing the game of hide and seek on down the road. I know she will come back to me in a heartbeat, there is just the little hang up of the ex, still being nursed into the grave by her attentive sweetness and loving care.

The last I checked they had been divorced back in 1998. When he answered the door, he was short by one foot. Though rather more so, he had become an amputee from the knee down. He had developed M.S. and lost his job, before losing even more. Apparently, a sense of stubbornness is another thing he has. With M.S., you have the severe cases where the person is gone within ten to twelve years, and the milder cases where the whole ordeal could go on for even twenty-five, full, slowly anguished, and drawn-out dying years.

With the double whammy he was dealt with, it's anybody's guess as to when he can no longer even bathe or use the facilities. At that point I intend to come rushing to the rescue with all of the sincerity possible. Oh well, unless another hot Norwegian blond comes along first, I guess that'll work for me. Maybe I'll look up her sister the next time I'm at the library! I won't love her, but "what's love got to do with it," as I once wrote for Tina Turner.

Back to the times at hand, we would go out on the weekends, then after getting back in the '68 Chevy I would torch one up, and the sweet, sweet, sweetness of our love would shine like the moon. This went on until Father did everything that he could to frighten me into getting work. The paintroller company had given me the axe. There had been one too many complaints from the girls. There were two sets of work stations. One supplier, or material handler, was to provide for one group, while the other would tend to the other group of stations.

I was switched from my regular duties over to the other team. Their material ran out faster so there was a different pace to it over on the farther end of things. I had brought a book once, and read about a one-fourth page or so before getting back up to make the rounds. I was never calmer or satisfied with my ability to reach each of the stations in my wonderful and suave fashion. I believe someone narc'ed on me as after two- and one-half days of pure peace, my boss apologized and said to ditch the book. It was then back to a harried frenzy ever after.

So, the boss calls me into a meeting and as those were piece-workers, they could become very disappointed if the materials were late in arrival. With piece work, you see, one may qualify for bonus money based on how many additional items could be made, over and above the set rate which would often just be a low average. The big boss was present in the conference room as well as the union rep.

I was done. You can always call the union headquarters and request a review of your termination the rep had assured me. The thing of it was, she was never home. I mean the actual union rep failed to answer. After rising to the top of that height she went and got a way better job, yet managed to stay on as our union head. After the second call, I really felt like it was for the better that I not return.

After starting there at the paint roller firm, a couple of the gals showed me the chemical burns they were treating. I was told it was really nothing, and that one just needed to get the special salve and keep the affected area covered for a while. The other thing about it was quite more than a common rash. One's skin could bubble up and permanently morph. I got some under my fingernails and still suffer from that minor deformity to this day.

It was now August. The local County Fair was in full swing in my girl's area. At least in the area where she attended school it was. This was a huge swath of land bordered by the local drag strip on one corner, and the freeway up to the north, kitty-corner over from that. All the way in between were farms, and small houses, some of those with huge yards bigger than a football field. I picked my girl up, and we were on our way. This was a fair that was more centered on livestock, and exhibits rather than carnival rides and games. We perused the offerings and basked in the warm Sunday afternoon sun.

All was well, and the world was a beautiful place of peace, serenity, and love. That was until I got back on the 'I' to take my girl home. Within seconds, the bright lights were flashing and I was being pulled over. The same exact thing happened to my son on the 4th, coming from the opposite direction. Local drivers should be warned. On this particular otherwise fabulous afternoon I reached into my pocket only to realize my driver's license was nowhere to be found.

It was cool though, as the Sherriff, was willing to base my release on available information in his system. He acknowledged as much once he returned with a ticket and a goodbye. About 17 mph over, if I recall correctly. Upon arriving at home, I searched through the dirty clothes in the lower chamber, quickly finding my wallet in the pair of jeans from the day before. Well, that is what may happen if you prefer wadded up bills placed in your front pocket, over clean crisp cool ones from a wallet.

I tried my hand at some small-time pot pedaling once more. Since cool people don't push weed on others this adventure turned out to be as much of a bust as the first one back in 1975. I made one sale, again, and had nothing but weed on my hands. That is not a good thing for someone that is borderline manic-depressive. The inevitable, something that may occur every two or three years, or fearfully more often, was just around the corner from such an unwise action.

I had been out of work for some time. Without the routine of my daily early rising and laboring intensively for the piece-workers, my internal clock was thrown off. I was awake for days. At one point, I had decided to check out a hotel room located nearby. I picked up my lady and we stayed the night. She just needed the right reason to give her mother. The very next day my battery was dead. Father come on over and gave me a jump. He was not pleased at all, but said little.

I went home and laid upon my bed with my girl in the living room. I had just laid with my head in her lap for comfort as I had gone sleepless again the night before. Mother had taken a job at a local department store and was not at home at first. I seemingly dozed off only to open my eyes to see little bro holding a pair of scissors just above me with a menacing look upon his face. I totally freaked inside, as he quickly, and quietly moved back into his own room.

He denied what had happened, and I had had it. The car wouldn't start again, and needed a jump from Father once more. He griped about it, and then pulled around to the front of the house. Once he came close enough to the front end of my '67 Impala, I moved directly in front of that so that he could ease up without any question as to when to stop. He didn't.

He not only rammed my legs; he revved the engine a bit with my knees wedged in between the two vehicles. Now with my car starting to actually move backward, I started to freak a bit. With the car in park, things began to moan before Pops finally eased off. He got out and said, "Let's do this."

Still in shock and with my feelings more hurt than anything, I said nothing. Once the cables had been clamped down, I turned the key and started it up. After fetching my gal from inside we were off.

This would mark the third consecutive day without sleep for me. I was beginning to lose touch with reality. I got on the freeway and just started to drive. It didn't matter to where that we went, anywhere from there was going to be just fine. At one point we found ourselves on the other side of the state line. I pulled off of the main system, and continued on over a blanket of beautiful, freshly laden snow. California was the place I ought to be, so continued heading in a southwesterly direction.

Previous to this unplanned-adventure I had placed an old pewter cross I had come across on the rear view. It was on the edge of the old rotten apple orchard just behind the big store that I saw it just lying there upon the ground. It would dangle in such a way, along with handmade faux poppies from the vet outside the local bank. It offered a sense of security so far from home for us. That would turn out to be a false sense of security at that. Coming around a sharp turn in the deep snow, I hit an icy patch, and spun out.

The car had flown over the ditch, with the rear tire now resting on a flat type of hidden boulder. The front end was now nestled against an old oak tree. I revved the engine yet to no avail. The tires just spun. Finally, out of aggravation and a sense of hopelessness, I gave the gas one final burst. Final it was then, as the rear tire exploded from spinning on that rock. I got out to make an inspection of the situation. That, a vital step I should have performed from point one.

The fresh and beautiful newly fallen snow offered a buffer against the harsh cruel world. I removed the cross from my rearview mirror and hung it upon a broken tiny branch barely visible at all, sticking forth from that large oak. It hung directly above the hood of the vehicle, and that action offered a minor bit of solace to our now stranded disposition. Within minutes, a car pulled up. It was the Sherriff.

They took us in to the local headquarters. It was a place known as Berles County. We would spend the remainder of the evening waiting for our parents to arrive. In the morning while we were waiting, my girl displayed her total disgust and disappointment in regarding what I had done to us. I was in no mood, and grabbed the wooden handles of her cream-colored woven material purse, and slammed those down on the table.

One handle snapped, and now my gal was taken down additionally. She has never forgiven me for the purse incident. Perhaps more so metaphorically, rather than based on the value of that favored item her mother had purchased for her years before. I mean since she glued it back together, I wanted a flippin' break.

To this day, I swear I would purchase as many handbags as she so desired in as many styles, designs, and with any material that caught her fancy, even gold, if she would please just forgive me for that one small act. Yes, and in addition, the other really super big ones that she has been so queenly enough not to harp on with those other more minor actions seemingly already being forgiven.

Her folks came, and since I wasn't being charged with taking a minor across state lines, any attention focused on our being there, had waned. I got up and walked out to the street. The Sherriff's area had a large yard around the perimeter. I decided, somehow by a sailor's type of instinct, to walk across that, and to just keep walking until my parents passed on by.

Within seconds of arriving at the edge of the grass I noticed Father's car turning toward me. He quickly pulled over and let me in. Within a few days the shop my car had been towed to, called with a price. I had enough, and we got back in the vehicle and drove all of the way back to that area. It was such a relief to be in my own vehicle, now well rested, and on the road back home.

It was making me slightly nervous to keep a pace with the folks so about a third of the way out I punched it, and moved well ahead and out of sight. The rest of the trip was a minor joyous pleasure. Whew! I still rue to this day, the bad decision to not have those ball joints replaced. Gentlemen, heed my words, ball joints are almost always worth the trouble, especially if you can mount them yourself.

My girl's folks now knew that I at least suffered from insomnia, with additional complications. To what degree they understood that it was borderline, and as far as any mental illness being quite "along for the ride," I am still not sure. With her now back in school safe and sound, I simply needed to keep a handle on things at home. Within weeks, we were back to going out, and other than the purse issue thing getting in the way at times, we were back together and in love.

So, come fall, Pops is saying how it's going to be just a cold, cold winter. With that right around the corner it will be especially so for one without a job. The next day I was hired at the local candy company. I was a fool to rush into that job. I should have more keenly assessed my options. Certainly, somewhere, somehow, something would have opened up for me. The thing was that Joe worked there, and I was in like Flynn in no time at all.

1981

As the position was second shift, my girl didn't take it lightly. With her in school all day and me at work, we could only see each other on the weekends. The turn our relationship went down was disappointing to say the least. Just when I began to fall in love, she had somehow turned cold on me. Her distant bitterness harmed me from afar.

In a state of distress, I longed for us to be together more often. I went out to see her after getting permission to leave work early on one evening. It was not just that I caught her with another man. It was more so that she was willing to create a further distance between us while the fruit of our separation was still so ripe. I believe that she sensed that only pain and heartache could await her down the road.

It would seem that her father had begun to have second thoughts about me as well, and decided to play break-up king. I mean it was the drummer in his country band that did appear on the horizon. I sped up only to see them move away from each other, enough to assuage my immediate concerns. My mind was torn asunder. Again, the more I truly loved her, the more I surely messed up, and the more therefore she edged away from me.

Whoever got things going on that end was immaterial. It hardly mattered. I was genuinely and deeply in love, and needed to be with my girl as much as possible, even if that would only be on Saturday, and Sunday. I insisted then that this fleeting *affair* be abruptly ended. I saw from this fellow's stance and attitude that he was quite willing to step aside for my sake. I explained once more that I was pressured into taking that position, and would duly work on procuring first shift employment as soon as the time was right. I mean I truly didn't wish to job hop once more so quickly and all.

A television show came on. It was one of those investigative offerings that delved into the facts about what may be considered everyday life. I cannot recall the title, but sat down immediately to watch. The subject was about the potentially harmful effect of one psychotherapeutic drug known as Thorazine. This was the very same product that I had considered not only dangerous, but mis-prescribed to myself throughout the spring, and summer of my junior year in high school. The main subject of the story had been taking it for about five years.

Things did not seem so frightening, as he talked from the comfort of his living room sofa. Quickly however that changed. It became much too obvious that this man's life was made nearly so unlivable, as to wonder how he possibly managed his way through each and every day. With things like doing laundry, and bathing oneself, no doubt grand, and somewhat insurmountable hurdles, he took us outside where the real show began.

You see, he had been beseeched by violently wild, and uncontrollable spasms that caused his arms to flail about wildly, and precluded him from doing anything at all. All in one shot anyhow it did. The monumental action now displayed upon our television screens involved his attempting to mow the lawn. Every few minutes, he would stop the power mower, and go through his ritual, with arms moving about up, and down, as though he were now possessed by an invading evil spirit. The whole affair of mowing, he had said, took about 2½to 3 hours to complete.

Suffice it to say his yard was merely average to small. I began to grow sick, both from his plight, and what I now considered my narrow escape. He was on this prescribed medication for all of those five years believing an adherence to that subscription was so very well necessary. In shock I arose to digest the whole of it.

That'81 fall season faded into coldness. Winter's icy sheets of bitter reality so quickly claimed the day. With the drummer boy from her pop's band having retreated to his corner, my girl and I grew closer. Although, not indifferent to my being away from her, she eased off from her demands and recovered from the minor emotional trauma perpetrated against her by myself. We were soon back together just as we had been before.

Christmas was on its way. My gal decided to give me an early present. She was to be 18 in 4 short weeks, so technically it was against the law. I would later meet a fellow hitching, who was coerced into joining the army. His situation involved everyone knowing the truth of such closeness for himself and his dear sweet lover. Before his lover-girl actually had her birthday come around, the baby bump exclaimed in a well-pronounced fashion just what had been going on prior to said roundly shaped evidence being so obvious.

He went before the judge and asked for mercy. Considering he was soon to leave for military duty, he had done what he could on his end. Such an arrangement having been intentionally made in the interim hindered him not. The judge banged the gavel, and he would be a faraway father, free from any harsh and troubling punishment on the local side of things.

My gal and I here though, took a sleeping bag that I had cleverly stashed in the back seat. You can say I got my gift early, and she got hers as well. So, there we are behind the garage on the edge of the cornfield. One thing led to another, and bam, it was over. I mean, for a minute, man, I actually believed that I did it alright, at least on that night anyway. We apparently got more than a little carried away though. I had mentioned to her even then, "It would help if you didn't go into that chant the way you do." It went something like this with a panting breath, "Give me your baby, give me your baby, give me your baby, give me your baby…" What could go wrong, I was asked? That was quite obvious.

1982

The year started off uneventful. That would change oh so quickly. Joe had sold me his '72 Mustang. I had believed it more than likely had poor handling capabilities in the snow. I was willing to give it a try. First, I needed to uninstall his stereo system, replacing it with mine. Once the transformation had been completed, I took it for a test listen.

I went once down the block, then after, turned quickly around. My own cassette player kicked. As I approached the intersection just down from my place, I came upon two school students walking in the roadway. Apparently, not all of the walks had been shoveled after a thick blizzard had covered everything. We were in the middle of a serious cold spell that followed a foot of snow. It was as low as 4^0 or 5^0 at night, and we were lucky to see 20^0 in the day. From just behind the heads of these young teens emerged a car of the same brown color. The piles next to the sidewalks were at least 3½ feet or higher.

I had no time to react. It was an unmarked intersection. (That itself changed by the next summer) My foot came up off the gas, but in my shock, I was unable to brake. She moved right into my path, a mother picking up her daughter from school. After I hit her broadside, my vehicle continued on until it rested against the snow bank on the opposite side. She called her husband who quickly arrived.

If only that neighboring community had done things in the proper fashion. This was well before schools allowed students in, from any other zone. We lived on the border.

That woman's child should have gone to my old grade school about a mile to the south. Why that other town's principal allowed this breaking of technicalities, I don't understand. Wishful thinking in hindsight is all that such a thing could be for me. You'll see near the end of my life story how once again fates gnarly grasp twisted its ugly knuckles upon me. Alas, I would not be here in my office typing, if not for these strange and harmful happenings.

Here with this new tragedy, it only took Father's clever jiminy-rigging to work things out. He took two pieces of small wood to prop up my fan belt cover. Other than that, it was a little mooshed. You had to double check the hood latch after checking the oil as that would stick, and pop up as well. Her total for damages was $2,000.00. Mine was still pending. Next, my girl had some news.

"You know that gift I gave you for Christmas," she hinted, "Well, it's the gift that keeps on giving, if you know what I mean." She had *missed* so we put two and two together, and it came up one, or three to be exact.

So, now I had a crummy low paying job, a $2,000.00 vehicle repair bill, and a bun in the oven. Over at my girl's place her father was getting irritated. Even though, all that he did in the winter was drink beer, and go ice-fishing, he needed me out of the house. We should have been quieter. By then, we knew good and well with her having *missed* again that we would soon be parents.

I mean, all way too soon. Pops called out, "get him out of the house, or you can go too." I had had somewhat of a falling out with her family overall since I lost my union job. The lateness of the hour only added to their disappointment. We left in a hurry.

Back at my place the next morning, I made the announcement. She got booted out, and plus, her pending enlargement. When the younger of my two sisters had moved back in, a wall was erected in the basement to make a room for her. Now my sweet, sweet lovely would take up residence in that same area. It was only natural. There was a bed neatly in place, and we weren't married.

Things were looking up. One night, after we went month after month without as much as a kiss, I could no longer hold myself back. We made out. I then let her know that I just wanted to catch the score from the earlier game. I fell asleep. In the morning, Father poked his head in, and realized what no doubt had transpired. Within days we were booted.

I had saved a small amount from my crummy job. We took the low costing one bedroom on the north side, utilities not included. We soon found out why the rent was at such a friendly number. The mice had a secret tunnel carved into the floorboards of the closet. They ruled the roost under the darkness of midnight. The most that I could do was put on my steel-toed cowboy boots, and chase them back through their entrance into the basement. Ants as well, had a way in.

I'm nearsighted. I had dropped the wax grabber from some bakery on the floor, not realizing how a smear of yummy goodness could turn so bad. The next morning the wax paper was clearly visible. I soon believed that I somehow had dropped coffee grounds in the same exact location. The coffee grounds then had gained the mystical ability of movement.

I dropped to my knees then pressed my face closer to the floor to clarify my vision. The coffee had legs now, (yes indeedy Miss McReady) and small antennae. After I freaked a bit, it was all cleaned up. I discovered that their secret entrance was in the bathroom. As far as I could tell, they crawled in from underneath the sidewalk, then after making their way across the basement ceiling, they moved into the bathroom through a tiny little hole. A hole no doubt, that the mice had cleared for them previously.

Another thing I found. If the oven is on, the radio from your would-be father in-law will melt, if sitting atop the back of that oven. As long as you like the station that's melted into place, you'll be alright. I had to make a decision. After unloading every pot, pan, baking dish, or tray that she could spare, Mother tried to convince us to get married as soon as possible.

My girl and I had already looked at rings previous to our new condition. The lower costing set was about $1,250.00. I felt that if we prayed to God, for him to consider us married, that such a request would be good enough, at least for now. No wife of mine would have a cheap-ring wedding. We prayed on our own in the same way, for the baptism.

I took my girl out to the quarry. It had been a while since we were in the old neighborhood and it was nice to be back on my old stomping ground. Some new construction was underway with a road being put through on the eastern edge of the water. We drove in as far as possible then parked. A guy my brother knew and the younger brother of one of my old classmates had just come out of the brush. We said hi then moved on in. Under ordinary circumstances, such a coincidence of meeting would only be a quaint happening. Here it was a bit more.

There wasn't much going on that night so we didn't stay long. Upon returning to the vehicle, we found that a bolder had been used to smash the passenger side window. My forty some albums were in the back on the floor.

Now all were being played on someone else's phonograph. Those music loving bastards, how dare they! I raced over to the home of the little brother. His sister that I knew was right there in the drive at the time. "Let him know then," I told her. I truly couldn't afford to mount much of an investigation. As long as those buggers were on their toes, and constantly looking over their shoulders, that was all that I could get, for now anyway.

We went out to see my girl's family. I stopped at the gas station. We got back on the freeway, and sure enough, the hood popped open at 55MPH. It just bent itself back and folded like a napkin. All of the wires were cut and it no longer would start. Rats. We got towed back into town, and the dying remains of my Mustang would then be housed indefinitely in my parent's garage. What more could possibly happen?

I left work early to handle a marital affair. I mean to try and salvage our relationship. There was only one thing left of a serious nature. The company made fudge. Just inside the kitchen three huge industrial size mixers were stationed. They needed to be hand dried for the next day's operations. This wasn't the first time that I had left early, you'll note. My baby was feeling lonely again with that being a night job. I thought my boss had my back, but apparently not. I was fired.

I hadn't slept in days. Back then it only took three sleepless nights for me to begin feeling trippy. Since that time, I've actually made it up to four, before things began to collapse in on me from all directions. I went out for a walk then ended up downtown. I stopped at a home just beyond the large buildings made of brick. What happened there should have tipped me off as to how far strung-out I deeply was.

A fellow in his back yard allowed me into his home. His mother gave me the water that I had requested. I hadn't eaten all day, and never am very hungry during these tragic episodes. Trying to walk it off merely caused a few pounds to drop. That did nothing for me psychologically at all. After I noted the rooster figures on the kitchen wall of this family, I began to go back in time to my very own home in the early sixties.

After commenting on the birds, as it must have come out very strange, the older brother after entering from the living room ordered me to leave. Now I had three young brothers chasing me out of the home. My heart jumped as I fled as quickly as I could. I made my way from the area, soon coming across a small-time shoe store on the edge of what is known in these parts as the West Side. Some evil force took over my actions. Of that I swear. The place had an item that I still considered one of the most fantastic creations ever conceived of, for short white guys anyway it was.

They were elevator basketball shoes. Now, basic elevator shoes from the old days had a secret internal inner sole that allowed a shorter fellow to pretend that he was now 5'2½" instead of 5'1". I decided to try the things on, while still completely pleased and amazed. It was after I had both shoes on that some strange force took possession of my thoughts. I moved quickly and out the door.

As if by a predetermined calculation, a bouncer with a billy-club appeared from just behind me, insisting that I remove the gems from my unworthy feet at once. He raised the weapon as if to strike, offering one lone option. I readily acquiesced, and dropped to the sidewalk, quickly and carefully removing the special footwear so as to not cause harm to these nifty, handsome shoes.

I fully cooperated with this security officer's demands, and waited for local law enforcement to arrive. They placed me in the back of a squad car, although because of the nature of my crime, the attempted theft of an item valued over $1,000.00, I was turned over to the sheriff's Department, as that crime constitutes a felony, and I would be held on bail.

After being turned over to that local sheriff, I was quickly placed into a type of holding cell. I so readily came to understand it was their torture hole. I was not quite familiar with such tactics but learned so soon enough. For one, it had 2-to-3-inch roaches crawling around on the cell room floor. The uneaten lunch from the previous tenant was situated upon that very floor in front of the metal bed.

Most of the roaches seemed to be retreating to the far wall under this platform that consisted of no mattress, and with no available cushion whatsoever. I finally had determined the empty milk carton would do just fine for my needs. If I washed some water toward that far wall, although the dead may come splashing back toward me, at least those that could still crawl, ran quickly toward that far wall. Without my spectacles the fuzzy dark movement was about all that I could make out.

Just a few more splashes, and my work would be done. As long as those still living understood how the game was played. I believed that I had a system that I could work with. From out of nowhere a Deputy with a mop and bucket came from around the corner. "Look, Mr. Penn is flooding his cell," he accused.

"Oh no, I'm not," I replied, hoping to somehow use the opportunity to find different accommodations. After clearing the floor in the hallway the Deputy opened the cell door.

I felt that my one and only chance had surfaced. If I didn't make a break now, the resealing of my cell door could be for the night, so I needed to act quickly. He set the keys and the door was opened. I made a mad dash beyond him. Before I could drop to my knees to beg for cleaner accommodations, I was tackled to the floor. From behind, a shot rang out.

My head snapped back as blood oozed from my brow. As far as I could tell it was meant to be only a warning shot. It ricocheted from somewhere inside, or even out of the empty cell before me. I had knelt before it as an act of compliant obedience. That convenient area was now was being used as some kind of storage closet by the sheriffs. Well, there was not quite enough of those stored materials scattered about to *take one* for me.

The bullet came piercing back in a New York second. I was quickly ushered to even yet another unused cell. It had conduit running along the wall, yet with no wiring inside at all. If you've been in enough older homes you will note, they as well, have conduit on the outside of the walls, and not buried beneath the surface. This building was no doubt erected around the turn of the century.

The roaches now were using their conduit tunnel to have at me again. I was offered water in a Styrofoam cup. Quickly tearing that into generous pieces I pushed the first haunting roach back inside the tunnel. I tore and placed, ripped and pushed, until I had blocked their doorway. After closing off the passage, I asked one of the prisoners in the block just over, how it looked. I was offered a mostly clean towel to stop the flow. After the profuse bleeding had stopped just enough, I showed this fellow what had happened. He shrugged it off through the Plexiglas that kept us apart.

Within minutes, a duo of transport officers arrived to shuttle me to an emergency room. Or at least I had thought. Either they were taking me out to the country to dispose of me, or the one driving had forgotten the off ramp. The passenger grabbed the wheel, and with a quick thrust, yanked hard. The vehicle flopped around until the driver regained control. Thankfully, we made it to General Hospital without further delay.

This was the place that so many came, for any needed care at all. After so many years of people using it as a free service it has closed. Alas it was said before its eventual demise that those on welfare had driven it into the ground. Thankfully back then they were still in service. I strictly mean that to hide the shameful actions of the unwarranted assault, a plastic surgeon was summoned to perform his handy work. Once inside the establishment, I was immediately given ASAP care, and passed right out. I had fallen asleep even before the repair work to my forehead had begun. Finally, finally, after all of that, I fell to sleep!

What I awoke to was not so certain, at least at first. My ear felt as though it had filled with blood. With that vital substance now congealing, the interior of my ear canal felt clogged. I pulled on the affected area only to have a part of my face came off. The surgeon, who I now noticed to my right, slapped at my hands, not once but twice, before I relinquished my right lobe. After regaining control, the man smoothed the facial skin that had come up from my skull, back down across my forehead toward my eye. After a smoothing once more from this physician I passed out again for the duration.

Once recovered enough, and now in court, I was wary of my options, I tried to plead guilty but with asterisks. I certainly had committed the act. Yes, I had taken a pair of shoes just beyond the threshold of this business. That constituted theft. The fact that I was totally out of it after not sleeping for three days, meant to me I was even innocent at the same time as fully guilty. The fact that the shoes were valued over $1,000.00 meant the act again, would need to be treated as a felony.

He accepted my plea then offered two choices. I could go to the 'House', or since I was perhaps, still not quite right, I could spend 30 days of observation at Central State hospital. I chose the latter. The two main prisons in our area are down in the middle of nowhere. Most of the others on the bus down to those parts would be doing hard time. It was a quiet ride to say the least. My stop came first and I entered the great walls of this kinder discipline. Upon being given my room, I was told about the week of iso'. In order to determine my state of behavior they would make daily inspections. The head of the operations must have been a drill sergeant in his past life.

Although, I dearly loved to hear the sound of the boot heels marching closer, the guy could be the coldest damn son-of-a-witch one could imagine. He, as well, had a slight softness underneath the military approach to life that his world moved to. He was completely irate that I was trying to grow a few leftover beans from the previous day's dinner. Silly me, cooked beans are dead, therefore you know they couldn't possibly grow. It is the hard, dry items in plastic bags in the grocery store that may actually sprout, given the proper opportunity.

I made it through the isolation portion of my observation, and was allowed some freedom. It was a very serene and calming atmosphere that the main room offered. Every night after lockup, a fellow just a bit older than myself, would play the same song. Was it for me I had wondered, or a dreamy wish of his own that he indulged in. You see it was <u>Thirty Days in The Hole</u> by the rock band Babe Ruth.

On the Sunday before Labor Day, we were allowed clean-air time in the yard. I had found a four-leaf clover so tucked it behind the cellophane of my cigarette pack for good luck. I surely felt it as a sign from above. The next afternoon we engaged in sporting activities for entertainment. The winners even received a small amount of cash that could be used in the canteen and such. A large African American fellow was a super athlete. In the footrace, he came around and lapped me. I had never until then witnessed such an awesome athletic ability. He could have easily played linebacker for any team in the N.F.L.

I lost, and lost, then lost again. Only one event remained. It was the wheelbarrow race. This fellow checked out the goods, then without ado or warning, pointed to me and smiled. I had a chance now. He had wished to go first. Perhaps his speed played into that decision, as we could then make up for lost time with my being in front. I dropped down as fast as possible, and my feet were up. He drove me like a teenager with his father's Porsche. I suddenly fell facedown for a second into the grass. I still would not give up. Just like that in push-up fashion, I recovered and finished. We were hailed as the winners and my heart beamed with a radiating gladness therein.

It was just before, that such high spirits were in such short supply. Other than the nightly ditty from The Babe, not much else could do it. Weeks later the time had come. The day before my set release the call came in. I was working out in the gym when a guard made the announcement. It was a boy. Jason Argos I, had been born. He so named, after Jason's ship, the Argo. Argos should be pronounced like dose, as in, "a good dose of your own medicine."

After telling a genuinely nicer guard he would be sorry if he ever saw me again. I was allowed to leave. I was taken back to the place of my birth and formally let go. Upon seeing my girl, I was 100% back to normal. She had been staying back with her parents until that magic moment. We all three spent the night with my folks, then, returned to our little crappy apartment. My life was nearly complete with happiness. It being the start of the recession I was unable to find work right off, however.

Things would not so easily come back together in other ways. As far as the name, Jason's Mother was afraid to use the cool made-up name that I had offered. It was at the last minute that Mother offered my middle name as a substitute, so the boy became Jason William. As for my not being there, I would, over the coming year see that my lady now had something to hold over me, as long as we both shall live. It was the case that when she really needed me, I had let her down, and wasn't there by her side for that special moment.

No matter how much you do in the meantime to make up for such a failing, the big one will always be there, waiting to rear its ugly head. Such a memory will remind you that you did totally suck. At least for that, now frozen in time moment, you sucked big time anyway.

The next day we were back home in that dumpy little apartment. I'm sure that it helped to get a break in more ways than one. With my not working we had to have the phone disconnected. A knock at the door was unusual nonetheless. It was my mom, and sister. A drunk driver had run a red light and killed my woman's aunt. This couldn't be good. I insisted on keeping the boy while she attended to her family matters.

Within hours, came another visitor. Her brother had stopped over indicating that the guest of honor was needed at the get together. I agreed. If the entire family is feeling down, there is one person that can change that in a heartbeat, the baby. I handed the boy over, then, slumped into a chair for a lonely weekend.

1983

We decided to move. My girl and I needed more room. It was fine starting out in the smallest lowest costing apartment on the north side but our family was bigger now and the time was right. So, it would be goodbye to late-night 'mousecapades' with I donning steel-toed cowboy boots, and maybe just some underwear otherwise. It was so long to large gatherings of piss ants posing as coffee grounds on the kitchen floor. There would be no more being frozen inside our home when the afternoon sun heats the cold stillness of the waterfall *flowing* from above the door. Yes, it would be goodbye to all of those miseries, and hello to a newfound greatness that our fresh start would surely offer.

It was the end of March, so it was befitting that our young lives should move forward on the anniversary date of our being so profoundly booted from my parents' abode. We found a place just down the road a mile or two. It was on a main street, so bus service was ample. We had a large and beautiful park, a half block away. The place was what may have been considered a Polish flat at one time.

With an official Polish flat, the entire house was jacked up with a fresh new ground floor being poured underneath. Depending on the lay of the land one may be able to access the front door from street level, or by descending three steps or so. In either case, the rear would have three to six steps to descend, or a ground level entry.

Ours was the prior. It included a huge kitchen with space that most young families would find a challenge to fill. With the majority of these fabulous enclaves, the storage space lying at the far corners was more than adequate. The enormously inviting reaches of our back area, had a main seating section. The laundry area was a room all its own. With two stationary tubs, and space for a washer, and dryer it was just what the doctor ordered. If only we had room in the budget for such mechanical wonders. With a dollar store purchase or two, a clever person could have had loads of decorating fun in that back space. Since America had not yet fallen to such drastic lows, such an upgrade was not in the offing. Just off of that back space was a long, long room.

That dining room offered up much of the same quandary. We had what appeared to be a homemade hutch, apparently abandoned by the previous tenants, and a golden chair, bequeathed upon us by my parent's next-door neighbor. That oft pilfered easily moved item so taken by the queen of our castle, ended up in the dining room again, and again. Somehow, magically, my girl's mom copped us a matching sofa that was to be the main seating area in that dining room until we could manage to score some additional pieces.

It made so much sense to my girl, since our son's bedroom was just off the dining room from where she'd casually nestle in my stolen man-chair. It was just so natural for her to drag it on over. I however felt so lonely in our huge 14X15' living room with only the simple hutch for company.

So, back and forth we would go. One night after hanging out at the rehearsal studio I stopped in with my homeys. Lo, and behold, she had done it again. I for the first time realized how bad I had been about it. I mean if we could come in as a group and be okay with it, then why couldn't I come home and be just as nice when the man-chair had been commandeered on any other night in question? There was one other factor that made me stop and think, my bass playing pal got an eyeful when we first walked in. My girl was in her short-cropped nightshirt and he got more leg action than he had been seeing on his own I had fathomed.

So, he comes home to a beautiful woman with her chair in the dining room, and he's thrilled. I just needed to digest what went on, on my own for a bit. I was beginning to realize that I had taken things for granted, and needed to show more than just some love and support for my girl. No, it needed to be even more than eternal gratitude. Too bad the year was 1983, and nobody was hiring. I could have really used some big-time money to emphasize my newfound appreciation for my sweetie. What truly meant so much to the very core of my existence was now my woman and my child.

I was on another upswing. This was not a positive up for me at all. In the past I had utilized these up times to write. I would learn the hard way that life isn't easy. It only appears to be when we're riding the highs of our past efforts. When we are so very young, we learn to ride the highs our parents grace upon us.

Our very family, our friends, and anyone group or person in our circle offers forth a spiritual goodness. The key is to move a dependence on such glories into our own actions. For highs in our life, we need to be reliant on our very selves for a daily and spiritual form of sustenance. To work and toil toward such goals so as to have formed an abundance of altruistic virtue is vital. With a keen respect to our reliance on those necessary efforts, we're eventually allowed to maintain such a richness of splendor, a grandness of jubilation, and even a miraculous elevation of joy.

I, blindly and ignorantly, had failed to fully comprehend the value of even the most necessary components of existence, and how a man's life is measured not by his possessions, but by his gains otherwise. These hard-fought lessons were far from understood, as I was moving speedily into a mania of no return. On the third night, my girl had had it. She made secret arrangements to go back home. I had been issued my final warning while at the other place.

The life that I offered was so much less than mediocre. Things were lacking to such a degree that only our true love could keep us together. I was on borrowed time. I left again just to walk around. I returned home to find a note. The very same neighbor that took my woman back home to her parents had pity on me. She let me move some things up to the attic, where I actually slept for the next few weeks. After the dust had cleared, my girl was back home with her parents, and I had moved into the roach motel.

It was an old cowboy type motel from the old west that I made my way over to. What I mean to say with my fun title, is that it had a drinking establishment just next-door with two wide doors that connected this pair of old relics. It was recently torn down so I went to see if any roaches were crawling around. Apparently, with no humans around, nor any food for that matter, they headed for the hills. Those old rooms from this turn of the century establishment each had a bed and dresser with enough room for one's own chair. With no screens on the windows the roaches thrown from the window could easily make their way back up to your very own room for some type of buggish revenge.

Because of my kind and sweet hearted ways, and the size and sheer numbers of the little buggers it was just so much easier to give them a nice little ride like that. At first, they would somehow seemingly by instinctive, open their wings a bit. These beetle type bugs which could apparently fly so many eons ago, would then casually drop to the ground. I, each time that I snatched one up, would make my way to the window, then each and every time I'd say "have a nice trip see you next fall."

The roaches were actually easier to deal with than some of the local toughs were. It only took one too many and for a guy to say the wrong thing, for the fisticuffs to begin. One of my new neighbors was getting it bad on one occasion. They were much too far away for me to intervene in any way, and who's to say if the fellow didn't actually deserve it. The sight of his head flying furiously back from an apparently mighty blow is still with me to this day.

Some bad news had come through. The buddy from my wild Memorial Day, the fellow that lived down the street from my bass playing pal, was found dead. He was sitting in his car. After at least 12 to 16 hours, the police finally checked on him. The only thing that came to mind was that he was waiting for someone with connections to come back with some 'caine. Whoever it was then that took note of his waiting, decided to jack him. What compiles the entire ordeal into a heap of troubled sorrows is the way they later found his best friend from grade school.

It was around 7 to 10 days after that shocking discovery. The word was that this old friend had had a falling out with his woman. He temporarily moved in with his folks. Since the chum that they found, had lived half a block down all the while, it only made sense for the two to have gotten back together, right? Or does it? Because so much is speculation, and I myself hadn't spoken to either of these two for years, I felt it wouldn't be good to offer anything to anyone.

So, the friend that was apparently waiting all the while for his childhood pal to come back with the stuff, takes his father's police issue hand gun, and ends it all, inside the attached garage of their home? Sadly, it all ended that way, yes. It still rocks me to this day! That one pal again, was the guy with the '67 T-Bird that I hung with, on the 'gas station termination' day, or rather, it was the entire Memorial Day weekend.

I had a few bucks here and there and was able to stop in any old place and have one in my new neighborhood. This was the same exact area that my half-brothers had resided in for all of those years. Since small tappers were still going for under a dollar a glass some pocket change would perhaps get you one. At the Iron Steed one day, I saw the dude with twin brothers from the 'lakeshore-vision' that we all shared. Yes, it was that dude. He was the fellow that rode his bicycle with Brownie and I after we skipped eighth hour to head the lakeshore. He finally got around to letting me know that he worked just down the street at the kill plant. My new brother in-law worked there as well, on first shift.

Dude said he could get me in, so I was on my way. At this particular plant they mostly *did* old retired cows, although I actually saw a pair of longhorns in the pen one day. Those older bovines were always turned into cured meats rather than offered as fine cuts. I knew all too well of what went on, yet it was the mooing at night that cried out to me. Those old and lonesome milkers would call out to me in the damp chill of the midnight air. The late-night lowing spoke about what actually did go on in that building, even more so than the actual labor that I had just completed.

Those leftover mooers were called downers. They were those that called out to me so incessantly in that darkness of night. Through my unscreened window from the closeness of their pens, their eerie beckoning played on. Because of the piss and crap all over the damn place, coupled with the age of these old gals, some could not manage to stand up when the call came. Their transport would have to wait until the proper equipment could be facilitated.

On my way into work, the sight of open trailers filled with empty bones of previous kills sat down below in the lot. The tinge of red, hiding the harsh work that my brother in-law along with his co-workers performed, made for an ugly sight.

At night we only did one thing, we sprayed. On went the fire hoses, and we aimed at everything. Certainly, some shoveling was required, yet for the most part the boners, as they were termed, did a fairly clean job. The bass player from the band that I had started, worked with me there too. We saw each other and laughed. An old girlfriend's brother, Tom was there as well. Word really made the rounds, I guess. It was crap work for crap pay. $4.75 per hour is what we got, so with only five to six hours each weeknight a good solid budget was required.

One night one of the downers revived itself somehow and then escaped. It moved in freedom, coming closer and closer to my home. The cops gunned it down in the stillness of the night just outside my window.

I now had just enough to visit the better tavern in that area. A few of them started making wisecracks. I, even back then was a little hard of hearing, so it didn't dawn on me right away what these jokers were up to. They chuckled and laughed then said some more before finally, it seemed, they called a braver friend. That punk bastard, even though he was older than me, and that is exactly what he was to me, was unlovable.

I therefore believed that this fellow's very own mom didn't care to at all. Well, he got things started. The chuckleheads made some more unfunny stuff, while one got on top of the pool table sticking his rear end out. I have never in my life encountered a group with such a bland and completely not at all humorous sense of comedy. I mean they weren't asking me to engage in an act of buggery, nor were they calling me gay at all. Yet here the younger punk of the group walked up as if to begin that very act of sexual strangeness itself.

The older more serious sucker that had just walked in told me, "You're done." I began to finish off the last of my swill when he grabbed it from me. Placing my glass on the bar top, with the bartender ignoring the whole ordeal, he pushed me out the door. That however did not suffice. He followed along until we stood in front of the furniture store nearby. He made some shitty-headed comment then pushed me. The first shove failed to satisfy this short little scrapper.

Apparently, he needed his money's worth after being called on over to brawl. I flew backward with a powerful thrust with his second more rigorous effort. My buttocks, I could tell, had shattered the thick plate glass of the window just behind me. *Ha-ha*, I thought, *Now he's really in trouble.*

His eyes got wide and he backed off and fled the area. I immediately knew why. A piece of the glass had cut its way into my trousers. Because of the science and physics of the situation, that jagged edge worked its way deeply into the side of my left buttock. As I arose and moved away, the triangular section dug in so deep that it was ghastly. I walked carefully away and tried to assess the damage. Based on the blood covering the point of glass, it had dug in about an inch or two. I made my way up to my room and dropped my pants carefully to the floor. It was as bad and ugly as I had thought. With no first aid kit, I would need to improvise.

After half hour, since the profuse bleeding had failed to slow, there was no other choice. I had to call Mother. She woke Father and they came and drove me to a hospital. Upon awaking the next day, I realized a good-sized roach was on my arm. One had also crawled through my congealing blood, a quarter inch thick on the inside of my jeans. The blood thirsty bugger never made it out of that mess. He was now stuck like the dirty rotten little scoundrel that he was. "How could I possibly dispense with this little turd?" I wondered. Maybe they won't be seeing so much of that one any longer, and indeed not even next fall after all!

For being unable to fulfill my responsibilities at the kill plant for a few days it meant that I would have to pay a sort of penance. As my punishment I would need to go to the main kill station down the street. I climbed into the jeep and we drove on over. Once inside, I could see that there was little difference from the boner house. Save for one fine aspect that is. High on a chain hung the last kill of the day. It had just been halved and was nearly up and onto the conveyor system. I would survive.

After about halfhour, the floor was filled with a reddish punch of blood and water that extended to the ankles. By about 7:30 that evening the levels began to come down, and things were more bearable. "Remind me not to go into that bar ever again," I thought to say. Yet there were no people that I knew at this water-spraying kill-floor location. With the stitches still on the side of my ass, I guess those would need to suffice, as a harsh and painful reminder.

I had a cold soon after that horrible set of affairs. I felt that perhaps a beer would help me to feel a little better for work. I sat down on an empty stool. A half breed Native American girl was seated next to me. She was visiting down from the 'res', and had beautiful brown hair that highlighted her more than ample bosom. She was in a very special mood, and seemed oh so friendly. One thing seemed to be leading to another. As a tried-and-true minute man, I still had time to score and walk to work a mile away. As every minute passed, the chances we would move upstairs seemed to increase. Then someone showed up at the door.

This young lady, about my age, was telling him that he had spent all of his money so he needed to get back to the shack. She repeated her order, and as though he were well trained, he moved from his spot just outside the door and went back home. "Who was that?" I asked. She replied it was just her boyfriend. That was it. I may have had an affair or two in my life, but it takes more than your being broke from last night's drinking, for me to do your girl like that. No sir, I was out of there.

I quickly moved down the road to the fast-food joint. I was still really buzzed so I stopped at yet another. Well, now I was stuffed yet still really buzzed. When will I learn? One thing that did come to me from out of nowhere was a memory from my half-brothers' home. They had lived just down that very street and around the corner a ways as I have mentioned.

The memory that came flooding back from the deepest depths of my cranium was about how we had all vowed to be vegetarians together. I hadn't at that point recalled all of those days. The one thing that mattered most to me though, had come home to roost. I was once again a fully-fledged veggie. Yeah baby!

Awhile later I decided to check out the store that I would see from my seat on the bus. A 48 ounce can of carrot juice was on super sale so I decided to give it a try. I had little money, and with the 'nocooking' rules at the roach motel one couldn't really stock up on too much food. I crossed the street and made my way back toward home. Who should be walking right in front of me?

If it was a Native American girl with a boyfriend, she had better have a good sob story for me to still really want her. No, this time it was the serious fighter from the *near* bar-fight. Here I was right behind him holding a heavy metal object, and he had no idea.

Just that fact alone offered a high degree of satisfaction. I needed to calculate my moves very carefully if I was going to whack him. The thought of one strong blow to the back of his head with a punch or two thrown in if necessary, so easily came to mind. I just couldn't do it. I simply could not do that to someone, even if he somewhat deserved it. I felt a little ill inside letting him off so easy. I guess that I'm not the type to take advantage of a situation handed to me on a silver platter.

As far as calling him out for a fist fight, not only was there too many people on the sidewalk, if one or both suddenly fell into the street it may mean a more serious injury than a big 48-ounce can could cause. No, I would take the high road. I really am not the type that fairs well when having to watch his back either. Just a side note: someone was killed by a reckless driver so close to that area, only a block down the way. That was just last week.

I was at the far corner for the big '*Monday Night' Football* game. It would be the Washington Redskins vs. the home team. I needed to milk the small-time change that I had. The excitement of nearly every moment of that very special game had me wired. The beer just added to the buzz. They went back and forth throughout the second half. Finally, with minutes left on the clock our team scored to make it 45 to 43.

People were buzzing that didn't even hardly care about the sport. It was that awe inspiring. I'll never forget the way I was treated out at the bar, not so much by the revelry of the crowd, and their common interest, but by the nearly greatest play of the team's entire history, scoring wise anyway!

1984

One of my very own instances of tragedy involved my getting into it with a motorized vehicle. In hind sight I am ashamed to have jumped to such a conclusion about that particular automobile. I was on my way to the rehearsal studio that my old band was playing out of. I began to cross the street very near the corner but began to veer over. My mistake, a car crossing the main drag, punched it to make it fully across, four lanes of traffic. It was now headed directly for me. Thankfully, I had gotten that one ballet lesson back in 1963. With the finer footwork of a Mikeal Baryshnikov I flew high and straight into the air and so swiftly out of danger. It was after landing safely, that my temper so readily got the best of me.

I made it, and in one fell swoop, I managed to punch the driver's window as hard as humanly possible. Without putting much thought into it, like a lightning strike, I punched that window. Not only was the entire vehicle still intact after my brief encounter, my pinky was now broken as well. That move was not well thought out, as seeing that when you look at it, it is mainly me vs. a speeding vehicle, any interference should have been a given a logical, and most sternly actuated no! The car continued onward as if nothing had ever happened. I continued on as though I had just cracked a knuckle.

I made my way down to the rehearsal studio. Something inside me was just not right on that strangely unusual evening. Nobody needed me to get them buzzed so I meandered on home with nearly a full quarter ounce bag. Once back at home something said to eat it. I mean to just start stuffing the entire contents into my greedy mouth, swallowing, chewing, chewing some more. I chomped and engorged myself until nothing at all remained in the bag. I had been awake for two solid days under one of my manic spells.

I quickly passed out falling into a deep and comforting slumber. Upon awaking I experienced such a tranquil sense of satisfaction that I still recall the gentle feeling of blissful contentment to this day. I so quickly realized that I could be cured, and cured indefinitely until…until that is, I drank too much or imbibed otherwise, using any non-prescription goods available. Alas, one must drag through the river to find the other side. Within two or three years I would be back in harm's way, if you will. A lesson hard learned is one that never leaves. It never leaves without the bitter scars, and tragedies of such a sorry life as mine.

Update: I just read that eating weed does not allow for a buzz. The molecules need to be released in a special fashion through heating. I guess I was just tired enough on that night to pass right out!

With the recession over I managed to find work for what I would term a Magazine Company. It was more of a mailing firm sending out periodicals, and gazettes and such. For the most part we ran address labeling machines. Some work involved coupling multiple adverts into one nice group. Once assembled, it was a short hop to the binder, then back again. Imagine little mechanical hands reaching out to take just one piece of paper from the slot, then dropping it down onto the stack.

A suction cup would draw the paper advert forward then the hand, again, would move in and grab it. As long as it was finely tuned and your stacks had been neatly and carefully placed into the pockets, things ran like butter. It was a family business being run by the son, and daughter for the most part. Sissy had little to no tolerance for anything other than an honest effort or outright perfection. That's why she loved me so much. That is until I messed up big time.

Although, not so unscrupulous, the way a group of us were brought into the picture, did somewhat bother me. We were all sent there by the temp service. It was my neighbors who turned me on to the idea. We worked a nearly full week then on Friday the daughter called us over. She said if you all want to be hired full-time, here and now, just say so and it shall be granted. There will be no need to discuss anything with the temp service.

I will call them being thankful for the effort, but letting them know your term is over. (Wink, wink) You may know that such an agreement definitely goes against the contract signed by such a needful employer. What the temporary service will offer is a buyout of the contract so that it's a win, win, maybe anyway. Most lowly paid grunt workers aren't really that special however.

I was a fool in hindsight, but I was new to the program so didn't feel at all comfortable with how things ran. I mean over at the bar for lunch. The guy would cash your check on Fridays, as long as you ordered something. One particular evening, things were jumping. I had hardly the time to even request one beer. Before I knew it, lunch was over. He finally walked over with my cash and thanked me.

I was already feeling a bit ill hours before. I hadn't had anything to eat since the night before. Here it was 8:30pm and I now had the slightest of buzzes besides. I went to the long tall slender daughter, and notified her that I indeed would need to leave. She started to become outraged. I offered to come back in just a few hours, but she took her long, long arm and pointed it at the door. "You're done," she angrily ordered, "out!"

I walked into a bar on a late Sunday afternoon, figuring to maybe buy one to catch the game. It started out that way, yet when the local team held the opponents to no score on that subsequent drive, a glimmer of hope appeared. Soon enough our team scored, and at that point I looked over to one of the more *'hardened'* fans and quipped, "now all that they need is 17 more points."

"Yeah, sure kid," he chuckled at first to himself, then by hitting his pal on the arm getting his hardy involvement in as well. I laughed along out of merriment, but had to wonder what had happened to their boyish joy and enthusiasm. Just like that, no doubt due to the alcohol, I did decide that I needed another. So, soon enough indeed, I would order up, as the home team was about to get the ball back already.

They then would therefore score so quickly again. Indeed, they obliged, and would be setting out some hardnosed defensive work soon enough. In no time at all they only needed 3 points to tie and a full touchdown to outright win this game. You better believe I was at the giddy level by then. One can only be entertained to such an extent before outright laughter is the one option remaining. It becomes such a ridiculously humorous affair.

Now with those two hardnosed fans still sitting by in amazement, I just continued to laugh as the team all too easily enough, scored the winning touchdown. The *'Magik Man'*, at least the name, was born on that day! Although, we were not from Green Bay, it was still a delight to see him work his thing. Sometimes the best sports are about talent and execution rather than any sort of alliance whatsoever. Just ask those folks over in Poughkeepsie if it matters so much where the team is actually from.

I was just getting by after that time in my life. Because the Magazine Company didn't want to deal with it, I was awarded unemployment compensation. I hadn't slept well but hadn't quite gotten to the point of being whacked out. I took a walk out of boredom. At one point, a Hispanic man with cowboy boots and tall heels moved from his home then walked behind me. I still remember the click of his heels as we both ambled along. I took a shortcut down an alley then blacked out.

Okay maybe I was little whacked. The next thing I know I'm across the street, and in fully believing I'm about to be robbed, I rushed to the front porch of the nearest home. As I neared the door, I tripped and fell, grabbing on to the front door, I asked the man inside to call the police. "Someone's trying to rob me!" I exclaimed. I was sure he had merely complied with my request as a paddy-wagon pulled up from around the corner in no time at all.

In hindsight, I truly believe that evil spirits came to me while I was in a stupor, and entered my head. This is based on a theory that I now have fully developed. We could never be crazy on our own, yet it would be all too easy if demon spirits were at play. You know what I mean. Impkins, devilkins, gremlins, troll dolls. Yes, even those figures and more, could be at play in your mind.

As we're made in God's image it seems that it would have to be something so otherworldly to so truly and deeply affect us so. The fact that I had a complete blackout for a minute or two, is not only somewhat puzzling, but more than a wee bit discomforting. The deed was done anyhow, and the police had been summoned. Within two shakes of a lamb's tail, they swung around the corner.

Both exited the paddy-wagon and approached me quickly. One grabbed my arm forcing me toward the back door of their van. I locked my legs in an effort to explain. From out of nowhere the sucker that had my arm, cold-cocks me. My foot went back against the curb, but I was otherwise unfazed, I mean other than the broken nose.

The damn-ass bastard takes another swing and knocks my front tooth half out. I still was mainly unaffected so this fluffing damn German bastard takes his walkie-talkie and smashes it over my shoulder. The audible break was not from his communication device. I now had a broken collarbone as well. "Now get in," the sh*thead says. I crawled into the back and slumped to the floor in a heap.

They drove me to the hospital where I was born, and dumped me off. Because you cannot put a cast around the collarbone, I was told all that they could do was offer a strap. I was to have my shoulder strapped back as much as possible for any healing to actually occur. My tooth was moved back into position as much as possible, yet the gum had become so separated from the tooth itself, that a portion of the root was now visible. They suggested I see a dentist.

A week later a letter arrived from the hospital. It was awful soon for them to bill me, I had thought. Upon tearing it open, I was so disappointed. It wasn't anything from the hospital after all, it was a freaking ticket from those sh*tty headed damn-ass, cop-bastards. When I went to the trial the judge made some kind of remark about my being '*different*' or something. I made sure to wear the strap brace outside of my shirt. Since I had been a good boy in the interim, he would hold it open. As long as I could stay out of trouble for a year, the minor charge would be wiped off the record.

A few other freaked-out things happened that year as well. We had what was termed the deep tunnel project. These sewer holes were at least 25, if not 30 ft. high. The entrance lay just down the hill in the old parking lot of a now abandoned building. I was still out of work so turned on the TV an odd and unexpected explosion had just occurred. A man was dead.

His body lay mere yards away from my doorstep. A high price to pay for sewer lines indeed. It gets just a little weirder. Just as had happened with a cow when I was staying at the roach motel, a bull this time had made his way outside the confines of the packing plant. He had made it halfway up the hill from that newly dug, deep, deep sewer hole. The cops then gunned him down in the middle of the street. Just a short distance more, and I may have been able to assist him in some way.

Alas, I was struggling to eat well myself, and did not have access to any hay bales. It stayed just as strange on that hill for a while just after. I came home to find the World Series of American baseball had begun. From out of nowhere the most serious earthquake in a very long time began to erupt. It was shocking to say the least. Yes, directly in front of me, as I sat in awe, an earthquake began to tremble! Wow!

262

1985

My drummer buddy had gotten another case of Brew from his father that worked at the local place. Pops only ever had one word of advice for us, and that was to make sure we didn't drink it all in one place. I talked to dude on the phone and we agreed to meet at the park nearest his home. I arrived after getting off the bus before anyone else had.

I walked up to the hill and looked out over the parking area. Not one vehicle that I recognized was there. I strolled around the grounds until I came upon the basketball court. I took one look at those hoops, and then wondered "did I still have it?" I took a good start then jumped as high as possible. It was once again that most of my finger reigned high above the rim.

"And now for this one," I recalled thinking. Without anything at all possibly holding me back, I leaped for it. Yet once again my left foot, the leaping foot, landed in a depression just before take-off. I lost my balance while in mid-air then came crashing horribly down. I hit upon the pole with my left foot. Once again, I reeled in pain. I crumpled over onto the grass.

It was as I pulled the blades out with all of my might that a sense of deja vu came over me. The intensity of sheer agony along with my need to tear, and tear at the ground, revolved around one fleeting yet not even clear enough memory. This was indeed not the first time that I had gone through this very thing I was sensing, though dimly as if only in a dream. Just as the pain became nearly unbearable my buddy walked up to assist.

"Call an ambulance," I cried out, and he seemed to resist. I repeated myself then explained enough for him to get on it. No one had cell phones back in 1985 (at least not those that were smaller than a Hugh-Gass walkie-talkie) so the people running the swimming pool had to actually make the call. Since I had been quite audibly writhing in agony, they got right on it.

In no time I was being seen and had a half cast on the bottom, heeled portion of my foot with a full wrap around the whole of that. I called Mother to come fetch me and she arrived forthwith. Where the hell are the freaking crutches, I wondered, then asked a little more politely why she would bother to come all of the way out to the hospital without those. Am I supposed to fly around with my foot like this, I wondered?

She made me wait all alone then backtracked the two miles over to my older sister's home. I had already told her that's where they were. The pain itself had for the most part subsided, so as long as she returned with the damned things, I believed that I was going to be alright. It was soon after, that I felt the burn of life itself. When she came to realize that I was living in the old foster home that my older siblings had stayed at, she immediately grew cold.

When I asked her if she would pull up to the corner gas station, for some cigarettes, even that was somehow too much to ask for. I reminded her that I needed to be off of my feet for an extended period of time, yet to no avail. Why she suddenly could not drive the half of a block, while turning around after seeing the old place was beyond me. Apparently, too many memories crunched back in at once, and it became a cranial overload. I perhaps thought I could guilt her into forking over a few bucks, since this was a rooming house with no cooking, yet even that was like pulling teeth.

There is no love, like no love at all, I do declare. I went in and lay upon the bed. My only concerns at that point where for sleep since she did get the prescription filled for the pain pills. Since that was the depth of her current abilities I needed to come to terms with the morn and all that it would offer, once that time arrived. Mother finally forked over a fiver, and was on her witchy cold-hearted way.

Upon awaking, I felt much better about things. Without any food, I had only one option. I could starve all day, day after day, and then die, or I could walk the seven fluffing blocks with my crutches, all the while going against 'doctor's orders'. I was in no hurry but needed to pee. Since this was nothing more than a front porch that I was shacking up in, for a mere $20.00 a week, the only way was to go outside, then back in and up the stairs to the second floor. That alone took most of the energy that I had.

After a few more hours I felt that I could not go any longer. I would need to swing my way up to the main drag for some kind of nourishment. It was one of the hardest hours-plus journeys of my life. It took that long, and yes, took that much out of me. As long as I stretched my cash, I could at least go another day or two as it was.

Having lost all of my good graces back at home nothing other than death itself would bring about much assistance. When I fantasized about being in the old cellar bedroom, back at my childhood home, it only brought a mental form of anguish. Here, on the poorer side of town, things were all too real. I had run into a couple of new age hobos in the area. They seemed like good enough guys at first. One could probably say such a thing about most anyone on their best day. I mean theirs, not yours.

I needed to make my way again back up to the local food store. I emerged with a negotiable amount of sustenance. Upon hitting the corner who should appear? The hobo brothers it was, no less. The big damn German bastard ordered me to hand over everything. Do you believe that those suckers would commit the crime of robbery for $2.86? No doubt they weren't just homeless, but big drinkers as well. Father arrived, and bailed me out. All of the way back to the old home he did.

Upon recovering I managed to become employed at the local candy company. I had recalled putting in one day at the old place back in 1979. It was some of the hardest work I ever did. The job involved accepting large heavy sections of dough through the ceiling of where I stood, from where that very fresh mixture had been crated, and processed.

It was then transferred down to me through a trap door. That was coming from just overhead in the floor, from those above me doing the harder part. I merely needed to be at the ready to pass it along, every minute or so. This doughy mixture went along on the conveyor until finally it was flattened, rolled out, and cut into one of the layers of a pea-nutty bar. After a long hard day of that, I was completely spent.

Apparently, the usual guy involved in such movement needed a break, and took off just that once. Whew! Here, as a matter of relief, I would be utilizing my forklift skills to load refrigerated trucks. The forks would shift from side to side, so it was easy enough to maneuver the pallets filled with candy onto these semis, in double rows upon the floor. The actual candy we loaded were Raisinettes®.

These things would come in from California as fresh as a raisin could possibly be. The stacks could be six feet high by four feet wide, doubled. When those huge deliveries first arrived before being moved up on the elevator, it was quite an experience to be so close to them. I am telling you with all honesty, the shear liquid energy oozing from the very *essence* of each and every raisin could be felt from feet away. Duly consider that raisins are actually dried-out food items!

It was a dramatic rush, to feel that still moist energy, move beyond the initial shipping packaging and into my appreciative mind. It was as though these juicy dried fruits were bursting with a watery vibrancy, one that could crawl right into your skin. I am so certainly sensitive to such energies. Wow! There was only one catch.

I was only called in because Nestle's outbid us for the contract, and there was only a short time left to fulfill the remainder of the order. It would be all over in about seven weeks. Seven weeks of loading yummy candy onto these constantly running refer trailers. The other big name that we worked with was Chunky®. Other than the pea-nutty bars I had assumed that not much was really going on for this century old firm. Alas, I would rock it splendidly while I could.

One interesting sidelight was that one of my old pals from high school was the night-watchmen. He, being one of the fellows that had torn my military-style green jacket from my very body back in the day. I would take my lunch outside on the dock and he would be doing his rounds ensuring that no squirrels or any human candy thieves were not lurking in the darkness.

If one of us had *any*, we'd torch up right there while seated comfortably on the back of a truck. Those little get-togethers were nothing compared to the average Friday night we had so easily become accustomed to from our teenage years. The supervisor was an older gentleman that had served in Nam. He was a clean sober hard-working guy, until Friday.

No doubt this was how it had to be, but one imagines considering each, and every detail it could work no possible other way. I mean every Friday like clockwork, he would send someone to buy a case of beer, yet not until having determined that there was every plausible reason for having done so. First it was a guy's last day, then it was because we lost the contract, the next week it was my birthday, and so one. But it never ended.

The main worker, aside from myself, had been in a motorcycle accident. He was coming down the street at a reasonable speed when a car emerged from an alleyway and pulled out and struck him. He was badly injured for a short time, but had recovered with only the litigation to be settled. His recovery called for, you guessed it, another case of beer.

So, soon it was all over, so we had another *case of beer Friday thing* to end it all for the last time. That was my very last day, so of course from 8:30 until 11:00 we sat in the tiny shipper's lunchroom and partied. I will never forget that group of guys and the best job I've ever had. Simply because of them, I mean. You will read about some of the dicky-sh*theads that I have worked with otherwise. But with that group it was just so fabulous. That old factory soon enough closed, and would never again put out even so much as one additional layer of a nutty bar.

1986

I had the chance to go back to school. I had messed up the chances that I did have with common labor to the point that it only made a natural sense. Why of course, how could I have been such a fool? It's what I should have done so long before. I had to swim the stormy seas of tragedy before reaching the welcoming shores of formal education, I had gathered.

As soon as I was seated once again, in the place of so much comfort, I rubbed the desk lightly. There's no place like home I gleefully considered, none at all. I chose computer science as my major, and started in January. That summer I returned to work around the corner from home. The building had housed a car dealership back in the day but was now home to a second-hand store.

It was the perfect setup. I paid $20.00 a week to live in the foster mother's entryway, or enclosed porch. She even brought in a carpenter to add some shelving and an attached cabinet. From the used-item store I bought a wind driven mini pipe organ, and I was nearly near-Vanna. She turned the letters on a game show. If you're near-Vanna then, that's a good place to be.

I could also run behind the ancient competing auto dealership situated right next-door. The only catch was that one needed to squeeze through the chained-up fence to finally make it into our store's parking lot. One day, I had lingered a bit too long at home. I jumped up and out the door. Before I could get to the fence my slightly loose shoe wiggled, causing my toenail to get hooked up on the steel of my extremely handsome work shoes.

That action caused the nail to be shockingly torn from the toe. I sucked it up with nearly a tear in my eye and made it back in time. With my toe's blood well concealed beneath the steel, it congealed so quickly. It is so now, just the thought of toenails and steel-toed shoes gets to me all over. Our assistant manager at this store got a clever idea one day.

One rule we had before baling any unwanted clothing items was to carefully and neatly remove the fur collars from such old-school ladies' coats. "Yes, yes certainly," he had assured me. "Some of the girls, it seems, come here specifically for the vintage items," he added. These were what I considered to be 'Pointer Sisters' if you know what I mean. I indeed did come across a few of those older fur-collared coats, so soon enough, and was eager to please.

So, a $3.50 coat becomes a $3.25 fur piece. How splendidly clever our assistant manager was. He upped the ante with his latest brainstorm. We would take the old salesman's office, from the original building's use, and turn it into a vintage room. I got to help paint it. It was cute, and quaint, yet when dealing in the used-item business, any one thing can maybe help with sales.

On the outside of the kitchen-sized doorway he had painted an old-timey, 20s style, marquee type of outline. Proudly displayed in special lettering just under the point of the marquee was an easily read moniker. That's right, outside of this former salesman's office above the entryway read 'The Vintage Room'. We were so soon again back in business.

Here it was the summer festival grounds. My good brother had just played up on stage with his wife on vocals. Who should be walking right at me? Yes, it was them. I think he's in California now. For me I only have the song I wrote performed by Manfredd Mann's Earth Band. You may know of that group yourself, from the film with Bill Murray called Stripes.

That number from about 1966 goes, "Doo a diddy-diddy-dum-diddy-doo, I love her she's mine that's fine, wedding bells are gonna' chime, oh singing doo a diddy-diddy-dum-diddy-doo." Or words to that effect, I do sincerely believe that very song contains. Mine goes, "How ya'doin' out in California? (If you know that high pitched _California_, add that here) I've been there many times before but only in my dreams. California. How ya' doin' out in California now that you've made the grade? I've been there many times myself, but only in my dreams!"

Just imagine now, and I am not trying to be proud, and blow my own horn too loud, though just imagine being so cool that everything, or every other thing that came out of your mouth was going places. It was going all of the way downtown, then all the way around uptown. It then was moving over to the train tracks, and all of the way to Hollywood. I mean if I really wanted to…but no, I exaggerate a bit.

They did finally start to call me though, Willy Hollywood, or WillyWood. I'll get to all of that later. I could only think "will I?" Why, I'd love to. Whatever that will mean one day, when the time comes, I'll know it. It won't at all be like anything WIL.I.AM does I don't think. Around this time a dude had a used Les Paul Gibson '*copy*' guitar. I was going to get warmed up baby but good, and things seemed to be coming together with my studies as well.

Back in school again I could manage things between my loans, and the job. Saturdays and Sundays were mine, plus a weeknight or two for good measure. One Saturday our usual boss had off. He and his family would be traveling out of town for the weekend. The overall business manager would come in when needed, and this was such a time.

He as well, had a trainee with him who would be taking over the west-side operation soon enough. Normally, we were required to get the final okay before punching out for home on any given day. On this day I walked around, evaluated the need for any attention to be applied, and took action where necessary. I stood at the time clock for just one minute.

After punching and saying goodbye, I walked. Yes, that's right, there would be no stopping me on that day. The sheer joy of bouncing out of Dodge, was delightful. I walked out with another employee. She usually got a ride and mentioned yes that she still did, but needed something from the gas station. I joyfully strutted around the corner then into my home. Aaahhh, life was good.

The next day, a Sunday, began with a calm and cool morning. I moved quickly to work, but became distressed. My boss had not gone out of town after all. There he stood just inside, and was talking to two law enforcement officers. Once in the building they dumped it on me, and oh so quickly. A bandit hid inside the maintenance stairway area that led to the roof.

"Once you left Will, he decided to make his move," the manager somberly explained. "Well, Leon is dead but as far as rich, well he only got it in the butt for whatever reason, apparently he felt that Leon could identify him, then shot Ralph for good measure, I mean he already had the money, they just turned that over to him once there was no other choice," my boss had sadly explained to me.

My heart was taken from my very chest. I knew neither of these fellows very well, yet Leon was a good-natured type of guy, the kind you knew you could get along with. He was someone that seemed reliable, dependable, and friendly. I heavily moved into the back area. I sat on the mechanics stool moving behind the baling machine.

There was nothing anyone could do now. Ralph already had his wound well-tended to, Leon was out cold. I thought in a state of empty heartedness "I did have to punch out and leave at some point yesterday." The guy couldn't actually see me, and how I was a man and everything, from behind that door.

He would have simply waited until I left if he knew that I was a guy. Whether it was with permission, or without it, right? I mean, he didn't want to have to kill anybody really, did he? It isn't easy though to have been with someone so recently, and for them to now be gone. It would take a while to get over it all. Something much more personal that I needed to overcome was all too soon in coming, just after.

1987

During the summer at the second-hand store, I was allowed to work extra hours. I felt that I had gotten in good with management, and was truly appreciated for all of my hard work and dedication. That had been the case until I came in under the influence one day. I worked like a maddog going through the donations as quickly as possible to determine the salability of these used items.

Once we had an official WWII brown leather bomber's outfit complete with a leather Air Force cap. No good it was. The actual was too ripped, broken and otherwise torn to have held any actual value. The old cooling fans from the 20s and 30s, were the best thing to work with because you could plug them in right away to determine their status.

The mustier clothes could get to you after a while, but it was more movement than actual labor. On that day because a truck was coming in with used product, I hauled ass. Just before lunch my boss, Jack, called me off to the side to have a serious discussion. He did not in particular site anyone condition, that he was here and now referring to. He did however say twice, "you better…you know, knock it off, you know."

Up to that time I didn't realize that anyone would notice that you had dropped some acid just before coming in to work that morning. This reminds me of a joke that Jack had mentioned one day. His father had the car in for repairs. The two rode the bus together that day. All at once his father shouts out, "bus driver, stop, you have to let my son, jack-off!" I was more than a fool in this situation.

Having done such an immature dumbass thing cost me more than anyone could ever imagine. It not only sent me into a manic state, where I wasn't sleeping well at night, it got me fired two weeks later. This all was going on just before school started back up. Jack was good about it. He was as good about bad news as anyone had ever been with me.

He himself was a Vietnam vet. They used to drop Agent Orange out of airplanes down onto the jungle floor. He told me he and his fellow crewmen would stop at the drugstore that sold over-the-counter speed. They would pick up any other vitals before launching into the sky to do their thing. He had wondered, off and on, if his wife had had so many miscarriages due to his exposure to that harmful 'weed-killer' back then.

Anyway, we walked over to the restaurant/bar, and sat and had one. This moves into a more tranquil setting at first didn't click. The beer was a distraction, while he and Dave let me know that I was done. Apparently, they could feel my stress and tension, right through the air. I managed to enter the first week of school that year, doing well enough to get by anyway. That didn't last long.

After running into an old lady friend from grade school, and having her take me to my bank, I went up to the sixth-floor cafeteria. You could still smoke indoors back then so lit one up. I was cracking jokes, and making fun with a few of the younger students. I was so freaking wired, and high, but it felt really good.

The next thing you know two security officers seemed as though they were rushing toward me, and no one else. I panicked and ran. You see, I had been thrown out of the rooming house by my half-brother's foster mother. I was now living at the homeless shelter. When I went to my parents' house Father instead of answering the door, turned off light after light, after light.

I finally lost it, and picked up a rock. Hurling it against my parent's picture window, I chipped it and thankfully didn't have it break on all of the way on me. Within seconds, the police were there and I was in cuffs, and hauled off. I spoke to a counselor from jail that dealt with mental health issues. That here and now before me was the whole problem.

She apparently gave out too much of my private information to the school. I was let out of jail in time to start the semester, but now the dean was more than aware of my condition. As well someone had complained that I was living out of my locker, and took my pants off in front of her. Well, I did do that, but had on a pair of shorts underneath.

All of my clothes were being held at the rooming house, and I didn't want to have the chance for Betty, the foster Mother, to go off on me again. Had a neighbor not pulled her back she may have sliced me with a knife. So, here it was, school security cut me off at the front door, and took me to see the dean.

He let me know that for now I was suspended, and would need to show proof of having been on some type of medication before ever being readmitted again!

I went back to the homeless shelter where I had met a friendlier sort of fellow. He claimed that he had a hot lead on an open room over on the westside. He had been giving it some consideration, yet said I was welcome to it if I was that hard up. Seeing that he himself needed to get things together, a little more, before moving on, I was now saved from any further desperation.

1988

The new place wasn't all that bad. It was another cowboy hotel with a bar on the first floor. My room with antique furniture faced the corner. I had my weights, and I was at home. Hefting about 90lbs every day before noon, got me going. I would plug in my electric guitar and jam for about an hour or two. Things seemed like they would be alright. Other than having to take a dump underneath a delivery truck on one walk away from home downtown, it was going fairly well.

So, soon I was freaking again so bought a bus ticket to L.A. Things were going along nicely on that trip for a while. As soon as we hit Des Moines, I disembarked and failed to get back on the bus in time. I stopped at a local tavern to try and come to terms with my newfound plight. Some dirty rotten, not quite drunken bastard managed to lift my bus ticket off of me.

He was just the one that was saying that I may be able to negotiate with Grey Hound to salvage any value from that mostly unused ticket by requesting a refund. What a mother-fluffer. I went around to a hotel. For unknown reasons I decided to color my remaining funds with some Kool-Aid powder that I had brought along.

It was both an innocent venture into fun and games, and something engaged in out of boredom. The next morning, I went to the local café. I only remember one thing. A woman with the curviest most gorgeous hips was a waitress there. Oh yeah, one other thing, one of those people called the local sheriff because of my funny money.

I was placed in cuffs and brought in. Even though they fully believed that the cash was only colored for fun, I was told that they would need to keep it for evidence. They sealed the clear plastic bags right in front of me. The cold-hearted suckers then drove me to the local nut-house. After a few days, they set me free. Apparently, by then I had returned-to-normal enough. I hitched just down the street from that facility.

A very nice girl picked me up and drove me to the end of her journey in that direction. From there two truckers helped out. One took me to the state line. The other managed to get me close enough to where my mother was originally from, to call for help. I was taken to grandfather's home. He and my uncle helped me out from there. Within a few hours I was back on a bus going in the wrong direction. At least as far as California was concerned, it was wrong. Oh yes, it was oh so wrong.

Upon returning to the old cowboy hotel, I was deeply hurt. The facility was supposed to have let them know that I would be back soon enough so to not worry about any due rent. The message that they claimed to have gotten was just the opposite. They packed all of my belongings into a storage closet and rented out my room. That is to say, the items that weren't claimed right off by other tenants were in the storage closet.

I kept those other neighbors cool until I could return for as many things as was reasonable. I nearly gleefully managed to move back into the old rooming house. The old manager, my half-brothers' foster mother was no longer in charge. The fellow that had taken over vaguely remembered some trouble with me, but I assured him that was a just a minor occurrence, and all was in the past.

I finally got to live upstairs, just across from the bathroom door. Although, apparently, I wasn't the only person who was nighttime toilet 'challenged'. The new neighbor on the corner, the biggest room in the place had a potted plant. I mean the room was really that big. The window led out onto a porch-type of surface, that was just wide enough to sit on. So, we were goofing around one day, and the young girlfriend says, "as long as you don't try to use the urinal ever again."

"What urinal?" I queried.

"That's what I mean," she shot back, then giggled. She pointed over to the potted plant, and claimed her Romeo was at least trying to use that as a urinal. "I did my best to stop him," she added. For all intense purposes, we can imagine that she failed. Whew, it was he who had actually used the emergency facility and not myself so much, when I was somehow deep within the throws of some type of drunken blackout.

One day not long after, I stepped out onto the porch of the old rooming house. The weight of the moment was ominous. I could feel the heaviness of the burden my neighbor bore through the very air. Like a thick heavy fog, it hung suspended around us now. He claimed that this would be the last that I'd ever see him. Upon asking him why, he laid out the tragic details.

Although, stupidity is all that dumbness can ever be, in such a case as this, only a deep wrenching sorrow could be made from it. He continued on, letting me know that he'd be serving twenty, and that he would voluntarily give himself up at 2:00pm sharp the following day. Just as he had promised he would begin his long-term stretch voluntarily.

He then laid out the scenario explaining how his bro had gotten a full thirty. The two were at a bar down the street. It was just a couple of friends out for a couple of drinks or so. With not much going on otherwise for these two bachelors, it would be a couple of tappers then back home. If it weren't for the asshole, teasing-guy taking advantage of the situation none of it would have happened.

They were ripe for the pickin' and he snatched, and grabbed, picked, and poked until one thing led to another. After leaving, the dumber of the two, and no doubt drunker, said, "I've got my gun in the closet at home, let's go get it."

"Let's not let that god-damned bastard get away with this." The more casual and normal of the two, and I mean under sober conditions, was just over his personal limit enough, to bend.

He had let me know that at first, he did what he could to talk his friend down. Soon enough he caved. Then he stuck with him, like only a fool could, right up until the end of things. After retrieving the firearm, the two stood outside the window carefully aiming and picking just the right opportunity to fire.

Bam, he did it.

Dude pulled the trigger, and a man at the bar fell dead. I don't fully recall the most essential details. Yet upon further review, it was determined that the dead one now was the wrong one. At some point my neighbor not being able to bear the brunt of personal guilt thrust upon his world, gave himself up. If I recall correctly, he as well, offered up his buddy simultaneously. You can understand now, how the weight of his circumstance could be truly felt.

Like a fog rolling in from the lakeshore it was so dark, heavy and mournful. I too was brought down by it. If not for a moment, then repeatedly, to a lesser and lesser degree, with each reintroduction of the memory, I was taken less, and less aback. However, I felt less and less bad for this drunken fool, and his thin-skinned comrade as well. He in turn with each recollection would have less and less time to serve, of his long, long twenty-year stint in the big house.

It seems that sometimes it can be as though strange forces enter our lives and pit us against each other. I will go into further details at the end of the book so that each and every reader has the opportunity to be on guard about this silent but deadly creeper. It indeed isn't one individual but an unknown number of evil beings that can somehow enter our lives with a stealthy silence that can only leave us with regret.

None of us has seemed to come to terms with this unreal reality. We seemingly can be as puppets. One pull of the string, from these invisible shoulder gremlin types, and stupidity reigns. Angry flares, then uncontrollable rage may be on the agenda of these rapscallions. Recall my theory on homeless types seemingly 'talking to themselves'. In my best judgment, they are indeed not at all alone.

The band that I had started way back in 1964 was finally calling it quits. That was where I was headed a few years earlier when I was nearly run over by a speeding vehicle attempting to beat cross-town traffic. The studio, the same place that the Van Halen brothers had auditioned for Dave and I, was a good half hour walk from the old rooming house. The two buildings were actually lined up perfectly from each other.

It was at the edge of the old warehouse district that this cream-city brick building stood. The old original group had decided to reassemble after recording one song with a replacement guitarist. It didn't last for even one full rehearsal. After moving the equipment in, the stuff simply sat on the floor idly. After a few weeks the room sat empty and finally then, once again for ever, quietly still.

1989

I moved into a new place. Well, it was actually the old war widows home from WWI. It was attached to the old post office on one end with the Movie Palace from my visit for the film *Chitty-Chitty, Bang-Bang* starring Mr. Dick van Dyke right in the middle of this multiuse building. It was Mother that got me in along with the Girl Scouts. Since she was a troop leader, they couldn't really say no.

The other film was from back in 1973 or so. My friend's dad, the one that brought me down to Mussel Shoals that year (and a Southern Baptist as well) took exception to some of the graphicness so duly offered in the apparently PG film, Judge Roy Bean. It was probably the large woman wearing only a night gown while running into the darkness that got to him.

Could I actually see her buns as she fled? I recall not wanting to, as she was more than a little overweight! As for Mussel Shoals, that local is mentioned in the Lynyrd Skynyrd song 'Sweet Home Alabama'. The name of that musical group actually comes from their all too real, all too dramatic, all too cool to be true, in the flesh, gym-coach from high school.

So, the theater out front was on its last legs. They showed only re-releases for $1.50. Even that lowball, and pleading figure couldn't save them. Probably due to the damn bastards at school ruining all of the movies that the other children hadn't seen yet! You may know of such people that go on and on, spewing out every detail even though you've so sincerely begged them before, to please not do that.

A workout center was located just around the corner from the apartment's main door, and just before where my phone was. That would've been in the lobby of that old movie house. The apartments themselves were quaint little places with a built-in dresser just outside the bathroom, creating its own separate mini room. The bath had only a tub with no shower, so I got permission to paint that area.

After laying down a super thick coat of paint, I managed to attach a shower nozzle that was specifically made for such a purpose. It took some duct tape to keep it from coming loose, yet was what was needed. You know what they say about duct tape "if you can't duck it, then f**k it." The super-small kitchen had a mini built-in fridge which had quite obviously died decades before. There was just enough room to place my small dining set next to the window near the big, standard type mini-fridge.

Just outside that window was a landing that created the flat tarred roof over that gym just next-door. One day I woke up to see the local bartender (now obviously a coke, or opiate addict) standing next to me while I was in bed. He was eyeing up my stuff, deciding exactly what he would steal. I immediately rose, and with no clothing on, what so ever, pointed to the screen he had popped open.

I quite authoritatively, and most demonstratively ordered him to 'get the hell back out'. He, from a flat-footed position, dove right through the open window. In one fell swoop he was completely out of my home. I raced to the door to catch him. He reached behind a parked vehicle from just across the way, and pulled up a crow bar waving in warning.

I called the cops yet to no avail, he was long gone, and no doubt back at his place. To think that sucker served me at his place of employment just weeks before. He had seemed okay and actually a friendlier type of individual. One can imagine then what addiction really does to a person. As far as taking away any decency, or humanity left inside such a person, it becomes quite apparent that truth is a harsh cold reality.

The owner of the entire complex needed some work done. It involved the skylight on the other end of the building that had housed at one time the old local post office. It was now an ambulance garage. I let him know that the dry wood was sucking up the paint like a dying man in the desert. I meant one that had found some succulent cacti to suckle with.

He requested that I stretch it the best that I could. I promised to do my best, yet claimed, "I already know it's not going to make it based on the simple math." I still shudder when I pass that place up, due to the half assed job he forced me into. My girlfriend from 3rd grade now works for him. He is one of the wealthiest business people around. What a cheap motherfluffing bastard!

1990

One unusual occurrence played itself out rather oddly for me there. They were tearing down an old Laundromat and two houses in order to eventually erect a library. I saw that the old doctor's office/house from about 1896 was now empty. Some around here like to plant orange lilies by their garbage cans. I considered what would soon be taking place.

I so quickly had determined that wrecking crews would have a grand disregard for any old flowers out back. I enquired about a transplant with my building manager. He was merrily pleased so I began the move. There along the entrance side of my old apartment house were some plantings with just the correct space necessary to add to the beautiful growth.

I appreciated being able to salvage something from the old place. After perhaps four or five trips my jolly work was done. Soon after, I had noticed someone had broken into the other home just north of the old Laundromat. Out of curiosity, I went up and pushed the door open further. Slowly, like the sleekest of cat burglars I made my way up the stairs. The reason for the previous unauthorized entry was quite apparent.

Someone had ripped out all of the copper tubing for the solar panels! I carefully surmised that no other valuable item was present. I then looked over the last remains of the tenants that had moved. Now you need to understand that I was a bit down on my luck at the time. I had a headless Steinberger, white bodied bass guitar on layaway, and my TV in the repair shop.

So, what do you believe that I uncovered in a box, sitting on the floor? There where the parking lot for a library would eventually sit a nice surprise was offered. Those were books of course, along with an approximately 1956 movie camera. Those were more than just what I had needed. What joy I now held in my poor and lonely heart!

The one book was I Buried My Heart at Wounded Knee. Since my childhood friends were part Native American, I quickly made my way home and began reading. Soon enough, I, within about 2½ weeks, had the book read. Soon after, I had my TV back as well. Days later the coolest bass guitar ever created was home with me too! Steinberger tuning involves threading the strings in from the top.

Upon locking the assembly, things would stay so very well in tune. I was in a blissful state of heaven. The guy from down the hall, and his brother and friends, felt that I was much better on bass, so have favored that instrument more so, since. Not having a music program in our grade school one can imagine so very easily that I play for fun and not at all for profit.

1991

I was up late one night. I decided to walk down to the lakeshore. Along the way I mentally worked on one of my inventions. With so many these days having cell phones, perhaps the time has come and gone for my little doohickey. It was to be a colored hand-held pager for night-watchmen. Along one side of the slightly larger than fist-sized device, would be an array of colored lights.

Red would mean one thing (no doubt an all-out emergency) blue would mean yet another and so forth. This would allow for a predetermined communication in silence, in case a *'perp'* or two, were stealthily lurking somehow in the building. On my way back home from my cranial/on foot adventure, I noticed a spider out of its web, crossing the sidewalk.

My first thought was *what in the world is he doing at this time of night, and walking right into my path?* I took my cigarette pack and carefully slid him inside. With a sense of respect and a delicate concern for his safety, I made my way home. What do you think happened when I neared the stairs to the apartment house? A spider from upon the door lashed out at me.

In jumping a good 2½ to 3 feet in the process, the thing had me startled to say the least. It landed just before me at the top of the porch. I freaked a little, but the thing was so small it actually became merely one of the trippiest experiences ever. I thought about scooping him up as well, but he scampered off to the side of the porch. Once inside, I placed the other nightwalker in an empty shampoo container.

Days later the neighbor was over with one of his buddies. We played some music, smoked, and drank. I looked up at the ceiling and what do you think I saw? Now that other spider, the one that just moseying along at 12:00 midnight, was still behind the sofa safely snuggled inside the plastic bottle. But here up on the ceiling and walking in surprisingly perfect circles, around the covered ceiling light, was one that I so quickly dubbed 'Dancing Susan'.

She walked around again, and again. The others were not too enthused, yet I laughed a hearty laugh, considering. Her perfect circles, around nine or so, offered a humorous amazement, at least to myself. Ha, ha, ha. Are other people afraid if spiders are above head level? I have to consider such a prospect based on the lack of outright enthusiasm with those two.

One neighbor at my new digs suffered from depression or loneliness. She would hear me crank out either on my bass, or with my stereo. She would then crank out her own tunes, or call the cops on me for mine. It was one of the officers himself that had informed me in a gentle and hushed tone, that my sweet, much younger neighbor girl, "Needed peace and quiet."

I immediately drew concerns of a mental nature, if you know what I mean! Oh well she was young and sweet, and gentle, and somehow fractured by life itself. I finally stopped, nearly altogether, then only playing with headphones for the most part, out of a sense of compassion, and respect for her. Nonetheless, I am now mostly deaf. That condition being a lasting lifelong effect of my previous high volume, and melodic needs.

My neighbor's buddies were over again. This time we drank at his place. Near the end I tried to bargain for the last beer. The neighbor was fine with it. It was his two pals that thought otherwise. They ended up not only grabbing the last beer from right out of my hand, they chased me out into the middle of the street with the bigger one punching me in the face. It was a glancing blow and didn't hurt at all. There are just some people one shouldn't drink with.

The other neighbor was over with his buddy again. His pal had plans, and I myself had planned to stop for one around the corner. His buddy left and I said, "Well that's it then guy, I'll be leaving too." Something deep inside this young neighbor of mine caused him to feel abandoned. Not only was his good pal not wanting to hang out all night, the only one left in his life, myself, was bailing as well.

I, perhaps in a heartless fashion, didn't give a rat's patootie about his nighttime plans, or a lack thereof. I had to be encouraging at the door just a bit, and then boom. Somehow in the rationalization that neither of us should be alone, just yet anyway, dude snaps. He kicked the lock completely off of the door, with the still attached door knob punching a hole into the wall, as it swung violently past my face.

In hindsight, I can certainly feel a bit of letdown in the guy's heart, I had already let this fellow know that I had about 5 bucks and was going to stop in for one around the corner. So, I bought a brass face plate to cover the torn apart wood around the doorknob. With permission from management, I as well, professionally repaired the hole in the wall. It was a good thing that not only did I have some written material with pictures explaining minor wall repair, but I was a big fan of 'This Old House'.

I had felt that I managed to keep my good standing with the owner. Yet that was to no avail, it was only a matter of time. It was a certainty that management considered me a bad influence on those others. I did my best to keep that in mind for down the road. All too quickly, in addition to my young neighbor getting the boot, I as well had been evicted. I quickly went to the library and scanned the rental availabilities. I was now formally at my end.

1992

A place in my price range was available back in a city I had lived in before. It was there in an old neighborhood to the west of the main drag that I ended up once again. It was a place with a reasonably low rent. Some of the things in that city, in that particular neighborhood go back to the 1800s. Our super huge house was from about the turn of the century. It sat nearly kitty-corner from the old Schlitz Brew House.

It was made illegal at one point to corner the market on which beer you sold. So, keeping all of the profit in one spot for any one brewery was considered an unfair marketing advantage. The old relic across the way harkened back to that different time indeed. It was often closed and in between management, so it indeed did not become a favorite rest stop of mine.

I would have to say here that the decline of certain American cities was being increased by our importation of inexpensive foreign goods. So, not only would the coolest former brewery taps not be able to manage, but families as well would begin to experience the slide from our nation's greatness toward something just under that. Factories would close again, and again. With nothing to heal the wounds of idle times, things could begin to fester.

It was the onset of the crack-head area, er…I mean era! As far as the overall move for me on my end, it all went so smoothly. My drummer buddy and I began the operation. With a rented truck and our hard labor, the change of venue was made. I would start over. I would begin my new life. There were no limits to where my fabulous mind could take me. The world was my oyster.

Within weeks, I was back with my old pals from the area. My buddy was still with the gal with a certain personal connection. If you'll recall she was originally with my good brother's Doberman Pincher-trainer's brother. Apparently, this *way-bigger* brother, of my own sibling's pal, was not the fighting type. He allowed his woman to be taken quite easily. I shut it out of my mind the best that I could.

Those were personal issues, and I was not in the loop in that regard. That old buddy from my previous stint in that area lived just a quarter mile or so across the way. We began to do more and more things together again. This time around, rather than blowing our small piles of cash at any of the other local pubs we would stay away from those.

We as well took to drinking in, to save time and money, and oh yeah, to get buzzed too! Those two lovebirds(?) had a new friend that came around to party. He was known, as Miguel, and not Miguelito. That would have been a character from Wild, Wild West the television show. You knew then not to go to certain places verbally when dude was over.

I mean, as in referring to 'Mr. Miguelito Lovelace', the character from said show. You as well could never refer to any additional work on television or in the movies, performed by any actor, with more than a nonspeaking bit on the show. You in addition were not to mention any touchiness in regard to monikers, nicknames, or anything really from our individual pasts at all.

I mean, that was as long as our tales of adventure didn't include 'little' people, anyone named Miguel, other than he himself, or the TV Show the Wild, Wild West! Let's just say here, that he would have been more than merely suspicious, even balling up a fist underneath the table. We merely had to prevent any slippage when it came to our new buddy's true moniker. If not then, the hammer would drop!

Miguel would later relate to us his most angry moment ever. This was not only an effort to warn us of his erratically explosive, potentially hot-tempered side. It was rather a chance for us to truly appreciate his gentle and sensitive side as well. His trials and tribulations had all started at school back then for him, so many years ago.

A bigger boy was giving him a hard time. He felt that he could take it no more. His only option, it was felt, was to bring the family gun to school to get this bastard to shut the hell up, once and for all. He smuggled it onto the bus. He carefully hid it in his locker. When the time came, he just couldn't pull the trigger. After toying with the idea of merely brandishing the firearm throughout most of that day, he could take it no more.

He merely needed to sneak it back onto the bus, without detection, and to reenter his home. He felt that he was now doing so correctly. That would have been in a fashion just as casual as it was when he had left that very morning.

He was so close now to letting it go he could almost taste it. That is unless of course that sucker started something on the bus home.

That was it. His decision was now final. He readied himself throughout the ride home. He wavered back and forth, from telling himself no, to reaching for it just in case. Finally, his stop was next and the potentially life altering episode was over. This hotheaded fool that sat before us had certainly elevated himself from an event!

We simply needed to sympathize with his teenage plight and to have cut him some slack. Now with the fear of an angry uprising no longer sprouting from the emotional depths our generally meek and humble older buddy, we could go on as one big happy group. As long as any mention of the old TV show Wild, Wild West was kept to a bare minimum, we'd get along anyway.

1993

I managed to gain employment with a service that offered rides. This system that they had rigged, perpetuated the ever-present need for the continued flow of temporary workers. Only those that could manage a car loan would otherwise make out in such a well-heeled fashion, or should I say wheeled. Our main duty, which was monotonous and boring, to say the least, was to check empty clear plastic containers for unwanted, and minute particles of foreign matter.

Even though, technically they would have been encased in clear plastic, such particles were certainly a no-no. The time of year in which I began this particular position had one perk. We were making those plastic containers for ketchup, and peanut butter. The company was behind at the time, so paid us double overtime for the Thanksgiving weekend. I chose to work Thursday thru Saturday. That was some good money for a short while.

Life had somehow become, if even for a moment, a bit more than drudgery. Even in my veins, I could feel a surge of energy flowing through me like a beacon of life's goodness itself. I rose to challenge, and worked to gain. My mind opened wide to the possibilities and potentials. Alas, I did not manage to acquire an auto loan.

One of the most tremendous experiences at these new digs I had moved into, happened one early spring morning. This was a huge two family converted into a four-unit house. The evidence of such an expansion was shouted out by the now sealed door in my kitchen. There was a movable lower hutch type cupboard along with the cheaply constructed sink area.

Anyway, I wake up one morning to find that I could not see anything out of, either the kitchen window, or the small window in the living room. I was nearly in a dream-like funk, beginning to grasp for some reality. Anything, something that would relieve me from this delirium, would simply suffice, I considered. There was nothing near to reach for.

That is, other than a glorious, fantastical, overwhelmingly-white growth of flowers. You see, the neighbors on one side had a huge apple tree. On the other side of that large building right outside the window from my small living area, sat a cherry tree. It took me at least ten to twenty minutes to take it all in. Afterwards, I simply sat there wanting to laugh.

I had never before been graced by such an elaborate and overwhelming sense of whiteness.

To behold such an innocent grace and wonder, so early in the morning was delightful. It was wonderful, and even spectacular. I would so quickly trifle with words like, 'Dreamy'. I'd say the entire experience which lasted a good hour was even stupendous. Perhaps 'a view with a glorious-bright-touch' could best describe the whole dramatic scene.

Just when a playful and wondrous fantasy world, offers up its illuminist persuasions, a harsh cold reality could be at hand so soon after. It was a normal evening just before bed. The old two-story had beautiful natural wooden floors. My double bed and coverings were finished out the look. With a few pieces of art for the walls, my room would glow. I awoke that night from a deep sleep.

Rather, I tried to wake up. From out of nowhere I felt two hands choking me, nearly to death. My first instinct was to run. I thrust myself forward. With the energy of a man about to do or die, I ran. I ran for my very life. I ran toward freedom. I quickly hit the wall. It was actually my nose hitting that part of the structure that fully had me roused. I turned and pawed at the other walls.

Nothing was visible, and I was still mentally in a dark cave, fleeing my attacker. I moved and touched, touched, and groped. Still after all of my efforts nothing seemed safe or familiar. I continued to feel and grope along the cave wall. Suddenly, from out of the depths the light switch was near. I instinctively flicked it quickly. "Oh light, beautiful, beautiful light." It was never more soothing.

My racing, weary mind wrapped itself around every particle available, around the glowing and brightly colored elements of my 'well decorated' boudoir. I so lovingly took in the now screaming redness of my discount pillows. I reveled at the fact that I had been sleeping the entire time, and so very safely at home as well. It was at first that the bold, bold red of those unusual night things flowed through me like a river of life enhancing ichor.

Then with each following appreciation for my modern and comfortable life, I was being elevated from the vary depths of such a cranial hell, as to make it truly comparable. My appreciation was so tragic as to have me fleeing. Yes, from even in very own home, and through the very wall I did attempt to flee. Though, yes, with one quick flick, I was back to the glorious heights of a fabulous, and spring clean living.

At least as far as my housekeeping, it was certainly that clean. Just a note; *the nightmares have come back recently. I just tore the hanging mirror from my bedroom door, after not being able to get out of that room. I stood there and nearly peed my pants. Finally, after tearing that item away from its holdings (an item that came with the place by the way), and free from its stronghold, I was able to feel for the doorknob. I had been in another state of half-dreaming, and half awareness! Pawing, tearing, clutching, and cryin'. I felt and scratched at my exit way. Now I make it a point to leave the door wide open.*

My drummer buddy and I stopped for one. An attractive blond was seated at the bar. She was definitely a Viking girl. I mean she had long blond hair, and that Viking look that only true Norwegian girls can possess. We hooked up for just a bit. I'm not quite certain what she indeed had gone through, but she was what one may consider a recent divorcee. The only question I could ask myself was "which of the two failed to keep up with the other?" She had claimed to be a former speedboat model.

Although, her images did not appear in print, she most assuredly was a hot little speedboat queen. At the local shop in her area, it was once upon a time her responsibility to sell those fast-driving hotrods of the water-world. She claimed it was with 'one wave of her arm' after she had climbed in, and that salesman's spiel began. So, quickly then, all of those little speedsters would sell. She reminded me enough of my one true love, and I was hooked. We kicked it for a while. It was all fun and games. Alas, it was not meant to be for us. She went back to her world, and we haven't spoken since.

My first tomato plant at that new home however, was a sad failure. My good buddy said that we should have a race. Whoever has the first tomato grow, wins. I beat him by ten days. Thereafter the scrawny impostor of mine withered with a limp frailty. It was that the dirt was the color of tan pants. I vowed to fight back with all that I had. I collected some worms from the brick alley after a rain, and it was on. I took an old pair of jeans to start out and buried those.

Next, by coincidence they had cut down several trees at the local park. I rushed home, returning with food-store bags. After filling those to the brim with saw dust, I was back on top of things. My good buddy donated some rare tiger-striped Canadian red worms, from his grass patch. By the very next year I had the richest, blackest, deepest soil that one could imagine.

There was a place down the way hiring. My good buddy from the area, his gal, and Miguel had worked there for a while. It was a walk-on number. Such places are often so desperate for help that all one needs to do is smile and show up on time. At least as long as one holds their own in such regards. The company made advertisements. Those were mainly created from thick cardboard.

It was near the end of our latest get together at my place that things got out of hand. My buddy let them know that he '*needed*', the last beer. Finally, it was time to pop the lone remaining cold one. So, quickly an argument broke out. My buddy jumped from his seat moved to wall on the other side of my upstairs neighbors, and quickly punched a fist-sized hole into it.

Recalling how I had already gone through a similar situation at the other place, I went from shock to recovery fairly quickly. It would be then therefore a matter of simple repair as opposed to a total loss of my security deposit. My buddy scolded the other two saying, "Oh well, you two should know better, how many times do I have to tell you?"

I got out the patching material and went to work. One day I had my own conniption fit. I don't recall what was on my mind, but I suddenly and for no good reason, punched a hole in the cheaply made cupboard. Damn! I got permission from the landlord, and replaced the fiberboard with a thin sheet of plywood. Whew.

I need to mention here, that no doubt, well before the new landlord, and his business partner brother bought this place, whatever cheapo landlord that did own it, bought what was quite evidentially what one would have no other choice in referring to as *bargain-basement-paint*. When your every movement involves the lowest costing materials *certain stuff is gonna happen*!

Those two colors were puke green, and vomit pink. The staircase was pink, and parts of the kitchen were green, including the inside of the portable cupboard. I was in good standing with both of those owners as the one's girlfriend commented how beautiful my flowers were. I merely had added to what was already present.

I happened to be in the yard one day in the evening. I look up and who should be walking toward me from the back-alley way. It was both brother-owners, and their girls. It was merely a few perennials that got me the 'lifetime' reference from those two business partners. Sometimes apparently, a little color is all that is needed to cheer everyone up.

We had an illness in the area that was water borne. I had been drinking fruity-ades made with tap water all along. My favorite thought was the root-beer, noncarbonated mix, with sugar. I know I got the stomach malady well before the 'no-drink' order was issued. Since I had felt that I had gained a certain well-earned immunity from this bug, I simply continued making the ade with my very own local tap water.

I was a fool. The sickness involved overwhelming gut pains that throbbed and pulsated throughout a person's entire system. That was only alleviated by frequent trips to the porcelain throne. The entire event transpired over the course of about twelve hours. The next day one would feel well spent, yet without the gut-wrenching spasms. It all happened again, in just such a horrible fashion.

This next time around it wasn't half as bad, yet feeling like you're dying from inside out is never a simple walk in the park. I talked to at least one person that lived just blocks away. She also had it well before the call to drink only bottled water went into effect. Our city spent millions on an update to the purification system. What then was the supposed culprit? A group of cattle from upstream somewhere!

1994

Alas, some things are just not meant to be. The house was sold next-door. I had raided their garbage can the year before, planting all of those rotting apples in my flower beds. Here the first thing to be done by this new fellow next-door was the complete removal of every single tree branch on my most favorite growth at all. At least back then it was so special, and that an item owned by my former favorite spring neighbor.

That ravaging of my gardens very lifeblood went all the way down to the trunk. Indeed, as far as the cherry tree on the other side, that was taken from us during a severe storm. Torn asunder into an unsustainable stump, it would flower no more. It made me appreciate even more so, the year it bloomed so bountifully, offering up such a merry and gay morning time delight.

We had a new buddy from Oregon. We met him at that local sweat shop. One didn't just perspire doing this type of work. It was a dramatic form of laborious toiling that was required to perform those duties. Basically, we needed to rip the outside of the cutout adverts made of a thick cardboard material.

The hardest to work with were the 6" foot stand-ups. Those were for Halloween. Imagine Frank, The Count, Elvira, and so on. Another big job involved mini football fields for large window displays. The big, big bar down the way so quickly had our work up and on display in their large window section. We also did tickle me Elmo that Christmas as well. He was the most popular gift for the holiday season that year.

Our new buddy from Oregon soon needed a place. I want to be honest here, he drank a little too much and would end up in the gutter. Not just literally, but figuratively as well. I offered to let him stay with me on one condition. It would only be temporary. The first thing that he did as a roommate worked out well. Now stop yourself here. What special things could a new roommate possibly do, to make his presence even more than merely welcome?

He had somehow met a pizza delivery girl. From out of nowhere on his first night over, she rings the bell. I would say that most close relationships of the roommate type, temporary or otherwise, work out well if enough pizza gets involved. The fact that he managed to come by these pies vis-à-vis, a 'favor', didn't alter our overall appreciation of this tremendous and powerful act. I mean not even one little bit.

The fact that this delivery girl was a former high school classmate simply kept it all in the family. Before things got too cozy though, I needed to remind my new roomie from time to time that our setup was only for the interim. Once he had saved up enough cash, I would need to give him a rebate on what he'd paid me for rent, and then he'd need to be on his way.

It wasn't long, and with my support he was back on his own. He even moved into the old rooming house that my half-brothers had lived in, just down the way. That didn't last very long. In no time he had gotten the boot. I don't recall really whatever became of him. Perhaps his statute of limitations wore out and he went back home to Oregon. I had troubles of my own in the meantime.

1995

I got a new job from the temp service, mowing lawns at a cemetery. I was told by the full-time staff that, with about only one exception, we could drive directly over any new style, flat type, grave markers without any concerns. Apparently, this newer design was created for exactly that purpose. The cost of trimming around the upright style must have gotten out of hand.

It was June and I was feeling great. Being outside in the sunshine all day was exactly what I needed. That temp service otherwise would send you to the stadium to pick up trash. I have never in my life experienced such a privileged sense of sloppiness engaged in by a group of such slovenly piggish bastards in my life.

I mean to be honest here, these were simple baseball fans. The fact of it was, the better the seats, the more profoundly disgusting the mess that lay across our paths truly was. The pesto resistance occurred one day, when a freaking entire pizza was thrown to the flooring, with perhaps one bite taken out of it.

I can only imagine one instance when someone would accidently drop an entire pizza. That would include the World Series, and a home run to close it out. Suffice it say this would have been May, and not in the warm sunshine filled days of October, when the sport's playoffs are actually conducted. One small perk was finding things that people carelessly lost.

Though again, perhaps those careless, and callous fans simply threw those fine, fine items to the flooring because they know good and well, when they come back for the next game, the entire place would be miraculously clean, and free of full-on entire pies and the like. I repeatedly asked myself if something was surely broken within society. Images of Roman times played themselves before me!

The good things to find were either money, or a good watch with a broken band. Although, on baseball card giveaway day, numerous, still pristine cards, in nearly untouched condition, would be lying about, here and there. It was good though now, at the graveyard, to be away from such callously tossed, and unwanted remains. Those boorishly dreadful mother-fluffers, would need a different patsy to clean up their sordid mess!

I mean specifically, those that treated the area like it was their very own personal pigpen. If only I hadn't run over that one and only freaking flat grave-marker. Yes, that would have been the only one, in the entire graveyard, that could have been damaged by the riding lawn mower when taking a certain angle down that slight slope. The ground had a dip, and was concave enough so that you can just imagine.

So, yes then, as you were passing, the blades would be lowered, and zzzzz. So, easily the lettering and numbers would become slightly less pronounced. I was told insurance would cover it, but I needed to be more careful. Well, why didn't they have that all figured out in the first place. It would only take pulling up the sod, filling in the depression, or denoting that site, and letting people know about it beforehand.

I got out when the going was good. My next job had a slight bit of prestige. We worked with the company that laid the drainage system in the winter home of the New York Yankees near St. Petersburg. Here we were at the old 'official' Playboy club in local area. Yes, the very one formerly owned by Hugh himself. This place even had its own airport to boot.

We would be laying the drainage system on each of the 18 greens, so that according to the experts, one could play on a reasonably dry course, five minutes after a total downpour. This job had everything one could ask for. I hadn't had a good car since 1983, so getting a ride out to the place with a half hour of pay was sweet.

Working out in the sun with pros from Florida was cool too. Working with this newer technology offered a bit of prestige all of its own. That temporary position ended on a good note. What was the exacting reason for my newfound level of self-esteem? I read in the paper the next year, that after a few new paintings were hung, the place sold for a $240,000.00 profit! Now that's prestige.

1996

The decision was made. I would do everything that I could to once again set up child support with visitation. Even if that meant paying for all of the years that I was denied that rightful benefit of such a legally required visitation, I vowed to suck it up and take it like a man. I only had a phone number to work with, and my girl's mom had moved to Arizona. I don't know all of the details, but her father had passed away suddenly and unexpectedly.

I called someone for help on the situation. I was told that the first thing to do was to turn myself in to an agency. I would at least then be on the rolls of deadbeat dads. The other advice offered was to check for public records. This was before the dawn of the internet searches that are possible these days. It is so easy to check through such things in today's cyber-world on one's own.

My first actual and pressing need though, was to enroll in school for the new semester starting in January of 1997. I then called again to make an effort to appeal to my son's stepdad. He was afraid of me, or more precisely I had gathered, afraid that if I was coming around so frequently, my ex would fall back in love with me. The next logical step would have involved an affair behind his back.

The sheriff called just after my attempt at reconciliation. I was told by this local law enforcement person that I needed to 'leave this family alone'.

I said, "Hey, if my son lives there, and I'm calling him, then I'm not bothering him or anyone else." He again insisted that I stop calling. I simply repeated my stance. If the boy lives there I have a right to call. Who the f*ck does he think he is anyway? I mean dude, and the sheriff too! Both were trippin' big-time dog!

1997

It was time to stop living the starving artist's lifestyle. I would be going back to school again for sure now. I waited for the turn of the calendar with an eager anticipation. I felt the stance of an overwhelmingly grandiose sense, of heavenly appreciation. I was growing in a true sense of some type of heavenly offered, masculine superiority. I had put my foot down on career choices, with no other options remaining. This time, as opposed to my earlier stint back in school, that episode being brought on by desperation more so than desire, I would choose something oh so easy.

I mean even I would feel that it was child's play. I refer now to the cold realities of my existence. I refer to any and all loss of brain cells, and a diminished sense of the total and utter genius level of intelligence I had maintained up to that point. Those enthusing traits of mine, now being something from the past, I needed to come to terms with my present. Here and now, then and therefore, rather than computer science, I would be taking up accounting.

It was as though now, that I had a chance to start my life all over again. It is as easy as one can imagine with a small caveat; auditing would not be quite as simple as I had secretly wished. Perhaps I merely had amused myself into believing such a course was only a meager form of mere child's play. Somehow in the interim, I somehow had magically moved to a more convenient location on a bus line.

The bus stop was actually just across the street. I would sometimes have to run to catch it. Huffing and puffing afterwards I should have seen the signs. I mean of the onset of COPD. It was for blocks, once on the bus, that I was out of breath. I was more intently waiting to relax enough to study in truthful reality. All too quickly, I would immerse myself so deeply into a hypnotic sense of appreciation.

I had gone back to school now after so many years of things not quite working out the way I had truly wanted. I would make every use of any potential study time. I vowed also to study on end before any tests, or exams were given. This time around, I as well, vowed to incorporate more than just a few well needed changes in my approach to academic studies.

Going back to my first stint, other than a Dr. of English telling me my report on graffiti, in comparison to pollution, was simply brilliant, there were not too many highlights. I had promised myself that this time around I would do everything that I could, to get all A's. Therefore, once I caught my breath on that city bus, I would check over what homework or notes I had taken.

In addition, with this being the next time around, I vowed to change my appreciation for what I could turn in as far assignments go. Instead of tripe, and trifling, my efforts would be well thought out and honestly well worked on. I promised myself that I would truthfully give every full bore, head-on effort that was even remotely possible. I swore that I would ever so humbly, conquer all that stood before me.

When assigned something I would either stay at school and do my best there, or come immediately home doing likewise. For anything beyond only the commonest type of homework, I would take what had been worked upon, and push it further, creating what only true genius could easily offer. Once I, and I alone, had deemed a work *complete,* only then would it be sincerely, and actually ready for submission.

With these logical, yet oh so necessary, changes in my approach, I felt fully confident that the results would be just what the doctor had ordered. It turned out to be a sorrowful basket full of broken dreams with my first go around. That nightmare haunts me still in the deep recesses of my pure and gallant heart. I vowed to be most excellent with this next attempt however. The first term paper type report had been issued about the first week in October.

Rather than jam it into my locker forgetting completely about it until just days before it was due, I would begin right then and there. Expediently and in a forthright manner I labored. In giving it then my very best effort, victory would be mine. (Refer to the animation figure: Stevie Griffin, if possible.) That much I had promised myself. What I meant was, that no available minute would I allow to pass me by without taking full advantage of that supremely precious moment.

Thus, the schooling of, or rather, with my true sense of greatness along, a brand-new awareness of my identity had more than formally begun. One of the classes was business law. I actually enjoyed looking up some of the cases for research. We had full access to the local university's law library, if need be. We also had access to more than a few old Law Books in another part of our very own Academy. That course not only ended up being very enjoyable, but professionally satisfying as well.

The hard times came the next semester with Beginning Bookkeeping. It was for the most part, to be a course with only work being turned in, and no actual 'other' in class activity. One came to realize just how much the difference was in expectations, compared to a lecture course, or one with instructors and questions being allowed.

I am quite honestly one-fourth Polish. That means if you live on the north side like I do your brain will often go dumb, like the other north side Polish people around here. Even though I am the first one born in this area in my entire family, at a moment's notice I can just go local. I truly do believe that such an unexpected lacking involves a physical, though more so a mental type of carry over.

At the drop of a hat, I can truly become as ignorant as one could ever be. We were, for all intense purposes, only supposed to sit in the room for a small exchange and turn in any old work, while receiving things she had just handed us back. She was a full-on CPA, and as harsh and stern as any German woman could be. We 2-yearstudents were only going to be Certified, or Degreed on the lowest level, at least upon graduation.

Not like her highness with her CPA credentials. After the second time that I had summoned her over she seemed to get really super-pissed. On one hand she just walked away, while refusing to help me. On the other, she had claimed that my chances of being hired would be greatly enhanced, with the ability to actually type.

I caught her both ways, if you know what I'm saying. First off, I found a way to redo any work previously handed in, without actually redoing it all. She walked away in disgust when I went on about starting the entire chapter over, since I was already finished with the very next one. What a damn witch. I was flabbergasted.

Upon arriving in the computer lab, it had hit me though. Why in the hell would I redo anything when I only needed to print up (or place onto disc what

I needed) then turn it in? I actually didn't need to start back over from scratch, since she only wanted one aspect of the work to be clearly correct. I found that I could all too easily fudge the rest.

As far as closing the month professionally it would not be quite necessary after all. That is why I still consider her to be more than a slight amount on the cold side. When it all became so clear, I was superbly thrilled, and remained so very happy, indefinitely just after. If I propped open the month in question, long enough to make the correction, the month that I had just completed would never have to be touched at all. The mistake itself didn't carry over financially. So, no dollar amounts would actually be affected.

As far as my typing skills being honed, I found a Temporary Staffing Agency teaching a one-hour course per week for only $30.00. I soon began bringing my unfinished works to school to get those songs, or simpler rhymes neatly cued, and ready. Learning to type correctly was quite like learning the piano. The keyboard of a computer though, is much quieter when mistakes are made. With a piano anyone within earshot knows just how much you really blew it, baby.

I really began to enjoy those lessons to the extent that I was absorbing a powerful energy. Yes, it was one that I could even type into, or rather, tap into, for any God given length of time going forward. Truth be told, I did hammer out a few typed reports back in 7th grade or so. That would've been on the '47 Royale that Father had brought home from work. His employer sold anything outdated to the workers there.

I had even begun to make up children's names to just keep up with my skills. I would propose a girl's name such as *Aurange Lilian.* The girl would be called Aura, while her official first name would sound more like the fruit of the same color. *Winchester Bulldog* would go down as a cool boy's name. Though, how about *Maverick Wild-Horse,* for a handsome young lad?

He would of course be called Rick, outside of the family, and close circle of friends anyway. This went on for months and I finally achieved the score of 43 WPM, my highest rating since that time as well. My future great-grandson 'Thor Sledgeman', will be thankful one day for all of my efforts! Although, Jason Argos I will always be number 1 for me, I feel that proud strong people can use any name they damn well want to.

1998

With one of the other accounting courses required for completion, we were required to enter at least, if I remember correctly 1,000 keystrokes per minute. Those involved numbers and not letters. I was flying and my hands and fingers were in tune with the world, at least the world of accounting anyhow. Things got down to the stretch. I had some unfinished work that needed to be handed in late. That was in the more challenging course of auditing.

One had to be able to take a car apart, on paper at least, and move each and every component back to its original grouping. To even begin to comprehend what auditing involves think about a receipt from the food store. You have now eaten all of that food. An audit of your consumption would involve the receipt, rather than anything else. Overall, an audit is an on-paper determination of the amounts and values of the assets and materials in a building at any one given time.

In addition, anything tangible on paper would need to be proved out, as far as the actual existence of those noted in the real and physical world. That subject reminds me of an old story from New York City. Dude had fudged on his tax return. The audit came. What this fellow had prearranged is nearly laughable, save for the sheer and outright audacity displayed by this soon to be busted business man.

He had it worked out so that after a semi-trailer from the yard had been gone through, that material would be quickly and casually moved to an empty trailer in the back. On and on this went. The agents from the I.R.S. finally smelled a rat. Suffice it to say he was busted, and the agents tended to look for cheating scammers even more so going forward.

That was actually the easy part, as far as an audit with tangible physical objects to observe. It was keeping track of the other hundred things one had to remove from a completed item now for sale that was the truer challenge. Imagine a piece of artwork. You walk up and that aunt of yours that loves art as much as you truly do, offers this mind-blowing proclamation "that, oh that's a jigsaw puzzle."

"Yeah, we just all put the thing together last month or so."

Your mission should you accept it: account for each and every shape, formation, coloring, and slight or serious mixture of hues, comprising that now well framed piece of artwork. As long as a person remains cool the actual amounts will so easily begin to present themselves. You may disassemble the entire work to begin your task. Beware though, you will indeed be required to put each and every item back into its original place, before the work is truly finished and complete.

Remember my motto: one is still using four letter words when speaking things such as; work-done-over, quit-tata-outa-here. So, do please begin, if need be, saying those only two apropos offerings. Yes, I mean finished and complete. I believe the entirety of such maneuvering all at once, was a little fuzzy for a few of us. I sat down with the instructor. He easily laid out the few things that I needed for his satisfaction regarding my final grading.

To fully complete the course, he would let me slide into home plate with a terse and well documented downgrading for my last offerings. It was a simple matter of taking care of business from there on out. He also let one know, based on past quality, what you would end up with, after the late work had been received and accepted.

My finally succeeding was so much a moment of pride, as it was indeed one of utter and total relief. I felt as though a great weight was being lifted from me off of me. It was verily lifted my soul, from my mind, and from my very existence as well. I was all too easily and quickly brought back down to earth by the lady seated next to me at the celebration ceremony. She wasn't just graduating with me.

No, a bit more had gone on for this eager achiever. I inquired about the extra tassel adorning her handsome cap. She replied that in addition to her new accounting degree, she was a return student who had graduated from the business program. That alone quickly prevented me from possessing any false sense of undue or egotistical pride.

Suffice it to say that aside from my computer science work from '86/'87, I had all A's, and yes, that auditing class with the late work, which should go without mention here, as being a bit less than stellar. I was ready for action though. Was the world actually ready for me? The damn bastards indeed were not. I applied, applied, and applied somewhere again.

After about 2½ weeks, I crawled into the local tax preparation office of an internationally known conglomerate. It was with my tail between my legs, and my heart weighing down upon me heavily. They called soon after and I was in. Just like that I was hired and given my office headquarters. It was one of the lowest days of my life. I had just applied at the 2Letters Square Co. as a tax professional. My first office would be in a community along the lakeshore.

1999

They had me filling out practice forms to start. Those were Dick and Jane type of returns with forged W2 forms. I didn't mind, if you've got to start at the bottom, as long as it's a beautiful neighborhood with plenty of middle-class wage-earners what could be worse? I considered the next offer to be the best of both worlds.

I would be working fastidiously now, in the lower income area for people desperately needing the cash flow. My services could now be offered in such grand fashion as to lift me up in a fashionable form, and take me to a subliminally quiet place of serious and staid solitude. My new boss, the manager of the closer office in the older neighborhood was glad to have me. She was generally a nice person yet had her pet peeves.

For one, if I had decided to get buzzed before work, and talked in a slightly slushed-mouth condition, I had better not have the one remaining beer in my coat pocket for the walk home. She was honest enough their Captain Bucky. She claimed if stupid stuff comes out of your mouth, the first thing on her mind would be, "is the rest of the beer in here?" I mean the backroom/clothes closet.

I think she kind of got PMSy, during some of her harder months though. Indeed, then I was appreciative of the truthful warning. She had fired that former employee for being a bit sarcastic, and mouthy. Because she knew he only did that when he was under the influence, she checked his coat. Sure enough, he had a still unopened beer, just like I told you, in his jacket pocket located just around the corner on a hook.

I assured her I would never get so bored with my day, or tax work, so that I would've consumed even a little bitty drop before punching in. No, no I didn't see myself getting buzzed at all for any part of the day, since it was early on, and we are just starting to get busy. She appreciated the outlook, and claimed we would surely be busy, at least off and on any way, for the coming weeks ahead.

We at least had an amicable understanding, and a mutual respect for each other's spaces, in order to start off our busy week. We would joke in that restroom of an office—if only we could turn the actual bathroom into another office, we'd have another desk available for crunch time. Things would cool down though, soon enough I had found.

Since I was the day person, she pulled out the hard stuff come March. Those would be started returns that were given an envelope then filed away. At least fifty or so would be waiting patiently for completion. I was to pull the entire stack from its hold and begin calling. Many of those returns were from men with children living in another home.

Not only did these fathers often have child support withheld, when they realized that they couldn't make it on such a low income, one thing often came next. They would usually request that their federal withholding be lowered. With few, if any dependents to claim on a tax form, such a move would often result in an extremely low return being available or worse yet, an actual amount due to the Feds.

No doubt more than a few of these taxpayers wanted to know if they were getting enough back to cover our fee. For those very fathers paying child support sometimes they actually owed more money to the I.R.S. than they could ever muster together on any given day. Yet these poorer blokes had earned enough, so that not filing was not a legal option.

I felt for them, but that's life. My theme is to never have kids. I can proudly say that I have never had a child that was actually planned ahead. Now that I've had a chance to think about it, I wish that I could go back in a time machine for a do-over. This world isn't good enough for any of my kids I tell ya'. Are ya' with me peoples? Not quite up to par for my general standards, this crappy place called earth truly isn't. No, 'tis both heaven and hell together, that we experience here on earth.

This format of paper product movement, in and out of those file drawers went on for years, although we moved down the street a few blocks, to bigger digs after year one. I was finally so at home at a place, so that I could have really bad gas and it would not have mattered. I mean on Sundays anyway.

That was a day of the week that I just mostly sat there reading a newspaper from the gas station next-door. I believe out of the years, over on Madison Avenue, I only dealt with any actual taxfilers on a Sunday, about three or four times, if that. It was a formality for us to be open. With my being single it was only a matter of my reading the paper here, or of actually doing in there at my desk.

The cold season changed, and I finally received a company bonus. At about $412.00 that meant I would go from $7.65 per hour up to $8.34. At this rate, I could afford a new pair of shoes one day. I had picked up a vintage 1982 Ford van. By the clutter of leaves in places supposedly covered, I would say it had been parked under a tree somewhere for at least a few years. It started. With that being my main concern, I was fine. As long as it continued to perform that one main function, I'd be all set.

I went to the temp service and applied. They got me something at a hospital working for a contractor. It turned out that the fire inspector had paid a visit and found troubling places above the ceiling tiles. Each and every space in that area was supposed to have been encased in a special fireproofing material. Because some rooms were supplied with pure oxygen, a fire could possibly race through the structure, so very quickly, so that extreme measures would need to be taken to avoid certain catastrophe.

The head man had let me know that it would not have been the first time a little spot was missed, but now because patients are nearby, instead of the blower we needed to make a paste, and apply it by hand. Each of the necessary ceiling tiles was removed, and we went to work, climbing up on a ladder, and patting the special compound in place. I went back up a second time after collecting more of this sticky paste, and *shreeet*. I ripped my pants.

There was just one baby little problem. Having been on a budget for so long, and devoting all of my energies toward school, I neglected one small aspect of my wardrobe. Those whitish garments that I was told are actually pea catchers, or stoop sitter protectors. (PS: don't ever sit where someone has once stood without wearing underwear.)

I mean here, that I really didn't have any to speak of. I had a few pair of jeans alright. I just needed to go get to them to adorn my slightly embarrassed self with a greater force of protection. I simply couldn't have young sweet nurses walking by and checking out my junk either. Dude was cool about it, and I jumped into my 1982 Ford Econoline van, and sped home.

I managed to smooth things over with this contractor from out of state, and it all went well. I was even making $2.00 more there, than when doing taxes. That job played out and since it had been so long that I had had any extra money to speak of, it was easy enough to stay on a good strong budget, albeit one that did not include undershorts! I made do, the best that I could, in anticipation of landing the big one. As Father said back in 1981, "Look at the calendar, it's going to be a cold hard winter, isn't it?"

I went out to start the old girl. It was damp and humid, yet as cold as a witch's buttock. The sucker wouldn't start. I did a foolish thing at that point. Having the doghouse function aroused some of my concern initially, as soon as I saw the leaves on top of that ancient antique engine. So, I had already purchased a can of starter's fluid, simply out of my very own ancient and antique reasoning.

Because that '*doghouse* thing', or engine cover, was inside the vehicle forming a hump under the dashboard, spraying the little whore was easy enough. The other aspect I wanted to reconsider immediately. You see, this particular model had a left-handed key start. That means one could spray with the right, while turning on the ignition with the left. As long as a person was deadly accurate with the spray it would be a piece of cake, anyway.

Having had the flu as a baby back in 1961, an illness that left me with a lack of total balance and utter control, I often can't do anything correctly. At least I can't often perform delicate procedures requiring a steady hand. The little witch of an engine caught on fire. Luckily, this last storm that streamed in off the lake, with its haze of moisture, also brought along some snow.

Just enough of that fluffy good stuff, was present on the grass next to my spot. I eagerly picked up as much as possible, yet needed another, and yet another scooping. Finally, the internal blaze of my vintage van had been extinguished. That fire melted so many of the required mechanisms, and necessary rubber components. I quickly called the junkyard, and ole' boy was history. Alas, without full-time work, keeping things in fine working order would not always possible.

I had a chance to move into a better place. It was a nicer one-bedroom type of place in a better neighborhood that was so close to the lakeshore so that I jumped on that b*tch like a red-hot mama at a Floridian Spring-Break frat party. I had recalled walking by on one of my manic episodes in the summer, so knew that it was a beautiful place in the warmer times to be.

During those wide-awake times I would walk, and walk, walk for days, losing even ten to fifteens pounds. The recollection of having been past the old place so very long ago, by now, was a dear yet distant memory to me. The actual reality of living inside that aging facility was somewhat different. The swimming pool was drained and empty.

I found out that the air-conditioner ran like a maddog, but didn't quite pump out the cold air as it should have. Yet still, on any given day it was so beautiful in the general area, that those distractions were easy enough to deal with. I was working for the largest professional tax service in the entire world, and was truly going places. At least I had felt that way for a change.

I would be driving now to work, rather than dealing with the fussy ancient van. I picked up an old 1988 Olds for about $485.00. I quickly ascertained that the nice gal down the way knew it would be a fair deal even with the repair job. The gas station just around the corner from her place redid the bearing on the right side for about $120.00. I was back on the sweet, sweet road again.

Upon returning to my humble abode, a true sense of peace would overtake me. This small lakeside community was named in such a cute way. That certainly was helping things. Does it work for you? No doubt indeed it does. The world was ready to smile upon me with open arms and a heavenly sense of devotion. I was all too eager to smile right back at things.

The warning had come for potentially high winds, with possible funnel cloud activity. I called my drummer friend. "Don't answer the door, they're going to make you evacuate," I had warned him.

He claimed that he knew about the situation, and was on his way already to his mom's just to the west. One other thing he imparted, "A freight train just went by, so loud I felt the picture window might shatter."

"Well, that was it, good thing it passed already," I countered. He said that he was just getting ready to go in any case, no doubt for a quaint and simple visit with Mom. I wished him luck and smiled. What we found out later was shocking. A guy near his home checking his oil had the hood torn away, yet another vehicle parked nearby was flipped over, then it moved east. I had yet to work in my old tax office situated across the street, once again, at that point.

After being transferred, from the better neighborhood I was still working out at that older place a few miles down the road. Plenty who were there that evening in my new neighborhood remembered the dramatic sequence of events all too well. They all got down on the floor hiding under their desks. A good thing too, because then it came.

The entire thing was no doubt allowed to escalate because of the huge open area provided by the airport. This section of town was just beyond, and up the hill, from this vast and open wide expanse. It blew all of the windows out on our business alone. Every last one! I had a chance to investigate further the next day. It lost some traction before toppling two trees and then hopping over the street to die in the lake.

What I saw later was a bit more shocking. Just down from my buddy's and across the street, not much more than a stone's throw from the gas station, lay the wreckage. It was déjà vu, all over again all over again (as Yogi Berra would have offered). An entire garage had been rendered into scrap. Recall for me here what I had witnessed in the aftermath of our previous funnel cloud encounter!

Well, this garage was much larger, and seemingly sturdier than the victim down the street from my boyhood home. Nothing more than a heap of rubbish, was in the place of what once stood. Amazingly no other structure was harmed. With these housing plots being slightly larger, this other neighbor's garage, was just enough out of the way, to come out unscathed. Whew!

Winter then did arrive, but not too soon. I switched temp services, and landed a real accounting job. Here I would not only be plying my trade, it was the type of work that I enjoyed. With accounting, only one main aspect is considered for the bulk of services. In the small business bookkeeping world, all one needs to do, is categorize everything.

It's all money in, and money out. All of the categories used are in one section, or the other. (It is in addition, a very real and basic necessity that one scrunches down their shoulders, and writes really small in the available spaces to actually qualify as a true-to-life-and-genuine Scrooge-ian bookkeeper.) I quite frankly never felt more comfortable or at home with an employer. As far as Frank goes, you will find out soon enough how it worked for me.

In any case, any 'money in' could be from loans, sales, or sales of service. Money-out would be for utilities, rent or mortgage, supplies, goods to be sold, taxes, and payroll. One extremely important aspect involves what I would consider to be more like personal record keeping with a flair. That category would be assets, owner's equity, and any debt which would be countered against that total amount of 'in the good' finances.

I was feeling at home, and loving it. It was my job to sort the paperwork, and enter the numbers into the system. The company used the same software that we had at school, so I was right where I needed to be from day one. There was just one tiny situation. Our receptionist/office manager had a small teeny, tiny, oh so wee, yet somehow enormous, little thingy or so, with her self-esteem.

She had a deep seeded fear that the clients wouldn't like her, at least as much as they would Steven or now me. Once the ceiling hit the fan, she then would go off big-time on our boss. This little old lady (not from Pasadena though) would then change into her running shoes, and storm out. It wasn't the actions at all that found and left me so dumbstruck.

It was the way that she seemed so normal in a strange and eerily bizarre sense of being. Who knew what may set such a person off, at all. She had warned me when I first started that I should never just get up and approach an individual who had just walked in. No matter whom that very person was. The fits of anger went on only occasionally.

By the end of the first summer, we had caught up for the most part with all of the monthly work, and any of our other things were going swimmingly. One tidy little number did pop up just then. Our boss the owner had a bit of a situation going on with his diabetes. He would need major digit removal, and the surgery had been merely postponed while we were so busy.

At the end of the year, Frank the taxman would come in from the town over. He had worked for the same business as myself, doing taxes years before. That special surgery for Richard would wait until that very work was completed for the year. The taxes finally were complete, and we all got back to our regular routines. Soon enough, the scheduled surgery would be a certainty.

My drummer buddy was with a new group. They were heavy metal players that had gotten back together for one last shot at stardom. We went into the studio to cut a single with the old vocalist, just for old time's sake. That went well, and they got a response from their ad for a replacement vocalist. Practice began and the makings of a full C.D. were implemented.

'The Master' as I call him was not only a teacher of the guitar, he had a recording studio in his home. That was out in a remote enough area, so that passing delivery trucks wouldn't ruin the recording at all. I call him the master because of his numerous 'How To' books such as The Songs of Black Sabbath by Troy.

The lead player from my bud's new band was a former student of his, one who now could pass that knowledge along, and recover some of the initial costs of being at the pro level. One thing The Master would never tolerate was an avid wannabee. Only professional level guitarists, or just below, could kiss his royal ring, if you know what I'm saying.

I felt good about the group's prospects going in. There was though one small drawback that they seemed to be dealing with very well. It was the chicken scratch on a huge chalkboard in the rehearsal area. That form of brutish communication was quite necessary. I myself got dizzy just looking at it. So, with the brother as the bass player, and a local guitar teacher on rhythm, regardless of the communication drawbacks, I felt the sky was the limit.

You may know that Ozzy's first lead guitar player was a local teacher. God and circumstance took him from us all too quickly when a helicopter mishap occurred. To round out the metal group that I was working with a new vocalist was finally chosen, and things were well underway. A good vocalist can get a band signed in seconds. The jury would be out.

There was a situation at my small business bookkeeping job. Frank the taxman came to me and whispered secrets of his, in gently phrased and hushed tones. The thing was that he had asked Steven a Vietnam vet to do things, but Steven drew the line when it came to the separation of powers that we possessed. So, Frank was so pumped and spiritually uplifted now that I was on board.

He had found something of questionable treatment from years past, and wanted me to tend to it. I assured him that I would look into it, and took a mental note of the situation. That would have worked for me back in grade school as far as telling myself to remember. Here I was now over 40, and my memory had begun to slide. It dies for me just a bit, each and every day now.

I am _enubilated_ to extremes when the sweetness of memory showers itself upon me. Here and there, I do recall such a sweetness of memory, and other times I leave it parked just outside the back door. The fact was that someone had listed a complete set of dinner plates as an asset, rather than a goods-for-sale item.

The difference being that those types of assets often have the costs spread out over years, as opposed to matching the cost vs. sales, profit in. That would be always within the very same year of said purchase, if that was indeed the actuality of any such affairs. As far as assets, most can be declared for the full cost in the year of purchase, as I attempt to refer to here.

By electing to utilize the other option if so desired, it will play out differently. The thing was, when Frank came to me the second time about that discrepancy, after realizing I had failed to make the change, I did feel more than sheepish and remorseful. Our business made it a point to indeed, maintain the separation of powers, so Frank himself was not supposed to make any alterations to that part of the books.

He was more than a tad weary and dejected with my failure. He was visually upset that I had yet to make the change. That moment set the table for our future relationship. Although, he seldom was in while I was working, his disappointment was nearly palpable. Thank goodness tax time is only for a short duration in the winter. The separation of powers would so quickly be a geographical aspect of our existence too. Yeah!

2000

Earlier in the year, when coming home from the accounting office, a traffic jam developed in the far, right-hand lane of the freeway. We all sat there for at least twenty minutes. Our quite necessary delay was due to an unknown factor, and seemed to stretch for miles. Because it was still early, around 3:45pm, the movement of vehicles from behind in the middle lane started to slow a bit. I checked, and checked, and rechecked.

There was just enough of an offering, here and there for one's mind to begin toying with the idea of moving over and out of the trap we were in. First a hint of space, then nearly enough, then an "ooh…ooh, good thing that I didn't jump on that one," is what played out before me, in an inviting sense of chance. Those possibilities were beginning to show themselves to some of us, again and again. I saw a clearing moving forth, but stopped myself.

I had too easily ascertained that not even a Porsche, or Maserati, or Bugatti could have worked its way into such a tiny spot. Yet here was one now just after, and at least 30yards in length. It beckoned unto me to jump on in so much so, that I did what came naturally. I looked back and saw that things were just dandy in the rear then I turned to look ahead. I never made it any further.

With a jolt, and a crash I turned to see the '82 Cadillac just in front of me was at a complete stop. What the hell, I had just surmised the entire situation, why are cars in front of me at a standstill when they had all just passed me going thirty, forty miles per hour? It didn't take long to figure that equation out.

Some bozo up ahead, squeezed his non-sports car into that super-small space, so that each car behind him had to jam on their brakes. That stupid asshole! Well, considering that I came close myself, to jumping into that spot, I guess that he is here and now, clearly forgiven. I truly mean that we cannot at all possibly be El Cerebro the Magnificent.

I hadn't quite afforded myself the chance to buy auto insurance in time. Not only was my hair permanently embedded into the shattered windshield, with my hand having torn out the shifter handle from its mounts, the car was a total wreck. Soon enough a sheriff had moved in. He forced my car from the rear, off to the side.

Those law enforcement vehicles come equipped with a battering ram on the front bumper just for these types of situations. I braced myself, then took what could be considered my last ride in that heap of torn and bent metal. The gentleman just in front of me had the trunk pop open. It may have needed a simple pull-out to get that to ever close again.

With the tailgater, (that stupid little bitch was riding the woman's tail in front of her, perhaps in an effort to force that lead car into closing the inviting gap just up ahead, and behind that other lead car)in my sincere opinion being the one that I felt had caused it all. By leaving a thirty-foot gap behind her, what else were people going to think?

Her closeness to the car just in front of her, may have been skewed by all of that room screaming from behind. That driver, the one with ten feet in front, and a thirty foot opening behind, had the rear, left, corner-panel pop out, from the tab and form fitted seal. Something that was created during assembly, no doubt, I had felt. Something so easily popped back into place I had figured.

I was left with one of two options to maintain my driving privileges, either come to an agreement with each victim separately, or put up a righteous amount to be held on deposit with the Department of Motor Vehicles. The older car had the lower repair bill. It was basically totaled, yet perhaps with just a little work, may have been drivable indefinitely.

The newer car had bogus charges that could not have been the result of our unpleasant encounter. I put up the $2,300.00 deposit for that lying witch, and called the other fellow to come and deal with me. Luckily for me, the tax service had paid me my annual bonus. I so surely qualified in my second year of work there.

The man in the car just ahead of me arrived at my home with his wife. I had invited them over to sit down and hash out an agreement. He had seen the entire incident from both sides. He knew good and well that someone had shot out from my lane, then moved quickly into his, all of the while I was doing the same exact thing from behind.

We didn't bother getting into it. He was there for one thing, the $1,700.00 I had offered in exchange for his dropping the hold on my license. I had created a contract for us to cement the deal beforehand. Just add this, he required, "The terms of this contract are binding as long as this check for $1,700.00 clears the bank."

I truly was sorrowful for how our encounter turned out, as his car was a vintage 1981 Lincoln, although not quite a Caddy at all, it was once a very fine car. I quickly agreed to his easily offered requirement and wrote out the necessary wording for his satisfaction. Here, this man was innocent of any wrongdoing and was simply at the wrong place at the right time.

I truly appreciated everything that he was going through on my behalf. It was a tremendous relief to have this innocent, good-natured person on his way, and somewhat taken care of. That little tailgater would have her turn next. In the meantime, the state decided to require all drivers to carry auto insurance.

I was embarrassed yet had to agree with the new legislation as there was admittedly a sense of lax behavior in that regard on my part. Some would not be able to afford insurance or they would have purchased that precious item already. Others would scrape together the money, and continue to drive. That was life. You do what you have to do in order to survive.

I went out to stop my son's entry into the army. That was something done to stepsons by the stepfather, at least in the old days. I mean that it was a part of the kitchen table talk that would occur well after all of the dishes had been cleared. That was an action based on a sense of poverty, or any real lacking duly present in such a household.

My son's uncle answered the door. It appeared that because of Little Richard's family, my boy was held out of kindergarten. I would say that he no doubt hadn't gotten all of his shots, something required by the local municipalities of grade schools. Since they were living in the old "*back-house*," the older place behind the new and beautiful home, closer to the country road going by, it meant that maybe they were living in a type of poverty all of their own.

I can only blame that stupid bastard and his god-rotten parents though for how things had fallen apart for me in that regard. For causing a well-imagined trauma to my boy, only an overwhelming sense of success, and status would seemingly appease these sons-of-witches. Was that the reality of my son's existence? How does someone possibly ever flunk kindergarten to begin with? I was the bad guy, my son the victim.

The boy's uncle did his best to assuage my angry feelings. He claimed that it wasn't so bad since the Jay was now an honor roll student. Well, I was at the college level when I was only 11 years old. How that little factoid of his being a year older than all, or most of his peers could be so easily dismissed is beyond me.

Such a situation could not be good to someone that was a total and utter genius at a young age. Whether or not it was me, or my son that was queried on their true feelings about the subject, I have to believe that *disappointment* would be the name of that truthful and sorrowful tale. I vowed to go and find him once school started back up.

I had worked for the U.S. Census Bureau since April. My accounting work was only 30 to 36 hours per week, so it was nice to have the additional opportunities for income. I started for the US Census Bureau just in time. As tax time ended a new count of the population had begun. It was desperately needed income for many reasons.

I had just purchased that 1988 Pontiac for $485.00, with the simple and necessary bearing job on the right side. After that additional $120.00 in repair bills, I was back in action. I was a crew leader for the Census Bureau and after being hired, was allowed to teach the overall course for beginning enumerators at the local high school. The hearing for the accident soon followed.

These hearings are not held in front of a judge, but for a judicial representative of a lesser standing. The room was small yet comfortable with a conference table and wooden chairs. We were seated and the claims began. The victim from up north brought her dad. She laid out all of the facts which were bare.

She was hit from behind by the car to the rear, after I had indeed hit that dude's car, pushing him forward. The traffic jam was another matter. I explained how I had waited for twenty minutes and finally saw an opening. The smaller slightly inviting version, just ahead, wasn't really wide enough for any car to easily move into. "That bozo," II said, "Had caused it all!"

The judicial assistant had one comment, "Yes, he stopped, but you didn't, Mr. Penn, and that's why we're here."

So, even if cars suddenly aren't moving in front of you, it is still your responsibility to brake in time. As far as the damages, he asked my witchy victim exactly what she had with her. "If this then is the only evidence you have," holding up the estimate, "Then I'm sorry you will receive nothing," he coldly informed her.

"In addition to that, she has had the repair bill padded," I added in. "Do you see the charge for a door repair?" I queried.

"Ah yes, and what is this for?" he grilled her. She stumbled, and mumbled, but had nothing really to offer. It was that I had tried to get her to agree to that lesser payment well before this, based on the estimate minus the door repair fee. She had turned it down flatly.

I did some quick math and made a newly fresh and well calculated offer. Just to show her how much of a little bitch she really was, I offered to settle for the bumper repair plus $25.00 for gas to drive up from her cushy little lakefront town. One of her claims was that one of her dogs was so rattled by the whole affair that certainly a little extra compensation was in order. She did so even to the point of wooing a mechanic into dishonestly padding the charges. God help me!

It was too bad for *pooksie*, that I didn't agree. To this day what really gets to me is that one woman can drive 10 to 15 feet behind another vehicle while on the freeway yet feel that other people are responsible when her dog gets all shook up from an accident. A minimum ticket for her driving too close would have sufficed. I did walk out of those festivities with my pride held high, and my 'make-my-own-hours' job from the Census Bureau ready to tackle.

Not too long after the whole nightmare, my drummer buddy's new band had a date. I would heft the drums as usual and enjoy a night out with the guys. We made our way into the new spot. The owner was eager for his new business to do well. He offered 'other' types of music and metal. The guys, of course, fit into the latter category.

It wasn't long and we were up. The anticipation of the early crowd began to grow. One lady in particular was excited. She sat down next to me and introduced herself. I mean rather, she introduced her little predicament. You see, it was that the gentleman that had just made himself comfortable next to her, had begun his spiel. "He is much too young for me," she explained.

"Well, I'm certainly old enough," I assured her.

"I mean I just turned 40, and you…must be about…32. Oh, I hit that right number alright. It was most certainly an attempt at flattery. I honestly knew that 32 was much, much, too young of an age to have guessed. She was pleased enough to come clean. She was 38, and soon to be even older! I'm with the band," I explained, "even though we have most of the stuff in, I may be required to jump in at any moment to help out."

She didn't mind at all and we bonded smoothly. I had no idea how much our paths had already crossed before, in so many ways. The truth and reality of life involves one very clear feature for those who never town. You will so often go out with girls that had crushes on your friends back in grade school or vice versa, get hired by a school chum's father and such, or even try to pick up a close buddy's drunken mother. Just be careful there, Captain Bucky!

I had talked to my new Lady right off about the band's previous show. With a twinkle in her eye, she smiled indicating that she attended that first show, and sure enough, an image of her near me was conjured. The fact that she was into music and live bands allowed for a rapid sense of comfort. I felt warm and at home with her near, and it was pleasant. We moved forward quickly, and I mean we went on a date the very next day.

I arrived at her home with a sense of glee and joy brimming from my heart. Her mother was there with her younger daughter. The sweet child begged to go along. Had I been thinking on my toes, I may have wrangled a four-way date for all of us. As it was, I hadn't realized what I was getting into. A rocky relationship with my dear, sweet Lady Lauralie had begun.

In seeing how her daughter wished to be a part of the group, we both made small moves to that end. The first weekend we rented a movie and stayed in. This type of activity set the mood for the remainder of our relationship. We would often stay home on Friday evening then do something as a family on Saturday or Sunday.

The first outright argument thereafter, didn't take long. Within weeks we were at it. One thing that I have found from our troubled days together, if both are sensitive people, and both can be needy in that respect, it becomes very difficult to maintain a steady and loving togetherness therefore. I hadn't previously considered myself needy or shattered in that respect. Duh, go back to 1978, and my brief but well titled nickname!

These otherwise normal and loving relationships become impossible or nearly so, to maintain, unless one or both can detach from the needful aspects of such a pairing. It is required I feel, to attend to those emotions and feelings that somehow now may become neglected. If a couple can be honest with each other, about such needful feelings and emotions, a sense of closeness then can develop.

As long as a sense of openness and honesty prevail anyway, a true feeling of closeness should be had. If there is too much need, a rift begins. The key is to catch it early on, and modify the actions. Again, I've always said, "I just wish I had kept a couple of hundred-dollar bills in my wallet for such demanding circumstances."

Although, never to be an introductory approach to a solid and loving relationship, the cold hard comfort of cash often cannot be denied. A little extra spending money goes along way when it comes to changing a bad subject. As long as a Hydra of future neediness does not develop, one may be able to dance fast enough to charm the beasts of such everyday living.

In hindsight, I do feel that I could have played her like a fiddle. The reality was that my own hurt feelings had gotten in the way of my seeing the needs she held out to me. Those were issues indicating a soft and delicately fragile psyche that lies just beneath the surface of such events. Such needs were so readily exposed as being born and derived of her past challenges.

I have since come up with an ultimate game plan, one that I truly believe would work for so many. It involves having those two one-hundred-dollar bills on me, in my wallet at all times. This emergency money could be pulled out at any given time, then utilized demonstratively for such extreme occasions. The truth of it was, and she had come clean with me, she suffered from good old-fashioned P.M.S.

With my new cure, I would merely have to open the billfold, produce the offending items, and plead for her forgiveness. "Is this what's causing a problem?" I would ask.

"Here then, I'm sorry, please take this and get it out of the house, please do, please do, do, do, do." The act alone would at least change the subject. If a fellow is in over his head, he might always ask the stepchild for some advice.

After all, if those big bills were for ice-cream, and fun things, maybe the young girl could talk to Mom about how the annoying funds could be spent. Depending on the income status of the household that needful amount could be reduced to $100.00, or even increased to $1,000.00. It's the healing power of the green stuff that matters the most, in under such emotionally extreme circumstances.

Now, to come up with an extra couple of hundreds would be the real trick. I at the time had to have a reserve for car repairs. Therefore, I was in a bit of a pickle. It wasn't long and my Lady started to go off on me again. She had been sitting at the computer surfing things for some time. From out of nowhere here aggravation began to escalate.

I could almost feel the negative energy flowing into her, and then right out. Again, and again, more, and more outraged she became. Then she threw it down. I was out, I needed to be gone. With my sensitive nature, I was devastated. My feelings were hurt so that I went into a tirade. I would take everything that was mine and leave. That included the bake-n-rise pizza in the freezer as well.

You know that I am super-pissed when I take the pizza with me. Within days, or even hours my Lady would call. She was sorry, and needed me. This situation developed into more than a habit. I began to note that the more I was truly needed back over again, the more Lady Lauralie had dismissed, or nearly so, our little snits, teeny spats, or occasional rows. She so easily dismissed those trifling, along with any minor differences in mindset that we had encountered.

It was like we were more than back together in an instant. Even before I had picked up the phone, we had become one again, even mystically so. It didn't matter. The sense of unity, the feeling of being loved, the thought that I was needed, is all that I could possibly fathom. As I would get into my car and race over, an adrenaline rush took over me. My broken heart would mend so quickly once again.

Something of interest to certain folks occurred back then that may offer a value to certain individuals in coming to terms with it all. There are a number of coalescing factors that I feel do indeed come together when all is said and done. First let me give the lead in. We have in this area both deer, and coyotes.

When walking along the seashore one day I had the chance to strike up a conversation with one of the locals. He spoke of the legend of 'Big Red' part dog, part coyote, or dog-oaties as I call them.

I spoke of a day that I was out late with no city buses running any longer. About 5 minutes out from the town's edge. A huge, no doubt mix of whatever, ran up into the brush as I approached.

That is when that large beast brought out the honest to God legend of the mightiest canine in all of the land. "Sure enough," he had said, "That may very well have been him." We then spoke of the common presence of those wild dog-things in that stretch of the woods. "For certain," he assured me. I finally let him know then at that point, of my brush, no doubt, with Big Red just months before.

On yet another day I was coming home from work, about 9:15pm. From out of nowhere, a coyote came running across the street directly in front of my vehicle. This was no country lane, mind you. It was a four lane, letter identified, highway. That designation comes from a street sign indicating that vehicular value authorized by the state itself.

In addition to the four lanes divided by a piece of land down the center, or meridian strip as they are more formally noted, there was as well, a parking lane. I reacted angrily based on instinct. Well, that sucker stopped and growled giving me a look like, "Oh yea, you wanna' go for it bastard?" So, he would have thrown down in a second if it came to that. The truth was that he was searching for yummy smelling garbage cans to raid.

That assumption is based on the two square miles of houses he had just been through. Sadly, he later took to chasing a deer. I mean, in order to get away, the female deer had to run in front of a moving vehicle. In order to escape the hungry wrath of that wild beast it was a necessary suicide. The carcass laid there for a day. It indeed was picked up and moved before that sucker could come back for more.

Just after, as I was passing through the legend teller's neighborhood. I saw trash containers lying mysteriously in the middle of the street. It was that this gentleman from my walk that day had claimed that those buggers will escort him and his dog all of the way home. They also refused to leave until their invading competitor and its master, were both tucked so safely inside.

At least three from the seashore, he had said, would follow them across the main drag and down the half-block to his yard. They would even circle and sniff a little before going back to their underground lair. Because of the of Hugh-Gass doe lying so cold and stiff on its side, I decided to give "Big Red," or whoever a very small break with just a small piece of veggie pizza.

Bam, a cop pulls me over, demanding to know why I was in the brush, precisely where that coyote ran in and under cover. I was honest and told him the truth. He was nice and kind and offered that as long as it wasn't too much, he had guessed that it would be okay. I mentioned the doe, and promised to go easy on the treats.

It was when I went to make an offering to those down the way a bit farther that things got interesting. I pull over and get out of my vehicle. I walked up to the edge of the woods, and ever so quickly after tossing the small slice down, pulled out my thing and took care of business. This was directly across from where my honey-bunny was born. So, what do you think happened?

Apparently, the next town over has spy cameras everywhere. What I have surmised is that one person back at the shack, is constantly watching. Then when anything in particular may be of interest to a patrolling officer, it would seem that the detailed info is radioed in. Then with the officer(s) in question speeding over to check out the sito' (short for situation) an investigation could begin. I mean, as soon as I zipped up, the cop was on me.

I explained to him the same thing as I had to the town over's police. Because his area only has these strange garbage bags lying perfectly in the center of any one given street, on any one given day, I of course offered that logical reasoning. He was the same way saying, "Alright, as long as that was all you were doing, you're good."

I truly do believe that their spy camera did not pick up any golden streaming or anything else out of the ordinary that I may have been engaged in, on that particular late evening. The reason that this becomes vital information is quite relevant. The act of police using spy cameras as a deterrent is truly quite a story. My opinion is due to the fact that such a pretty little scenario comes straight out of the futuristic science fiction novel 1984.

"Are we there yet?" The kids may ask from the back seat of an auto during an especially long road trip. We no longer need to ask that about our futuristic world! What I believe is that we need to be drawn closer to God, no matter what the circumstances. If the end of our world is nearing, at least the world we know and rely on in any case, we need to buckle up for the long hard ride. This will be no test drive baby.

I decided it was time to go and see my son. I drove the back country roads reliving my times with my lady by my side. The fresh clean air, our deep love for each other, it was all coming back so beautifully and readily. I had taken her to school one day after we were together all night. I was also pulled over in that downtown area without a license.

Good thing it was a cool cop. He saw how old I was, and just gave me a warning about my headlight. It must have been days after I bought the old 1967 Impala. Here though, I had a much better vehicle. It wasn't the 1982 Ford van that had the muffler fall off, after I made an attempt to contact my son previously. Remember the fire inside the vehicle, under the '*doghouse*'?

I didn't have to pee right then when the licking flames surged from my van's engine. Yes again, it was so very cool that there was enough snow on the ground at the time. Here I pulled up to the local high school. I got out and asked some older looking fellows if the boy was around. One smarty pants asked, "Why are you here to kick his ass?"

The others shook their heads with a no reply. Oh well, it was back to the drawing board.

One night in particular during this fall time period was of note. The plans had been made in advance with my Lady, and I only needed to arrive on time, and we'd be good. With my job letting out early enough, I would just need to drive the short way over, and all was wonderful. I would merely need to mind my Ps and Qs once and a while, and be on top of all things positive.

It was opening night for a special film. We would be going to see Harry Potter for the first time ever. Of course, it was Carlee's idea. We stood in the theater with at least sixteen to twenty additional adults and nearly thirty children or so, average age about 9. Those youngsters were as eager as we, to get things moving. Then finally the doors opened and we were in.

That fact that I hadn't gone to see a new movie since the rerelease of Jurassic Park, with some friends and one of their kids, let's you know just how big this newest release truly was for me. Remembering correctly, or not, I would say Jurassic Park was from 1986, and the re-showing I saw from 1993 or so. My viewing of Star Trek, whatever version that was, came back in 1992 or so.

Yes then, in two decades after dating my first true love, I had been to those two, and the second runs or so. One was a scary comedy with John Candy. I am clearly remembering now the rerelease of Star Trek; I had just gotten off the phone with my drummer buddy. So, in more-so reliving some of the excitement from my childhood days, I would say that I was surely pumped.

The actual excitement in the entire theater line itself was more than quite appreciable. Life is so surely good sometimes. I was in love, our togetherness wonderful, and that's all that mattered. We visited my parents for the Christmas holiday, and things could not have ended that year any sweeter at all. We had made it through the first calendar year, not quite six months, with a few bumps and bruises, but we were still together.

Frank the taxman from the accounting service was upset. He let me know in no uncertain terms that I had let him down. He now hated not only Joyce, the defiler of her own name, but now Steven, and myself as well. He proudly and with angry undertones, let me know of his disappointment. "But don't worry about it," he scolded, "I took care of it myself."

"I'll know better the next time, than to ask you for anything," he added as well.

I was just like, "Oh, oh, oh yeah, I forgot I'm sorry, but as long as you've taken care of the whole deal then we should be good."

Again, it was like, "Yeah, no thanks to you it's all taken care of." It was that dishes set but was listed as an asset if you recall. With depreciation being used each year for something that had already been sold, it was just too much for the old boy. Whoever did that work so many years before, apparently had surmised incorrectly based on guesswork.

2001

My car was in for repairs. That was fine, as Lady Lauralie would be picking me up after she left her job. There was a fresh pile of snow dispensed by the late winter sky that morning. It wasn't too much and the air warmed up a bit by afternoon. My Lady had arrived and we were off. Moving east Laurie mentioned that she needed to stop and pick up a few things. After turning south, we came upon a citybus that was stopped at the bottom of a hill.

The only troubling situation involved one aspect of our approaching. There was a driver of a car beginning to, for all intense purposes, peek, if you know what I mean. You could tell he was just dying to see what was behind that bus. Well, it was us. He moved back and forth in an attempt to gain a vision of what he might face moving forward.

I sensed he was really gearing up for a good look at us this next time. We began the decent toward the corner, with the bus still in idle. "No, no don't do it!" we began to shout. It was too late, he had committed himself. From behind the front of the bus, he began to creep out. First the nose of the car, then that retracted. Then a little more of the car showed its face, but not quite enough for him to note our presence. The third time was a charm. He pulled out just enough to see us coming right for him.

Although, only going about thirty, after my Lady pulled her foot from the gas, she feared locking them up, so pumped the brakes. The only option for the curious one was to backup. At first, he tried to speed up then threw it in reverse. It was too late. With all of the slush, and partly melted snow, we moved right into his front end. My lady's car was totaled. We pulled off to the side, and phoned for help. The young fellow was apologetic and remorseful. If only he could have heard us calling out to him.

Within minutes, my Lady was working her magic. Not only did she score a temporary replacement vehicle, something covered by the perps' insurance company, she somehow managed to find a replacement car of the same make, color and model. This replacement vehicle was actually even one year newer than the wreck, and for around the same price.

I was never prouder of a gal of mine. She was calm, strong, steady, and even persistent and it all paid off. Wow. That took the weight and pressure of the situation, so squarely on my shoulders. Her ability just lifted it all up so gracefully, working each of the pieces together to form such a wonderful tapestry of execution. She charmed the pants off of somebody, I'd say.

I was so well satisfied. I believe it was a completely new feeling in special ways that I was having. Laurie's true calling was to have been a secretary, or some type of business associate. I could see that quite clearly now. Well, as long as she can continue to shine like that for me, I'd be fine. If she can continue to work it, in any way possible, I would be a happy man. Sadly, this was just another day in the life of the type of person that Laurie was.

These types are considered crisis people by modern-day psychologists. They live to conquer. It is the tragedies in life that they thrive upon. It's been noted that many of these individuals are potentially shopping addicts. They will create a crisis by over shopping. Once home, they realize that what was purchased is so wrong. The victory and achievement come when the item is returned, and the exchange completed.

The warm weather of spring had arrived. Although symbolic in many ways, I suggested that we replicate our very first date, this time with my Lady's daughter along. Even though we had spent many Friday nights together playing Monopoly, or watching old movies, it was still nice to get out once and a while.

As a matter of fact, my lady would often allow me to kick back at her place, while Katie and she went out shopping. This was such an ideal setup as I would either take a nap on her couch, or during football season move it on over to the Silent Spring House to watch the game. Here though, on this glorious fall Saturday, the idea was to bring back the innocent magic of our early get-togethers. With our young charge in tow, it would be a symbolic restarting of our relationship.

This dramatic field trip is one of the most popular in the area during the changing of the leaves. It involves scaling a bell tower situated high upon a hill, just past the apple orchards, pumpkin patches, and llama farm. All in all, it takes at least twenty minutes to a half hour to fully ascend, depending on the crowd. We made it with pleasure. The view allows one to look over to the city with a true sense of awe and wonder. We did it. We were now officially one big happy family. The remainder of the weekend went well.

There was one tragic happening in our lives that my lady most assuredly needed me there for. She had ordered furniture from Sears just before they closed. I let the deliverymen in, but failed to hold a sharpened eye toward the quality of the goods, or lack thereof in this case. She was livid. Upon further review, it did become apparent that all or most of the wood fiberboard, had warped before being assembled in Mexico.

I had to agree with the final analysis. So, yes, she had every reason to be upset. She called and demanded a return of merchandise, which was set up for that Wednesday. Her mother was to stay there while she and I were at work. Not only did these blokes forget the nightstand, her mother dropped it on her foot dragging it out as she called to them.

Serious medical attention was necessary. I felt horrible, yet could only block the tragic event from my mind. We would be sleeping on her floor for at least a week right after. Now what? We decided to go to the classier place in town. We would be buying a real-wooden bedroom set. Rather than dink around with any lower quality issues, we needed to play for keeps now.

This better stuff isn't just so really wonderful, it's as heavy as hell to move around as well. Since she had gone through the heartbreak of a bad buy, I felt it quite necessary to purchase a nightstand of my very own. Simply though, it was to have a nice place to set my glasses on, before calling it a day. Never mind that we had been sleeping on the floor for the last eight days.

Absolute luxury now bathed us in a special sense of high-end, middle-class comfort. When the new stuff came in, we truly shared in the joy of ownership. With the way I owned my nightstand, an honest appreciation for the natural high-quality furnishings were warmly shared. I started by oiling 'er down with a citrus product.

One needs to clarify here, there are indeed orangey things out there for household use, but nothing glows like a brand-new bedroom set that's been properly lubricated with the strongest orange solution on the market. I still recall with a sense of deep satisfaction the wet look I had created, as well as the strong pungent aroma. Certainly, it is required to *not touch* said precious items, until well dried. A good three hours if not a day should do it.

2002–2003

I was lying on my bed talking to Lady Lauralie. It was then that I noticed something on the bedroom ceiling just over my bed. It reminded of the day that we had pulled out everything from Laurie's closet. There on the wall at her place, behind where the tent was stored, a dark discolored blotch was visible. She had told me that she had liked to keep the heat down when possible, to save on the bill.

Both residues were reminiscent of the dark spotting that occurs when you hold a cigarette lighter to a surface. I had believed that that was actually carbon, so what is this now visible on my ceiling, I had wondered? Laurie claimed that some dark spots appeared on the very corner of her bedroom ceiling once before. Management had come in and painted over the blotch after she complained.

We went to the State Fair that August. Things didn't start out too well. We parked freely on the street in front of a home some four blocks away. This would give us money for other things like food, and maybe a ride or two, not counting the games one could play to win his sweetie or daughter a prize. When we got in, I needed to use a port-a-potty. I did so, utilizing a *no-touch* move that not only involved having no underwear on, but as well, sticking one's rear end back to retrieve the unit. Then with a quick zip, the *no-touch* method would be completed.

As soon as I had failed to stop at the porta-sinks, Carlee went off on me about washing. Well, not only is that not the duty of an otherwise good-natured young girl, nobody tells me what to do! I said that I didn't need to, and meant it. Lady Lauralie now was urging me, and I still protested. I mean you cannot tell anyone about the *no-touch* move in public, while people are shouting at the top of their lungs to wash up.

I quickly relented, then hoped that it would all go away by changing the subject. It did not. It did not completely anyway. Four two wonderful hours though, we were one big happy family. From out of nowhere Laurie just started going off. As I have mentioned she was the type to over-shop, only to realize once at home that at least one of those items just wouldn't do. So, back to the store it went.

Here now she was doing that to me. I could only take so much and stormed off. When I got back to my car, I saw that *Little Miss Travels Light* had left her house keys in my vehicle. I started the car nonetheless and went straight to her place. After letting myself in, I placed the keys inside her file cabinet. I then, after getting back home found that she had left messages on my machine.

Calling her cell phone, the message I left was "they're on file, under key." Hours later she finally called back, at first defensive, and then so loving. She explained how they went to the Sherriff at the fair, and managed to get home alright. I told her that I thought that she would understand to ring a neighbor's apartment, then to walk right in, and to take her housekeys out of the file cabinet, filed under K, for keys.

So, a good neighbor indeed let her in, and let's be honest, I had to consider how I had gone through this type of petty argument time and time again. Somehow this just wasn't right. I would become angry, we wouldn't talk, then from out of nowhere she would call and make up again. I got into my car and raced toward the freeway anyhow.

I felt the freedom of life and love itself as I made my way across the river to the south side where Laurie lived. She had asked me to rent a certain movie for her daughter. I hoped the fact that that flick wasn't available wouldn't cause another spat. She opened the door with love and an apology, and we were together once more. Ahhhh, life was good again. That lasted about a month.

The next time I was told there would be no make-up. She even, near tears, stated that she was sorry we had ever met. There would be no quick drive across the river ever again for me. Since I had already given her the nightstand that I had paid for, nothing would need to be taken from her home. What little I did have inside was waiting on the floor, on my side of the door.

A local female police officer escorted me up and it was over. I mean once and for all completely over. I would never again feel the glorious uplifting energy of *flying* in my car back toward her loving, caring embrace. There was more than something so wrong about the whole ordeal to begin with. Alas, life is long, and as long as I am good, things would magically turn out, or would they?

Certainly, save for one little detail. When we both went on the internet after Sears closed, and she still hadn't gotten a refund for the bedroom set, I distinctly recall answering one of the questions wrong. It was "did you actually receive delivery of merchandise?"

I answered, "Yes," because technically, it was there for 36 hours.

Because Sears was closing, we were placed in a different grouping. I know we did talk, and I did apologize for that little mess up. But here we were broken up for good and I'll never know if that issue was resolved properly. Sweet Lady Lauralie did mention that she put in for an appeal for reconsideration with the Sears Bankruptcy Team.

Things were getting tense at work now. Joyce, with Big Dick still recovering at home from his tragic digit removal, now needed a new person to get mad at. Because she loved Steve so much, by default I became her new verbal punching bag. My heart went out to her when she had brought in a photo of her estranged daughter.

That girl married a man from up north old enough to be her vey own dad. I'm not sure what actually caused the rift between them, yet did that even matter to any of the rest of us? To help to keep myself from shouting back at her, I had placed not a cross which may have actually worked better, but more of a charm, on the left side of my desk.

That way, when she came in for the attack, I would naturally turn me head, and I would at least glance at the lucky charm, or consider its power as I turned to speak. Or so I had all too easily thought. Her sneak attacks were so stealthy that I was caught off guard each time. Again, and again she would have no one to pester without Big Dick there, with us the only two, as often was the case.

Frank, the taxman for the most part, evaded capture in such a regard. Big Dick though, had made it early on a regular thing to stop in at least once every two weeks. He was still homebound and not getting around much. I had now been offered the duty of his yard-work assistant. It was just that back in the day, a client was going broke and out of business.

This fellow paid for his last bit of service with a 1963 Skidoo speed boat with matching skis. The boat was parked next to the garage. The boat cover had a hole in it. The garage had gutters added on, to keep the water from dropping down into the speed boat. I clearly recall viewing early '60s magazines (saved for posterity) with the girl on skies waving toward the shore!

Richard had quickly recovered enough to get into his mom's old 1974 Caprice Classic. We took the boat cover in to be repaired. My job was to now get up on a ladder with a tulip trowel while lifting out all the debris that the squirrels had dumped. Most of that unwanted refuse came from the three oak trees surrounding the garage. I needed such brownie points as Joyce, the defiler of her own name, not only got Frank the taxman to be against me, she or he blabbed to Big Dick as well.

He sat me down at the kitchen table and pulled out some wine. He claimed that one of his buddies made it for the church, so it was really, truly special stuff. He poured two glasses and asked that I do my best to not let Joyce get to me. I promised that I would, but to no avail. Joyce already knew how to push my buttons. The charm had failed, and with her sneak attacks I was a goner.

At about 5, and 115lbs. you can only imagine that *going-off* was quite a natural thing for her. With this latest case, she had hidden a company's paperwork on the side of her desk. With her low self-esteem she just couldn't bring herself to enquire about a certain feature of this brand-new business. It was uncomfortable for her to play the serious tough role, when it came to our, oh so necessary requirement, of needing more information to truly do our job correctly.

This new business was like a gas station or bakery out in the middle of nowhere. The farther from civilization, the more likely any one business can erect a Western Union sign right next their very own. The only question we truly had? What was the one reason that we couldn't go on? It was because of the time frames involved.

Such a thing involved the delay in reimbursement from Western Union for money-grams and such. Because of that lag time we had a situation that involved us not having a complete picture of the business costs, and any kickbacks received. How could something so simple even become an issue?

Well, Joyce brought it out and dumped it on me in October. It was 9 months of paper work, and it was still missing that one little feature. Steve had quit and moved, and a new replacement had been hired.

I don't recall all of the details, but old gal went off on me, then she let me know that I was done. "Oh, you little old witch, eat sh*t and die b*tch," I angrily twisted out of my *freaked-and-a-half* mind. I stormed out and went and bought some 'Steel Armor of Protection' beer. That stuff is over 8%, so you can just imagine.

I drove with a maddened foot upon the gas pedal to the woods. I popped one open and began to slam. I stomped, and tromped, I was frazzled, yet not becoming dazzled. What would it take to overcome my violently eruptive rage. Now I certainly don't mean physically violent, merely that a wild beast when provoked will move into his primal self-defense mode.

All of that while the rise of blood pressure, the raging pulse of that very blood through the veins, the tingling of brain neurons firing off, all of that must be returned to a normal non-defensive resting state, for a true sense of calmness and peace to have steadfastly returned. Normally, I would have brought some actual lemon juice to tone down the harsh taste of that stuff.

Here there just wasn't time. Frizzum-frazzum, riffumraffum, were the only sounds that I could think of. I popped yet another tall-boy, and the potion's magic finally began to set in. Even after slamming two, I was still just a tad upset. This would be a three popper. It was that last one that got me over the hill. Now what-the-flock was I going to do for survival?

2004

I was desperate for work. I signed up with a nearby temp service and they sent me to a local packaging plant. It was a snack company. I worked the end of the bagging-line for a while. It was a nonstop gentle movement of the snacks off of the line, and to the side. When I saw the forklifters moving so quickly nearby, I didn't know if I could safely hang at that level.

I mean, after a well-deserved and well merited promotion to forklift driver anyway, that is. I in the meantime was quickly moved to the crunch mix area. I was the station master in that zone. What were washing-machine sized boxes—would move up from the automated system. Let me just tell you about that setup a bit.

It was like a pair of mechanical arms would reach out, and pull out these big boxes of mix from a nearly bottomless shelving array. When being initially received these huge containers had a bar coded label slapped across the side. The incoming merchandise was then entered into the system so that each and every one of the hundreds of boxes, scaling at least 30 to 40 feet, would be in a retrievable state by that style of electronic identification.

Afterward when a box that passed my way was fully emptied by the manual dumper-man, a fresh new box would already automatically be on its way. Here and there they would get jammed and stuck in the storage area. The techs would then have to come to figure out the safest procedure to take. My job was to remove the black band from the incoming product.

The cardboard top would then be so easily removed. Imagine a super big train set with no engineer. As the official station manager, I would open the huge plastic bag, gracefully pulling it nicely down around the box top. I would then push the button for the train to go back into motion. Repetitive it was, but not hard at all.

I would be okay here until something better came along. With my rent being on the low side, considering how the pool was drained and not in use, and my air-conditioner on the fritz, I was easily able to squeak by for a while, in a state of faux middle classiness. Because of my basketball injury, the pain was too immense to consider applying with those folks.

I was a term temporary employee so set my sights on creating an upgrade for myself through the checking of the want ads more and more. As the end of our contractual commitment of our relationship grew closer to the end, I grew stronger in mind, mightier in commitment, and more focused on a well-deserved elevation of pay-scale compensation.

The snack company job being finally over, I was thrilled to be done. It helped me to get through that fall and spring but was not my cup of tea. As I passed by a newly created former co-worker, he eagerly offered up some news. The snack company extended the contract, and I needed to do was enquire! Thankfully I had gone to the library, and checked out the newspaper there.

One opening in particular stood out. I walked in and was hired based upon my warehouse experience, and the fact that I had moved things with my buddy including his drum set, but with a rented U-Haul, and not as an hourly employee. That's not to mention all of the apartments moves performed as well, with those types of rented delivery trucks.

I was driving on a midnight run that very week. These trucks would be anything and everything just up to those under a semi in size. The pickup had four wheels in the back so we called that red Dodge the *dually*. Those types of fun monikers and such were so quickly dispensed by all of those young lads from the eastern area around here.

It was mostly college guys from around the area working for the summer, with a few of us older gents thrown in for good measure. We mainly got tent erections. All of those tents, just like the trucks, came in many, many sizes. Imagine the numerous fairs, festivals, parades, and other events we could possibly have handled so very, very well on any given summer day!

The new neighbor from downstairs knocked on the door. One of his connections was over. He had an ounce of weed going for $85.00. I should have never opened the door. What started as a deal too good to pass up, was actually the beginning of a whole new slide. It was a fresh pool of dung that did await me just below.

On a downward trend of spiraling loss, I wavered, I collapsed, and I finally fell into. This was a trend that would coil around, snake, and descend for me into a darkness of despair. Dropping me to the farthest depths of my seemingly once recovered existence, this new predicament so assuredly took over. As I mentioned, back in 1997, in order to be accepted into the rehab program I needed to be clean.

Upon arriving at the two-year school back then I was notified that they kept a file on me. In order to enroll once more I would need to offer substantiation that I was medicated. Not a problem. I just needed to score some meds. I arranged for a prescription to be issued and returned to the school. Here now nine years later, eight after that graduation, I was about to sink to a newfound low.

I felt totally fantastic the first night of my stoner highness. That was how it had become. For perhaps a week, or even maybe longer, I would be in a state of heavenly bliss. The ecstasy of fonder days from my youth would bath and fondle me in a sense of free flying cranial delights. The harrowing, harsh downfalls always came later.

As high and as far as my sailing mind could wander off too, the depths of desperation would always wait just as deeply below. My friends from high school had mentioned 'burnout' way back in the day. From what I was finding in the here and now, within two or three days of being buzzed, I had lost my ambition.

I didn't really want to play my bass or guitar, and found myself sitting slumped in a chair like some bad antidrug character from TV. Somehow, after all of the years, even to myself, that was exactly what I had become. I was a lone stoner with no reason at all to even exist, other than for common lazy pleasures. Though, was it really that way? Was it truly so desperately lame?

Is that what I had become after all of life's struggles had been wrestled to the ground, with me a total loser, and not a proud victor of life's travails? Was I that well below a common standard of normality, that I myself was somewhat repulsed? Oh well, I simply had used up all of the good times, and needed to quit. Just 25 more grams to smoke and I'd be there.

To be honest I smoked a little back when I was with Lady Lauralie, and once again when I was terminated from Kay-bar Systems bookkeeping service. If someone out at a bar happened to be puffing on a good one, and kindly offered to cut me in, I surely obliged. Here I was though, with more than I had purchased for personal use, since my one true love and I had first gotten together back in 1980.

Just a month, I thought, *Just one short month, and the thing will quietly die down, I'll step away from the pipe, and things will be back to normal. That is what I had hoped and prayed for anyway*.

Things began to move along wonderfully. I was held over for the winter at the tent erection company as a *small job* delivery man.

I would go to one job high as a kite, quickly make some deliveries in the smaller truck, then rush home, take a shower, put on my special clothes, and be off to do taxes for those other wonderful folks. That lasted 3½ weeks. I hit the wall right near the end of my stoner blitz. I wasn't sleeping well and was near the cliff. After two days without sleeping a wink, a new wrinkle reared its ugly head.

During times like these, I would often go into a cleaning frenzy. That was the indicator of my manic side rearing its ugly head. Here I had decided to bring down the special New Orleans Saints curtains in the bedroom. A light poured through that hadn't been exposed since the day that I had first moved in. That window would not stay up without a board propped up underneath.

I immediately considered such efforts weren't worth the benefit. The window remained closed, and the curtains in place until the moment here at hand. Then and there, with my bedroom seeing the first rays of sunlight after all of those years I totally freaked out. I still keep my current bedroom completely dark with my new deep red curtains. Because it has two windows the black Saints curtains had to be retired.

What I was witnessing here in this case though, sent me into a panic. Everywhere now in this bedroom, was a nightmarish and ghastly growth. Black and crawling, moving, creeping, this nightmarish growth was seemingly advancing. It was on the TV, on the walls, and so hideously thick, up and down the window itself, that I still get anxious just thinking about it.

I am currently doing my best to drink enough to forget that trauma. (Just kidding)That's how you get 'self-induced-oldtimer's-disease'. I mean by drinking the nightmares of your life away, you jeopardize your sense of conscious awareness down the road. Just in case any of you recalled suddenly of something that you'd like to forget; I'll mention Father's plight here. He finally couldn't be trusted alone in the world.

The street's paved on both sides, I like to say. If you cheat to forget, you'll really, really forget more than you'd care to. My mind couldn't deal with it. This overwhelming and all too sudden, so bluntly administered truth about the very place I had considered my refuge from the harsh coldness of the world outside, was all too clearly mind-blowing.

My sanctuary from the harshness of the stiff and crushing realities of the cold existence outside of my cradling protective domicile was truly more of an illusion than anything else. I wanted to both cry and go insane at the same time, if only one or either would make it go away. So, the landlord patched the roof after some cajoling, he however left the hole in my bedroom ceiling just above the foot of the bed. Let me explain in detail why I lost it so totally.

Half way or more up the window sill were jelly bean sized mold mounds. They were layered over, and over each other. Because of my arthritis I took soothing super-hot showers, apparently adding to the collection of growing dark matter now before me. I grabbed what I could from that home then headed for the basement. Once that first load of wash was in, I began to relax a bit.

One may consider a musty old cellar to be the last place to find solace and comfort, but there it was. The open space was relieving, and my duties as a homemaker were being fulfilled. I needed to think now, "Is there anything more, anything I can do quickly before I race out to a hotel?" I decided to grab the TV stand and take it to the dumpster. The rest I would work on bit by bit, while planning careful moves from the sanctity of that very hotel room.

My first decision was to not pay my rent. That was mistake #1. Because I had failed to go through the proper channels, specifically to turn in a complaint about the hole in the ceiling, I had no standing. I moved down to the lower chamber, and if my ears heard right, the apartment manager and his hired gun were planning for a showdown.

I stepped closer to the doorway of the handyman's storage room. "Hey," I called out.

"Yeah, yeah, yeah," Will answered back.

I said, "Look sucker, not only are you going repaint my bedroom, you're going to install a new air-conditioner, and ((punk mothafluffayou're gonna) went unspoken) pay for my hotel fare too!" I swear to God sucker, also went unspoken.

"Oh no, no," he shot back, "You've got to pay your whole rent, you've got to, and I'll see about the hotel cost."

That really pissed me off. I don't know if I've ever been so upset in all of my life. "No, I don't damn it, no," I shot back, and stormed off. To be quite honest I had failed to note this condition, so I had therefore been responsible for it getting to that state.

Even though he fixed the hole in the roof, yet left the hole in my bedroom ceiling, I was the person living in that home, so I was the individual responsible for the general upkeep and maintenance. So, therefore, even in his knowing good and well that rain leaked into my bedroom, he nonetheless could not be held responsible for my mold.

He was not to blame for my having to quit cigarettes, or any other physical maladies I may have endured from the continued presence of such an eager domestic invader. Again, the ceiling hole is where all of the millions of mold spores poured through, then after collecting on the damp window behind a shade, and black curtains with a New Orleans fleur-de-lis design, had grown to the size of jelly beans.

Finally, then breaking open and pouring out a million new mold spores, so on, and so forth, over, and over. It is the tenant's responsibility to maintain a sense of cleanliness, and not the landlord's duty whatsoever. One must be diligent an all cases in order to maintain a receptive and hallowed place of comfort and slumber. Bachelors beware! There are never any excuses when it comes to cleanliness!

The horrible memory of that entire time actually involves Lady Lauralie. As I lay upon the bed one evening back in 2003, If you recall, I was wondering what the slight blackish mark that I was seeing near the light on the ceiling really was. The hole with water dripping through when it rained was right along the edge of the wall.

It was just enough over for me to catch that bit of water in a coffee can, until Will, that mother-fluffer finally took his finger out of his ass long enough to at least patch the roof. I just needed to monitor the situation as best possible. The thing about this time in my life was that the serious effects of the lingering hole in the ceiling had occurred at Laurie's place, and not at mine at all.

One evening after that phone call we had been in her bedroom sitting on the bed when from out of nowhere, in a shockingly dramatic fashion, she coughed out two full handfuls of clear liquid from her lungs. It was that she had just spent the night at my place, with her daughter being at grandmas. Here she raced to the bathroom dispensing the phlegm into the toilet bowl.

She came back and expressed her wonderment as to how that may have come about. I was in shock. This circumstance at such an extreme level, was merely a precursor to my own troubles. It was about a month or two later, after her lung trouble, that she pulled the old camping tent away from the wall in her bedroom closet.

Upon seeing that a small round blackish spot had formed upon the wall, she then determined that to be mold then tossed the tent. Because she had claimed, living on the very corner of the building without a lack of proper insulation, no doubt, there was the same blackish marking on the ceiling years before. I didn't put two, and two together at first. She complained to management if you'll recall.

Again, as far as I know they merely painted over her ceiling blotch. That was just as my very own bullshit landlord did. It was not until the whole episode had played itself out in my troubled mind that it fully came together as one string of related events. Was I busy, or was I lazy? Was I tired, or was I lying to myself, deep, deep, so ever deeply, into the dark shadows of my now so troubled mind?

Eviction proceedings began. I had been, day after day, cleaning my way back into my home. What I found on the third day was a bit disappointing. Will, who was actually a part owner with his relatives, had simply painted over the yuck. He and his homey even painted over the natural wood trim around the window, that very same off-white color.

The window itself was now spotlessly polished, with no remaining residue on any of the walls or surfaces. Where was that bastard? Oh well. I was thinking now that it's inhabitable I may as well call it over and done, as far as my tenancy. Because I now had CPOD I sure as hell wasn't going to pay the full rent. I was still too steaming mad.

Back at work doing taxes, I felt that I needed to go home to finish washing everything. I thought if I hurry, I can just get the wet things in the dryer, then I could race back to my tax desk, perhaps leaving time for another load after work. I was hyper. I jumped in my car looked left and right, then backed out. Right into a brand-new car quickly moving past, I moved my vehicle.

I mean compared to my piece of shit mobile, it looked new. Anyway, it was like I was set up to take a fall. I was morally, and financially defeated. I walked back into work, and slumped into my seat. The woman called the local police but was helpless. I had no insurance, and really with the two jobs was barely making it, neither offered insurance, and all of the money that I had, went to pay for the car.

If I could, I would do anything possible to make it up to that woman. I mean I have had hard times, I have had rough times, but eventually most of us believe there is a light at the end of the rainbow. One can only pray for others to forgive them so often times, especially since she no doubt had uninsured motorists' coverage.

The officer stated that because the accident was in a parking lot and not out on the roadway, it was out of his jurisdiction. Because of my photographic memory, things such as that will always haunt me. Let us take due note of this predicament. Most states have an insurance requirement to drive lawfully. Many cannot afford it. Those folks should live good lives and pray with faith. That's about all that you'll get in such a case!

I went to court and Will told the judge I was a good guy, and that he really didn't want to see me go. "Then what the hell are we doing here?" was the judge's question.

"Well, there was an issue he had claimed, but I looked into it and there was really nothing there, to cause him not to pay the rent anyway," Will had answered back to the disgruntled justice.

"Okay," the judge replied, "I'll consider this matter closed, though you'll need to pay the amount of rent owed," he offered up to me.

Whew, I was relieved. To have to sacrifice so much of one's life, for a bit of faulty righteousness, was more than I had cared to go through ever again. Life is indeed so much more complicated often times than we are prepared for, at least initially!

2005–2007

When I came home in the summer time at that seashore apartment, it often felt even hotter than it truly was. That had everything to do with the neighbors having a pool. They need not be in it splashing around and having fun and giggling to make me feel so very warm, or even hot. The fact that my air-conditioner did not quite blow out cold air, (until at least I ordered Will to replace that growling juice user), was truly the real and genuine factor in my summertime discomfort.

In knowing that I'd be on my way up to an all too warm home was enough to make me sweat just a bit before I had even left my car. In addition to the paint, Will actually did finally buy me that new air conditioner. That new machine was so ready to offer a sense of electronic relief. It blew cold air from a seemingly heaven-like source. Aahhh, I can still remember with pleasure, the feeling on my face that first time out.

Although, living the life of Riley one doesn't ever get to keep their cake and eat it too. So, therefore a brand-new situation had arisen. Black bastard ants were now marching across the living room floor. No doubt a small enough 'hole' was left unsealed around the new air-conditioning unit so that they could squeeze past. Then no doubt, after munching delightfully on whatever scraps they could find, they would go and brag to their best buddies.

One day I opened my sugar cupboard to find a shocking occurrence. It was that some sugar had spilled, and in my bachelor sense of housework, I had merely managed to push it into the very corner of that area near the cupboard door. So, here, and I do have a bit of a temper, a mother-sucking big black one, was eagerly gnawing at that smallish clump.

I was like oh you punk little bastard. This sucker reared his head back, as if to growl a righteous and menacing roar. It was unbelievable. He then bit off an actual piece of corner wood from the seam in the connected cupboard wall. He was so involved in his sugary delight that the little tough guy would even rather die than give up on his engorging ways! I was using Father's good luck approach to house pests with live capture.

Those black dandies were taking advantage of an old softy, all while utilizing their very best advantage of concealed entry. I felt like being even cooler one Saturday morning as far as those fierce little rascals were concerned. I got up and sat in my man-chair as usual, then looked down to the floor with some consideration. It was that five ants decided to party in my forgotten beer glass. All of them OD'd.

What made it miraculous was the perfect circle they were in! So, yes, there was Dancing Susan, the circular ceiling spider from my old war-widows efficiency place, and now the party boys from next-door! A rigid sense of cleanliness is always a first priority in a modern home. Take urgent and vital notes I declare once more all of you bachelors.

The easy keen option is to have those Friday night cleaning parties with the single girls from work helping. Those would be the casual singles from work non-dates that I've heard so much about. Truth be told, those girls loved helping their buds from the office or so, in such a special way. Though, don't forget the sixer, Captain Bucky.

I decided to go all out that new spring with my planting. I had been receiving mail-order catalogs for years offering all types of pre-grown plants, some from seeds, others from a bare-root. I had gone into my own world imagining how wonderful these things could be if they actually turned out the way that one would've hoped for.

Since I had been working at the local GM plant, I mean General Mills not Motors, I had saved about just enough to splurge, and try and cover more of the parking area with any and all possibilities.

First, I would plant pumpkins and hang those from the tree branches. Alas that left just enough of an opening to see naked arms, and necks having so much fun in the water, yet I would be happy enough with that.

I as well ordered high growing daisy type flowers and planted those along with some tomatoes, green peppers, and enough California Zinnias to cover each parking spot on either side of mine, with a wonderfully colorful growth. My layout formed into a replica of the Ohio state football stadium. At least half of that large and great facility was replicated anyway in such a fashion. In such a bounty of brightness was where football competed.

After hanging last year's crop of California Zinnias from the basement ceiling, it was time to harvest. I carefully removed each group of seeds from the dried stems, and placed them in sandwich baggies based on color. After ordering from the catalog, I went to the local garden center for the vegetables. I, as well, bought some decorative bricks for a walkway in between these yummy greens to access and harvest. Things would be nearly just as good as the best fantasy garden could ever be.

That summer played out splendidly. I was not making a huge amount but often had at least a few hours of overtime. Come fall, most of the other tent erection employees went back to college or were laidoff. I was fortunate enough to be kept on. Two of my pumpkins from that year had held on as well. I mean to the vines hanging from the trees at my parking spot.

The one was so large it may have fetched even $4.00 at a local store. That strange bit of jungle type growth lasted until Labor Day. Some turdy little sh*ts cut through the side yards and spotted my prize beauty. When I had returned from my own bit of partying later that evening, the shock, and realization set in. It was that a large park was situated just around the corner from the neighboring retirement home.

So, these punkish rascals were in a hurry. They cut through not only our place, but the area that was a no man's land just next to the house on the corner. Had I caught them in the act, I would not have been responsible for my actions just afterward. It was my bullsh*t neighbor with the pool that let me know just what had happened. Rather, he made up a story to engage in a neighborly sense of borderline infringement.

He took a chain saw and cut down all of my, extra biggest-of-them-all, sunflowers that I had used to help create the final curtain of obscurity that my overheated summertime body did so require. I jumped the fence upon taking due notice and went to have at him. He answered the door only to claim, not only was it his property (total bullsh*t) but that he had no choice because bees had attacked his grandson.

His son came from the living room to exclaim, "Dad those weren't bees." The lad even repeated that again, because his very own dad was such a stubborn jackass. There had been some lone bumblebees that I had dug up from the ground during my planting. Bumblebees are harmless, and they had proved their loner status by burrowing into the ground individually.

How this bozo could have possibly known that they did so was beyond me. The crabby man claimed that I had been under the influence and decided to pick my pumpkin and toss it in his pool. That sucker needed some reckoning, but first I needed to go to City Hall to find out who actually owned the land used as a soft buffer in between our apartment complex and the houses to the rear.

Hah, that son-of-a-witchin' liar. It was actually the Electric Company, so neither of us had any rights of domain regarding my beautifully created fantasy world. Please take note: pumpkin flowers only bloom from about 7:00am until 8:00am. So, it is each morning when abloom that those huge lovelies are available. If you ever become a fan you will need to set you alarm no doubt, at least on the weekends anyway.

So, the evil, lazy neighbor kids did their part, and this old crabby bum-fluffer did his. Since boys will be boys, I felt only one choice remained. I refer to something that would offer any vengeful rectification whatsoever. I do mean here that specifically, non-aggressive combat should never be undertaken lightly. One must consider how a definite form of battle can be engaged in, with the precise and coldly calculated effects so deeply longed for actually activated.

I had just the thing. It wasn't just what the doctor ordered it had a side of lime and some lemon wedges too. Here it is then. I would photoshop giant bumblebees holding machine guns marching toward his front door. Since his wife was okay looking enough, you can only imagine what giant sized bees would be after!

So, after a scene depicting the bees ringing the doorbell, I would have included a shot of one those humungous beasts having his way with the old gal, right there on their living room floor. *That'll teach him*, I thought. I still need to pick up the better software to make it look so frighteningly real! With my army of trained bees, victory would be mine. I would begin to control everything. Well, at least my hard feelings anyway.

2008

I had come up with an idea for a movie. It was all about a girl from Erie Pennsylvania that dreamed about the big time. When I would go into my fantasy, there was one person that I allowed to become the star. Her name was Amanda Bynes. She had started out as a Disney child then had moved into film.

Whether I was at work performing any of the menial tasks, or sitting around at home, she would be the one that I wrote for. It came to light in the late summer of 2008 that she would be making an appearance at the local mall as a part of a clothing line promotion. I immediately felt that this was somehow a sign from God himself that things would work out for me.

I was scheduled for a few short hours of labor that Saturday morning, even further allowing me to consider that I was about to knock on fates door. A true sense of joy and prestige made for an enjoyable breeze through my tasks at work. Upon arriving at the mall, I was not quite as certain. I created a handmade sign to hold up that included my phone number.

The line itself was so long that I thought to bribe someone up ahead for skips. $40.00 was enough to sway a young lady in line with a boyfriend who had just recently needed medical care. He had told me quite honestly that he had dire needs prescription wise, so our agreement was actually best for him as well.

Once I had made it to the check-in table, they informed me that no additional articles would be allowed beyond that point. My phone number at the time was 744–4444, or something rather close. I felt it would not have needed so much of an effort to get a hold of that, considering the star was already holding a pen in her hand.

I was allowed to have my extraneous additional items that I was holding moved across the way, on my behalf, while I approached with the photo to be inked. I went through my spiel with my phone number, and repeated it again.

I did my best to use a relaxed and positive voice. Alas, she has not called me at all. I did realize at one point soon afterward, that what I had been doing was using her as my mental model, and nothing more.

Whether one is aware of what is happening, or purposely goes about creating a story line with someone in mind, that is for the most part, all that occurs. It becomes convenient for an author to have someone real and solid to imagine. I was just a tad embarrassed, about how things had worked out, yet am well over it by now. I simply need an agent that sees the truth, and light of day, is all.

Things did not get any better just afterwards. I was back on a manic high, and had overslept. I was still wide awake at 7:00am. The night before my co-worker and I, a fellow I first had met while doing his taxes years before, needed to go to a far-off adventure park. After a quick setup there, it would be all of the way to the state line for a massive takedown.

A larger tent, with so few employees had never before been accomplished, at least by myself anyway. The nearly monumental task was nothing more than a case of proper planning and logistics, and some careful and well thought out maneuvering. When we finally arrived at those fairgrounds, it was just before darkness would descend.

Getting a Hugh-Gass tent down, is easy enough to fathom as far as the simple part. Gravity takes over, and with a few careful details tended to, the thing drops on its own. The hard part would be the disassembly, followed by the roll up. Imagine gargantuan hohos, or ice-cream cakes. Just as you roll up a sleeping bag you fold and fold, and fold again, depending on the size of each section.

The joyous pleasure comes just before you roll them onto a pallet. Then on to the next one a person would move, until finally with each of the pallets loaded onto your truck, it's Miller time. It was 11:17pm and we were back on the road. Let me tell you something, for some of us there is nothing sweeter than a well-gassed vehicle, and an open road.

My homey needed the window open to stay awake and fresh. The wind was bouncing off my side of the vehicle then was striking my right arm with a fury. It helped not that he chuckled when realizing I had forgotten my hoody at the first job. I was finally ready to pass out, yet torturously half way between a distressed wakefulness, and oh so comforting unconsciousness.

The misery lingered, slapping my arm with such a wicked fierceness, I wished to cry out in a dampened and cold state of misery. For 5 full hours this painful pendulum of merciless suffering continued. I dared not protest as we had nearly come to blows the night before. His boyish laughter only deepened the wounds of that discomforting, drafty, and oh so frigid assaulting of my unclothed arms.

On that previous evening after 10:00, we became trapped inside the stadium grounds and had no way out. The barricades were present to keep curious revelers at bay. I rushed to flag down a private street sweeper who would be moving back and forth endlessly all night long. He had just passed us as we circled in confusion.

I ran my ass off, and even hurt my feet in doing so, only to hear some honking while my partner drove over the curbs managing to free us from our well laid maze of blockades. I was never more so angry with someone I had worked with. Luckily for both of us he had some control. I mean, if you allow me to over exert myself, all of the while you're calculating a much better plan, don't expect me to like it!

Here I just needed to hang in there for the remainder of the long trip home, and I'd be free. Finally, at last, we pulled off of the freeway and into the drive at work. Hallelujah, I slipped into the comfort of my own small car, and delightfully drove home. Once at my place, I showered then sat at the kitchen table. I wasn't hungry, I wasn't thirsty, I just wanted to sleep.

I couldn't. I got back up at 5:10, and hit the 151. For those inexperienced teetotalers, 151 is a type of rum that is precisely just that, 151 proof! I slammed another and another. This is what is known in the world of sorrowful troubles as 'self-medicating'. I not only had never done it before these recent hard times, I honestly didn't know how easy it would work.

I did realize however the perils that did lie there within, if such a procedure was so casually undertaken. I therefore thought to call in. I was scheduled for another night-move for this outfit, and to start at 1:30pm. I wasn't sure if I could bear it. The fellow that answered let me know that he was not authorized to accept call-ins. He advised me to come in at the right time, and to work from there.

I hung up, downed the last shot, swallowed the chaser, and dozed off. I must have slept through the alarm. I rushed out still wearing the nightshirt from that morn. I raced to work but had been abandoned by my crew. After reporting to El Capitan, or Stratego, as I called him, I was given the go ahead to proceed on my own.

I moved through that city, then into the next. The fact that I was half mile from my destination only causes me further mental turmoil, and an additional sense of emotional harm. I was what happened next that was even more than bizarre. I stopped at a place that we had worked for in the past. There I cannot understand just what went so horribly awry.

Apparently, even though the booze can knock one out, it doesn't make you normal at all whatsoever. If I could go back in time at least I would apologize to some. So, I enter the place, and they have not one, but two receptionists. One was a woman, the other a trainee. I was so desperate to find that actual work site just before entering that more formal drinking establishment, yet after meeting this Incan type prince character from South America I turned strange.

After giving him a big *alright* I walked up to a couple of classy black dudes, and queried, "when did they start letting brothers from up in the hood in here?" I honestly don't know where that came from, but in hearing myself say such an unkind thing I quickly snapped to, and got out of Dodge. I hurried to my car trying my best to move out quickly.

Just as I was leaving, a cop pulled into the parking lot. It only took 3 minutes for him to arrive from the starting point of my having entered that establishment. F*ck 'em all anyway. I pulled out of the lot, and he was right behind me, with the siren blaring. I stopped the vehicle, and waited for the other shoe. What an asshole. It was as though this pricky f*cker just lives to be this dicky, asshole-bastard to people.

He seemingly just makes sure that it's the right person before going all 'German Bastard' on those poor individuals. So, if you have the appearance of someone that attends Sunday service on a weekly basis, he won't be abusive, and stomp all over your rights. Yet if one hasn't had a haircut in the last three months his strict German punk-ass bitch side, is all over a bro'.

So, first he tells me to get in the back of his car, then has mine towed before he even questions me. That is why I say "f*ck 'em all." What kind of scam they have running I sure don't know, but I was getting railroaded. We enter the station and the bullshit begins. As the one holds a mechanical breathalyzer, like a football on the one yard line, with the readout facing no one, the other asks me to breath into a little hand-held component.

After doing so, he cups it tightly then, in flexing his arm behind his back in an obvious game of keep-away, he nearly dares me to do something about it. So, now it's the other assholes turn. Here he is still hugging that thing like he's about to win the big game. Well, I know when I'm being set up. There wasn't much that I could do, but wait to see the judge.

After the full charade was over these bozos agree to drive me to the work site. They let my homeys know that I'm under special restriction, and to make sure that I don't drive. Here it gets worse. I walk back to the station house to get my keys. I run into these clowns, and the one pulls his gun on me. After realizing who I was he chilled but said, "Naughty, naughty, you're on special restriction. You need to get back to your babysitters."

Well, I answered, "I'd like my keys."

"Keys, we don't have any keys," this evil German m*ther f*cker claims. He had purposely left them in the ignition of my car. So, now one of my bros needs to loan me hotel money, in addition to giving me a ride to said overnight location! I went back to work the next day after not sleeping so well.

The young guy that actually took my place as the assistant manager, at least as far as job duties were concerned, got into it with me over some minor issue. My brain was still fuzzy from the previous day and I was moving a little slowly. One of the duties of the assistant manager was to get people moving in the morning so they weren't standing around talking. This was different.

I had been sent on a job without all of the order so needed to return. Dude just needed to back off so that I could clear my thoughts. All at once while he was bitching about something with a slightly wise-ass attitude, the payroll-bookkeeper walked up on us. The next thing you know before I could get in the truck and drive off, I'm called into the owner's office.

The payroll lady sat in with us for support. I had to believe it was for both of our sake. No doubt they were talking behind my back using snide remarks. There were to be no secrets as far as the manager, and the payroll lady had been concerned. I was told quite bluntly I had come to the end of my rope, and with a "thank you, but no thanks," I was dumped from my employment right then and there.

I would be walking to my counseling sessions, two miles each way, as required by the court system, in order to get my driver's license back. It was a painful lesson that I had to learn, even though the Gapman, and Bucher faked my breathalyzer results. I can't wait until I get my hands on the software to make their very own comic book. Just thinking about it riles me up all over again, especially the way I'm sitting here without a job once again.

One good aspect of not having any job whatsoever at all, back in those days, involved my finishing up of the screenplay. I hacked and hammered at the keyboard diligently, month after month. I spent the entire autumn season, and the beginning of winter bringing my story to a climax. Finally, I had completion. I entered a contest along with 2,999 other aspiring writers.

To no avail that effort was. It was the recession, and so many desperate people had entered that event. I as well, mailed it to several agents out in Hollywood. What I learned was that those businesses will mail back the entire packet with a sworn affidavit stating that they closed their eyes, not even peaking during the entire process, so not only did they not want the thing, they did not even lay eyes upon it.

Thus, their statement goes, "We have the contents for you in this return envelope, once more, unlooked at!" For the most part, each winner of one of these screenwriter contests has his, or her, screenplay considered for production out of perhaps, five or six of those on-line talent contests. The other thing that I did discover is that if one could find a writer that already has an agent, and lure that individual into co-writing, you have a chance that way, of getting into the act.

Should my book sell, I believe I will place an ad in a Hollywood publication. I have a brand-new idea for this experienced person to help with, meaning I could use his agent for my already finished product should he approve of the new co-written offering, before I ask for permission to date his agent, er...I mean utilize the services of.

Things had started off for the training session at my only job, involving the upcoming tax year for 2009 fairly uneventful. It was now November, and two months removed from my dismissal from the tent company. I was super glad to have something to hang onto. The one thing that was of concern was how the two courses from earlier on, had been omitted from my file.

Those had been administered by an arm of our business picked up, to merely validate any connection to investments. We quickly sold them off, and they were still ours until the end of the year, yet as a formality only. Within weeks, there would be no connection whatsoever, and any claim that I had, as far as actually having completed those courses back in August, may have forever been lost. I was duly suspicious.

2009

Although, our good boss from Minnesota had moved on, and her evil replacement from my first two years had come back home to roost, things seemed to be coming together as they had in previous years. This replacement actually went out on dubious terms as I had recalled. He was nothing more than a cheap mother-fluffing bastard as well.

I can finally forgive him after all of this time, but I indeed had made an evil plan of revenge just after his cruelty had destroyed me. I know that it is sinful to allow one's self to hold grudges, yet time and time again I would find myself lying in bed contemplating some well calculated moves. So, this rouge cheap-ass manager wannabe finally has his day.

When I first started there, I had heard that he wanted to hold off on this, he wished to cancel that, yet the big one that he was denied was the maintenance of closure for every single office in the entire district, save for one. That would have been the main headquarter facility, had he gotten his way. Such a slimmed down tactic would have only been until W2s, those forms one's income was established on, for the U.S. Government, had begun to be received.

At that point, in his opinion, we could slowly trickle in as Tax Professionals a tour regular pay.

He was told 'no' as far as his grand scheme went. He then pouted, and had what one may term a woosie-fit. So, nothing more than a fussbudget he was, and prone to bad reactions when the big boss, that woman from Minnesota, would feel a business minded need to rein him in.

One featured aspect of his being the assistant district manager was that 5 out of 6 of the tax offices would run out of paper. This caused the necessity of bumming from your closest allies. If they even had any to spare that is. Any such availability would have been a nearly miraculous occurrence. Only sad, lesser busy tax offices, those that weren't paying out big employee bonuses, had any paper left on their shelves.

So, it wasn't just that this selfish dumb-cluck wanted most of us to earn minimum wage, until at some point it got busy enough to have us earning more than the training wage that we did indeed receive in November-December, he wanted to score personal brownie points with headquarters in Kansas City.

My feelings at first, where for the most part neutral, for this assistant now promoted to the top position. That is, until the scenes of our darkened history began to roll out so deeply inside of my head. It started early on in December when he refused to alter my educational standing which did definitely play into my base pay, and overall standing.

That was my status on paper anyway, with the company. Was this a mere computer error or something so much more? I began to wonder as things rolled along. My feelings of fear, anger, and dread began to fully crystallize when upon starting on January 2nd. Things went against company protocol, and all of our understanding of how things should proceed as we usually had before.

It was for the ten years previous to this date that we employed the use of company mandates and standards. Here though we were informed that unless we were actually performing the full-on duties of a tax professional, we were to continue to receive the base training-pay at minimum wage. That indeed was strictly against the official process offered by upper management back at headquarters.

What would it possibly be next? An older fellow and I found a way around the cold-hearted bugger's new rule implementation. By doing our first return early on, we would have at that point, established our 'working' status. It had happened that a nice young lady had a few years to file all at once, so I found myself busy enough to stay active, rather than in the learning mode from then on.

The fact that that two newer victims of his, were hacking away at practice returns for weeks on end, was only a minor discouragement. Someone needed to turn this f*cker in to headquarters regardless of who he particularly hurts. What exactly set me off on the day in question escapes me. The fact here was that we had a new office manager.

She was a gal that had spent years in retail management, and filing and posting, or whatever activities that big-time department store office personnel engage in. She was not yet very comfortable in her position with so many different duties. She was more afraid of who I would dub, and so properly and accurately so, as 'Count Trakula' with her even being one of his evil demon brides!

So, dude puts me on suspension then had the nerve to call my home talking bull-rotten trash. Well, after being harassed at home by his invading phone, call I just totally snapped. Had I known before I picked up, that it was her that indeed calling, I would have run from my home not returning for several hours. Alas, I regrettably did, out of an outright sense of curiosity, pick up, and listen.

I listened to the cold-hearted son-of-a-witch go into some meaningless ramble about what I can't even recall anymore. By the way, he lived with his mom, and did nothing other than live off of his father's life insurance policy otherwise. And I mean that was when he wasn't doing everything to poop on us common workers. In his vainglorious search for more brownie points, no one was safe.

Otherwise he would have been sitting back at home with his momma *chillin'*. Did I mention that he only pretended to move to another state, all while managing that distant office, located more than 500 miles away, from his home. I guess it seems more of a normal thing with so many working from home these days. Recall though, that this was more than 10 years ago.

To top this all off, my new landlord was being an asshole. He was supposed to have come to inspect my place, as I refused to sign a new lease with him until he did so, I waited and waited, day after day. If you recall the older bastard Will, who was only a part of a family group, refused to pay for my hotel bill, a place that I stayed while he and a helper cleaned the mold out of my bedroom.

He merely painted over the woodwork around the window rather than actually sanitizing anything. Now the new owner was intentionally avoiding me, refusing to come and inspect the place so that I could move forward with a new lease. He did finally show up after weeks of delay and we were good, or so I had thought.

The fact that I had been filling out my rent payments with a few letters missing no doubt played into what would happen next. His real name was Schmidt, but I was leaving off the c, m, and d. After three months when nothing came of it, I thought that a secretary or someone must have been doing his rental deposits.

It was already bad enough that I had spent hundreds or nearly so, placing attractive plants in front of my parking space to block out the vision of my neighbor's pool. That sweet beautiful, colorful and glowing floral life didn't just perk me up with brightness, it helped me to ignore that playful splashing that was so relentless on those hot summer days.

I mean, I really, really did have so much invested in that parking space. So, Mr. Shit comes in and shreds everything on the Electric Company's slim line of property along the fence, leaving nothing but wood chips, and an all too clear view of each, and every neighbor's home along that entire area. He as well, filled in the long-ago emptied swimming pool.

What would happen next did not come at so much of a surprise. After seeing that yet another family in the twin building down the way had been booted, I now had guessed at what Dave truly had in mind for me. The others who were evicted took soap, and wrote on the windows. In no uncertain terms, they indeed let everyone know just how they had felt about Mr. Shit.

Within two weeks my notice was received, and I had begun a search for new digs of my own as well. I decided from point one that I would not take a step backward in regards to accommodations. The fact was that a place down the way from where we lived back in 1960, when I was born had been available.

In addition, one identically structured was even going for $5.00 less just beyond that area by a few miles. The old man at the farther place chose me as the tenant over a lady with one child. I sit here now in splendor seated at my desk in my office. It's a good thing that I was offered this fabulous two-bedroom too. As it was, it was just <u>two weeks</u> after my new landlord had his wife call up to verify my employment at the tax service, that I was put on, '*Suspension*' by Count Trakula.

His office is still here right around the corner from my new home. It burned for me for so long. It was that I couldn't sleep at night on a few occasions. The owners of the very best place that I've ever had have both passed on, but the sons seem willing to hold onto this four-family for now. The handier one of those was just here recently placing leaf guards over the gutters.

With forty-foot pine trees, debris and pine cones, and other things can get clogged up from time to time. It's a good life when you have good landlords, I'll tell you. The thing that still gets to me a wee bit is how this sucker of a manager tried to ruin my very life. I mistakenly put in a claim for unemployment, not understanding how things actually worked. Perhaps I would have lost all hope otherwise!

The Count had placed me on, 'Suspension' rather than firing me outright. It means that you don't qualify for unemployment. One either needs to be called back to work, in which case a person wouldn't need those payments, with that other option involving a full termination at some point down the road. In hindsight, I honestly felt that he had tried to completely destroy me in every way, shape, context, and any form possible whatsoever.

I received a letter around April telling me that I owed back over $4,000.00 to unemployment. Because The Count's mother's house is 65 miles down the road, he apparently didn't receive his invitation to the hearing. The tax office is open at least one day a week during the off season but ole' boy doesn't do the hard work for that company.

He is more of the inspirational speaker type of boss. I was however finally awarded full compensation as his lack of presence that day offered only one option. Then and therefore, I wasn't required to pay back that money after all. So, dude tried to ruin my life, and cause me to be homeless, and I mean even to the point of suicide. Had I not been mistaken about my status; I no doubt would not be here typing this for you now! Whew! That was one mistake that I was truthfully grateful to have made.

The very second day that I lived here was one of the most peaceful I had experienced since living at home with my parents, no doubt, with little exception. Near the lake my waking hours had been filled with a sense of joy, and the appreciation of nature. Here though, without the slap-whap-slapping of car tires across the roadway sections, the morning time offered such a deep serenity, that I was now reborn.

Even without a job, and The Count of Taxation just blocks away, I had truly reached such a peaceful time in my life, that I was grateful to God himself. The gamble in regards to a better class of housing had paid off then. In addition, there was an eerie sense of things situated so nearby, as to cause a sense of mild concern. This area just across the way had been constructed as an experimental zone.

The other community bordering this one, refuses to put in sidewalks. This then offers the illusion of having a bigger yard. It as well, causes people to jaywalk in the street with their dogs, and such. So, this new zone came up with a clever and novel way of blending things in together. They decided to place most every sidewalk, with little exception in between the houses on the sides, and in between the backyards in the rear.

This setup offers the even better illusion of open space. With all of these families planting trees and such, throughout the years, it has become a fantasy world, for me at least it is anyway. That very first day I had felt that the *Stepford Wives* were inside there somewhere, baking cookies, and otherwise keeping house. The fact was that it was spookily quiet. Nothing was stirring, other than a squirrel here and there.

Spring turned to summer and I finally found some work. Out at the world's third largest outdoor arena they needed help. I worked gigs like Pearl Jam, missed Aerosmith, got to do The Dave Mathew's Band, and even loved it. The agony, at least for me came at the end of each show. As the massive crowds moved onward and upward, they left behind a disgusting disarray of everything from wallets and cell phones, to even clothing items.

The question then became what type of unruly mob consisting of such piggish brutes, dumps anything and everything right then and there on the grass? "Oh right," I had gathered, "The type that knows good and well, that we'll pick it right up, especially just before a repeat performance to be held the very next day."

We would return the next morn, regardless of the day's agenda, to attend to the outside perimeter of the facility. That was when our duties could potentially take on a new and so extremely special meaning. I had found that after collecting at least twenty-four beers or so, when seeped in a sink full of cold water any questionable of those units would have been exposed, vis-à-vis any tell-tale bubbles escaping and making their way to the surface.

One additional note needed to be taken and adhered to, involving an age-related aspect of those well welcomed jewels. Those would have been hidden cast-offs, undiscovered by anyone else for way too long. I do mean much, much too long. Yuk! I must admit my most well pleasured moments of grunt work for this facility involved something a little more off the radar.

Having been a clean former user of weed, for the most part anyway, it was always a true joy to come across some of that type of action on the side. The most wonderful of those occasions involved walking up upon a partially lit bowl, with perhaps only one puff being drawn from the device. How buzzed can anyone actually be? I mean come on. Within yards and minutes, it was a small bag of the good stuff as well. Life doesn't get any better than that I'd say.

In between shows at the outdoor arena, I felt that it was time to walk one of the three junk bikes that I had collected down to the nearest repair shop. It indeed was not at all near, more like three solid miles away. These highbred what I would term, stuck-up bicycle repairmen, refuse to even consider touching certain low-end machines. (Think, K-Mart Blue Light Special)

My Kent with ground down bearings in a case, failed to make muster. I returned home to my serious collection of '*recovered*' bicycles. I brought back the oldest, highest end machine that I had. Upon seeing the '71 Schwinn the main mechanic shook his head and said no, "Again, we don't fix any bikes that have bearing cases, and that there is another one of those."

I brought back the Raleigh, nine miles later I got the same response, "Nope, no good, that's the same deal." Walking 18 miles in one day is good exercise. Especially if you don't have a full-time job! Starving artists have nothing on me. I can go to the library and pull out books on natural herbs and spices. I can walk all night, and all of the next day. Of course, I would rather ride!

Come Fall I found a new gig of my very own at the costume warehouse. This was run by a bunch of cheap bastards from Seattle, or somewhere out there on the west coast. The word was if anyone ever managed to make it to $16.00 per hour that person would need to be terminated. Unless of course, they were a member of upper management, that pay structure was no doubt up to $21.00 per hour, or so.

One fellow had actually reached that high plateau, and was at the top of his game. He had made it as one of the elite workers down there on the bottom end of things. He lasted less than two months afterward. They *downsized* eliminating his position, sending him packing.

One thing in particular had me wondering after a while. Could someone have the same exact voice, say your name in exactly the same way, as she had throughout the years, going back to grade school, yet even more so in high school, and not even be that same person? I mean like her cousin maybe, with the same exact name or something? Is that even possible?

I realized after years that she was a weight-watchers success story. There would be no more lying in bed wondering about her anymore. Things went along smoothly and I was held over for the end of the year inventory. That was cool because I had other plans for that new year. With this new place still coming in at $525.00 sans utilities, I was set dog! The only question was,

"Should I open my own tax business, or could I manage to find new work in that field with an already established outfit?"

2010

That new year finally fell upon us. I had actually set out to create a home office in the spare bedroom here. When I claimed that I was done with jack-diddley little apartments I meant it. This place not only has a 13ft. by 19ft. living room, it has two 13ft. by 11ft. bedrooms. That's just the right size for a place to become my beautiful home office. Why, I'm sitting in it now, you can imagine.

My good buddy from the old neighborhood had given me his grandmother's old dining table. He had used it in his basement as a party place, but had a vase leak out onto the table top, causing some discoloration, and damage. It has actual wood inlay so may be worth having repaired. I have used it for merely decorative purposes only.

With a nice lace table cover, and an old silver-plated tea tray, the display is set. A miniature tea set with clovers for the artwork sits atop that silver tray. In addition to that distraction, I picked up an elbow curved desktop for my computer. An on-sale cane back chair from Sears, highlights one wall along with an old Miller sign given to me free of charge.

Out of desperation that action was for certain. That came from an older gal just down the street from this particular buddy's place. Rummage sales in poor neighborhoods apparently end up in outright giveaways. In addition, I just so happened to see an old file cabinet for sale, and after spray painting it black, it sets things off in such a perfect way.

After my new bedroom set was brought in, the 'on-sale' baby dresser joined the array of miscellaneous other pieces simply needing a home. Two 'on-sale' black and wood-toned kitchen chairs, round out the ensemble. Those, along with my *special guest* black-office-chairs allow for a true sense of professionalism. The big, big plants though are sadly dying. Back in the day when with Lady Lauralie, I was invited to her apartment complex's annual outdoor bash.

The plant-man with his especially painted bus ala 'The Partridge Family' was our privileged guest. The one chosen by me had to have suffered relentlessly by living on that very vehicle for who knows how long. It is one of those common spear-type multi-colored plants with about five to ten points emerging from one close root patch. I've found these plants to be easily overwatered and killed. I have two casualties and two intensive care patients, all separated from the original.

The thing is that this plant originally in the west window at the other place, sprouted about two feet in a year's time. In the second year or so, a small four-inch spike emerged. Within days, dainty little bell flowers had formed and opened. The next year the bounty had increased to three flowered spikes. Then came the move.

When the prime beauty failed to perform again in the spring at these new digs, I was at a loss. I finally separated the mighty beast, yet that allowed for the over watering. Alas my magic finger has turned into a brown thumb! I need to remember this is an office, not a hangout. Just before my final preparations for my own tax business could be implemented in that space, I noticed a want ad in the paper.

Professional tax preparer needed. I applied and was accepted into the fold. One caveat about the tax business, you always make exceptions for your lead pro, and by default, the new guy either gets laden with burdensome smaller returns, or is required to sit back waiting. You may be expected to handle any loose ends that may need tending to, as well.

Ole' boy just about apologized, yet based on some hesitation in his voice during our interview, I knew just how things may play out, or actually fail to. His star performer finally took care of his personal stuff, and was back in the fold. Finally, upon returning to my summer work for the one of the largest outdoor arenas in the entire world that summer, I was offered what in all intense purposes would be considered a promotion.

From a common scrub, to an outright usher, is what I had become. My car simply needed to hold on until I could make other provisions. This was that old 1988 Olds. When sitting at a red light, the people next to me would roll up their windows, making faces in disgust. It was only the good clean smell of fresh gasoline they were breathing in with my leaking fuel pump.

Any man that had worked the old-fashioned full-service joints, such as I had, would have felt the same. Whew. As long no one flicked a lit match under the back end of my car, I'd be alright. When I found the wallet at my feet, I had some overtime to perform. After the husband of Gwyneth Paltrow from Coldplay ran past, I thought the hard part of my evening was done.

The thing was that I was told that I needed to shield the then husband of said younger movie star, whose dad was I believe a director. The hubby would be leaving the stage area, quickly trotting by my station. Afterward, very quickly ascending to a mini stage placed just beyond the amphitheater area, he would perform the very next number, in between the good seats, and general seating area. That mini stage was set up just before that grass only seating.

What should I find upon making a quick sweep of the area once fully cleared of fans? I had warned a few off the young ladies that they would not want to be caught between here and there during that extra special time of tonight's proceeding. The next day, I drove over not too far away, and the gal that caused that slight bit of agony, gladly accepted the return of her precious item, that being her wallet, with a gracious smile and pleasant thank you.

Indeed, I had vaguely recalled her face from the prior night's event. Quickly enough that summer outdoor music season was over all too quickly. I returned to my work at the costume warehouse in September. Just four more months was all that I needed. I would go back to doing taxes, making about $20.00 an hour, rather than the straight up $10.00, the warehouse offered, and bling.

Things would be made right. All that was askew before, would be corrected now and just precisely so. Things would be altered to be proper once again. All of the minor adjustments to a clinging salvation would be so coolly and in a calculated fashion, made true again. Any sadness, despair, longing, or any such sense of needfulness would so easily vanish. Maybe, anyway.

2011

As the previous year hadn't quite played out as I had wished. I believed a little innocent scheming was necessary for this year's efforts to bring fruition to my goals. Now, based upon each tax service, and their very own special rules, as long as you don't upset the apple cart, one can play the field so to speak. If caught with your pants down on a steamy Friday evening, oh well, que sara, sara, as Doris Day sang in one of her very special movies.

Remember now, I'm the one that pondered a deep and loving marriage with my lovely sweet. With I myself puttering around in the yard all day. This flick in particular with Jimmy Stewart, is truly a splendid film for children under the age of thirteen. You'll have to look it up on your own, as I wouldn't want to needlessly spoil it for you. That would have been circa '55, '56. If memory serves me, she goes into that loud, loud number in that film while railing at the piano.

So, in any case, I planned it all out to two-time this other firm, as I was for the most part, brought in as an extra man, and a backup to the dude that had way too much private stuff going on, on his side plate. It was then with some disappointment that I ended the tax year feeling rather low. So, here now I would not only entertain such thoughts of multiple services, I was indeed in training with the third biggest outfit in the area.

Each Saturday morning, I would rise and make my way over to the main office. We had our briefings, and all of the going over of things it was felt necessary to touch upon. I got my wish and worked out of the office in the old part of town, two doors down from my former employer's local gig. I would walk to work each day at that location, then drive when necessary to the 4th largest tax business in town.

The only catch was that the old 1988 Olds wasn't just old, it again wasn't just leaking gas from the fuel pump. That sorry sight was going to the junkyard. 'Twas not such a good situation for a driving smoker to be in, I'd say. Having quit 11 years before, nearly to the day, I was fine on my end. I merely needed to watch out for any of those hard puffing pedestrians flicking a well-smoked butt too close to my car's undercarriage.

In no time I had saved enough to go shopping. Neither employer was any the wiser. As long as one didn't move clients over to the other's office, or especially to a home office, it was off the record, and somewhat allowable, if not outright excused. It was at the world's 'largest' enterprise that a certain unnamed individual, had handed out business cards to his people for the very next year's returns to be snaked over to his home office instead.

His well noted legacy stands as a warning to any other tax pros entertaining such brainy ideas. As long as your favorite tax filers love you that much, you may be okay under such pilfering circumstances. I would say here that such low-level cheap bastards lack one keen aspect of a good business person. That would be an appropriate level of self-esteem!

I have three used car dealerships within walking distance from my home, and had been casually on the lookout for my next mobile. When I hit the place up the hill, I knew that I had met my next true love. It was a 1988 Chevy Cavalier. This was no discount-priced *rumbler*, mind you. This car was indeed the racing version of that very simple model.

It came stock, red with black racing stripes, and boasted a 3D decal, in bright yellow and orange colorations on the sides behind the door. I mean, this was so cool for a slick $3,000.00 plus, and it even had a twin identical car that lived down the way from me. I proudly drove to work at the newer tax service. The two gals that I worked with were both of Mexican descent.

The elder, a former migrant worker from Texas back in the 1950s was a sincere, and sweet older lady, that was wise, yet quite open with her approach. She was always giving one the benefit of the doubt. The other, more of the Spanish type, wetta they call that, for white, was just as keen yet not so sly. When they went into their questioning bit, a part of me started to doubt my judgment.

I could only hope that it was from a motherly standpoint that their concerns had been raised. When I tried to pull away from the snowy curb outside of work that very night, and needed assistance from a friendly man picking up his bambinos from school, I had my very own questions about the wisdom of my choice in cars.

Work soon began to wind down for both tax services. I had no choice but to go crawling back to the costume warehouse. They brought me back in, with a smile. There was only one caveat to my continuation with this business. The gal that was a peer just months before, had gotten my promotion, and was now over me. She is the one that got to sit at the computer, directing my movements.

She is the one that would send me back out on the raise-lifts for further review. I could only resign myself to do my best, and hope for greener pastures. The fact that she was a very friendly person and easy to get along with helped my brain come to terms with what I had chanced and what I had indeed given up. Being another year older, with chronic pain in my broken, or 'bad' foot, and the increasing effects of arthritis helped me not a bit, I suffered in silence.

Secretly taking pain pills, at first on Wednesday, then with a double dose on Thursday, and even up to three by late Friday's eve, did do me a world of good. I was a man damn it, and a tough one at that. So, I refused to let those circumstances interfere with my livelihood, or any other part of my life. Even when my lower leg would numb up nearly to the knee, I still stood tall and proud.

My new car however was a beast of its own design. Running late one day, I changed lanes, and punched it. Hah, I moved ahead with such a quick burst of speed that I nearly became a thrill rider for a second. Getting myself and the auto back under control, I moved to the freeway, and off to work. I had believed all the while that the exhaust needed to be reapplied to the manifold. I took the old baby in, to the muffler shop.

Upon returning I felt more than somewhat leery. The mechanic, an hombre de Espanol, had a look on his face that one could only describe as that of perhaps of someone having just seen a ghost. His forehead was ashen white, while his cheeks were ablush with…something anyway. It was the hesitation in his voice that was the cause for some alarm.

Upon further review I had believed that he rose the car up on the jacks, then revved the engine manually to listen for leaks. What he actually said to me was that perhaps the whole engine needs to be removed from the transmission, then reattached, rather than simply the exhaust reattachment as I was looking for.

My car was returned to me for further consideration, yet with things not quite being written up and offered, I had to wonder exactly what was up. My thoughts went back to my co-workers and their seeming doubt in the value of my new machine. About three blocks from the shop something horrible happened. This is an experience that no car owner ever wants to go through. Before I hit the corner with the gas station only a few blocks from my home, the thing went on me.

Imagine two gerbils running in a wheel underneath your hood. Now add two squirrels to that equation, only the squirrels are vigorously shaking coffee cans filled with rocks. I think you see what I mean. That can be the most shocking, and world crushing noise an auto could ever make. I pulled into the station and poured some S.T.P. from the back that I had already purchased. Those initials stand for Stop Teasing Pollacks, by the way. Upon restarting the beast, it was only more of the same.

No doubt, when I had punched it the week before, it had set the stage for this predicament to occur. Then when the mechanic was revving the engine it gave way, all at once. Those rumblings spoke volumes, but with just the beginnings of what was so soon to come. Drat, I would need a ride from my parents to work.

That wasn't too much since Mother's family had come from that area and we still visit to this day going down that stretch of the freeway. Out on the main drag however, it was now slightly dicey. The city had put in roundabouts. For those folks not in the know, roundabouts are circular roadways that allow for people to move into the mix, while allowing others to move right out.

All of that keeps the traffic flowing without outright stop signs. After Father had unintentionally changed lanes while moving through the snaky esses, I was just a tad weary. After the second go through, indeed involving an un-signaled lane change again, Mother suggested a loan may be in order. Whew, the last thing a person could want is to show up late for work because Pops hit another car.

The fellow from the costume warehouse where I worked, the one that was on a ladder one day, and held it in, thus not going afterward for three full days afterward, had a would-be son in-law. I feel that I need to go further into my setup on this topic. He did some minor construction type work, and even some heavy contract-type of work as well.

One day he claimed that he needed to finish a job he had started. Well, three days later he finally finished up, if you know what I mean. Yeah, that's right, after holding it in. It took three additional days for things to kick back out. It had already 'kicked back in' at that point, so to say. So, my workmate suggested that I go see his would-be son-in-law, so I surely did so.

What makes this such a very small world is rather quaint. It turned out that after seeing a family photo, I realized who this young suitor's dad really was. He was none other than Vito the Italian hair dresser. If you recall, Vito's daughter would come in with the monthly paperwork at the small business, Scrooge-ian-type, bookkeeping service.

That was my first *real* accounting job. Yes, that first placed that I had started off at. Ahh…do you know what olive green surely is? I say again, when it refers to the beautiful skin of a fine young Italian girl, it retains a meaning all of its own! So here, out of my needful desperation, Mom and pop pick me up the following Saturday.

We pull up to the used car place which was situated directly across from the *other* tax service, and right next to the restaurant that the owner of that business had treated us to. That was following April 15th of the previous year. We got out of the car, introduced ourselves, and began the search. The first car that he showed me was a really handsome grayish silver muscle car. That was a 2000 Sebring.

He popped open the hood and I could see that the engine was on steroids, or at least it had been, at one time anyway. Once bitten twice shy? I think so. My heart longed for the hulking beast, yet my mind said that this is a loan, choose something a little less…er, intimidating, or frightening. Anyway, the very next vehicle was a used 2001 Mitsubishi Mirage.

I had already vowed over and over, to never own even a used foreign car. Could I possibly go against my own commitment after having the damn Germans kill one uncle in Normandy, and after the Japanese sunk the elder uncle in the Pacific back in WWII? I would need to take a test drive to be certain.

This car, I have to admit, was as smooth as a pair of silk stockings smuggled as contraband during WWII. On each turn it was as though I was dancing with the most lovely, and wonderfully light, and graceful, Japanese woman. I insisted that she repeat such a performance, and ever so quickly the second turn had been reeled in.

I did certainly go for another, and then another. The fact that it was nearly a sensuous experience only offered the feeling of that memory repeating itself again, and again, and again. Over and over in my mind those cornered turns return to me with such an elegant and pleasant sense of finery!

That was it. Mother turned over a check for about $3,200.00, and we were off, each of us in our own different directions. The freedom of not smelling gas, not listening to furry small animals shaking coffee cans filled with rocks, and the continued smoothness of my new hot ride, brought a sense of pleasure and relief. Soon the goal became to lift the loan monkey from off of my back.

There perhaps was one quick way to go. I mean to go all the way down to the casino, Jack Dabner! I took a half day from work and slid into the local joint feeling up, and ready to roll. Rather than dice, my game of interest had become 21. I took books out from the library, and after determining that one in particular suited my approach I went to work.

Although, the author had some doubts as far as my style of play being an actual legitimate method, I found all too quickly that I was beginning to lose my memory and couldn't possibly win, counting cards. With that method, one keeps a keen awareness as to how many low cards are still out, versus how many high cards.

This is especially so for the number of aces, twos, and threes remaining to be played out. As the casinos have been quite aware of this legal strategy for some time, they've come to using three decks at a time. Some then, suddenly consider that any portion of the remaining cards should be tossed, in favor of a new set of three decks. Here now, while receiving my cards and doing my best, within a few hands knew that I was in over my head, and would need to switch my approach.

That first night I did fairly well. I came home with about $800.00 additionally in my pocket so went back the next night. The forces were with me once again. I mean, I had a red-hot dealer and could do no wrong. She smiled and seemed to delight in my advantage. After about an hour of ridiculously uncontested wins a man from across the table noticed what was happening.

He laughed with glee, and shouted all too loudly, "Hey look, he wins every time, everybody do what he does." We went around for one more and the crowd was stoked. After pulling all of the chips back, the feeling of this being one of the most fantastical experiences was had by internal psyche. It as well, was treasured by each and every person at this full table.

For me most certainly, it was in such a special way that I became glorified, reveling in victory. That guy and his outrageous proclamation to do whatever I was doing, blew it for me big time however. I played just one more casual round then excused myself. Mr. Big Mouth, of course, was all too disappointed. He should have known better.

I came home with all told, about $3,200.00 in my stash. The wonderful ride of sweet, sweet gambling winnings had come to an end. After returning the next evening and feeling that the flames of fortune had died, I walked back out with $2,500.00 still in my pocket. Suffice it to say the car was all mine by the very next day.

I would then need to save up for the inevitable repairs. Like all other things that cannot be stopped forever, those surely came. Although, it would be the greatness of glory experienced from such close contact with a smooth-running machine would lead the way for now. I am now a bigger fan of all things delicate, especially those smaller more fragile mechanisms.

2013

Spring had sprung. I saw an ad in the local paper for a rummage sale. The fact that said sale included a men's 10 speed bike was what got my interest. I had now gone through a total of four garbage bikes, those being so noted by the method of receivership. Each of my 'found' bikes had that one critical condition.

They each had the very same with the pedal bearings having grounded to a grinding and grungy sort of disturbance, there was only one option left for a man such as I am, and on a budget besides. Rudy, the bike fixer was supposedly in possession at any given time, of extra Schwinn parts, as well as anything in particular that he felt was reusable.

With those other machines in my possession being no names or discount K-Mart specials, from companies such as Kent, or Huffy I felt the only readily available choice was to go to this yard sale and to take a look. I drove over to the old neighborhood by the lake. I get out of my car and walk up. Low and behold it was my other Raleigh's twin brother.

I'd say they're both about '76s. I pulled up and the taller man, and his average size wife were manning the table with the Raleigh parked beside them. I had for decades automatically considered this to be an English import. I have recently discovered it may be considered just as American as a Schwinn would be. That's because Americans did finally buy out the company.

One noted difference on the American versions is clearly labeled on the wheel axle. "Bearing Cases," the red label loudly announces. So, we went with cheap imported gears, stopped using the more expensive style of center-pull brakes, and began using bearing cases. It may be that 1975 was the very last year for a true British Raliegh to have ever been righteously constructed.

"Can I test drive it?" I inquired.

Old boy is like, "Here you look short, I'll lower the seat."

"Oh no, no," I shot back, "This is just the right height for a man with long legs." (An old man at the mall just explained that the rights to Raleigh had been purchased by an American enterprise just before my vintage collectibles had been created.)

I just need to find a '74, or '75 from England to round out my collection. Indeed, such preposterous inklings did this taller man maintain, I merely needed to mount, take the test drive, then dismount without racking my balls. I wish to be very precise here and now with my claim of height correctness. Such a distance is determined by the straightness of one's leg, when the pedal is at the lowest point.

This action should come naturally without any undo straining whatsoever. The bend of the toes should comfortably offer the strongest surge of downward power, without any extraneous exertion at all. The height of the seat therefore has nothing to do whatsoever with not falling down, or worse yet, rupturing the family jewels!

So, again, the seat was at the perfect position for my legs. Dude, was like, "Yeah, but as a shorter man do you feel that it's actually such a wise idea? Please. Number one, if you know anything about riding, it's all about the pedal to seat distance. Yes, it was a 27" men's 10 speed. Hello! Do I really look that little to you funny man? Jeez! I am 5'11" ¾, you know."

So, I get on, go about 20 yards, it's fine, no mechanical issues were present, the wheels were not too warped. It stopped fine enough. I was sold. I told him straight out, "this is never going to be a cool bike." I meant, with the small scratch on the body, and the tiny tear in the seat, please. He said, "Oh, it already is a really cool bike."

Whatever dude, maybe to an old grandpa, or the original owner, standing right here before me, but give me a break guy. So, guy is holding firm to his overly optimistic $115.00.

This slightly taller man's wife was filled with a familial joy, as she described serving up hot chocolate for the little kiddies, using those small, Irish tea glasses. (I like to call them) I couldn't resist and picked up a couple of those while I was at it.

All was good. It wasn't until, out of a sheer sense of guilt, (over his rip-off price) that pops is actually getting in my way as I tried to remove the back wheel to fit it into my sweet little Japanese honey. Understand, that is how I would get home from the auto shop after dropping off the car. With one quick wheel application I was once again mounted and riding.

Admittedly, I do need to be careful of my crowned jewels when coming to a complete stop at intersections. That should be a given for us just under six footers. Apparently, not for dude, and no doubt one of his sons. Suffice it to say, the bike really does almost look real cool with the brand-new white handlebar tape that I've recently applied. Rather than dicker and play around, since I wanted to get the whole ordeal over with, I pulled out the exact amount of cash and turned it over.

Now because the damn rip-off (I use the term lightly here) is feeling guilty because he and his little sweet one is probably going to the Bahamas, or at least Hawaii, he's now bending over backward to assist me. So, come on guy, just back off and let a slightly shorter fellow do his thing. With the back seat down, and the wheel removed, yes even a men's 27" ten speed was going to fit into my sweet little foreign jobber. As long as he quit trying to help it would.

I finally got him to ease up enough so that I managed to slide the whole works in, and shut the trunk. It gets harder every day to get on the little bitch, but it was an exact fit as far as my leg length goes. The nerve of such a fellow, although he was at least 2 or 3 inches taller than I am. He apparently failed to read the manual in regard to such intricate specifications being properly actuated.

2014

Although, I managed to become gainfully employed within two weeks of my termination from the costume warehouse, things could turn rough at any point in time. The main factor on many a horizon, at least for so many lower-class beings, is any unforeseen yet quite necessary car repairs. It is that one must think ahead, and do whatever is possible to avoid disaster down the road.

The temp service needed snow removal personnel on those very special days after we got dumped on overnight. I've merely made it sound fancy when the truth was, that what we did that for those apartment complexes, was done the good old-fashioned way, with shovels. The very next time coming up to an intersection with a green light, I continued on at about 35mph.

The street had gone unplowed, and a beautiful white blanket of snow covered every surface. Bam, I hit a huge deep pothole at the very worst angle possible. The dramatically pounding effect of impact slammed against my brain. Here I was working maybe 30hours at the new warehouse, and so desperately willing to engage in such additional hard physical labor.

Again, so many know of the back-and-forth hardships that come with used car maintenance. So, now this happens, and I'm back to even. I hit that stinking pothole just before our entry onto the freeway. Oh sh*t! That same day on our way out to the site, a fellow just ahead of us somehow became distracted, allowing the tires on the driver's side, to move over just enough.

The previously plowed snow was from six to 16 inches deep, settled in unruly, haphazard clumping, along the sides of that freeway. He was in the far-left lane, we were in the middle lane just behind a semi. The young fellow overreacted when grabbing the wheel. There was just enough residual moisture and icing still left upon the roadway so that he began to spin out.

At 60 mph, that can be one of the most freaking things to witness in your entire life. I would pick up the other men of the crew at headquarters, and was driving them now on out to the location. At the point this younger, less experienced driver got spun around my mind panicked slightly. With his car jetting out sideways and backward at a frightening rate of acceleration, my mind panicked slightly.

While my heart began to sink, I braced for impact. I mean it was like the snow bank spat him back out. It was just like a watermelon seed at a backyard family get-together. He flew sideways right into that semi in front of us, so that his rear windshield was completely smashed. As the trunk of the vehicle was low enough to just clear the gas tank area, the rear corner of the cab's step is what did the actual damage.

All that I could do was to change lanes, getting into the right lane in the nick of time. We were all just totally blown away, and thankful as hell to be still moving smoothly. There was not even time to look back. No siree. We had our own basket of laundry to attend to. The memory of this catastrophic event still haunts me to some extent.

It is more so in the winter when the sight of his spinning vehicle returns to my wild imagination, then suddenly comes flying toward the semi, all at about 60mph. I recall keeping my cool, yet am so nervous just before I change lanes. It's all in my head though. I want to make it a point to let people know here and now, you always take your foot off of the gas when correcting for snow, or ice.

This method will allow the weight of the vehicle to bear down heavy on the rubber tires, reducing the chances of a spin out. One should learn the other rule as well as far as turning into a spin, or is it the opposite? Do you recall my bro with the old Caddy and '62 Pontiac convertible? Those cruising weekdays were mostly about gaining experience, and not so much about having fun.

I could barely make ends meet as it was, now a low-income person's worst nightmare was upon me. I put off a visit to the repair shop as long as I could. I would readily soon regret that knuckle-headed decision. After about nine days I got around to taking it in to a local shop. I told the guy twice, "I am fine with the right side having old parts, just do the left side."

I did some window shopping for about forty-five minutes then stopped in to check the progress. He imparted that the parts had become wedged together, and that he had spent the whole time tearing those apart. I reaffirmed my wish to have only the left side worked on and went back out for a walk. I could see that he had put in some good toiling, by the sweat on his brow, and was perfectly fine with a larger labor charge than usual.

When I finally returned about another hour later, he was writing it all up. The total came to $2,200.00. "I told you not to do the right side." ('You damn mother-fluffer' went unspoken). Here I was a man of little means other than to cover the barest of necessities, and this bozo is like holding my car hostage for a doubly grand amount!

I maintained my composure and pulled my credit card out. My mind was racing for an answer otherwise, but came up empty. I just needed my car. I had to make it to work the next day simply to cover my rent. I would have time to consider my vengeance once I was pulling safely away. What could an innocent consumer do to recover from such treacherous skullduggery?

"Enemies for life," is an initial response. Calling a lawyer? Most, I had felt, wouldn't want to take such a small-time case. I ended up filing a report with the better business bureau. His response was to claim that I was a rambling, incoherent nutcase that didn't know what I was talking about. I still have plans to picket his establishment and quite readily so.

I will walk back and forth repeatedly from one corner to the next with my large bright white sign, and lettering in black, and red. 'TOTAL RIP-OFF', it will say. Plus 'UNAUTHORIZED REPAIR WORK PERFORMED', will grace perhaps even an additional sign or two. Maybe those will be carried by a loved one or so. Wait, what if I pay those who've been ripped off in the past, to help out?

When I talked to Mother about this place she had recommended, I was just like, "What the hell?" She then informed me that I was confused. The place she frequented was around the corner and had only a slightly similar name. She mentioned that her and pops had sold the motor-home, and threw in $2,000.00 to ease my misery. I was still rather hot about it. Here it was that my mom was now getting totally ripped off instead of me. It was still such a tremendous R-E-L-I-E-F, any way that you spelled it, and I was glad to be able to move on.

2015

I decided to switch teams. After working for a year and a half as a part-time loader, I had felt that I had paid my dues. It was April and at that exact point I went and applied with Kelly Girls. Well, that was what they used to call it back in my time. They recently removed the Girl part and added Services. They just needed everything from my arrest in Lewella Springs.

Bucher and Gapman, those bastards, if their miscarriage of the law was going to cost me everything, I swear that one day, one day soon, or one day later, I will create that comic book based upon the real and genuine Dynamic Duo, and send one to every person with those last names in the entire tri-county area. I went on over to that other community, and they printed up the details for me.

No one was home in the little Kelly office when I went in to present the whole truth and nothing but. I decided to slip the entire wad underneath the door. I soon hoped that this one emergency action wasn't costing me my chances. They were housed right inside the business, and were frequently about, whether giving tours to new candidates, or conducting personal business with one of the new hires.

Two- and one-half weeks later when nothing gave, I felt that I needed to take strategic action. I went to Carl, the head of shipping. I had felt that we were on good enough terms to plead now for a favor. I needed to ask him to work his 'Head of Shipping' magic just one more time for me. It was, if he might give the ole' girls a pitch call, I mean those two from Kelly.

If he could put in a good word for me in the meantime that would work wonders too. With those two from the service, it was a good-girl, bad-girl thing, going on between the two. I knew good and well, which of those two was holding up the wagon train. That little witch. Carl happened to be training his very own replacement at the time that I poked my head in to enquire.

He only had one day left as that was a Thursday. Within twenty minutes it was a done deal. Hah, how do you like me now, Kelly-bitch? It was so cool; I was filled with a joy that had been somewhat absent from my life up until that time. Thanks Carl! I started the next Monday and was as high as a kite. The only thing that I needed to do was to go through the pain of mostly standing in one spot.

There was plenty of movement required, yet it was within an eight-foot span. One would take a scanner gun and enter the bar-code into the system, then determine what special treatments may be necessary. Some of that involved separation, additional wrapping, and even bubble wrap as well. I could deal with it on Monday, and make it through all of Tuesday.

By Wednesday I was on my pills. So, it was a dose of one tablet for that day, two for Thursday, and even three for Friday, just as it had been in my darkest hours before. I found out years later that such an act goes against company policy. The poor girl that was nearly dying from cancer was *walkedout* by security. It has more to do with forklifts driving all over, in addition to its being a warehouse filled with hazardous chemicals.

If someone dropped a glass vial because they were hopped up on pain pills, it would cost perhaps even $3,000.00. What would be much worse would be if such an item was a corrosive and got all over your hands. I suppose they imagined someone standing still, checking the severe chemical burns, and saying, "Oh man, look my skin is smoking!" It would be in their minds, like someone that can't feel pain, yet can still see it right before them.

It was a fact that when I first started there, at least three others from the costume warehouse worked there as well. It was once again, that same gal had beaten me to the *good* job. Where I left the other place to do taxes over the winter, she left herself, and somehow found this honey job on her own. The girl from receiving was in my department as well.

I noticed another fellow that eventually stopped on by with a big hello and smile as well. Things were looking up, and life was now good for me. Ahhh…honey-money, yum, yum, yum. When I hadn't been hired outright by December 15th, I decided to make a complaint to management. The damn bastard that gave me dirty looks when I first started on the dock was in charge.

He would always hire the women, and make the guys wait. What a mother-fluffer. Within three minutes after turning in a complaint about workplace bias, I was in. That damn bastard though, wasn't done with me! Some men, mostly

German bastards just cannot like me even a little. I still see them constantly. Three men are naturally cool, when out and about.

It's always the fourth, a damn German bastard, that gives me the dirty looks. Over disciplined they are, I would guess. Think boney fingers here. Hey fluffers, I am a quarter German myself. Maybe that's what actually gets to them. I'm a way cooler German dude than they could ever, ever, ever even want to be themselves! Hahaha.

2016

My dreams of stardom had for some time, even going back to 2004, involved the lucrative fantasy of riches and wealth. After being burned twice down in Vegas, I told myself never again. Never again would I risk it all without a thorough determination of the odds, the probabilities, and my testing of my skills on paper.

With the daily newspaper being delivered to my home, I had every chance to determine exactly what was required to pick only winners. After twelve years I was ready to give it another shot. When it comes to sports gambling what you want to devise is a method that is only based on factual data. One big thing to keep in mind is that each year is a new one, with players often moving to other teams.

In addition, bad years can happen unexpectedly, and any one other thing imaginable could potentially rear its ugly head. Any one thing too, could prevent history from repeating itself. I feel that only luck is in the offing during the first few weeks of any sport. I had decided after all of my research that my only chance would be with baseball. I carefully narrowed my choices down to the two best teams around. Boston and Baltimore were it.

After landing in Nevada, I checked in to the cheapest place I could find. Just off the strip by about two miles, that end of town has its own separate action. I put about $2,800.00 on each game while holding some out for a little 21. Both of those lousy buggers lost 2 to 1. Can you believe the best pitching teams in all of the sport played true to the promise, yet the bums up at the plate struck out like wimps.

With my dreams now crushed like cold hard ice I only had one thing left. As I lay dying on my hotel bead with the reverberations of loss, rocking my very soul relentlessly, only one thought could help me to recover. It would mean going against the promise of a ghostwriter and outing my compatriots and brothers in song, spilling the beans about the truer origins of so much '70s and early '80s music. So, now I had only one chance left.

I pulled $2,000.00 out with my credit card and laid it on the line. Alas I had to catch my flight back home, but the good, good fellows at the casino mailed my winnings home to me, and I was nearly back to normal. As most have lived the superbly wonderful life of total outright rock stars, I consider that all in all, they should be good about things when I out them as having used the work of a ghost writer.

Also considering that I was a minor at the time of our work together, I should be given some leeway when it comes to blabbing all about it to everyone. In addition, by our very nature, musicians and such are always a bunch of good, good guys and generous blokes. Let me be frank, I have only met just a few of those professionals that have used my work. How so many of my unfinished numbers became finalized is beyond me.

So, it was now that I had decided to come out with it, not only to avoid a sense of poverty, but to more offer the world a sense of greatness that is all my own. You will read further on, in the epilogue, of my sincere humanistic and religious beliefs. To make it simple and to give you a review, I believe that life is about being set up to feel guilty just after we die so that a tractor beam will be cast out, and set upon us.

With our then-being moved off to the side, and held in a temporary state of hellishness, our life in purgatory as we Catholics refer to it, will begin. Only one group is responsible for these demonic actions. That would be a group that I refer to as the 'insane dead'. These evil spirits have not only lost their minds, they apparently may have sold their very souls in order to gain the power and ability to enter this realm.

There are two main issues that they so easily pick at. Through a silent invasion, deep into the cavernous reaches of our simple minds they can affect us. Sadly, once they do indeed manage to cause any undue behavior on our parts, as we are creatures of habit, nothing more may be necessary. Our two weak spots are for consumption, and sex. Those are the things that we so easily fail at. Whether it's alcoholism, addiction, overeating, or cheating on a spouse or lover, humans cave and give in, over and over again. At least sometimes they do, anyway.

2018

It was October. I had read that most car companies would be moving away more so, from regular sized vehicles, and concentrating their efforts on those hulking beasts with bad mileage. I chose to take the opportunity to pick up the least expensive car known to man. That was at the time anyway. It was an end of the year sale, so this baby was going for a slim $18,000.00 or so.

"How could one resist," I say. There is one aspect of being single and juggling two autos. It's quite similar to having two girlfriends. One needs to keep track of things so very carefully, so as to avoid any sticky situations. I would like to point out that my new motor vehicle is the smallest 'BIG' car on the market today. It all started so sweet and innocently enough.

I brought my new baby home, then riding the bicycle back to the dealership, I removed the front wheel, then placed the thing into the back of old girl, the 2001 Mirage. Neither would be the wiser, or would they? The new girl got the garage, with the little sporty vehicle parked with a permit out on the street. The first thing to go on the Mirage was a tire.

Easy enough to get repaired, I considered. The way I was making about $21.50 per hour, little things such as a flat tire can't possibly interfere with one's spectacular new found life. I simply pulled out the new Ford, made my way to work, and dealt with the other little trifle the very next day. Things were back to normal, and everything was fine.

Fine that was until December hit. The little bitch had stopped starting, if even such a thing is possible. First it was here, then there, then once too often. I took the chance that it had to do with something inexpensive. The clowns at the repair shop, let me drive off with the little thing having been switched out, all the while she had been acting like a little whore the whole time, they had it.

So, she starts up at work, then it goes dead at the drug store down the way, and on the main drag. I was now losing it. I mean not just my sanity, but the keys as well. I will tell you some things were made to be the only one in your life, and unless it's some old collector car that you mostly just look at, that's how it is with those for those incapable of maintaining more than a mild interest the 'other' vehicle.

So, I went back and forth three times in between the drugstore, and the gas station on the corner, a quarter mile away. Unless someone came along while I was on my back under that Japanese bitch, the suckers just so totally disappeared. I finally jumped ole girl, using the spare key, then walked back once more for the Ford.

So, now I'm down to the spare set of keys taken from my own personal secret hidey hole, and the house keys which I wisely had separated, on their own keychain. I had doubles, and even triples of the keys now gone, but it still bugged me to no end. After going to the bank, the next day like a fool, after the little nasty tart finally started, I just gave up again.

This time around not even a jump would get her going. Although, I wanted to milk the old girl for everything she had left, it was just not meant to be. I called the junkyard, and had her towed. When I drove in with the new girl, the sucker says, "oh yeah, here, this was on your car," handing me a ticket from the day after they agreed to pick the sad, sad thing up.

A break-up was never harder or more filled with personal trauma, than it was for me anyway, and my sweet little Japanese honey-bunny. The new machine apparently had made someone envious. A one inch very deep gouge has appeared on my car's rear end. Only sad lowlife types envy another's physical possessions. Normal folks know to block stuff out, and to get back to work on their own.

It appears that someone has taken their car key, then while standing behind my vehicle, out of view of the security cameras, used every ounce of energy to make a 1 inch long by 1/8-inch-wide mark that goes all of the way to bare metal. I did give errors where errors were due! Even I went through those days feeling a bit sheepish about my work when I had first started. Oh well, some just can't handle the heat of close and investigative introspection.

2019

Things went along fine without my little foreign sweetie pie. The new 'least expensive' car in the world was treating me well, and things were otherwise running smoothly. One aspect of my work however did not play out so smoothly. It was when I discovered that not one of us at work were supposed to be on any level of pain reliever, over and above the over-the-counter type.

It was that a co-worker in my new department became all too clear about it. This slightly older gal that I have briefly referred to, had gone through those lifesaving chemo treatments just years before. Security was called to 'walkout' that older gal in my department years before, if you'll recall. They would not even let her go to her locker without a proper escort.

After her treatments and recovery, she finally returned to work. There was only one aspect of her return that caused concern. No one, not one of us was supposed to be on such a serious pain reliever, so as to potentially render one unable to properly perform one's duties. I however, knew good and well that taking opiates was the only way to perform my duties.

I don't just mean whatsoever. I mean at all. If you'll recall, by Wednesday I was in such severe pain it was agonizing. I thanked my lucky stars for what I didn't know up to that point. Whew, I did believe I had just dodged a bullet. I quickly decided that I would continue with things as usual, while being even extra, extra careful when handling glass items. I merely had to keep it cool, was all.

I recalled how I had dropped one tiny vial on the floor, although years ago. I was in a hurry to make rate, I recalled. After a safe and careful cleanup, I was back up and running. To think, my very existence, as far as I had come to know, was based on my having been cheating life itself, as far as the 'no opiates' policy here at work was concerned. I shivered at the thought of any negative possibilities.

It took several moments initially and then again over days, for me to come to terms with this new truth, comprised of such a newfound harsh and cold reality. As long as I didn't expose my pills to anyone at work, I would be just fine. I locked that aspect of my newer self into its secretive, designated, super-private cranial space. As long as I was sure not to mention those life savers in passing, as my co-worker no doubt did, I would be able to reach retirement in fine, fine shape.

I thanked God for my new car, all of my handsome clothing, my new refrigerator, my new man-chair, and for all of the other fabulous things in my life that I truly now appreciated. It was as though they were made of gold itself. With my work being often sitting at a computer, I found it much easier to squeak through the week.

By Wednesday yes, I would often take at least one measly oxi-3, and never more. By Friday it was certainly an overdose of three that got me through the week. Here though, with my desk available to sit at intermittently, throughout any one evening, I could go indefinitely and love it. I would be just dandy, and super happy, and so very well pleased, as long as I kept it cool Daddio!

It was when going out into the field that my toughest days were now ahead. When it came to the inventory, because everything was so computerized, it often did not come to light that our system did not match the amounts on the shelves so quickly and readily, as one may have duly appreciated otherwise. That was when I was often expected to execute a search and destroy effort. (If you'll recall, that was a costume warehouse mission that I was sent on so often times.)

On one occasion the computer claimed that 40 boxes of product Z would fit on a shelf. Later when to the individual whose work it was to place that very amount onto the designated shelving, it became obvious something was amiss, only a few options were available. So, those would only fit if placed onto that very shelf *sideways*, with the label obscured.

The order filler came along and no doubt panicked when unable to find the product. They put into the system that none where available at the designated location. I wish to clarify here, anyone determining that our products could not fit in the predetermined location was supposed to have called in a management team member for a 'systems-override'.

I would then go on one of my search missions to come down to the bottom of things. It mattered not that the product was actually present the whole time.

I either reloaded the product into the system or moved some. While adjusting the totals for location, and then offering any 'errors' my tasks would be complete. Any truly responsible parties responsible for any discrepancies would have *earned* those demerits *justifiably* therefore.

Certainly, there were so many, many of those occasions when I allowed for things to stand pat with no further action necessary. It was so that folks new that I was not out to get them. Here in that instance, all forty boxes had been front and center the entire time. Whew, I was extremely pleased to have found that much in value, still in one location.

The new folks, or temps, as so many were, simply needed to learn all of the secrets of order selection before being considered a member of our topnotch personnel. Some of our MIAs may have come from orders not filled correctly. Just as the department that I started in, was on what I will term piecework, so were those pulling the orders as well.

Considering that they had been exclusively hired from the temp service, at least when I had started, it was so that anyone individual may be brand-new at this. I would see the regulars often times, walking along with the newbies. It was a slow and casual pace at first. Once one realized you would always be a temp at that rate, it was time to pick up the pace.

That is when a little boo-boo may arise, such as when 40 units are overlooked, or in my case when I lost control of a tiny glass vial, and dropped that onto the floor. If you'll recall from my days as a temp at this facility, one gal and one gal alone, refused to go there. I mean she refused to become Wonder Woman. So, she was not executing superior packing moves.

With a graceful sense of placement, moves were not being engaged in so that her very existence finally played out as one of life's beautiful ballets. No, that wasn't her game. She somehow knew that such an effort would not come easily at all. Rather than to *chance* things, she simply worked at her own 'quick' pace doing the most that she possibly could. She therefore wasn't harried or frenzied at all.

The rest of us knew better. Yes, as long as the tiny vial did not contain chloroform, we would be just fine. Gloves would be donned, a special face covering applied, and the spill team would go to work when called upon. In no time at all only a wet spot would remain of what one did consider a hazardous spill site. The fine line between total excellence and frantic hyperactivity could be as slim as head-hair.

Dare ye' risk it all, to venture forth into the vast darkness of superhuman abilities? Some say aye, while still others choose to die! Or rather bid adios, and adieu to all of us now about to make lower-middle class wages. As I have inferred, some of our off numbers in the system involved mis-fills. If you have ever ordered something through the mail or otherwise, you can easily imagine the feeling of eagerly opening that just delivered package to find what?

That's right, you would be like all "what the hell is this, I just verified my address on the damn package, so what gives?" No doubt the person that pulled your order was either incompetent to engage in such work, or was merely in a hurry due to their numbers being a bit low. If just before such any such action was undertaken, a person was reminded of their lack of quantity mistakes may begin to occur. Again, as long as I was careful, attendant, focused, and aware, I would be just fine. The glass vials too, would make it through my hard laboring days, from that point on as well.

2020

I had just stopped at the eye doctor. Having realized that I overslept, I realized as well that after changing the wake-up time on my alarm clock, I had absent mindedly forgotten to actually set it again, to wake me up in an hour or so! I drove to the optical center hoping to be squeezed in, rather than having to reschedule putting off my clearer vision needs at work. Just as I had feared my next appointment was pushed ahead from that day 7/1 to 7/22. I looked at frames and had two selected. One would be for work, a pair of bifocal safety glasses, and one for my leisure time watching TV and such.

I entered my vehicle and wondered what I should do to kill the 40 minutes I had left remaining, before actually having to punch in. Here it was a question on several fronts. I could drive home with about just enough time left to turn right around and head back that way. In the past I had stopped at my library, or Lady Lauralie's library rather, a place her daughter eventually worked.

If hungry enough I may have stopped at a fast-food joint for some fries as an option. Oh, what to do, what to do, with an extra 40 minutes? Here I was not only on a diet and doing well in my estimation, because of the pandemic I believed all libraries in the entire state were more than likely still closed.

At work in the lunch room, we had three computers set up for employee personal use. They had been disconnected. I had arrived early in the past by as much as 20 minutes or so, and utilized that opportunity to engage in bill paying activities. Maybe I did some online banking making sure my available funds were adequate for any expected necessities. Yet here with no computers, the time inside that building was almost painfully unbearable for me. Yes, those computers at work had been unplugged, with the keypads humorously wrapped in saran wrap.

I would lately then, when too early, close my eyes and make it all go away. With the new faux leather sofa and chair, such an activity was a neutral affair. Because my supervisor was tired of altering our time sheets, she changed the earliest that we could punch from 3:24 to 3:28. There was no sounding device to indicate that such a break in time had started. If we punched in late, we were marked up as such.

When it came to being back early it meant that we may be up for some *unearned* overtime pay, sans a necessary adjustment. I could, all in all, without my favorite thing to do, paying bills with all of that wonderful moola, only handle about ten to twelve minutes in that break room. Before the start of my busy workday, I needed just the proper stimuli to move on into it. I was never in the reading mood like my younger teammate, yet I should have taken a hint. Reading always lowers my heart-rate and blood pressure to a calming level. Oh well!

I would so often sit and relax closing my eyes and blocking everything out. It helped tremendously that the company brought in that very brand-new black vinyl sofa, the two matching chairs, and as well, a coffee table, and the end tables. One of those was complete with a phone recharging station. Occasionally I would peek to note someone's presence. My main goal was to make it all disappear, as it would be a hectic chase for product soon enough. Here today that became the only question. Would I kill time here, or do it there?

I decided a beautiful joy ride would be just the thing. I turned my vehicle toward the baseball stadium. I then turned left on the highway out of town. Thinking, thinking I surely was. The nearest food store that I was aware of was just out of the way. I had plenty of time though, and it was a bright sunny afternoon with time to spare. I continued on and decided that it would be a banana I would buy, rather than a yogurt.

I still needed to take my morning pills with food. It was 2:35pm, and I felt that only a quick ten-minute drive awaited before my sweet yummy breakfast would be consumed with delight. That would be just before re-ignition and setting my headings for work.

I bought the most attractive banana I found. Before entering my car, I had realized something though. I had slipped the pills into the wrong pocket on the side of my carpenter jeans. I could readily reach the bottom of the lower pocket. My hand jammed at the knuckles on the upper. I struggled to no avail. No worry. I merely had return to the store, slip my leg out of one side of my pants, then while standing on the other foot, slide my leg out and shake. With the removed shoe carefully located under the other foot, once the pills dropped out, I would be home free. You can imagine that when in a hurry I so easily could forget which pocket was which.

No luck here Captain Bucky, a different individual had issues of his own. This being a not so popular food store well outside of town, it wasn't just slow with few bustling customers, they had as well, only one bathroom stall. I was at the mercy of this other fellow's predicament. Ten minutes had passed. I felt I should count my chickens, and move on. Wait, I would only have to perform the same exact procedure at work anyway.

Maybe he's almost done. Seeing that the self-serve assistant had not even one customer, I decided to ask her. After explaining each detail of my predicament, I said, "Would you then, put your hand deeply into this pocket, and retrieve my pills?"

She declined. Even though she was only about 5 feet, and 110 lbs., I admit it could have easily turned into very comical situation there indeed.

After a few more desperate moments I looked down and saw the red shoes. I was good to go, maybe. Thankfully, in short time, all was well again. I did note in retrospect the complete absence of foul odors. Dude was apparently there to buy laxatives! Oh well I entered my car, I swallowed the pill dry, and consumed my sweet yummy banana. Oh-oh, upon turning the key I could see I was running late.

I quickly calculated a route to the local Interstate. Things may perhaps turn out alright afterall. I had set my car clock eight minutes ahead so perhaps did indeed have the time necessary. Things were going well. It looked as though I just may pull it off.

Coming from the east there is a soft 90° turn moving south. I recalled the day a semi had completely detached from the trailer. On one other occasion as well, there were vehicles parked along the side indicating an apparent accident. Here it was again, as sure as shootin'. Though even with three parked vehicles and a motorcycle, there was no visible debris, nor any emergency vehicles, nor any law enforcement vehicles, or otherwise. I was back on track soon enough but wondered how close my arrival at work would actually be. It took us at least a mile to get back up to even 50 MPH. It was not looking good.

The damn Germans had speed bumps put in at work. They privately used an official road sign along the side of the building reading '25MPH', yet it was most required to decelerate to 5 MPH, to move carefully over both those speed bumps. With the parking lot all of the way behind the building, as long as there wasn't a first/second shift, combined meeting, one wouldn't need to walk quite the 300 yards or so, from the farthest reaches of the property.

One speed bump started that roadway at first. The city style speed limit sign was exactly half way between the both humps. That second one being at the end of the straight away. He crossed over that second bump before officially entering the parking lot itself.

I turned to park. I usually guessed first lane or second. Here, indeed I guessed wrong. Where I would have had a clear path on the second lane, a pedestrian was exiting the building. As he approached the crosswalk I stopped to wait. He signaled with the wave of his hand. I quickly signaled back. When I could see his shoes on the pavement, well beyond my car, I paused for an additional second then I took my foot from the brake beginning to crawl forward.

As I was approaching this area just beforehand, I noted that all of the vehicles on the corner-end were dark. The only way anyone could be in any of those vehicles was if they had something fall from the passenger seat onto the floor, and were picking that up as I drove closer. In addition, dark colored clothing could potentially obscure any actual activity in those readily parked cars.

The worst was about to happen. I easily noted that an entire section where I had hoped to park was blocked off. I can't fully explain why *what would happen* over the next few minutes, did indeed occur. It was as though this well laid trap had been so cleverly set, so that even the other victim of man's failures, fell right into it. With a lockstep and marching gait of his very own, he put both feet ankle-deep into the lot of it. I so readily mean that the red tennis shoes, the non-accident, the new I.D. badge scanner that worked for sh*t, every single and individual moment that played itself out that day, held a certain demise for both of us.

It was as well that the company ran out of two-foot-tall orange cones, so went to using the one-footers. I would have easily surmised the lack of any space; had they actually used the two-foot versions. We both were otherwise generally common persons, usually exhibiting a sense of good and kind behavior, I had to believe in any case.

Again, each and every action was all seemingly part of a well-set trap, waiting out ahead for me, on that tragically strange day. With all of these things hovering above and, in the background, all of the other trifles, trials, and tribulations of ordinary life stuck out like gnarly daggers, being thrown into the vast darkness of night.

Yet there was for certain, only to be two of us as victims. I wish to point out that when entering the parking area at that facility one may need to consider where to park, is any other person around, are there pedestrians, if not potential drivers about. I had my head filled with everything but the necessary amount of gas to finally apply here and now, upon finally seeing an opening of where to park.

My foot slammed down on the accelerator, squealing the tires just a tad. I lifted my foot then reapplied it. I had about 7 to 8 yards to go before the next 90° turn. After an additional 25 yards or so it would be a 'U' shaped turn. There were three open spaces to choose from. I performed my greatest parking maneuver ever. In noting that very aspect of my rushed performance, I grabbed the keys, and my lunch. I shot out of my supersale car, then ran a trot toward the door. As I passed the office worker for the second time, he went into lecture mode. I cannot explain why the next thing happened either. I immediately and instinctively had gathered his truer intentions. We need to here, take a look at the facts.

It was 3:28PM. Our shift started at 3:30. I was running toward the door with my lunch. I idled past the official crosswalk after seeing both of dude's feet on the ground well past me. I even gave him a few more steps for the sake of it. I immediately took my foot from the gas, and readjusted upon realizing my undue heavy application initially. That amount of acceleration was incidental to any of my true intentions.

So, yes, I accidently punched that pedal for a simple moment, it was nothing personal at all. This shabbily dressed employee did not work at our plant, so therefore had no authority, and his standing at the other building about 40 miles south, carried no weight otherwise.

Indeed, wasn't I 60 years old, and with his being about 30 years my junior, did he not fail to respect his elders? Was he simply trying to ensure that I was late? Some people due to mitigating circumstances developed over a lifetime, can become demonstratively police-like, or otherwise fussy when it comes to the lacking of certain protocol being maintained by others all about.

If those lacking in the maintenance of proper protocol, and not adhering to the expected level of superior greatness that such a character now demands in his everyday life, may so easily cross the line! An imaginary line of sanity it would seem for this fellow. Or it could be simply when the mood strikes that such character-types morph into a grade school principal. Here we were, and then the round 2 bell rings!

So, my initial response, holding up a fist, was in my opinion, the response to the true outer stimuli being offered at this quite inopportune time for myself. Although, it was even more like, "Look sucker, you don't mess with someone that's late, especially me."

Yes, that is about what actually jumped out of my mouth while holding up my fist. He went apish. In hindsight, I have him pegged as an anally strict disciplinarian. A damn, old-school German from the south side as well, I had believed that he was for certain, no doubt indeed. I being from the north there was an automatic personality clash just waiting to be exposed by our intersection of happenstance.

He took a small step toward me raising his arms, then flexing violently once and again. He then ordered me to hit him, not just once, but two times he screamed that order at the top of his lungs. I need to make it clear at this point; the only people invited to the quarterly meeting from our other plant were upper management sorts. Yes, it would be those individuals along with one middle-management supervisor that attended those quarterly sessions.

Here and now, his tirade, his wildness, his enraged sense of craziness, came as I was turning away from him to continue running to the door. As I came about, I saw three persons standing frozen in disbelief. All three were in total and utter shock.

They were seemingly suspended in a state of dismay, and held captive in the very fact of those abnormal actions being displayed now before them. Only the elder, the fellow with pure white hair had managed to get his mouth to close. The other two had apparently not experienced life to the same degree, in order to so easily come to terms with this psychotic nightmare, now playing itself out, to the strains of their astonished fright. Once I neared the door they must have intervened on my behalf, as he was off my tail. I had heard the loud clap of his soft toed casuals as he apparently applied the brakes.

Even initially and so very quickly he was right back behind me. I entered the building casually, used the hand sanitizer then pulled a Covid mask from the dispenser. As I was about to scan my badge in, he finally entered. He was now ordering security to place me under citizen's arrest, shouting, "stop that man, stop him."

From this, I ascertained his goal was back to having me punch in late. Rather than taking an assault charge simply to execute my very termination, he now would settle for even my late tardiness.

Security did nothing. They knew me all too well, going back to my truck loading days. As far as I could tell this fellow was new, and had never before attended one of our meetings. Here I quickly made my way up the steps, and down the two long hallways. As I made my way to the clock, I could see the time. It was 3:30 on the button. Two others punched in behind me in a timely fashion. Things would be just fine after all. I worked for an hour or so, then got the call.

I entered the conference room with some confidence. After all, this was the gal that was present when Carl, during her initial training, phoned over to Kelly Girls temporary service to get me in like Flynn. I explained to her, without going through all of the details, how I was running late, and needed to hurry to punch in on time. This fellow who was obviously here for the meeting, I told her, purposely tried to stop me to make me late, all the while sounding like a grade school principal. I merely held up my fist, and said he needed to leave me alone.

It was all to no avail. I was on suspension, and the next day quickly fired. It was the fellow that gave me dirty looks when I was a temp for the trucking company, that made the final call. The other supervisor in that area that I would see was always smiling, yes, even at me. One can imagine how for some reason they're not liked by someone that they've never met, or even spoken to directly on any one occasion. That I was now terminated was all I needed to hear.

I hung up the phone and went into desperation mode. Oh well, now I have time to go back to my book, and here I am now before you, hacking away madly like a death row inmate pleading for a Governor's pardon. Understand dearly enough though, I am not yet quite in a state of desperation. I can make it indefinitely for at least another decade or so before a sense of desperate poverty begins to settle in.

I can easily retire then, in 2022. With the low amount I would receive it would be a type of hardship and suffering, and no less for certain. However, I have just heard of an option that suits my situation to a tee. If I retire early, then come across some income or a grand inheritance of some sort, I will be allowed to pay back the government what I had received to that point. I could then by canceling my retirement, restart it at a more favorable, and beneficial time, as far as the monthly payments go. I however back then, two long years ago, spent that entire weekend in a state of financial agony.

It wasn't just the hangover. It wasn't just the sore body parts from walking around in the woods. It wasn't just the mysterious bruises from falling occasionally while slipping on the slick trails. It was all of it. All of it, all together, all coming at me all at once and, with such a vengeance as to put me into an earth rattling state of turmoil.

Up to that point, nothing as horrible and awful as any one of those things could be, none of those other occurrences that I've muddled through, none of the physical traumas, none of the harsh and last-minute terminations was as brutally final as this parlay into desperation so coldly before me now truly was. No, I proclaim to you with the deepest, keenest sense of hindsight one could ever muster, not one aspect of my younger life made me feel so desperate, such I was feeling now.

I have felt it necessary to go through these life trending, ceremonial separations in the past. There was the boy's mother, and our emotionally painful separation. First, I experienced the termination from the Small Bookkeeping Operation, and now this. Could it get any worse? On Saturday I recovered from the over indulgence of alcoholic intake.

On Sunday, I was overwrought with tumultuous agony and worry. Rehearsal of what I would do again and again, offered little respite from the anguish. I would be left in a weighty state of agony, only to merely go over the whole routine of possible pathways once more, and again. I mean as far as any of my options in all regards.

Here with my brand-spanking-new vehicle, my house full of knickknacks and treasures, with my visions set on a peaceful and even fruitful retirement, here with all of those key and reveled-in aspects of my aging self now at risk, I was more than a bit troubled. Just once more in my mind, to refine my approach, I would cross every bridge before me. Gaining passage across each and every trail, in order to fathom an escape from this horrid existence that I had created for myself, I would cranially fathom. Something, anything to remove this desperate grade of turmoil, would help to salve the cranial dilemma of my predicament.

I could perhaps move in with mother. Then again that would be the very last thing on the list that I would choose. She is the type, at least for now, to reach into Father's big-time earnings from being an electronics tech, then in dispersing those valued holdings out toward the needy, removing herself from any further concern. I can only feel partly responsible for any others in our small family group when it comes to outright need or an urgently tragic, and dire set of consequences otherwise.

If turned down from that final option, as far as accommodations, suicide was always in the offing. Without my special pills for arthritis, I do even suffer now when perhaps missing a dose, here or there. The doctor offered a refill on the pain pills.

However, I will not be able to afford my next visit, set for the very next month, August. I will save all of those 'emergency-opiates' that I can for now, avoiding any use other then what may be considered emergency medical needs. To be truthful and honest, hardcore users consider those pills to be a mere step above ibuprofen.

The prospects of a 60-year-old man finding a job, in this pandemic ridden environment, are desperately void indeed, if not then unlikely. It does factor in as well that my minor maladies have caught up with me in such a physically harsh and grand fashion.

For now, I will cling to the belief that my manuscript will be completed, and will be accepted by not only a fine and wonderful publisher, but by the general public too. It was just this Sunday past that we all in our family got together. Mother seems to have recovered from Father's death in May. That last thing needed is something so dire, something so traumatic for us yet even more so, to struggle through.

At least to me it is. So, I will hold on as long as possible. Who knows, instead I may be proclaiming my greatest triumph. Father and she knew, to some extent, of my unbelievably artistic skills. If I can only keep at it for long enough to put out something worthy of consideration, I will do just fine.

On Monday, I applied for unemployment compensation. I say who knows, if those stuck-up bunch of bugger-rats were not in the right, what's wrong with having them pay a little compensation? At least until I can get back on my feet. Truth be told, they haven't laid anyone off going back to the early days, working out of the founder's garage. So, yeah, that means that they've surely paid into the system without any employees whatsoever really needing such a Godsend. Or if I finish up my tale of woe and greatness, I will at least have climbed a mountaintop, claiming a moral victory by planting my flag atop that lofty peak of published literary performance.

I soon went to the local UC office to present a hard copy of my resume. There were cars parked from here to Montana. Police were everywhere. A man in line finally told me, "This line is for corona testing." I drove around the block to a wider street with legal day parking. Relieved I made my way around the corner. It would be a quick jaunt. Oh no, sidewalk repair, I'll just have to jaywalk around this obtrusive affair right in front of the officers, I was thinking.

I quickly made my way through the twists and turns of waiting traffic. In addition to the line going out of vision around the block, at least four more curled up in the lot of what was at one time K-Mart department store. Finally, I was there. I donned a mask, and would soon be seen. Alas, they were closed up good for that function.

I went to the other side of town miles, and miles, and miles away, far from the dispensing hand of the local freeway. "I just need to relax, that's all, it's a hill to climb," I assured myself. They too had the door unlocked, but only offered a phone number, as had the closer facility. I flipped a coin, and after some minor waiting, the gentleman on the other end of the line offered a reprieve. My case would still go through without the hard copy resume being turned in. Some relief bathed my fettered mind. I was only in a desperate panic-mode, that was all.

Another week or two and all the obsessing, the turmoil would quickly dissipate. If the infidels at the warehouse challenged my claim, a hearing would be held. If it was an outright denial that came through, plan 2 would be initiated. If indeed my claim was accepted, I would receive about $386.00 for at least 4 to 6 months. That would be time enough to recover and execute plan 2b.

On Tuesday I took a bike ride. "Should I, should I?" I asked. Go all of the way down to the lake. On a straight route it would be a candy dance. But past downtown, along the lake shore, and then up to the lighthouse, well I would just see about that. The first leg of the journey was quite pleasurable. I went on the angle street toward the taller buildings, then past the old neighborhood where my half siblings lived, then across the river.

It was nearly all downhill, so I had decided to go for it. Victory would be mine. After the river and the college campus it was more easy riding. Truthfully, I had to stop more than actually go. Up the hill so soon and after a quick move the beach was before me.

It got a bit rough, but after a combination of walking the bike and riding, I had made it. You know that you have a well-balanced machine if you can simply coax it forward by the seat while walking casually beside it. If it's so very easily pushed along with one hand, your machine therefore, is a well-calibrated finely tuned roadster. I set my attention to the beauty and splendor reaching out around.

I wish to take a side track concerning those well manufactured machines. Because of Joe's family for the most part, I had considered those old Raliegh's to be British made cycles. I have now gotten my original 1976(?)Raleigh's bearing case changed, that was indeed after a small withdrawal of some retirement funds. I just read that an American business purchased the rights of production. I believe that is when the company began using Shimano Co. derailleurs from Japan.

It is now that the stuck-up elitists at the cycle shop have sold out, and the new management has no problem at all, using preset bearing cases rather than creating an adhesion to the critical pedal area, utilizing the common grease packing method. Update: I now own eight bicycles of varying makes and quality, most needing bearing cases replaced. The 'coolest' is the 1971 green Schwinn.

My newer Schwinn, gifted to me by the bike-shop guys, falls just below the American made Raleighs. It shall require the same type of overhaul nonetheless. I now have nearly enough of those classic machines to outfit all of my kids, and grandkids!

Recall my mechanical 9-year-old neighbor if you will. My original 'found' Raleigh is only waiting for the dough to purchase a new back wheel, tires and tubes, as well as some handsome, handsome white handlebar tape. For those who are into the more modern and physically comfortable frames being offered, I will say that it is simply a matter of learning how to ride no hands.

Get that vital aspect of the ride experience down, and you won't need a sissy-boy's bike like some are riding nowadays! Nor will you need a girly-man's helmet either. I am sorry. Too many helmet boys spoil a good Sunday drive! I repeat, you get three feet, three feet, and that's it. There is no legal double riding allowed whatsoever. That would be along roadsides or anywhere else for the most part.

So, there I am, I'm driving along a sleepy parkway, as they are deemed in these parts, yet its welcome wending would be ending soon. I come around the main drag out of town. What should I come upon when turning off from that highway out of Dodge? An old man, at least three years older than I, is enjoying the peaceful tranquility of that pre-noon Saturday sunshine. There was just one aspect of his admiration for that grand and beautiful morning that set me off a bit.

The sucker was somehow recharging his batteries, though smack dab, with little wavering, right in front of my vehicle. I considered that he may have been daydreaming, or perhaps using some type of porta-musical device. I therefore beeped. His head rose up in an acknowledgement of my needful presence. He made no effort whatsoever to do anything other than to feel old. I beeped again.

So, now bicycle-boy, or should I refer to him as Helmet-Boy, stops dead in his tracks, five feet in front of my vehicle. With me right behind him his actions were puzzling if not outright provoking. So, I honked a third time. Helmet or not, he's asking the wrong person for directions to the roadside, I'd say Jack Dabner, by gosh by golly.

I truly mean it. Don't ever piss me off, or something may just go down. So, 'Tired-old-man' claims he has a rightful domain to the roadway. That popped it. One wrong move from Helmet-Boy, and I was going to throw down. While my brain attempted to calculate an entry into his weakness, I informed the rotten bugger, while pointing to the stones, grass, and weeds, that "you get three feet."

"Three feet," I repeated. He moved over enough for me to cool my hot-rodded jet engines. God what is wrong with some people. Other than some being old and tired, I just know these days.

Now, regardless of where you are riding, if that track is meant for motorized vehicles as well, as '*legal*' bicycle rider, then truly, really, lawfully, such a road sharer merely gets three frickin' goddamn feet! I don't know what the hell is wrong with some of you people. Wait, cops stopped pulling over kids riding on the sidewalk, while issuing tickets.

With such an encounter that for the most part, requires one to learn how to mother fluffing drive a two-wheel non-motorized vehicle in the correct and proper fashion, one would tend to believe that we could all get on the same boat in those regards. Yeah, let's all just ride wherever we want until we get bicycle riding tickets.

So, let us start once more from the beginning, you are required to use hand signals. You are required to make a left turn, while on the right side of any cars turning, from the *actual left turn lane*. That would be that actual and true to life left turn lane, created for those very vehicles now beside you. You are not allowed to ride side by side on bicycles. The gutter, if present, is considered a part of the three feet referred to.

So, if I am driving up behind you, you then, as a cyclist, are required, by law, to move over into that very three feet of space. I don't consider the lack of approaching vehicles to be a reason for you to veer slightly into my lane. I mean, come on Helmet-Girl, do you really need six to eight feet of pedaling space?

So, what the fluff? I will tell you what. I'll tell you in about one sentence, these '*helmet*' people have taken over our streets and roadways, yet without utilizing the required rules of proper maneuvering. No wonder they wear helmets, and sometimes Spandex. Although, that choice of gear is for a fashion statement more so than anything. Am I right? In addition, all types of elbows, and knee pads are implemented, to what? Ride a freaking bicycle?

I only get slightly upset when people insist on taking something that is rightfully mine, such as the pathway of my car, unless of course, you want to be in idiot and throw down, bucky-boy. Then slightly, I will kick your ass.

Some of the girls had on bikinis. Wowza, oh man, that's enough to wake you up in the morning. I mean getting back to beach while refraining from being such a Man-bitch, although here it was, actually nearing 2:00pm, at just the correct moment. I walked the bike, up the winding walkway to the preserve beacon. At the top a gentle protester banged a bass drum with one mallet. It was reminiscent of American Indian drumming, with the call to gather as the message.

I was home again. It was not that I had ever resided there. It was simply a place with a sense of peace, and goodness that I would allow myself to meld into. Think of Dave pulling me from the seemingly gentle waters down below. A summer street festival used to be held nearby, so the old hippie neighborhood if you wish to phrase it that way, was where I now was. I made my way to the good bar.

I rested my Raleigh against a chain lock-bar. Taking a seat, I just relaxed. In time a waitress emerged. I explained how the hill had gotten the best of me, and that I just needed to relax a bit. Perhaps I'll go back, and even soon. You see when I was homeless, and had just a few in my pocket, I had stopped in. After ordering fried potato wedges with skins attached, I went from pouring a generous amount of catsup onto those crispy delights, to nearly half the bottle. I plopped at all atop the basket of goodies now calling out to me with a reckless abandon.

The fries stood up to all of that complimentary goodness. I was stuffed afterward to say the least. Upon returning years later I came to realize the decision was made to go with the more standard shape of those well fried delights. I somehow felt guilty. Were others taking after me and having the big basket as their only daily meal? Perhaps I should refrain from any consideration to go back so quickly. After all, a man needs to be wise and to budget out his resources in order to fulfill his daily needs, rather to jolly about frivolously, partaking in such grandiose gourmandizing.

Tuesday of my second week of being let go offered a new day. After a gorgeous sleep I moved to arise, and then, a rude awakening was all about me. Without my pills, those that I was saving for an achy rainy day, my mind was ready, but the rest of me…well some of you may know of it well. I finally crawled out to the garage to take a look at those cycle breaks.

Did I mention, a little more than dangerous those were, and perhaps why I walked more than the hills required. Wouldn't you know it, the tool that I lacked was a metric 10.

Although, it was a rag tag group of true misfits I had amassed, as far as tools do go, I know better than to count on any one of those discards being fully functional, not at least when you truly need them to. With my needing to budget, and conserve the only thing absent was what I truly needed? The socket was $3.99, all that I needed to do was find the *minnie* ratchet, and I'd be good. By shopping the necessary food store sales, I would so quickly recover from that unbudgeted expenditure, and be back on course. I indeed spent the remainder of summer walking and riding. I mean, it seems like I did anyway.

It is early October now. The weather has been nice. We are about to hit the thirties, and forties this week for the very first time. The winds for now are howling desperately from out of the Southwest. By tomorrow evening, a sense of true coldness will have set in. If it becomes like other years, I will need to curl up under a blanket before bed time to warm up.

It's always better after a quick catnap in the invading coldness of the season, as long as you're warm enough. It is that, as a part Norwegian fellow, I must most assuredly partake in a ceremonious summer winter change over.

After awakening from a well-blanketedslumber, I am all set to take on the 'Old Man' himself.

I just got back from the library. Because everything seems to be somewhat remote, computer algorithms are notifying Temporary Agencies that I am the greatest thing since sliced cheese. It only takes a day or two for them to come to terms with who I really am. The fellow from last Friday I called on Monday. He let me know that I only needed references to go forward.

One must come from a supervisor at my last job, and one from a peer. The only thing is I have nobody's phone numbers. The last thing one would expect when all is going so smoothly is to suddenly need references from those you did believe, would watch you retire instead. Alas, the girl that claimed she would call yesterday at 3:00pm after I had completed an application online, still hasn't phoned yet.

The fact of my termination continues to invade and haunt my waking hours. I was working on a report that could have potentially saved the business at least $6,000.00 if not $10,000.00 outright. It has to do with the software being used to direct incoming stock to a storage area. For some reason the system has been repeatedly sending product to shelving that we know good and true, as being <u>filled to the brim</u>. This can only mean that the actual 'available area' factor has been disengaged somewhat, or disabled altogether.

Because some of the shelves are notorious for not having room, I've been left to wonder if those indeed have this x factor turned up, to a '<u>disregard the mathematical realities</u>' setting, or at least to fudge on occasion when the harsh truths of the space available will not at all accommodate. For this type of feature to truly be necessary, it would involve a fast-paced business that is receiving goods, even before the *sold* items have physically left the shelf.

In order to process the new merchandise, and find a home, it would then be necessary to tweak this 'squeeze factor' up high. So, the orders would so quickly go out for the night, and the necessary room would be created at the last minute for the *put-aways*. Although, it is plausible in some cases, they just fudged the whole ordeal. As a computer school drop-out, I do indeed know of what I speak!

What moron or idiot has this *squeeze* feature in that software jacked up so high? I can only think of one idiot who would be so bold, but that is just hateful thinking I believe. The thing is, if any one person cannot put the recently received product away where the computer is forcing it in, they must get that 'manager's override' to cancel out the first location that I have mentioned.

An optional shelf could then be manually entered with the manager's secret *special-access* code. Our department would take over from there, measuring every single unit on that shelf, unless of course an item could be found, that didn't belong to begin with. Did I mention that the computers and conveyor belts run the company, and we mere-humans were only doing our best to keep up?

I'm suddenly having this fantasy wherein this bogus manager that fired me is forced to go to work at the Sheboygan plant with his apesh*tty south-side German brother, and they then bring me back because of my sheer and utter brilliance. It's worth a fantastical try anyhow. So, by Christmas I hope to have my unemployment case resolved and the latest, and greatest report ready to send out to someone well over that damn German bastard's head.

Yes, I do mean the one that fired me! But wait. I believe that I was just on-boarded by UPS. As a *personal-car* delivery driver, I will make over $21.00, with a 68¢ kicker for mileage. Since I've parked the 2018 mobile, and only have around 16,000 miles on it, this new opportunity sounds like a winner.

Perhaps I won't even finish this bio, in which case, none of you would be even reading this. So, this gal there claimed it would last from about 11/15/20 until perhaps, even the end of January. My only concern is my having to take off for an arthritis appointment. They over-shipped the pills from the mail-order pharmacy, so I went ahead and canceled back in August.

That UPS gal also mentioned that I would probably need to hook up with the brown truck in my area, to load up on additional boxes on any given day. If I can manipulate the appointment in between deliveries and reloading, it sounds like a grand chance to make it work. I just completed the W4 online at the library, so it seems as though it's all downhill from here. Big Brown here I come!

I've been redeemed. I have just returned from being hired on by the U.P. Not the northern part of Michigan, mind you. This is a company paying about 20¢ more than the bastards at the warehouse. I am now officially a *Personal-Car* deliveryman for that one and only service. So, this may very well be a sort of goodbye for now, although I've pledged to do my best to put in at least some time every workday.

The official writer's manual from the library stated that unless you were of the rare type that could manage to put in the 1½ to 2 hours a day, on top of a busy, full-time, forty-hour workweek, that you should, after fulfilling that minimal daily obligation of honest writing, go shoot a round of golf or just enjoy yourself otherwise. Now let me rephrase that serious recommendation from an all-out author. If you've got it, write for 1½ or two hours, then go and have fun. Aye, aye Capi'tan, I here and I obey, was my very first reaction! I am still rockin' it big-time!

I just needed to find an old 40s set of clubs. I mean wait. I am obligated to be gainfully employed. I was just over at the second-hand store donating a little used pair of black vinyl steel toes. I had worked there you may recall, while attending the local two-year university, back in '86–'87. They moved down the street to the old food store, from the car dealership it had been in.

Quaintly, they put up a food store after tearing down both dealerships. Alas, the Mexican-owned food store put the huge beautiful discount store out of business. It has been leveled now, with the old-timey seven-foot clock hauled away as well.

I have the employer's phone here at a 100% charge, but it is locked out, and apparently void of any apps, or smartness of any type at all. I will need to trade it in tomorrow on Tuesday, as we will have Mondays off indefinitely. Luckily, I had paper maps in my vehicle to refer to on Friday afternoon. I have learned the route well enough to maneuver through the area without becoming completely disoriented. The locator app works upside down, so one may actually become ill and vomit from looking at it too often!

Things should be much better tomorrow as I intend to refresh my aging memory tonight again. Why I looked so bad that someone snatched my Thursday afternoon deliveries I will never know. The fact that I appeared to be a little careless by not charging the phone on Thursday night, leaves me in neutral for now. Oh well.

I just got into it with one of my superiors. He walked up and in a stern and disappointed tone outright claimed that I had just 'cut somebody off' and that it was not the first time that I had done so. I immediately became defensive, and when he persisted to make me the bad guy in all of it, I angrily protested. "Bullshit," I shot back.

This was the same young man that trained me on day one, and got super-pissed that I missed a stop sign, or two. I need here to clarify what being 'cutoff' means, he meant that I didn't let other drivers move toward the gate in the morning, after we had all cued up and waited patiently. Believe me, there was no set method of approach. The gate would open and we would file in.

The plain fact was, with his witnessing a minor and superficial road infraction on my first day of training, it was no *biggie*. I had not had anyone in my car for such a long time that I wasn't used to carrying on a conversation while driving, so was distracted by that factor. When he seemingly blamed me for having another driver's package on board, I was like, "Come on someone else messes up and it's my fault?"

"That's darn right," he came back with. The thing was that he had failed to warn me that such a thing could occur, yet it was still my fault. Right then I knew he had served in the military. I quickly tried my best to smooth things over, and we soon enough had moved on. That was after he expressed his lack of confidence in me altogether, as a seasonal Christmas-help driver. I thanked the former military man, and got in my car and left.

Things moved back over to a more normal approach, and I managed to reassure him that I was up to snuff. Of course, I threw in that my uncle died in Normandy the day before D-Day. The next person that I got to know there, suffered from stress, and failed to develop bonding relationships, at least those that could easily grow within the first few moments of chatting. She had let me know that she was actually retired, yet each year the company would drag her back in, to help with the seasonal deliveries.

I had believed that it was her way of apologizing before she actually seemed cold and distant later on. I was fine with her thinking at all, in a nearly angry, and oh so urgent way, out loud. It did not faze me in the least. Whatever I could do on my end to maintain a sense of organized procedure, I would do so with pleasure.

Although, back to accusations. I plan to create a scaled down model of the parking lot to measure for myself if I was the one cutting another driver off, or if indeed as I have it laid out, that this other fellow was nothing more than a line skipper himself. Every morning, we would assemble outside one of the driver gates as I have mentioned. This fellow with a tiny little super-small white car would always park in the back row.

I had recalled that he did once park in the front row, the third car down, yet every single other day it was the back row for him. I finally came to the conclusion that he must have an inferiority complex, based on the size of his tiny white vehicle. I even mean when compared to a much larger big and black 4wheel drive trucks, and any SUVs, that he apparently had a hang-up in that regard about.

Every day the gate would be opened wide enough to accommodate three vehicles simultaneously. The true fact was that when parked in the third spot over as I had been doing, the front corner of your bumper was indeed a bit offset from the gate's true opening by about two feet. Still, as I said to my superior, "There are two rows of cars, the front, and the back."

Therefore, again it is physically 100% impossible to cut someone off if you are in one of those first three cars. I know if I had a kite string, or some garden twine, and a pencil I could prove out my theory in an actual life size manner. One would simply need to hold the pencil down on the asphalt at the gate's midpoint, while another interested party takes the string or twine, and walks over to the very center of the third spot in the lot. Then while holding one's place tightly the string could be walked over to the very center of the first spot in the back row.

I guarantee that the measurement would be within two feet, either way. I am getting so obsessed about it for a very valid reason. I had just put in a six-day week, and could barely walk. My right knee was in such pain that later that day at the food store an old white-haired woman in their 80s felt that I was in their way.

Of course, having that many older gals in the food store at one time should have been a tip off. We had gotten a message the day before claiming that 'A-L-L' drivers needed to be available to work Monday thru Saturday. Even though I had felt that I would more than likely be laid off, in person on Wednesday the 23rd, or Thursday December 24th, I had just worked the previous Monday, and was fine with coming in.

I was having trouble sleeping on a regular basis. I had been using alcohol abusively. It was now just after Christmas. My holiday partying no doubt played into my loss of cranial balance. The very next day after forgetting to set the alarm to get up and waiting for a call from them, I totally blanked out the previous occurrences.

I woke up on a Monday morning feeling a bit groggy but had enough time to make it to work only a little late. I rushed in to work explaining that I had just gotten out of bed. Normally we would line up at the gate and proceed upon the opening. Here I drove right in. There were only two cars still loading. I recognized the taller brunette as having pulled in, next to me on many occasions.

Because almost everyone had left, something was more than just askew. I exited my vehicle, putting my hands up asking, "What the hell?"

The tall Norwegian woman was in one of her unfriendly moods when I arrived at work. She basically told me to shut up, but I countered, "No, you need to listen to me."

I informed her that I had called the phone number offered in the message involving total availability for the week, yet no one picks up, and I did try repeatedly three times, and at the end the message offered is "this phone has not been set up for messaging."

I had failed to realize at that point that it was still Sunday morning, and not at all Monday. After all, she had wheeled a few boxes over for the brunette that always parked next to me in the red SUV. As far as I could tell that was nothing more than pity-work for her. Since she went through all of the trouble of coming in and everything, why not toss her a bone?

Apparently, though, that brunette was a teacher's pet, grooving on some Sunday overtime action. I was asked at that point to turn in my non-functioning phone and safety vest.

Because I had refused to shut up like she wanted, not only did she _not_ inform me that it was still Sunday, she messaged me later informing that I was now on an 'on-call' only status. Later that evening after having considered that a huge drop-off had just occurred at work, I came to another harsh and cold reality.

Apparently, on Sunday I was up and got the paper, then went back to bed, and upon waking up again at 9:00am, had believed that it was already now Monday. I sat in my man-chair looked over some of Sunday's paper additionally, then drove off to work.

It was indeed still Sunday as I so harshly discovered over the coming hours. Even though I had only wondered aloud, "What gives, Daddio-," I was now once more, finished. You can only fire someone so many times in their life. I am done. I will write until I die, if that's what it takes! I will never bend over, or bow to anyone ever again. This is it!

The first week of deliveries for this outfit did not actually go so well. Somebody snatched my afternoon boxes so that I was done on Thursday after about 2½ hours. I neglected to charge the company smart phone that I had been using, as I mentioned, and it therefore died just after pulling up to the first house with the afternoon load. I guessed now that better people would finish out the year, especially on my behalf.

My arthritis doctor was kind enough to hold off on that annual blood test this last time around. That would normally be performed merely to denote whether or not my stomach has been bleeding into itself. So, the bill was only about $75.00, rather than the $325.00 that I may have had to pay with a full-service check-up. All in all, it was mostly a draw, and I would be okay. At least for now I'd be alright.

Things change, and it isn't good to hang on to anything so dearly. I managed, at my old employer's store, to pick up a cute little miniature tea set. Also, the most beautifully jewel-boxed mini porcelain thimbles as well, were on super sale. Since it was half price day, I ended up paying around $6.00 for what had been originally priced at over $20.00.

Sometimes life kicks you in the nards, sometimes it picks you right back up, and hugs you good time. Oh well, I'll either use the reference from UPS, and become employed full-time again, or get by until next summer with my book finally finished. May God be with me in my endeavors!

Upon waking up this morning I went to the library and am still rather stunned to realize that today is only Tuesday. The previous two days have so well blended in together, what with my having moved from a second shift position to a short shift starting at 10:30am, I have been thrown into a near nightmarish fog that I am still trying to work through. I am certain that I will be back to normal tomorrow, when it will finally be the day that I thought it was today. I sure hope this book sells, as I am not sure how much more of the steady working life that I can take before being terminated once again.

It's now finally Wednesday, December 23rd. I made a return call to the unemployment office. The gal was nice enough, but let me know that she could not include in her report that the 1st manager gave me dirty looks back in 2013 when I started there from the temp agency, as it would merely be my opinion that the bugger didn't like me at all.

So, perhaps he only had some dust in his eye on three occasions during that year and one-half term. I do have to admit that he was so very neutral after I was hired on. Other than his tossing my suggestion in the garbage and not getting back to me, anyway. Her question, "Did you actually witness him throwing it into the garbage?" Uh, does one need to?

I indeed had another to offer, yet as he never liked me to begin with, I would have gone over his head with that one. I feel the need to remind you that I do have one year plus in Computer Science, and an Associate's Degree in accounting from the same 2 year school.

The thing was that computers controlled everything, as I have indicated. For me to know that someone is being bogus about the truth, or for someone to pretend that the lame conditions were not just idiotic and Polish (I am a quarter Polish), but so not frugally wasteful as to beg the question "Who is the 'fluffed in the head' *moron* that allows for such incompetence?"

Such a thing would be 100% completely impossible, if the software had been created properly. If not only scientifically, but mathematically as well, it so boldly asks the question, "What idiot allows for such a lack of jurisprudence when it comes to a mere software program?"

Now it was, if each item on these very shelves in question were in the system as being located there, and if each and every item had been measured correctly, again science would only allow for additional product to be directed to such a spot if our indications were that such room existed. Honestly from time to time the producers of a product or two, would go with a different size package. If our receiving team failed to catch that factoid, our 'Control' team would come to the rescue.

My job was to print up sheets, then to do a physical inspection of the shelving in question. The thing was, it happened all too frequently, at least forty to eighty times a month. If indeed everything checked out, I was to then take a measurement of each, and every item in question. What I was finding was, that not only were all of the goods properly listed, the measurements themselves were close enough to deny any remedy through that easier avenue of approach.

So, yeah, increase the size of unit Z from 3 inches, to 3 and 1/8, so a box 6 inches across is still rejected the next time. Not quite. So, my work was labor intensive, with me standing in one location for extended periods, thus causing my improperly healed foot to ache and throb. This system failure occurring to the point that, yes, I am again taking 'un-allowed' medications, just to get through Wednesday. Something should be looked into I proclaimed. Suckers! It wasn't the pain in my leg from the knee down, talking to me loudly either Capt. Buckey. Damn bunch of fools! When we were busy, weeks, and weeks of this tedium would pile up, until finally my supervisor simply deleted it all from the system.

The only aspect of such a computerized tracking to have possibly ever caused these extreme cases, involved what I have again termed, the 'squeeze factor'. Upon further review I had come to the conclusion that such an option would only be used for pallet locations, and only in the case of fast-moving merchandise. Such a factor would allow to systematically *'put away'*, say, *a dozen or more pallets*, in knowing that those spaces would all be <u>cleared-out,</u> by early evening. Even that scenario begs the question "are we really that insistent on putting the cart before the horse." Or, is this company being run by a group of jackasses who are too cheap to look into better software?

I truly had believed that whoever had actually known about this 'squeeze factor' had long been retired, and no one else had even a clue as to how to remedy the situation. In looking at the costs of this idiocy I had calculated that $10,000.00 to $15,000.00 was being frittered away on useless busy work.

In addition to myself or another from my team having to investigate the situation, and the stocker being able to only place the goods on any other shelf with a manager's override, my very own supervisor had to be involved as well. Who knows how many precious minutes have been wasted on the front end alone, while these stocker employees needlessly wait for someone with the proper authority to come to their assistance, on the back end of things.

Truth be told, the head of receiving notified me that not one common worker could ever touch that part of the software that inputs measurements. Only an office worker was allowed that privilege. Considering this went on needlessly, at least two to five times a day, and that this circumstance would easily push people into working overtime, anyone even without an accounting degree, would become disappointed.

I did believe that the only one, no doubt, that even knew anything more than a precursory understanding of this dilemma of ours had again, most certainly retired. Now the costs of their stupidity are at 150%. That would be anywhere from $26 to $36 per hour or more. If you add in the pay from my former team's looking into the matter, and you can imagine it even potentially exceeds $15,000.00 per annum.

To be more than a little honest, I think we may surmise that big-time software companies would want to charge exorbitant amounts of money, along with a long-term maintenance contract to boot. So, was this the company's way of giving the finger to such enterprises. After I had looked into the matter more extensively, I would have offered just a few simple solutions. The fact is the company, rather than going to one of the larger specialists, could instead pay a professional Software Specialist and fly him in from another city, putting him up at the fanciest place in town, and even driving him to and fro in a rented limousine, while still in the long run, eventually saving money.

One easily remedied situation had involved the packaging department of one of our locations again, using larger containers than they previously had, and that action being taken without bothering to e-mail us with a heads-up about it! Let me make this more than clear. I think the selfish bastards ran out of the smaller containers. Then they got the go ahead to use the bigger ones. These plastic bottles were not even a quarter full.

Unless some strange and volatile chemical change could occur due to a product being confined to a tightly enclosed space, only idiots and morons would pull such a rank, amateurish stunt, with the nearly empty containers. I mean you authorize such last-ditch effort use, and don't let us know? Hello, it's spelled 'Inventory Control', dumbass, bullsh*t, mother-fluffers.

It finally dawned on me when I had determined that one of these unnecessarily huge, plastic white bottles was taller than the shelf opening itself. It would not have been the first time. Now if I measured that container then turned the paperwork in to my superior, she no doubt would have gone in and changed the specs on that particular product to accommodate the truth of the matter.

I did believe she may have had more than one reason to hesitate on such an act, depending on whether we would go back to the smaller containers or not, right? I still am roiled over my termination, yet wish to contact these numb-skulled idiots to address this troubling circumstance. That action would be in order to relieve myself, once and for all, of any further cranial turmoil, undue concern, outright consternation, or even the slightest tickle of a faded memory whatsoever. Perhaps in a well thought out letter, I will do just that.

The results of my unemployment compensation case are to come in next week, along with another $600.00 in stimulus money from the greatly understanding government. I checked at the library, and can have $10,000.00 plus wired to my bank just like magic. I intend to retroactively deposit that sum into a retirement account to make up for the $8,000.00 that I had removed just to make it this far.

I have until about April 14th to designate as much as possible as being a contribution for 2020. That's kicking the can down the road just a bit, but gets me to next Tuesday, if you catch my drift at all. I won't owe anything that way, on my federal tax return, and may even receive a refund, since they'll allow donations as a deduction this year, even though one doesn't necessarily itemize using a Schedule A form.

2021

It is now 2021. I lost my unemployment case, but have filed an appeal. I feel that the facts of the situation have been casually and carefully overlooked, and perhaps the board simply wanted to clear their docket as quickly as possible. Two factors stand out clearly for me. First, I was not even punched in when this character from the other plant approached me, and not the other way around. The greatest factor involves his screaming at the top of his lungs, as I turned to go back to running toward the door.

"Hit me, hit me," he screamed, if you'll recall, as loud as can be. This indicates that he knew good and well, that I had no intention of doing anything other than getting inside as quickly as possible. I mean, you don't need to order someone about, if they had already had intended on behaving in such a brutish fashion and manner, to begin with. He again, then chased me.

I have to believe that he outright twisted each and every facet of what did just occur, to his superiors, in order to try and keep his apparently brand-new position. I mean with three witnesses from his plant who stood there in total and utter shock over his outrageousness, his only option apparently was to lay it on thick with exaggerated details, so as to have me appear as an angry, and oh so hostile, aggressor.

The only one to even move a muscle I say again, only managed to get his mouth closed. The two others were just too shocked, too much at a loss, to even function on any of the most basic human levels. The services of a lawyer are offered to those in the appeal state so I have hope that the decision will indeed be overturned. I mean to say here good and well, I am not just a fan of Erle Gardner's Perry Mason series, I feel that I could go a round, or two, with the best of those Law Degreed Orators.

With a goal to finish up here, with this book by the end of June, I will be able to continue budgeting until something gives. I just mailed a check to pay the rent through that time period with the prepaid gas-electric bill being sent out next. That bill should arrive tomorrow.

I have now, only $7,000.00 ready to place retroactively in a brand-new IRA, yet the rep. was unavailable on the phone. I do hope he answers my letter. Such a move will indeed still allow me to break about even on my 2020 tax return.

Since no federal tax was withheld when I closed that account out, it was a bit dicey for a while. I chose that method to pay off the car that I'm currently not driving. You see I am back to using my accounting degree to its fullest, at least annually at tax time for now. Around $19,000.00 remains in total holding, meaning I'm good until Thanksgiving 2021 as long as UPS takes me back.

I think my memory is going, and although my manual was from 1969, I swore they mentioned that one needed to go with a manual placement of the bearings when replacing those. That is why I was so ecstatic when my little 9-year-old neighbor had a case the right size. The price with this new bicycle crew was so very reasonable too.

I now own seven bikes three of which need new bearings inside the pedal case. As long as people continue to abandon those suckers, I'll be happy to collect. As far as the *old* mechanics from my local shop, they apparently were told not to do simple repairs so that folks would buy new $6,000.00 bikes. Guess again amigos!

I'm having my cake while eating it too with these newer gentlemen bike mechanics. I have the second Raliegh slated for a rebuild come June. I will certainly need to calculate my expense accounts and any other financial standing before going ahead with those overhauling transactions. If you'll recall the How to Be a Writer's manual had clearly stated to go at it for about an hour and a half, and then to go off and play golf or something.

Well, how 'bout going all the way to the lake on that '75 special? Indeed, I can feel the cool breeze of summer even now as I type. Update, I continue to become confused in my old age, as far as that one-time British outfit. Upon further review, and a cranial comparison, along with an evaluation of the two in the garage, I now consider that my mere guess was nothing more than wishful thinking. What I actually no doubt have is a '76, and a '77 model. Both more than likely from after the sale of the British Raleigh outfit to the Americans.

I just got off the phone with the Administrative Law Judge. I assume now, much too late, that any time a 4G phone is on it is using minutes. It went dead at the 10-minute mark. Again, that former employer has never laid even one person off in its nearly 70-year history.

At one of our quarterly meetings the bastard that fired me mentioned that the company wished to get the number of people that quit every year, down from the low to mid-twenties, to more like under eighteen. So, seventeen quits in year, and they'll be happy? One can only imagine the steadfast pace of chemical movement engaged in, so deep within the walls of that briskly paced outfit.

The thing was that they publicly shamed you by posting your numbers on the wall for all to see. You then knew you had to kick some major axe just to get hired. My first numbers were in the low 80s. You better believe I busted a move and got those up into the 90s and low 100s. Just after I was brought on as full-time employee, the girl that worked next me after lunch let me know.

"This is it for me, I'll be done in 2 weeks, but that's alright," she added, "I already have something lined up." She was to be the replacement for the dude that had had it, every day for two full months.

If you now remember, that is what he said every Friday before punching out, "This is it, I'm done, it's over, I gotta get me a new job, uh huh, no more of this struggling, it's over, I'm outta here." Finally, true to his word he was outta' Dodge by sundown.

Update: I can appeal my appeal. The girl that wrote up the paperwork has so many discrepancies on her decision page that I think I have a chance. She claims ole boy had a suite on, and that he was a co-worker. No, he was a lowly supervisor but one that no doubt had a 4-year business major. He was shabbily dressed, and was wearing street shoes with super thick rubber soles. I believe him to be a descendant of south side German Jews.

If you know what Art Garfunkel's hair looked like, he being from the sixties singing duo known as Simon & Garfunkel. His 'fro was the opposite. With Art because he was already starting to lose some hair, the top of his head was more like a wooden bowl. Why one could have even placed, full-on just-picked fruit, atop his mop and those ripe goodies would have stayed in place.

This brother's 'fro however, was oddly shaped like a gorilla head. Do you remember how you only took a bath or shower once or twice a week when you were younger? Well, there's that aspect of one's young life, and this sucker's huge water melon belly. I assume that he always slept on his back, and that's what flattened his hair out. Due to his wild-man reaction to my holding my fist up (by my face, not his), and moving it back and forth, I would say that he was teased relentlessly as a child. They probably called him Ape-man, or Gorilla-boy, and now he suffers from post-traumatic stress disorder.

Remember how he chased me? I was only saying to him, you don't mess with someone who is late and running for the door, especially me Captain Cowboy! (You got it? You dig Daddio-? Are we all up on this, or are you going to need a reminder, or an actual man-type lesson the next time I'm running late? Okay pop, are we good?) All of that went unspoken, yet I had felt that I had made myself more than crystal clear.

06/27/21

I just back from another vigorous bike ride. I keep asking myself "why are people so goddamn stupid?" This goes back to a couple of weeks ago. I'm coming down a hill toward an intersection. A car off in the distance is approaching from the opposite direction. Crosstown traffic has the stop signs. I and this fellow have the right of way. This entire time that I'm coming down this hill at an accelerated speed, I have my left hand out, with even my finger pointing north. This is to emphasize for those stupid imbeciles out there, just what I'm about to do.

Just as I'm going into my turn, the bozo with his son in an SUV who was waiting to turn, starts to lurch forward toward me as if he is about to run me over. Then he has the lame ignorant nerve to roll down his window to cuss me out. I immediately threw down my vintage Raleigh 10 speed, and yelled, "let's do this." The sucker just laughs.

The guy in the car that was originally approaching me, yelled out to that dickweed, "Hey, he had the right of way, bozo."

The next Monday temporary stop signs had already been re-installed. Did Bozo drop a dime on my ass? (An author's note: apparently the clownish fellow went to City Hall to offer a beef about it, as the stop signs have become a permanent and year-round fixture on that corner.) Thanks a lot, stupid dumb-fluff!

I did recall those temporary signs from previous years. You know that they're temporary by the crossed flags mounted atop the two stops, now imbedded in the ground with no doubt. With sand and stones around the bases to keep those in place things would be good until the dig-out. The whole timing of it all seems suspicious. Now today yes, on my bicycle, I pull up next to a car turning left in a left turn only lane. It is just him, myself, and a car on the opposite side in her own left turn only lane. I approach the light with my left arm out, and pointing in that direction. While waiting astride my bike I hold out my arm again, just in case the woman didn't notice.

The light turns, and I and the driver that I am next to begin our turn. I took a curved approach toward the corner, so as not to be a hindrance to either person. What does the woman do? She sits there with her finger up her ass, and then honks at me as though I am doing something wrong. You know good and well when someone is honking to say high, or rather when it's just because they're a stupid bitch. I mean this for a reason. I snapped and shot back a different type of international sign language, if you know what I mean.

Let me please rephrase my approach to taking a legal turn from the 'left' turn lane. I am allowed to be directly next to you, on the right side of your vehicle, while in that left turn lane myself. As long as I hold out my left arm (I *point* left, as well.) I am allowed to make a left-hand turn from your left-hand turn lane. Let me get those not in the know to relax a bit. Yes, it could be a bit confusing, and even more than intimidating. Yet, look the next time. Where is the corner? Is it not safely the farthest place away from where you wish to travel with your vehicle? Though actually, you probably never had any intention whatsoever of going near that corner at all as a person committing a left-hand turn! Do you ever?

That safe place, the corner, when I am making a legal-bicycle-left-turn from the legally offered rightmost edge of the left turn lane, is exactly where I indeed am traveling to. Yes, I will be desperately attempting to near that corner, and out of the way of traffic as soon as my handsomely powerful legs can get me there. This law allows for the left turn without having to walk the bike across, which is another lawful factor. So, yes indeed again, bicycle riders are required to walk their cycles across lighted intersections, unless using officially mandated 'hand-signals'.

Now just two blocks away, I am approaching another intersection with a light. A gentleman who wants to do a right hand on red stops at the corner. I put up my left hand, just as one needs to do when riding a bicycle in the street, yet point in the right direction. The guy thought about it for a second, then went into his turn confident that I was turning right as well. Just after that I was in the middle of the lane with local law enforcement just in front of me in a marked vehicle.

Because I held my arm out and pointed left the entire time, that cop couldn't do jack. He knew good and well that I was driving legally down the middle of the roadway. These are not the only type of incidents with some uneducated drivers that I have had. The two things that I remember from Driver's Ed back in 1976 are #1: pedestrians always have the right of way, and #2: when turning onto a designated highway with more than one lane in each direction one must stay in their original lane.

That is why they have cutouts next to strip malls. Instead of making a left turn, and cutting across two or three lanes, those are conveniently placed, so that one can make a U-turn through them, and come around toward the stores, and such. It would be important to turn on one's directional as you're passing through the intersection. Not before you enter, and not after you're completely through.

This gives anyone behind you the chance to change lanes if they possibly can, rather than getting stuck behind you. Although such a courteous offering to the other drivers would certainly have a dependence on any traffic coming from the opposite direction as well. One doesn't have a lot of room for a U-turn through those cutouts either.

Again, if your city has those, especially directly next to strip malls, the reason for such an effort to have been initiated on your behalf is so you do not cross over two or three lanes after turning left, just to hit the strip mall. Again, it is so that you can enter a corner strip mall without having to *unlawfully* cross over those two or three lanes directly in the front of said strip mall.

How else would they expect you to obey that traffic regulation without the quick opportunity to come around after banging a quick one? I know it's no big deal if traffic is light and you swerve over three lanes then turn into the parking lot in such a fashion. It nonetheless is against motor vehicle regulations. I want to explain why such maneuvering mostly will not work.

A driver must first establish his presence in the closest lane when turning onto a designated highway. Then in using the directional to finally change lanes, that indication can be appreciated by those moving in from behind. The question is, have you ever had somebody speed up and pass you while using these prohibited lane crossing moves? If you are ever in an accident from driving correctly you may need to recall the rules so very, very quickly.

I mean here that I will stay in my lane then use my directional to move over right, even before my turn is complete. If you punch it from behind me, and take that farther lane right off, rear ending me in the process, you the unaware motorist will be at fault!

Each jurisdiction may vary somewhat from the next. What the law allows for in our state on any HWY, designated by a letter or number, is the simultaneous turn. That way, if we both want to drive down that same road, you turn, and I can turn together, while entering that roadway "simultaneously."

With us originally having been driving toward each other we would then initially stay in the nearest lane available. Once having established a presence in that closest lane we can both choose our pending pathways afterward, if those are different from the one initially turned onto.

So, I'm a block and a half from home, and this was in the other neighborhood with the cracked, then filled in swimming pool. I and a lady about my age (so there is no excuse, since Driver's Ed was being taught back in her day) reach the opposite sides of the intersection at nearly the exact same moment. I have my left blinker on, and begin my turn. I could see that she wanted to turn right at that intersection that employs only stop signs.

This roadway is not only marked with a huge freaking sign telling you that it qualifies as a local highway, there are three very wide lanes on each side. It is so that a bicycle can safely be passed, even with a very large delivery truck parked along the side of the roadway. That passing could be by two drivers going past simultaneously. Again, yes, together any two vehicles can, at the same exact time, turn onto a designated highway.

So, this woman freezes, and drops her mouth in total shock and horror. She can't believe that I'm taking her lane evidently. No, no, no, no, I was taking my rightful lane and no one else's. Not far from there we have about the narrowest four lane designated HWY in the area. This road does not even have the piece of land in the middle with grass, or trees, or flowers. It's just four cars going at it, two from each direction.

With all of those drivers carefully maneuvering down the road in an observant, and close proximity to each other, it is driving straight and nothing else. Another driver, a man, wants to turn right onto this street. I want to turn left onto that same stretch of roadway. Bam, this older fellow about my age sees my directional and we pull it off, as smooth as pudding on a cake. Yes, my sweet, sweet darlings, we completed the simultaneous turn with both vehicles doing at least 15 to 20 M.P.H.

Just to make things open to the truths we live with, and honest to the realities of everyday life, even the cops skip over lanes, and don't perform those turns correctly. Right in front of me, where the coyote, or dogoatie, tried to get tough with me one day, those coppers did the worst, most unlawful turn one could imagine. You again, are supposed to stay in the first lane and signal to move over.

If there is not time to get to the store you wish to shop at, you by law, must come up with a different game plan, as in using those cutaways to make your U-turn, coming back then, ever so quickly to then turn into the smaller side entrance of that area. Another officer from a nearby municipality recently pulled an unlawful move on me. I looked back and asked, "Is this sucker about to do an unlawful pass on my right, before I can even begin to change lanes?"

No, he wasn't in that much of a hurry. That cop was a strip mall cheater! All that he wanted was to skip over two lanes to make his local business entrance.

At least around here that is how it goes. When was the last time anybody has even seen a Driver's Ed book? Let me explain it for you one more time. I am allowed to pull up next to a vehicle in the left turn only lane, while atop a men's 10 speed bicycle. I would be situated on that driver's right side, so that I myself can turn left. I usually move into the crosswalk just beyond a car's windshield, in order to let my intentions be known. That way, those operators next to me can see me.

If I sense that they are looking, I will again point, yes even with my finger, in the left direction. I will then even point left a third time so that no one can be confused about my actions. If I am turning right, I hold up my left hand in the proper position, but for an added emphasis, I even point right. Yes, you have it correctly, I signal my turns with my index finger.

There is also one additional hand signal that is lawfully required in many jurisdictions. That would be holding the left arm out with the hand pointed down, as if to say "whooooaaaa, whooa Nelly, we're stopping here." In any case, as I move forward on a left turn, I give any other drivers enough space so that they can either turn left, well next to me with a good few feet between us, or bang a quick a u-ey.

So, that those turning left from the opposite direction can do so readily and with a grand sense of ease, I most demonstratively curve my turn toward the crosswalk. Any drivers can then accomplish their desired action without my even being a tiny bit close to them well out of the driving paths of anyone out on the street that day. Remember, I was pulled over by a cop, while on the sidewalk, and forced to license my bicycle. With that, I was required to learn all of the rules regarding lawful riding while on the very streets of my community.

People, don't ever mutha'-fluffin' piss me off, when you are actually the ignorant, and potentially unlawful individual involved. In an effort to more educate those drivers that have failed to learn the rules of the roadway, I will recap those few things a bicycle driver is allowed to engage in. Please consider checking with your local law enforcement agencies for any variations when it comes to the freedom of cycle riders in your zones.

Number one: It is required that a bicyclist turn left from the actual left turn lane created for mostly cars. The only lawful alternative is to walk the machine across any lighted corner at the appropriate time.

Number two: You are only accorded three feet of lane space, including the curb area. It does not matter how many bicycle helmets, or 'spanlax' outfits, or whatever else you have that allows for you to believe that your stuff don't stink. That especially goes for double and triple riding as a big no, no! (SEE STUPID FLUFFER IN FRONT OF ME ON PAGE 160–161)

06/29/21

I'm thinking about yummy pies and things right now. I just got back from the library after applying for work this past Friday. I was told that I would be contacted if they're interested, through my e-mail, or by phone. Nothing yet has materialized from that effort. As far as those pies, due to the weather, half the blackberry type fruits have fallen, creating 'a skid of blackness'.

Now I don't mean a pallet at all, I mean a potential wipe out skid if one needed to hit their brakes suddenly for any reason. Those yummy berries grow on trees, not rose-like vines. I've been thinking about bringing a ladder next year and harvesting those sweet, sweet treats, as the tree is really no one's personal property at all. It is however rather, situated at the end of a parking lot outside of several long empty buildings.

All you would need to do is trim the green stems from these darkened berries. That task would be easy enough while using a brand-new nail clippers. How about a gleaming white box cutter with a razor blade, inside to trim those green, green stems. I would probably add some of the more natural type of sweeteners for my deserts, like molasses, honey, or even some carob syrup.

I'm thinking now of the recipes I saved from last week. One is for oatmeal bread. The other is for an interesting cake that has well soaked raisins, dates, and even some diced figs added in for a very special flavor. Cherries compliment the fruitful delight with a sweeter more American accent.

One could remove the canned cherries from the more syrup like potion portion of the pie filling. In using that sweet more liquid aspect from the can for the frosting, a special and professional quality begins to emerge. I would only use carrot cake frosting for this recipe, as it has a very special texture, and professional tasting quality to it. One will be adding prep time if raw bing cherries are to be used. I stuff all of these recipes that I've saved up in the corner cupboard.

So, as far as the cake goes, you want it to be naturally sweet with honey and such, but scrumptious with all of that fruit I so longingly need, at the center. I am thinking of stiffening a simple homemade chocolate cake recipe, using real chocolate, but as well some additional flour or even some corn starch to blend in lovingly with all of those gooey features. It would be the type of cake that would overwhelmingly satisfy, with even only a tiny piece. Think common spice cake.

As Mother stated about my very first home:"the one thing that I miss about that four-family is the generous cupboard space." Mine in the corner is stacked top to bottom with those 'best' of the best yummy desert recipes along with any recommended stereo component articles the type of which I cannot afford right now. The true secret about that cake involves soaking the fruit for a month in some type of alcoholic solution.

The article names some fancy harder alcohol as the liquid to soak your fruit in, but I myself would prefer a much sweeter drink. I regretfully cannot recall the name of this German wine. You will know when you have the correct type by two distinctive factors. The first is the tiny sized bottle.

Secondly, the overly sweet taste of this candy like import, is so lustrous and smooth even babies would drink that magical potion, if allowed to. Stewed raisons in addition to the soaked fruit, may be the paste' resistance for those well-imagined delights.

One day though, even with all of the yummy recipes yet to be tasted, I will crank 'The William Tell Overture' even louder than Father had back in his day. He used to hot-wire the speakers from the 'Harmon Kardon' tuner along with an official 'Bell' amplifier. That would be Alexander Graham Bell's company, although he would have been surely deceased before Father picked those items up.

I need to remind myself to inquire about the soundness of the old records as a flood came in at least three feet high. The vinyl itself would have been intact, yet with all of the soggy album covers those may not have been worth salvaging.

Included in Father's collection were several Johnny Cash albums, one from the Kingston Trio, along with the soundtrack from 'South Pacific'. It was the Boston Pops does Authur Fiedler that I truly loved. Update: The removal of three feet of wall from our family cellar was a decorative measure, and not enacted simply from a soggy type of necessity.

I just want to add that all of the drivers out there today were attentive and kind. One was my scrawny Sicilian nephew. He walked up at the food store and said hi. He is an Italian water-color artist. He replicated the cover of a magazine for me that now does hang above my TV. It will need to be especially framed as he replicated the mother lion, and cub drinking from a shimmering pool nearly identically to the magazine cover. He, not wanting to waste time replicating the 'National Geographic' portion, left that space blank and free of any paint at all.

The drivers in the area were even more tested than a bicyclist ever could be. Seemingly by accident, the guys working outside cut off all power to this area for hours. No warning was given, and it went back on without any announcement either.

Not one, but two traffic lights lost power as well. Since no temporary stop signs had been posted I had to believe that this temporary loss of power had not been a preplanned event. Each of the drivers instinctively stopped at the corner then patiently waited their turn to move through those intersections. I was actually moved. I mean away from the anger I had held for a brief moment on Sunday. Well, they don't call them Sunday drivers for no good reason, right?

09/17/21

It's my son's birthday. I decided to give the boy's mother a visit. The timing could not have been worse. With Little Richard being so well handicapped I had felt that it was only a matter of time before he could no longer bathe, dress himself, or go on with what had become of his regular daily routine whatsoever. I was in error. Somehow, he apparently was still managing to get by. My old girl buzzed me in then proceeded toward the lobby. As my handsome figure came closer into view, she focused on the reality before her. She quickly went into shock.

Upon completely coming to terms with what was drawing nearer she turned and headed back inside. I was more than curious. We yelled back and forth through the tightly locked door. When she enquired as to my visit, I became cold. I asked quite plainly, "why…isn't Little Richard dead?"

"Why would you think that?" came back through the wood.

"Well, why did you get divorced way back in '98?" was my response. If this ex of hers was indeed just behind that door, I was creating an embarrassing and more than impolite scenario. I left unsatisfied. I shot over to the library. I e-mailed her an apology, explaining about my book. It was once again, so quickly over for us. Apparently, when a fellow is insanely jealous only his own death itself can relieve him of his inferior ways.

10/27/21

I had a few minor chores to tend to. I needed to drive west then slightly north-west for a block or so. I drove past the police station on my right. I headed up the hill just beyond, as I had so many times before. It was a sunny day with nothing but those minor chores on the agenda. I still needed to finalize my destinations to frugally go about things without wasting any petrol. There had been road construction in the area for some time. I recalled vividly the clump of barricades just at the corner where I would turn. I went into the motion readily.

When I awoke, I was up on the grass facing an empty field. I had glass embedded in my forehead, and scattered about my hair. I turned to the left to see one the largest dump trucks in existence. It must have been a military grade vehicle with a 3-inch steel body. An ambulance brought me in. The verdict? My brand-new vehicle was totaled, and I should be dead!

Epilogue

Summing to sum up the ideology and approach to life that I have evolved within myself cannot possibly occur in a few simple paragraphs. In coming to terms with all of the common history that I myself have lived through, I have found a new understanding of life. In addition to the personal conflict, drama, joy, ecstasy, friendships, trauma, turmoil, adventure, shame disgust, and even pride, relished upon myself through simple living I have grown. I may perhaps have even a much better insight therefore, into the very workings of not just mankind's mind and mental process, but even more so, that which is beyond so many of our common abilities to process and assess.

I can look beyond wealth, peer over close relationships, and see truths held distinctly out of common sight. With those issues being needful and quite necessary for many to function as normal human beings, it is necessary to look beyond the façade of life, to search deeper for a mere understanding of ourselves. As well, I remove myself from a sense of parental concern, and finally attempt to grasp those vital realities, that may not be so apparent, to any one of us, on any given day.

Having attended a Catholic Grade School, I can fathom and deeply appreciate the concept of miraculous wonders, and nearly unfathomable truths. I can as well, see the harsh cold reality in regard to hostility, anger, aggression, and all-out sense warfare, for what it truly is. Those negative concepts are nothing more than roadblocks placed here by the evil underworld, yet all too easily fallen into as traps, and then somehow adopted by mankind himself. It becomes as though these maligned undertakings were our very own and sincere desires to begin with. I proclaim here and now; man of his own volition is incapable of such despicable treachery.

As creatures of habit, it seems all too simple for ourselves to be lured into conflict, whether it be something as tame as an older sibling playing keep-away, or the more severe and serious forms of non-inclusion that take various forms in our day-to-day lives. Two feeble, unkind traits ever so easily fallen into include elitism and racism.

To come to terms with the fact that only one source, one body, one force, can have a separating effect on mankind I wish to appeal to your higher sense of being. Here therefore then what could be cited as the reason snobs look down their nose at some others, is actually an undue influence from an outside source, and not so much in inherent form of bloated and misplaced self-righteousness.

Yet as the very same origins that somehow cause others to offer a solid sense of disappointment, we each our very own selves, all have something truly lacking deep inside, that prevents us from being perfect as well. In some way, shape or form, we all fail. Whether or not it's by the end of the day, week, or month, at some point common human frailty takes hold.

We can't actually keep up a strong presence of glory for very long. At least not on such a pious and lofty level as our faithful and altruistic hearts, do so dearly desire. We therefore must forgive each other of our faux pas, and especially the big ones, feeling so deeply within our faith, that with the behavior in such extreme circumstances being unintentional, we have only one option. That would be forgiveness.

Please consider what I proffer now before you, it is the premise that one negative force, or one negative source, can play both ends so easily and readily, that we surely have legitimate reasons for a sense of disappointment in our fellow man. Some even do look down their nose on one end, while others fail to live up to common expectations on the other. Yet with my theory, actual and truly stupendous and wonderful miracles can occur.

If we can somehow see past our human frailties to move closer together, with God Almighty at our side, as our sovereign guide and bellwether of altruistic virtues, we shall rise in prophetic fashion toward the heavens. Emotionally, 'twould be at first, in any case. When such a sense of heavenly and virtuous bliss becomes us, only one destination surely remains. In awaiting our righteous finality, the heavens shall one day rejoice in our collective and unified harmony.

For those who are atheists, good living involves doing unto others, and a more common approach that utilizes human nature, and logic, rather than spiritualism and doctrine. Although, not borne from the belief in the afterlife, the kindness factor remains. Nonetheless, all too many cards fall the same exact way, no matter which long and winding road one utilizes to grasp things. The power is within us to come to the truth. Negative movements have no place on this godforsaken planet we call earth. We are then evermore so, obligated to find ways to bring a closeness of spirituality, regardless of any one perceived end result.

You can make out with more bears when you use a little honey, right? Wait, I think that goes a little differently, yet my approach is sticking to some of you, is it not? Imagine a world where instead of keeping certain groups at arm's length,(segregation) we do whatever is necessary to bring those individuals up to task with today's standards, so that we truly love and enjoy whatever contact we may have with them.

Be those encounters common, occasional, up close, infrequent, or anything in between, we are meant to enliven and enrich each other's lives, though more so spiritually. Just yesterday I ran into the dude from the chemical plant. Even though he no doubt is…I sat least $1/128^{th}$ white, it is his true nature that is appreciable. Some just got it goin' on, if you know what I mean. If you'll recall 'Laughie' from the costume warehouse, you may begin to understand. He even gave off a wonderful, nearly palpable glow as he passed by to plug up his forklift, that 1^{st}shift warehouse driver did.

Just like that, then, a bro would come around the corner, cock up his leg, as if on a treasure chest, then gave me the ole' "arrrr, it's the captain." Consider professional athletes for a moment. Do some of us hold them on a higher level than we do any common sort of gal, or fellow? Now, it may not be comparable to any one miraculous event, look at how certain peoples of our world can be considered, on both ends of the spectrum, while being nearly identical in other ways and fashions.

What if some of us chose to create these so-called miracles of which I speak? In offering waves of a crisp white elegance that speak of a unified oneness, for us all to partake in. would we bask in an ethereal delight?

Could it be possible that, not 100% of all the worlds individuals admire and love these godly wunderkinds, yet more like 90 to 95% of all of us, love and adore them for who they are, rather than what they are, or where their families originated from. That is a tremendous percentage of humans, to simply cherish who we've now become. Miracles would then be considered to have taken place. Therefore, I truly believe that mankind has been taking the wrong approach to success for all of these centuries.

The weakest of us, exemplify our greatest overall strengths. It is here that I am denoting the fact that by comparison we have no choice but to appreciate our very own greatness when others simply fail to live up to our tremendous levels of performance. This is my new theory. It is so that only by raising up those in need, can we ourselves rise above the commonality of our very own existence.

The formula is undeniable. Look at any grade school teacher to find the truth in what I now proclaim. With nurses the caring is merely to get someone back on track so that they indeed can get back in the game of perfection, or as close to that as is reasonably possible.

It is therefore thrust upon the extremely wealthy to find clever ways to utilize all of their wiles, conniving, scheming, and top-end planning, to beckon unto the lower class, calling them forth to a new life of prosperity, inclusion, success, togetherness and sharing, that again, becomes a part of an overall miracle that somehow resonates in the hearts of all men, so that so much of our gain from the experience is an undeniable elevation of our love, and appreciation for everyday life and living. Without these efforts we fall short. Then only hell awaits us all in the end, potentially.

Now bear with me, if this new feeling of goodness really truly takes a hold of our mindset, our overall understanding of how life works, and this newfound mindset becomes second nature, we would have brought ourselves up to a higher level of being, evolving into more than angel people. I for one believe that we were somehow meant to be in all ways shapes and forms, beings of a higher realm and existence in the first place.

Can human evolution involve a deeper sense of Godliness, and spiritualism so that we become after 200 to a thousand years, super-humans? This has always been a possibility from the get-go, I do say, here and now! It therefore should have come to pass already. We need to make up for lost time then, as well.

When you come to terms with who I truly am, if you indeed have not yet, it will be an overwhelming knowledge you gain, pleasant in the mind, and joyous in the heart in regards to my theory of enlightenment, and togetherness. It is when we can feel the goodness of people, seemingly through the air, that we have shed our bias, and concern for any difference. People are people, and they possess the same ability to please, love, cherish, adore, create, pitch in, and contribute no matter from where they may hail.

Then this happened. This world, this yuk, this everything that falls below a sense of positivity or neutralism, that is what is keeping us from our rightful place in the annals of history. A history that would describe either a person's coming to terms with the unmitigated truth of circumstance through contemplation, or through automatic consideration, or even through a visitation from the Holy Spirit himself!

This full-on understanding of the harsh cold realities we face on a day-to-day basis, would open our eyes to deeper truths beyond the social standings of any one group, beyond the failings of any one family. It would then be a natural occurrence, to raise up just and righteous citizens. Those newfound values, then moving beyond the standard platform of what was perhaps considered an individual's just due, and well-deserved take, would comprise the general experience in life. When it comes to the hording of wealth, and material goods those hell-bound sinners would awaken to a greater understanding of need. I speak of the outright and natural need that we possess for each other, rather than for so much fluff and comfort.

This certain aspect of our humanity hasn't changed one iota going back to the very origins of our weak existence. What I offer and represent here and now is nothing new as far as I can fathom. I merely choose to offer it from a different perspective, based on my own personal mind-blowing experiences, both high and low. From being such the "fabulous lyric penning rock star," to having bones broken, a tooth smashed out, or nearly so, to even having a ricochet bullet enter my skull, to the point that you perhaps bleed for me.

I mean even just a wee bit when considering the agonizing pain, I've been through. Then in coming with me to escalate to the grandest heights of a spiritual ecstasy, the entirety of the situation will formulate before you. With all of that, is it any different because I am a hard-working individual with value, does that make it worse, or better for anyone?

The greatest and most overwhelming aspect of our lives today, that I can possibly conceive of, involves the end of reproduction all together! Yes, I mean a baby boycott. Now ask yourself this question, "If I landed on the Planet Mars with my wife, and we then quickly evaded a Mars monster, would it be wise for me to say, hey…let's go behind that Mars hill and make out, so that we can start our very own authentically *living on Mars* family?"

I hope you are not that dumb and horny to say yes to that query. Think of it. Yet we here and now, are so ignorant and void, that we often play into the illusion that everything is so wonderfully hunky dory. Then yes, we finally do even go there. If not just a bit, then even all of the way, we tend to turn a blind eye to the harsh truths of today's world, while engaging in custom, rather than wisdom.

Yet look at us, from famine to flood, petty crime to assassination, from world wars to everything in between, we somehow blow that all off, like it's nothing, and do that very thing so many of us do. We somehow convince ourselves that it is okay to start a family. Yes, so many of life's troubles and travails may seem distant to us, but are they? Are they really? I claim to you here and now, that they indeed are not remote, not in the least. A minimum of 5 to 10 years therefore is 100% necessary, for the all-out baby boycott to have an appreciable effect.

Here, you'll need to forgive me. I have failed to properly introduce myself. I am William Penn, the self-appointed king of the world. I am your one true leader. I alone have the wisdom and knowledge to lead us to the promised-land. It is only I that can see with not only my eyes, but with my very mind. I am humbled now before you. I bow at your presence.

For some, they may need to forgive my earthly failures, before accepting me for who I truly am. For others, they are magically blessed and, overwhelmingly risen. They then emerging from a sense of spirit itself, draw closer to such a Godly form of goodness. Forever, and ever, and ever we can move so much closer.

I at this time wish to implore you to consider the whole truth. Not the fairy tale version that mother read to you as a toddler. Open up to the harsh cold realities before us. Let these finer keenly sharpened factoids about life dig deep, deep, deep into your mind. We are, and always have been obligated to each other. It is when we choose to overlook such worldwide trauma that the very gates of hell begin to open for us all. It is because the world itself is so wide, so large, and so far away from us at any given time that it becomes easy to ignore the truth. That is as well why religion fails us.

It is because we are so damn advanced as a culture, that to some extent, even our sacred institutions are hollow and void of an extremely needed sense of completeness.

Now it would be easy to claim that because certain peoples don't attend service that things are broken. Guess again. It all however, starts with family. When the fantastic mothers with open hearts and clever minds have control, it's all good. It's when things already started to unravel before birth, that this sense of disconnection of which I speak, has taken root.

In fostering an existence that somehow falls just short of the miraculous levels of superiority that we so readily need at any given time, we move away from the cold truths of our very existence. Again, rich, poor, tall short, those aspects of life have been rendered meaningless by our failure to be a constantly united group at any one given time throughout the day.

They will need to forgive me for smashing the wasp's nest, for resting on my laurels after becoming a major rock star at the age of twelve. They'll need to forgive me for the same, after being deemed a boy-genius at the tender age of eleven, and barely getting by on what I already had known, in order to graduate high school. They will need to be kind when it comes to my recreational drug use, and self-medicating through the use of alcohol. They may especially need to forgive my failing years, during my twenties and thirties.

If then, you've prayed to God, if need be and can overcome my shortcomings, you will take up non-aggressive arms, and rejoice at once, as our hearts are now most certainly as one. Even though the work may seem never ending and the task enormous, I feel that each and every one of you, are together with me now, experiencing a newfound brotherhood, and togetherness. Though, please don't let me assume anything unto your world. If I needed to be forgiven by some then, I as well then and therefore needed to raise my game to a new respectable level.

Now, when it comes to another facet of our existence on this godforsaken planet called earth, I truly believe that there is a mingling of thought that does go on in today's world, even on a daily basis. I even refer to those most vile and lowdown thoughts, as well as the type known as creativity, genius, and even in my very own case, songwriting. Do you truly think that inventions such as the steam engine, the motorized bike, or horseless carriage came about from thin air? In my view only the wheel could have been conceived of through a sense of common and simple logic.

All one needs to see is a fallen tree rolling down a hill to begin to understand how such a concept initially came about. With compression, the act of lovemaking is the closest thing in regards to the enclosed gasoline engine. If you are old enough, consider these features, the piston, something going up and down, if the young lady is enough of a virgin compression will occur, with possibly even some blow by.

What I do declare here and now, is that it is 100% impossible to go from here to there without some type of shared thought process. Let us consider that all creative scientists of the inventor category may possibly possess a minor, yet distinctive shared thought mechanism.

All one would need to do is concentrate, and consider any roadblocks into a finalized and well diminished and finished and finalized afterthought so that those impediments could not possibly stand in your way. In time because such things (inventions) do exist in the future, you will no doubt come across something that will at least, advance the efforts.

With my very own writing, although I do write from my own perspective and creativeness, I have to admit that more than a few of my works involved the mere act of dictation. That would be the writing of song lyrics. Well, sung words that are somehow simply playing in my head is what I would scribble ever so quickly. Yes, I merely dictated some of those lyrics that indeed and quite evidently, strangely and eerily were playing on their own, in my head.

In other words, I was merely jotting as quickly as possible those words that had somehow presented themselves unto me. With some of those songs coming through to me, even in the voice of another, I merely dictated. I was amazed, yet went with the flow. We can easily imagine then that any great invention from the future will at some point, wend its way back into a prior time. Then with its resting gently on the mind of a thinker, those mechanisms begin to slowly evolve, even becoming patented.

You may realize that the radio was being invented simultaneously in two different places. In such a case it's the one that hits that patent office first that matters. He would be the one to receive the glory, accolades, and especially any money flowing through. With such an exciting offering, a patent would certainly be necessary. My oldest brother had mentioned those facts to me back in 1964.

If you now allow yourself the possibility of this magical connection to be occurring inside the human mind, one that relies not on timeframes, language, or even being alive in the same century, you can take the next step forward, toward an ultimately potential truth.

We need to look to the Amish to understand, that of what I speak is nothing new at all. They truly believe that certain newfangled ways should be avoided at all costs. They consider that such actions can emanate only from one dark source. That would be from the bowels of hell itself.

Considering global warming, pollution, and the degradation of the earth to dig up coal, not to mention the severe illness of black lung, suffered by those early 1900s miners, it could easily be argued in a great debate that electricity is not quite all that it was cracked up to be indeed, at least at first rendering. No sir I say, indeed not the cat's pajamas whatsoever in those early days. Those are times that still cling to us in many shapes and forms.

Going further upon this path, we have the possibility that anyone in hell and on the earth at any given time could partake in this type of sharing, or thought transference. This again, is not at all a brand-new concept. How many pray to be relieved of sinful thought? How many consider the acts, and ever so readily, the thought process of some criminals to be so ghastly. Then how could those have moved here, to this earth. From only one other place I so readily proclaim. The key then is to come to terms with that facet of life, and to be on the lookout for any unsavory thought process in the making!

Sadly, with some negative actions, the fact that those have become more common place and standard, may make it easier for some to fall from grace. Consider organized crime on the east coast, or even the pettiest actions of minor gang bangers. The array is complete, and it is fully across the board. Certainly, we all know deep down what the price of a bad judgment in such a regard may be.

Even then somehow, it becomes second nature for some to engage in those types of callous activities. Do they not fear damnation? Are they blind to what awaits them in the great beyond? Alas, we can only pray, here and now for their very souls. From what I've come to understand the disconnection emerges more in adolescence rather than any other phase of our maturation.

You see then, the belief in transference of thought has been a part of our societal identity for ages. Consider here how the mentally ill were treated in old England, and other European countries. A true fear resided in the hearts of men, as those not in complete control of their faculties, had been placed in dungeons, to rot in despair and die. This is the greatest amount of evidence available that what I preach here is valid. What we offer now is a way to block out the radio station from WHEL. Why, you should have been made aware of that fact already, "It's all HELL, all the time."

So, through one medication or another, the attempt is to free the human mind from these demonic invasions. Whether the medical profession sees it that way or not, is completely immaterial. If you place a sponge in water, does it not absorb? Likewise, when you squeeze it out, does water not pour forth from its emptying orifice.

The end result is the same no matter how you conceive of its science. The sad reality with those overwhelmingly harsh psychotropic drugs is that some degradation of the brain itself may occur. The idea is then to ride out the storm in order to regain a sense of one's truer self. With that a sense of life's enjoyment and a real sense of partaking and belonging should reinitiate itself within you.

It is that I believe, way too many doctors are willing to settle for a mere stability even when the livelihood of the patient is forever sacrificed. Considering that this newer approach has not been utilized for more than 50 years or so, it is yet still possible for the psychiatric profession to further tweak and evaluate the ups and downs of dosage and viability. One aspect of any recovery may involve a period of one's getting used to that dosage, and any side effects that accompany treatment. With the most severe cases one may be able to recover from this period, and go on to study, and or engage in a sense of full-on useful employment. With those sadder offerings, the person may settle for merely living in the outside world.

The question then becomes who, or what entity is truly responsible for this invasion of our most treasured components. Some point the finger to only one source. Others, like myself, happen to believe in any number of misaligned misanthropes who possibly have their meaty fists in the stew. It was our 1st grade teacher that first opened the door to my way of thinking. She had described to us back in 1966, that the theory held that hell was filled with those in purgatory. Perhaps, the bowels of that realms itself is flanked with outright demons of human origin, and yet even a third category.

Just as some believe in aliens from another world, the Theologians there in New York City somewhere up there on the fortieth floor of some building, had left it open as far as what category to place the steeliest of their world. That boyfriend from New York had offered that theory. I had merely imagined the actual building near Central Park on my own. (It may actually be on the 39th floor!)

So, nonetheless, you can see I simply take these ideologies to the next logical step. To what degree our very own minds are susceptible in such cases is an unknown factor. The Catholic Nun had warned us of this. A potential invasion may begin if we failed to keep our thoughts clear. I mean super clear. As in newly cleaned window clear!

She encouraged to deeply imagine when necessary, using our 'mental chalkboards' if need be. Be warned again, should one fail to maintain that very sweet innocence with which we are all born, it is an outright invite for evil demon spirits regardless of their nature, and origin, to come on over and play in our minds. It may take only a moment of thought moved into the wrong direction for such an invasion to begin.

It is up to the mothers therefore, or grandmothers and such, to instill upon any public school students in their family, such an avid inspiration for goodness only. In teaching control, and eschewing anything less, the religious approach takes on a more generic status when brought into the home by public school mothers.

Now, with my belief, as far as the insane dead are concerned, the only question becomes can they reach us more readily based on anyone factor of their lives when here on this earth? Let's say they are from the same century; can that offer them a closer look into our world? What if such a steely demon were from our own hometown, could they more easily sit near us through that avenue? One other point I wish to make, these peoples would be normal folks on their way to heaven if it weren't for just one deep and desperate factor. It is their lack of sanity that weighs heavy upon their world, I say.

Yet how does someone become insane after death? When it comes to the entity that we refer to as the Devil, I feel that I need to impart a factor or two into the whole mix. First, he was supposedly our Good Big Brother Angel. There had been rumblings here and there, of negativity that even reached up into heaven itself.

In order to maintain the total and complete safe separation of that blissful Shangri La, it was proposed that an entity needed to accept responsibility for taking care of such a place, and to get things back into order. Only one took up the challenge, our good brother angel.

It was then postulated that this being was held in limbo for 40 million years, half way between heaven and earth. It was a place that had yet to completely form. If thoughts can travel through time, then so can the very existence of our being here on earth, as well as that of the planet itself, and the entire animal world. During this epoch period supposedly, all of man's failings, all of his occasional lack of love, or otherwise hatred, all of his blaming, the blaming of only one individual, bled back into the innocent past, until that once sacred past itself was no longer guilt free.

Imagine being in such a predicament and realizing the only reason any one part of the whole charade is going down, is due to the failure of one group, and one group alone! I wish to reemphasize that the only failures possibly bleeding back into the past are our very own.

Can we now understand the plight of the one that takes all of the blame instead of us? We this group, the only failures, and he the one and only person thrust into said position, by the Almighty himself. Are we collectively to blame, together with him, or is the only measurable faulting at all, of our very own?

What I wish to do now that you have come to terms with these truths is to look for ways of perfecting our society, and improving our overall approach to life. It seems that there is so often concern where attention is most needed, yet a lack of total regard across the board when it comes to actually making changes where needed.

So, I say, look for ways that we can unite and gain a sense of strength from more of a consorted effort. In regards to those aspects of common society and today's life they should be always readily available. Those avenues so readily reach out, and even speak to some of us, even in silent desperately spiritual ways.

When it comes to the grand awareness you now possess, one denoting a separation from the heavens, and some comingling of the very thought mechanisms that you so readily rely upon, are you able to feel yourself. So, truthfully then, is the distant and protected shores of the hallowed place we signify as heaven? What I refer to is nothing new again. This hallowed and sacred embodiment of all that is chaste, pure, and free from interference, is surrounded, figuratively or otherwise, by a fence, with the gates themselves guarded by an angel!

Is it somehow now, beginning to sink in? Have you already gotten to such a point, with now an even deeper revelation of the sincere and hallowed beliefs that I present to you? Take it all in, if need be, for a moment. We, the people of the earth, must be kept separate and apart from God himself, and all things holy, and sacred. It so being, we are left here on our own, with all of the steely demons, the insane dead, and any other facet of the dark side one could possibly ever come to terms with. Yes, I say, we are now left here to fend for our weak, tired, and fetid selves.

I am indeed hoping by reintroducing the very concept of our separation, to have each and every person that is available, come to terms with the fact that only humans can sin, in so far is the very definition of sin entails. It is our legacy then, and that of no one else. We therefore must band together to reach the level of an honored knight in and of God himself.

I say as well, we must somehow resurrect our fallen king, the good brother angel, whose lot in life can only be affected by one group. It is only members of the living human race that can bring yet even more darkness to that realm of our one-time Big Brother Angel.

Even though this next theory goes against modern teaching, I will not relinquish it for even one small moment. I do sincerely believe that terms like forever, and eternal, were necessary in days of old, to merely get all of the people on board with the program. I say ye here me good and listen strong my people, if we can pull together upon the end of earth's very existence, once the very last human has been risen from the depths of hell's bowels, even our good brother angel, can rejoin us in the great beyond.

It is us Catholics that place such a strong belief in purgatory. We were taught in school and church, once more, the tortured souls would cry out for redemption, yet even God himself was powerless to save them. So, I ask you, what could make the overwhelming greatness of Heaven, the one place of total and utter Idyllic supremacy, even more complete?

Why of course, the inclusion of one that in past times, sat near the righteous shoulder of God. I speak of the one the only, good brother angel, and how he could even return to being, return to being that which he was, so very long ago. Imagine heights of glorious appreciation, so well beyond even what our heavenly images, could at first fully come to terms with.

It is that I fully proclaim, here and now, that when each and every human alive, comes to full terms with my proposal, or any of the deepest additional aspects of my flowing message, he shall therefore, find it in his or her heart, to begin life anew. Folks would be renewed in the prospects that any past damage done, can be eventually recovered from. At least if any of us have any say in the matter those shall, and will be overcome.

I further shout out, even to highest depths of heavens reaches, that if we ourselves can follow through with such a miraculous transformation, so as to join in, with those of the highest power, reveled endearingly in the joyous proclamations of God the Almighty's sincerest intonations, how then could we fail to embrace the final piece of such an overwhelmingly perfect puzzle.

Please be kind enough to recall here and now that according to the teachings of the Catholic church, both blessed and ordained by each and every Pontiff since such theory has been proposed, that for 40 mil. years, our would be king was held in limbo. Then while the impurity of our sinful actions, the disgrace of our indiscretions, and the sharp and distinct infliction of that millennium ad infinitum, plays out upon a stage of humanity, all that is impure seemingly falls back upon one existence.

The harsh truth of woes and sorrows is thrust backward in time. Back to the only place able to receive such cold realities. In this realm it is for those to rest gently upon such a strength, bringing into a blissful state of harmony, all that can exist, with the one that they call the Son of God.

It is my sincere desire to reach every person alive today, and those that shall come to pass into time infinite, with this message of togetherness. It is that we must not simply embrace a wonderful thought, or gesture. No, we must rather insist upon, within our daily lives, from the lowest of lowly paid milk-maids, to the highest of sovereign kings that we unite as one throughout the live long day.

It is through this non-mystical experience, one both blessed, and carried forward by the immaculate grace of the Holy Spirit, that we shall be able to overcome such unrighteous intrusions from the evil underworld. For that matter, even from anywhere that those malevolent affectations should here in our world, arise.

This all-encompassing glory cannot be had when there are those in such untouchably high places that cannot be affected, by the altruistic and honorably sincere persuasions of those holding, what may be considered the lowliest of domains. Here on this earthly globe, we call the world we must be risen when feeling low. We must refrain from such a bold sense of behavior 'en braggadocio'. Yeah, as long as there are the honest and forthright among us, goodness shall reign on this earth, our home.

Even yet, the desires of either, or those who so readily who dwell in between, and who are both chaste and wise in origin, and free from the

441

inclination of favoritism or bias shall be our beacon. We have a chance at a realistic version of heaven on earth. So, then therefore do these choice entities speak for the greater good, and in moving toward the betterment of all, speak on behalf of God then therefore, himself? Is it I myself that even attempts the same?

One aspect of life that I believe would enhance our appreciation for all that surrounds us, involves free health care. Under my plan the government would negotiate healthcare prices, such as they do for retirees, and pay those costs as well. For this to work properly we would need disincentives to reckless behavior such as smoking cigarettes, or riding a motorcycle without a helmet.

Those would come with a penalty that becomes a copayment, offered up at tax time to the I.R.S. here in our nation, the USA. I believe anywhere between $100.00, and about $3,000.00 should have the proper and desired effect on most individuals in regards to maintaining a common format of a safe existence, with an eye toward personal glory, rather than a needful sense of show-*offy, 'hotdogishness'*.

So, rather than necessarily taking hordes of cash away from doctors, we would simply eliminate the Medical Insurance Industry, and maintain sensible caps on pharmaceutical prices. If need be at any given time, as long as any interested individuals have the grades and intelligence to succeed, we could offer government funded scholarships to those needful young persons.

As long as they have a true desire to enter the medical field in some capacity, things should come off without a ruffle. If such a plan as mine were given a phase-in period of at least one year, those individuals whose life's blood involves insurance company profits could devise a steady plan of differing, and yet still profitable investments.

Now let's be honest here about insurance. The entire motivation that leads folks into this business involves making millions and even billions from investing other people's money. It is so that we pay into the plan and in bulk, all of our money when pooled together and placed into the proper vehicle, makes the main body of individuals bloody rotten rich.

We're talking stocks, bonds annuities potentially, and anything and everything else that looks on paper to be profitable. It would then be possible with a nice lengthy phase-in period, to establish my more brotherly approach to healthcare, allowing those with massive investments to have their cake, but not ours at all, ever, ever, even once again.

What happens in life is that certain types become somewhat addicted to their wealth, so can tend to be heartless and cold. This many times occurs without one's actually realizing that they've become so Scrooge-ian, as to invite a hellish world of suffering upon themselves.

Once death's hand does finally come to call, it could be a rude reawakening for some. The only question in my mind is can someone get off in purgatory, based on a mere and innocent ignorance, or will it be considered the onus of those formerly holding piles of cash, to have known better than do have done so, all along? I honestly feel that monumental waves of greatness could be fostered by the very wealthy if done in the proper fashion.

I was just reading in Sports Illustrated about Ryan Lochte. The article went on about his careless days of successful youth, spoiling his bro's with slightly lavish gifts. I truly believe that his was a case of ignorance, since he was a fun-loving rascal that was simply being himself. Now that he is well matured at 36, he feels the need to return to the Olympics. Though now with two children the spoils of a victor will not be relished upon blokes and homeys of the coolest athletic type.

His regiment is one to admire. That would include swims of at least four hours, with him left in the actual *tears* of physical pain. I wish him well, and have a grand appreciation for his fortitude and might. It was Mark Spitz from my time that got me interested in at least viewing such swimming competition.

With my boycott of stolen television (pay for TV), I really don't see much sporting activity on the set, other than the standard fare. I indeed vaguely recall this Lochte fellow's triumphs from back in 2012. In recalling the other excellent swimmer, a Mr. Brian Phelps, we can easily see a plain yet keen domination having occurred going back to '72.

I just received the appeal confirmation for my unemployment. If need be, I will go on, and on about my race-walking and skipping steps on a staircase simply for the fun of it. Lo and behold, fast walking is a genuine, bona fide Olympic sport. If I recall it was an English fellow that year, back in '72 that was of the best. I do hope that I can continue to not be obsessed with this upcoming case. I just went through again, for about the 200th time, what I need to emphasize and highlight from my nightmare of an afternoon nearly 11 months ago.

So, if one holds up a fist from a distance of 3½ to 4 feet, while letting someone know that they're lucky, and I mean if the same person harassed me like the second time around is that an outright threat? If this individual is purposely trying to make me late, if I merely let such an individual know of my consternation, am I threatening?

I don't actually know to be honest, that I could prevent myself from taking such a blow-hardy, anally strict disciplinarian, as he was, and giving that rascal a good thrashing. In recalling that I was directly terminated for indeed threatening another employee, yet let him off so easy before turning to run, how would even you decide such a case?

I will once again add that the fellow that made the final call, had given me dirty looks when I first started on the docks for that trucking company. For a year and a half, I tolerated his quite obvious distaste for me. Upon switching teams and applying at Kelly Girls (the old '50s–'60s title) I did take note that he did on at least two occasions seemingly force his head to the side, while then staring intently at the wall, rather than to have my person even slightly in his field of vision. Considering that he was just at the quarterly meeting with this Ape-man, I had felt a case of bias had most certainly occurred.

Let's go on about Gorilla-boy a bit. As I have theorized, he was apparently tormented in grade school. He wore his hair in the shape of a gorilla head. Now imagine the bigger boys at school riding you hard on a regular basis. I am sincere when I say that this fellow, no doubt again a German-Jew from the south-side, no doubt one suffering from PTSD, or Post-Traumatic-Stress-Disorder, is no longer a normally functioning human being. If you recall the guy snapped and ordered me to strike him.

So, he goes from just trying to make me late, to trying to get me terminated outright. Recall his workmates from the other plant had become immobile with shock, once they realized dude was nuts! It was only the elder, that fellow with white hair, if you'll recall, that managed to finally get his mouth closed. The two others were still unbelievably unable to come to terms with what they were witnessing. When the rubber sole of dude's left shoe slapped down so hard just feet behind me, I did believe that they had recovered enough from a state of disbelief, to intervene on my behalf.

I thank God that they were present. I was the boxing champ of not only our neighborhood in my age category, 6–8, I was the best with my dukes in our class at school as well. I know I would have begun my right, left right moves and had him down in seconds. Because of his sh*tty headed ridiculous ranting I would have then let him have two more. I wish to make this clear as well, only three people in the entire world have the rank and authority to enter the grounds and dictate any one thing. Those would be the head of the entire business, the head of the American division, and the leader of our area.

Yet why would even one of those leaders stop someone from making it into the building on time, unless he or she were an anally strict disciplinarian as well?

The coming days may be tense and stressful. I still have about $25,000.00 in my IRAs, yet fear not being published, or ever working again for life. I have to tell my family or especially Mother as it is to her place that I may need to move. Winning the approximate $15,000.00 from UC will take a tremendous burden from my shoulders. Hopefully by the 4th of July I will have completed enough here on these pages to begin shopping the book. They can all know then, that I have been writing my life story as <u>The Boy with The Blue Pants</u>, or something close to that.

Update: I know this is the Prologue, and for all intense purposes the story has ended. In hitting upon the fact that my case's appeal's appeal was pending, I felt an urgent need to vent. The horrid witch that took the case was cold and methodical. She, without any heart whatsoever, took only the prima facie evidence at hand and thereby judged me as 'not normal'.

Let us once more consider the barest of facts. Someone who as a guest in our building (yes, an employee of the other plant) stops me at 3:28pm, going into a lecture on parking lot safety, even though I waited for this pedestrian to take two additional steps after clearing the walkway. I had and only temporarily hit the gas too hard.

I basically said, "Look sucker, you don't mess with someone who's runnin' late." I began to turn and run. Let us consider one more fact: a person with a four-year college degree, who no doubt was at his very first inter-company meeting, goes insane, and it's somehow my fault? Come on, I mean really?

I said to the UC gal, "This fellow has apparently been relentlessly teased as a young lad." They no doubt, because of his hairstyle started calling him 'Gorilla-Boy', or 'Ape-Man'. He apparently fell in love with his grade school principal. As he grew older, the rumor got around about his secret name.

Now the younger crew at his school began harassing this poor fellow. He 'takes no prisoners', takes no shit. He begins defending himself but with a form of physical violence. He now must appear before the woman he loves, the gal that offered her wise and loving heart out to him during those past altercations.

It would be time to pay the piper then, and therefore. This back and forth, with his being the victim, and victimizing, no doubt went on for years, and years. What if the new school rule became that not any one student, not even for schoolwork, could even breathe the words 'ape-man', or 'gorilla-boy'.

This woman shot back with her denial of my claim that I was unnaturally obsessed with this character's back story, and that all that I had offered for a defense was this ludicrous theory that somehow this character was mistreated as a youngster, and therefore became a somewhat dysfunctional adult.

Okay, I had over a year to sit and stew. Perhaps, even a bit, I embellished and formulated exacting reasons why an individual would go off and become a raging authority figure, when their little job title of 'floor manager' precludes them from maintaining any authority whatsoever over any one person. I mean no authority other than over an employee directly under them on that very floor that they manage.

Okay, so I did sit here stewing, day after day, after day, without any gainful employment of my own. I went over, again, again, and again, my thoughtful and concise testimony. So, what then? You the UC rep. is just a bitch who is a freakin' principal lover, just like that blast-hole? You fail then to take note of two people who suffer from mental issues, one who stopped and harassed another, while the other merely warned him to 'step off?'

Apparently, the entire world and all that exists for me in between, would like me to finish my book. I mean that is the only logical option left. Good thing I'm in the final editing stage!

I was just contemplating how wonderfully mysterious life could be, if it were not for man himself. I mean this man, that one, this other guy over there. Is it that, wonton sexual desire and vital nutritional hunger rule our very genetic codes? Can we not stop ourselves when it comes to satiating such animalistic rages?

Well, okay, I was a 12 year old lover. I failed at that young age to deeply appreciate the harsh truths, and bitterly cold realities that seemingly encompass even our most generic foundations of basic satisfaction and survival. Remember, I am not only your king, I love everyone, every bug, and other animal, and want only for an eternal and blissful happiness for one and all.

Now I don't wish to be harsh about our feeble-minded failures so readily prevalent wherever one should look. I still feel it is necessary to point out one simple fact. We, as humans, have had figuratively, 2,000,000 years to come

446

together as one and to unify so that a sense of heaven on earth is achieved. In our having failed, I sincerely and honestly consider that only sinners would bring additional '*sacrificial lambs*' into the picture. Most certainly we cannot deny our animalistic longings and tendencies. To reconsider such a proposition then, is somewhat expected.

To deny that we exist here on this planet that is for the most part half hell, would be futile. Just like the song by Ronnie James Dio with Black Sabbath entitled 'Heaven and Hell' we need to deal with both sides of the coin. It is because of tradition that parents fail to hesitate when such dreams and fantasies play out in our dutiful and oh so pure at heart minds, when it comes to childbirth.

One would be foolish then, to consider themselves above the fray. Your children will not be born unto heaven, no, they will be summoned as Super Heroes to try and move things in the right direction here on this lowly orb, dangling somewhere between heaven and hell. It's a place that we know as earth. The only question remaining, "Are you, a mere human, capable of raising such a wunderkind?"

You may come to terms now with why so many social programs are available. We already know we cannot on our own, accomplish such a monumental feat. It is so in our coming together that we are able to, as a united society, offer a peak sense of nurturing that any generic human needs. Wealthy individuals may attempt to purchase through local offerings, such caring, nurturing, and character building.

When we all together realize that only one option can work, we may then begin to rise from the ashes of a world we wanted (a twisted version of a song lyric). It is in the fear of societies woes, trials, and tribulations that we can be affected. Even more so, an infectious existence of something somehow lesser than human, an energy even, that can touch us with the hand of evil itself falls upon our world. It is so, that if we should even hesitate for one false moment, the frail house of cards we've built as our home for our loving family, could come falling down so quickly.

With all we've toiled for in collapse do we throw our hands up caving in? It is foolish to believe that we are somehow indemnified by our very own personal sense of virtue. We all have something in the closet. That would not be little sins. No, it is within the inability to notice our own lacking that the pit of our demise grows wider. Some of us already have a pile of stuff on our plate.

We would oh so readily admit that you wouldn't want your daughters over here with us. Here is another song lyric: "you cling to your treasure troves." It is easily understood that some wealthier folks aren't always so kind, or generous. Do they cling to those gemstones out of fear? Is it the truth that they cringe at the thought of being somehow less than they already are, with fewer accoutrements? With such an action, would one less bauble, or trinket to bless their day, really begin to cause such a collapse of identity?

Not only should we not need such people, we should have been preparing all of the while for our own frail adulthood. As far as everyday business goes, the same fear of subhuman invasion occurs for those types. I do believe, when even general commerce comes into play, a no doubt well learned approach comes into form. Such an invasion of purity however would be through the tough games played by those on the higher end of things. It is out of fear then, I do truly proclaim that "crummy, shitty-headed, bullsh*t mother-fluffers, do connive, plot, and plan."

That's when all of those business games begin. The remainder of any evil ways seems to have come from a sense of "well, if they are doing it, then why don't I?" I mean by overcharging on rents for the most part. You are going to hell for at least the weekend for such unkind, selfish, and unwarranted acts of brutal, at-sea type, of buggery.

Understand me here and now, I am not just a man that has stayed at the lowest costing rentals. I tend to consider those owners as the nice kind of people you'd even enjoy doing things with. So, let us start at the beginning. Rooms were $15.00, to $20.00 a week. The lowest costing one bedrooms were about $120.00, to $180.00 per month. Please do not consider that I am old and crotchety. I paid $465.00 along the lakeshore, and am only paying $545.00 per month, for a larger two-bedroom. My physical residence here goes back to 2009, with the rent at $525.00 per month. I sit here in my home office as a true king before you now for that keenly priced reason.

I, on a daily basis regale in the delights of my humble abode. I cherish any one facet of my very living here in this place of constant love. It is one of those types of business relationships established long ago by good, good people. Did I mention the lilac bushes? One must pay for the privilege of smelling those in the late spring, as well as the joy of leaving so very quickly and easily through either door.

I mean back or front. Hey for $60.00 additional per annum. I think we're talking paradise, Capt'n Bucky! In addition, I regale in the smaller amounts of available cash with which to buy decorative adornments for myself, and for my fantastically decked out home. I also have no deep or pending concerns involving well-imagined monetary needs down the road.

Therefore, I am relieved of a certain anguish in such a regard by the one, and only one factor, I only pay about one-half, to two-thirds of what most others are pumping out. I don't care how many in-house gyms, pool parlors, saunas, or other amenities you try to console me with. I will never be able to pretend that you're not trying to rip me off.

You could offer half hour massages by the most well trained, largest gals over 5'6", 150 lbs., and I still wouldn't, (wait, I need to determine the current cost and availability of such muscle rubbers), and I still...okay, the jury still out there. I only have one rule as far as that goes. "No man, is allowed to make this man, feel that good." I will repeat "no man, is allowed, to make this man feel that good." So, if those gals are at least 5'6" and can really, really rub...I mean, I may be at a loss for words under such comforting circumstances.

I want to wrap things up for everyone in one big nutshell. We are all born with original sin. That means that genetically we are feeble. Cranially, and psychologically we are lesser than we could possibly be then, as creatures on this planet. We are quite honestly half-animal, half-angel. When it comes to not being as wise and judicial as a good intellectual person could be, we can blame the animal side.

When it comes to over-thinking something to the point that we freeze up, and cannot function normally otherwise, I would say the angelic side is having trouble coming to terms with a sucky type of daily life. When we know good and well how things should truly be in the lives of others, as well as our loved ones, and ourselves, I believe that we could even go as far as to fathom that such an angelic side of our identity has made a profound and grand appearance!

Give 100%

Remember, my people, "I am El Cerebro Magnifico, your self-appointed king."

What follows is a list of my work with other groups, as well as all of my own unpublished lyrical works.

Songs I wrote or co-wrote:

The listing that follows is not only an incomplete offering of my work, it is hard to possibly fathom all of the hands that some of these works have had to pass through to make their final destinations. My most complete writing has been used by the English band Marillion, Van Halen, and Pink Floyd. Most, if not all of the remaining numbers needed to be completed, or handed off to persons unknown to myself.

Although the very claim can itself beg for credulity when considering that most of the one and done artists had merely a line or two as a starting point, it would not be so much of a stretch of the imagination to consider 'rock in America' as a starting point. *Sunglasses At Night* had at least two lines, yet is more of a comedic approach to lyric writing. Along with my country *instant hits* I offered, there was just a line or two that needed to be finished somewhere along the line. Nearly every one of those quick jottings would needed some finalization to say the least. Whether you believe that I am truly 'El Cerebro' The Magnificent (here instead of reading off the second half of my moniker, if you'd prefer to imagine Queen's *Bohemian Rhapsody*'s—"Magnifico!" that works just as well) or feel that my 200 years of American-born English heredity is what allowed me to pen these hits at the mere age of twelve, is of no consequence. The choice is strictly yours. What follows are my mostly unfinished, and unpublished-to date, works.

ArtistSong(s)
ACDC: Dirty Deeds Done Dirt Cheap, Back In Black, Highway To Hell Big Balls
Aerosmith: Jamie's Got A Gun, Lovin' In An Elevator, Walk This Way Rag Doll
Aha: Take On Me
Boston: Moe Than A Feeling, Rock'n'Roll Band, Cool The Engines
Pat Benatar: Hell Is For Children, Love Is a Battlefield
Phil Collins: In The Air Tonight, Sussudio
John Fogerty: Put Me In, The Old Man Down The Road
Deep Purple: Perfect Strangers, Vavoom: Ted The Mechanic, Soon Forgotten, Rosa's Cantina, Knockin' At Your Back Door
Def Leppard: Foolin', Some Sugar
Devo: Whip It Good, We Are Devo
Dio: Starstruck, Hell???

Dire Straits: Sultans Of Swing, Money For Nothin', Walk Of Life

Duran Duran: Hungry Like The Wolf, Girls On Film

The Eagles: Hotel California, Fast Lane

Foreigner: Rev On The Red Line, Dirty White Boy, Blue Morning Blue Day, Double-Vision, Cold As Ice, Feels Like The First Time, Hot Blooded, Juke Box Hero, Urgent

Peter Gabriel: Red Rain, Games Without Frontiers

Genesis: Invisible Touch, Land Of Confusion, No Son Of Mine

The Go Gos: Vacation, We Got The Beat

Guns 'n' Roses: Paradise City, The Jungle

George Harrison: Cracker Box Palace

Billy Idol: White Wedding, Eyes Without A Face, Rebel Yell, Flesh For Fantasy

Jefferson Starship: Find Your Way Back/We Built This City, Janey, Janey, Jane

Joan Jett: Bad Reputation, I Love Rock & Roll

Billy Joel: Movin' Out, Piano Man, Uptown Girl, We Didn't Start The Fire, Entertainer

Kinks: Come Dancin', Destroyer

Cindy Lauper: Girls ..., She Bop

Huey Lewis & The News: New Drug, Happy With You,

Lynyrd Skynyrd: I Know A Little, That Smell, The Breeze (The Breeze was my uncle's nickname from highschool, he was on the basketball team, and ran track, when people drove by, they honked and called out his nickname.)

Madonna: Material Girl, Keeping My Baby

Marillion: Market Square Heroes, He Knows You Know, Garden Party, Three Boats Down From The Candy, Punch & Judy, Assassing Punch & Judy, Kayleigh, Lavender, Heart Of Lothian: Wide Boy

Meatloaf: Paradise By The Dashboard Lights

John Cougar Mellencamp: Jack & Diane, Little Pink Houses

Eddie Money: Take Me Home, Two Tickets To Paradise

Men At Work: Down Under, Who Can It Be Now

Steve Miller: Fly Like An Eagle, Take The Money And Run, Abracadabra

Willie Nelson: On My Mind

w/Julio Iglesias: All The Girls I've Loved Before

Ozzie Osborne: Mr. Crawley, Crazy Train???

Robert Palmer: Bad Case Of Lovin' You, Addicted To Love, I Didn't Mean To Turn You On

Tom Petty: Free Fallin', Refugee

Pink Floyd: Have A Cigar, Wish You Were Here, Welcome To The Machine, Pigs, Dogs, Sheep, A Momentary Lapse Of Reason, Learning To Fly, On The Turning Away, The Wall (nearly all of it) Comfortably Numb, Is There Any Body Out There, Vera

The Police w/Sting: Don't Stand So Close, Message In A Bottle, Every Breath You Take, Roxanne, Walkin' On The Moon, Spirits In The Material World, King Of Pain, Synchronicity ('a dark Scottish shore')

Prince: Little Red Corvette, When Doves Cry, Raspberry Beret

Queen: We Are The Champions, We Will Rock You

Quiet Riot: Cum On Feel The Noise, Bang Your Head, We're Not Gonna' Take It

Kenny Rogers: The Gambler

Rolling Stones: Shattered/Waiting For A Friend (Shattered was my nickname at the end of my senior year in high school.)

Rush: Tom Sawyer, Red Barchetta, Subdivisions, The Trees

Sade: Smooth Operator

The Scorpions: Rock You Like A Hurricane, The Zoo, Big City

Bruce Springsteen: Born To Run, Cover Me, Hollywood Nights

Paul Simon: New Plan Stan, You Can Call Me Al

Styx: Blue Collar Man (Long Nights), Too Much Time, Supertramp Breakfast In America, The Logical Song, Goodbye Stranger, Take The Long Way Home

Talking Heads: Burnin' Down The House (Yes, my half-brother and I really did start my parents' bed on fire.)

George Thorogood: Bad To The Bone, One Shot One Scotch One Beer, I Drink Alone

Toto: Who's Gonna Take You Home? Africa

Tina Turner: What's Love, Typical Male

U2: Sunday (title catchphrase only), Bullet The Blue Sky (just a few lines)

Van Halen: Runnin' With The Devil, Everybody Wants Some, UnChained, Panama, Top Jimmy, Drop Dead Legs, I'll Wait, House Of Pain, Hot For Teacher, Love Comes In, Why Can't This Be Love, Love Comes Walkin'

In, House Of Pain, Dance The Night Away, Jamie's Cryin', Somebody Get Me A Doctor, Atomic Punk, Ain't Talkin' 'Bout Love, Hot For Teacher, Drop Dead Legs, Beautiful Girls, Take Your Whiskey Home (not a complete list!)

Joe Walsh: The Confessor, Life's Been Good To Me

The Who: Teenage Wasteland, Baba Oreilly, Who Are You, Rain, Squeeze Box, You Better, You Better You Bet

Warren Zevon: Werewolves Athunder, Lawyers Guns, and Money, Excitable Boy

(Singles)

Paula Abdul

Bryan Adams: The Best Days Of Our Lives

Tracy Adkins: Her Favorite Color Was Chrome

a-ha: Take On Me

Bad Company: Radioactive

The Bangles: Walk Like An Egyptian

Beach Boys: Kokomo

Edie Brickel & The New Bohemians: What I am

Jimmy Buffet: Margaritaville

Garth Brooks: Katey Wants A Fast One

Clarence Carter: Strokin'

Cinderella: We're Not Gonna' Take It

Eric Clapton: Cocaine

The Clash: Rock At The Casba

Charlie Daniels Band: Devil Went Down To Georgia

Thomas Dolby: She Blinded Me With Science

Eloy: Escape To The Heights (The early name of our neighborhood)

Eurythmics: Sweet Dreams

Glenn Frey: The Heat Is On

Eddy Grant: Electric Avenue

Greatful Dead: Touch Of Grey

George Harrison: Cracker Box Palace

Corey Hart: Sunglasses At Night

J. Geils Band: Centerfold

Whitney Houston: How Will I Know

Ian Hunter: Once Bitten (Twice Shy)

Chrissy Hynde w/The Pretenders: Brass In Pocket

Ram Jam: Black Betty

Rick James: Super Freak

Elton John: Alice

Kiss: Rock'n'roll All Night

Led Zeppelin: Feather In The Wind

Madness: Our House (Ours was in the middle)

Ricky Martin: La Vida Loca

Night Ranger: Still Rock In America

Men Without Hats: The Safety Dance

Miami Sound Machine: Do The Conga

Michael McDonald: Yamo Be There

Willie Nelson: On My Mind

Willie w/Julio Iglesias: All Of The Girls

Billy Ocean: Caribbean Queen

Jamie O'Neal: There Is No Arizona

Buster Poindexter: Hot Hot Hot

Judas Priest: Son-of-a-Bitch

Stacey Q.:2 of Hearts

Kenny Rogers: The Gambler

Michael Sembello: She's A Maniac

Bob Seger: Turn The Page

She Daisy: Lucky 4 U

German Group: Luft Balloons

DeftaLoneby: Been Strokin'

38. Special: Rockin' Into The Night

SuperTramp: Breakfast In America

Suzanne Vega: My Name Is Luka

Warrant: Sweet Cherry Pie (my favorite dessert)

Out of all of the big numbers, I actually wrote two that were outright thefts from previous artists. It is not that I actually knew at the time. Most of the entire group simply came to me from nowhere. Although, I am quite capable of simple belting out tunes at a moment's notice, and even sitting down to methodically pen, rewrite, and edit my work those two, Move Over Big Dog, an older country number, and I think All of My Love had floated through my head one day. Oddly, the two artists, namely George Thoroughgood and Roger Plant, decided to go ahead with updated versions.

I believe that it would be proper at this time to refer to that old early '60s animated show Tom Terrific. Recall that all of his thoughts spiraled into his funneled hat. He lived in a tree house. After the swirl of tornado-like thoughts would enter his brain through the top of the funnel, he would quickly begin to jot down outlines and plans involving his newborn theories onto his chalkboard.

ESSENTAIL REFERNECE TO ACTUAL 3:00PM CARTOON SHOW!

Songs or Poetry

The Mostly(?) Unfinished Works of The Incredible William Penn:

He asked me not to see him as the tragic fallen hero
This strong and weathered herder was from a place called Mazatlan
Then he offered me a treat from a cookie sheet from Mirro
He had so fully filled it with some tasty treats of marzipan
On long treasured days he was oh so reliant he
Was saluting tattered flags oh so compliantly

A random thought, spectacular mote
Richy sweetness, in a candy drop
A cool line eye, so fabulous hot
Creamy dreaminess, for a foolish fop
A foolish whimsy, a casual trot
Reverberations of the fading light's decay
In radiation giving off bright colors display
My spirit's risen, in knowing where to go
Brightness glistens, for an emotional over flow

The birds sing out calling, they taunt me from a nearby tree
As cats come on by crawling, oh they're never crossing me
Dogs chase me falling, so I'm never feeling free
Horses ride by taunting, in running much too fast
My needful task is daunting, my vigor will not last
Those things that I could alter, now solid in the past

Fallen ichorous remains, globules drop to the sea
An ethereal contact stains, celestial drips set free
To nearer to the sun, time to land the journey's done
The farther that you go, the clearer that you'll know
Mortal man held gravity, bounds us to the ground
An ancient myth, a travesty, seems like woes abound
To every oneelectic, from the sweet scents I detected
As the night was moving strong, I'm moving on and with my weakness

May this possibly be construed as success intense
May I clutch your dress, remorse immense
Stand toward me, lay your mind toward my heart
And yours in mine, so that we'll never part
Let us come together, let us be as one
With my shadowed past, I quickly come undone
How did you create such designs, can you really make sunshines
I'm gonna seek that girl and make her all mine
and as my wife lay each night, with a man now dying

White caps pop up like Alps on a billboard
Gum snaps forth like pancake batter poured
Mountains climb beyond our spectral reach
Reaches higher welcomes, downward so to teach
Our ready minds now open, awakened to the door
Bathed in tranquil senses, a richness so much more
Arisen to our virtues, we bask upon the shore

I drum things up at the expense of cordiality
I beg a favor, please oh please, for me (no fee)
Humming your song upon the sultry tips of June
It must be the highest of the higher moons
And when your hand grows old, goes cold
And when I look to you with longing eyes, bask me in serenity

Well I was walking down the street with a box of Rinso in my hand
To wash, and rinse repeat, until the colors come out grand
In swept up silent whisperings, we all move for the door
No need for desperate wondering, we all do know the score
As you're wiping off the spittle from a pugalist's shoe
Kiss me my princess fulfill such keen desire
An ethereal enchantress, fill me full with fire
I've longed for your dear comforts, as I'm so far from home
Exiled by rule in these swamplands, so far from home I roam
Touch me now you're trembling, and offer me so much
Assuring that your virtues, will always mean so much
With one smooth swirling motion, once again I am alive
'Tis in her deep devotion, and mortal virtues I've contrived
Her sweet romantic potion, will slowly now revive
Beckon unto me, and I shall be your guide
Just give your command, and I will so soon abide
With your cherished trust, I am at your will
Your valued honor bold, my longing ever still
Yet now have I cast my mind to the wind
And forgotten all of those wayward sins
I dainty waft of caramellic grace, now moving down the hallway
'Tis a jolly dance to marvel at, with lacy days and some of that
To taste delights and play all day, to sing of sprites 'til June
As I grow older the matchless inhibitions, the forces fully bold
I cling so softly and hold onto thee, so desperately

Wizard on my wall, cast in pose & standing tall
Wistfully sowing his seeds, under the starlight and breeze
Moonbeam tonight I'm free, indeed inclining, reclining
And oh so ever politely declining
Tonight I'll be, so soon team, indiscreet deciding, presiding
It' that we all should, thrust forward with good
Silence is golden, so the silver tongued man
Reached into the darkness, spreading glitter with his hand
Then beckoned into the dark night's abode
Please come with me, harken unto your newly founded home

As all of the regrets of tomorrow, sink slowly into today
There was a girl from Germany, she is quite a gal as you will see
If I came home with her now how tasty things would be
As soon as we come through the door
All of my thoughts go down to the floor

Deeply wooded valley, stretched out to shining sea
Up to the treetops of Amy Lane
Trodden trails and rabbit paths
Where sneaky deer and gophers, take their morning baths
Arching crescent, soon rolling out to me
Up on the hilltops I dance once again
Where butterflies lick daffodils, and chipmunks get their laughs

Sept. 30th 1989

With exaltations in their place, the mainframe was displaced
Forgotten world of yore, charred with past digrace
Entry for the good now, in the kingdom of Waheed
Opening new ground for the anxious golden seed
Triumphant reigning showers, with unrelenting power
Can we escape our wretched past, to hold on dear to love at last

Nov. 17th 1989

The golden graze with my eyes amazed
The misty haze is shattered, by a royal sceptor's glaze
Schooled with stalking shadows, chased down with frothy drink
With tools of haunting gallows, bewitching he should think
Remaining like a hound now, circle forward toward the sheep
Caressed by calling thunder, sinking ever slower,
Into the drowsy deep, ranging peaks are rolling
And drifting with the tide, an ambiance extolling
For faith and foolish pride, rumbling and knowing
Autumn leaves are blowing, tall willow branches sway
An icy wind is showing, how cold the demons play
Each and everyone is showing, that a conscience often speaks
In brilliance and in showing, a truer heart now seeks

Magnemotive forces building up with fear,

Teaming wild eyed horses, run toward what is so dear

Sitting so cool back they also chillin', the ornery start to cast the part

Now enters the warring demon, in my heart now so deep

My mind collides with mountains steep

Such fiery rage within the lair, my soul dear god will keep

There was a horse bright orange and tan

A freer soul not known to man

His proud clouds of dust had been seen by few

And only his lips kissed the sweet morning dew

Of where such a majestic roan horse hides away

And how he did welcome the start of each day

'Til one day upon that secluded hill there did ride

A group of young cowboys, and an Indian guide

Searching for quick ones to harness and cast

Though all had startled by a deep sounding rasp

Of a tall man of lightening and reddish brown hair

As he roped and he hollored and went on without care

Though one horse had gotten away from this mess

With sweet tastes of freedom, and his mother's caress

He stole into the darkness away from the pack

And as he moved onward deep into the black

Willowy wisps in the night, billowing wisps out of sight

Twisting the gnarls that were wretched

Deeply outlined the landscapes were etched

By hard stony fields, the granite marbling yields

Swirling the winds do now captivate, dried up it leaves in an unwinding fate

Dark shadows emerge then recoil, reaching out and up from the soil

In unwinding fates iron hand, fine gemstones now lost in the sand

I bought a gun to caress my brow, in the midnight hour

When it's more than hours, and hours that I'm losing

Not the pale of a dark and looming moon, nor cigarettes devoured

Nor the smoke that's inhaled, into the wee morning hours

Creeping out but all too soon, so goes dusk to break of day
And smoke that devours to bring to the ends
Our cold yesterday then so surreally it bends
Snuffing out now the gains of my inner delight
And darkens long shadows deep into night
Cast for problems one by one, reel them in now you've begun
To march right in to life's parade, or pull down fast beneath the shades
Rising up again for calling moon, the ship sets sail and all too soon

Papa's coming home tonight, he said he's picked it up now on a flight
But we don't want him here no more, nor shuttered knocking from the behind
the door
Oh, take away this day, take it all away, please it's just a dream that my
mind's replayed
It's been a while, yeah a year or two, there wasn't much that we'd ever do
I remember one summer day, that allowed a man to freely play
Oh then the old winter came, and that old man was never the same
Papa's coming home again, he said he's picked it up now on a flight
But we don't want him here no more, no shattered knocking from behind that
door
I shake again clutch at my coat, a heavy lump from within my throat
I choke it down the time has come, what is it that I'm running from
I'm on my knees now, it's so hard saying please.
Oh papa's coming home again, he's going to set it right
My papa's coming home again, tonight's the night, the night

Abject audacity, adjuvant capacities
Acute auspicious adorations, amoebic adorations
Bountys of bile, bring bold brawny Bedlam
Beasts from below, brought brash baggage with them

Anemic attractions, brotherly bromides
Blazingly blaring, back from yesterdays daydream
Going for joyrides, jauntily jingled jalopies
Clap for knifing kite strings, kilos of kilted kennel kickers
Long for love's lavish lust, lead lost liar's likely lines

I'll take all your wives tales, fancy stories
Saved for now in a box of glories, back to wild ale and crashing lorrys
My guile is tempered like a rock, but I'll not dig through empty quarries
I'm busy building up my stock, retelling tales of sages stories

No way, no way man
If teacher says I'm late, that she knocks me down a grade
Don't quit the party don't crash the scene, life has just got started
Absorbing now the green, we are all good hearted
And this is what I mean
No way no way man, no way no way
My girlfriends kiss had got me high, my curfew missed
So with my honored parting the shit would fly, doing cartwheels darting
So low am I now that I can't speak
No way no way man, no way no way
So don't be doing, kids what I did
For your very own parents just might flip a lid
We'll here a mighty call, no way the voices fall
No way no way man, no way no way

I toil for the master, digging his plaster
Dare he say faster, yet in need is the caster
Now digging the pit, on the embankment I sit
But out from above and over the hill
I'm given a shove, disquieting still
Dare he say faster, in need is the caster
Oh ever so faster, and faster I will

Tales of spring and sunshine moved across the air
Sprigs and boughs and green leaves dance across her hair
I recount again to be stronger, with the men
Rays of future's dimming, sun's now setting low
Sprigs and boughs and green leaves, love is letting go

As the raging defeat's at my veins, hide my feelings so deep inside
As crew sets sail for stormy weather, the captain's tied below
Contained in his own hold, they're bound for ports of pleasure
Captive minds now filled with thoughts of treasure
??????????????????????????????????????no measure
The captain shakes and quakes, deep down his belly aches
The thirsty morning comes at last, shores filled up moving fast
The captain's down below, his time is running low
Now his bad seers too really red, standing into day

Candle stick carnage, river boat garbage
Paddy waddle scene, insipid tepid green
Monarchy's repulsion, sinking sleek convulsion
Abbot Lexington, cooling steamy gun

It's 3:00 and the bars are closed, shouldn't be thinking of oatey O's
But the screaming man on the T.V. set, is feeling bold, and made a bet
The grazing goats will get theirs yet, when all is told and fortunes let
Us get on way down to the grinding stone
While leaving this whole mess alone
We've gathered for the massive throwing stones
This book makes light of day
As inner soles cause interplay, all hell breaks loose today
Bright fading moments soon decay
As Jack B. Nimble jumps back into the fray
The book makes light of day, as Interpols cause us wide dismay
All hell breaks loose again, quickly twisted into the fray
And Jack B. Nimble he jumps away, Fading moments to dance and sway
As the pages play out an odd and eerie play
Such fading moments are on display
You know what older wives would say, yon bonnies bright should be so gay
With those doctors playing Frankenstein
They've always got a change in mind
Parents playing god and goddess, seems they're under some duress
Yet Mommy always knows what's best, holding <u>soldiers</u> close to her breast

On the day that you were born, the farmers sowing field with corn
A smile that graced that early morn, today's the day we celebrate
Yes in the book we record the date, and with open arms embrace our fate
Casting foolish lots, to bet it all on little dots
They're easy games just made for tots
It seems my play is not for naught, nor all of those things that I have bought
And golden chains that mere mortal wrought, lurid treasure so many sought
So jeweled jaded and bemused, 'twas a thirst for alms I'll never drench
An empty soul I'll never quench, I lust for miles, but they gave an inch
Another acid nightmare from somewhere out in outer space
It's just another acid raindrop rolling down my cheek
Started pure and clean upon a mountain's peak
In my dreams I've got a princess, so close the door to hell
I can't go left I can't turn right, it won't turn out I've been turned in
So drop me off or turn me on, 'cause it's too late I know they've won
Just leave me behind don't look back, you know that I'm not blind
I'm merely dressed in black, remember the pillar the salty shame
An emotional killer, yet whose to blame, just don't turn back

Curiosity killed the feline cat, from back in English class, remember that
Those curiosities return all set for a fasting feline
Although she may have been feeling rather fine

The boy is waiting outside the door, who knows what's, so much more
So don't try to find the reason, answers are easy
Don't offer one to me, they change with the season
Please just let me be, crashing waves relent unto the sea
Foaming and receding as I am on my knees
With you I am pleading, please don't crash on me
Catapulting all the discard and debris, I see
But on tall and sturdy stands the tree
As the royal court so full of clowns
And thieves with virility decreases, maiden voices
Upon your feathered bed you sleep
And in the midnight hours that I keep
Hearing howling moans and weeping

Of the lonely shrouds hidden by the daylight
In our morning crowds, muttering mingling
Among contented souls, and those that hide their grief
But once again in shadows disbelief, muffled tears of silence

As my heart feels like wax which soon will be melting
Then those of humble substance, and those who drool like fools
My work keeps me living, as I know that I am true
Believing I'm fulfilled by sun and skies of blue

Twisting in your twisted minds, reversing all the power lines
Mining for such fallen finds, escaping from the laser and the visiting times
Searching for a rainbow, messing with the cock's new crow
Hypnotic in the afterglow, messing with the power flow
I always look for those who know, just drifting with the undertow

She's so good, and when I feel her touch
And as the bow breaks the water's edge
The perching watcher's wait from the edges of his ledge?????
As where we land thar is where we'll sing, so you frenchy-boy
Don't worry 'bout nary a thing, and don't go on about the whine too much
For the rums up on ahead, and then it's off to bed
So the captain's sets a wino's doff instead
She's so good and when I feel her touch
Just don't go on about the wine too much, 'tis the end of a sequence
See the breaks, and the bow below
How fast the wakes scene in the water's flow
It's off to bed, and the end to all you're shows
Quick now, before your *white* dream stampedes upon the herd
My dreams are so well built, that they're used for tons of brick

When you battling demons made of rum, and all the witches they come from
Deadened portals, bitches glom, drumming trumpets banging toms
There all so dead, and all so gone, yet not buried as they don
Cloaks of dragon's guilt with steel, slaying blackguards puffs of smoke

Take down the midnight royal curtain, blow the dust off from the moon
Trudge through marshes that you've been
Bogged by the darkness of a soggy June???????????

Too Many Girls? (NO)
World??????????????Too many girls, be??? Because there's only one of me!
123..........43, yet still there's only one of me.

Hey get up on it, there aren't even any customers
If you've just sold out to the lowest denominator
As then he heard his mother claim
There'll be no captain's cry for help, he said look the captains cry
Don't lock your cell phone when away at the lodge
Think back, and blow it out again, a focus overhead
seems to climax in the skies, I'm so lonely I could think of you
just like today when what we used to do
a close encounter, the softness of your dress
evolves into a hurried-scurried mess, and then I gasped
oh heart be still, for it is ye that carries me over

I'll think I'll catch a pig tonight, to fill his women up with fright
So don't come knocking at my door
Or you may wind up face down on the floor
And once your backup comes foe more
Wild-n-Willie Singer'll let 'em know the score
So villainous features will you let my people go
There's just one thing that you ought to know
I think I'm gonna catch a pig tonight, or am I just filled with vengeful sight

Don't buy your shoes at the discount store
Do look out for the one behind the door
Need no lawyer when they kick you to the streets
For something only victimized, unseen
Playground swing sets blow running free
Such things in my mind I wouldn't want to see

You're Psychedelically out of this time
You're perilously out of your truly absent mind
Yet while you think that you're okay
Millionaire nightmares coming faster than a hurricane
A millionaire's problems with thousand dollar dreams
There's no way that I can solve them
With simply conjured patriotic schemes

Oh, you love each and every girl, so why would you even lay a witch
Yes, you'd walk right through her door, and play her into the corner
But you dig a dirty ditch, go on complaining life's a bitch
As surely you do jest, upon a hammish actor's quest
Although you'd like to smash those that fell, there's not another magic spell
To break through the drowning pell, and tho' it's just as well
The way we're on our way to hell, it'll all be good as we're set free
So we'll hear nothing of such misery, remember swiftly the chimes will toll
The long forgotten love you've sown, the rivers fast the hearts so deep
As the children romp to see, fallen heroes near treacherous peeks so steep

Don't let the deep thought of constructive activities
Muddle your otherwise needed thought procese
Badger your dwindling thought capacities

When all of the trees have lost their leaves
And the nights are cooled by a northern breeze
Don't hang your head and mope around
Just dig down deep for what for what you've found
When the scenes of summer lay in your head
-or-
When the summer scenes cast a longing play
Don't you sink your head in a wrought display/decay
Just hold on know, hold onto me
And dig down deep for what you found
Yes dig that deep philosophy
When the icy grip/wind tears/digs into flesh
And the howling of war without the rest??

467

Don't hide away, away from me
Dig down deep find what you need
Dig down deep and find a way/make it stay
When the howling wind doest cast a spell
Across your house as that burning smell

Got so bad, you're never gonna' be so good
Cuz you always lie around, you're high
And then your dream it dies
Tonight your dreams are up in smoke
If you're so hyped on tryin'
Give that guitar another stroke
Quick fiddlin'ain't no joke
Cool hot licks that do invoke
So serene, sublime, reach quick in time
It's gone with yesterdays
You need only change your ways

A sister's profit, with a margin's wink
Miss Briggington the eye, I can take that look
And I can make her look just like a saint
Come by breakfast, or over for tea
All set up with cups, she is family

Streams by an English river, the gimmickry of hair
Outside winds feigned the really tall buildings
The magnificent sheen of sunlight
You knew that it would come to this
And now you face the wall
Ride the case of mummy
And the Indian's horse
Yet you insist there, moaning and groaning
It's the ceremonious juices flow
With no one on T.V. illicit in sympathy
Was I awake when I awoke today

With no time for others and their party fests
His boys rise and tear asunder
Taking vengeance upon the earth
And all who should happen upon their hallowed territory

One more chance, a lotto tickets dance
Willy's a double agent man
He's sold part of the script
In the hope of some type of
Eternal matrimony, which of course
Having been nullified by said sale
Could no longer exist, in so that it had been to fruition

On peaks anew, as fields of flowers that I plant for you
Of paddle balls and jacks, and kicks those daisy games
So neatly spread like a joyous piece of fruit

The sun shone brightly on a Saturday morning
Cuckoos calling from out on the lawn
A bit of steam from a quick bath I'm drawing
I always am ready just after the dawn
As here I wait for your caress, your loving motions relieving stress
I'm yours, in hours now to impress, with nothing showing no lock, or tress
It was such stress, not the designer's dress
In the glaring scene of unknown possibilities
Kept now hidden from the light, dip back and out of sight
Just far from reach, the best are best to keep

As she stared me down with a critical eye
I had to wonder, what did she see, espy
A shade of deep virtue, or a casual lie

New blouse new shoes, going out on a Saturday
Gonna' see a new movie, can't come out to play
But you've missed the end, then still call me friend
I school I see you, you just run away

Then you call me up at night, and tell me of your day
It's just a strange twitch of envy
Pierce the night to scratch the surface
Of a daylong dream, it's ripped its image
Now bleeding falling down in front of me
Which of the starts could be unright
Snatching murmurs open, rip up the seem

Oh those sugar lips, those succulent drips
From the edge to the tips, on luscious long trips
From her smile to her hips, my heart really skips
Those sweet sugar lips, filled with succulent drips
From the roughly tattered edges to the long extending tips
Around the world in seconds inside holy hallowed ships

I'm so alive in the morning, so alive in the day
And until I am yawning, I constructively play
'Til she's gentley fawning, 'neath the covers I'll stay
At night when I'm resting, and all else is away
A curiosity's testing, but will she obey
With a new moon now cresting, to keep bad doggies at bay
Then it wouldn't need testing, as I instructively say

Awakened from a tranquil nap
I hobbled out, into doubt
The peace which rocked me gently to sleep
Snatched in the night for hobgoblins to keep
Donning a long coat, and warm woolen cap
On a pre-gauged route, was up and about
The road is bleached 'neath its own bed of snow
Yet my pulsating senses knew where to go
Toward rocky tors high, near a low gentle sweep
I ravage the wind with my axe
Men tremble weakly at the size of my racks

Cold sight of butted cigarette, beckons me forward it's not done yet
Guilt looking for remorse, welcomes luck...come again
Gone too fast I realize, it's in the past...with what underlies
The golden moon, a truthful glow...come chiming in the afterglow

Plagued by thoughts not of this world
Gone and come from this never land
Back to the future it's hurled
It's a tough scene, one never planned
It would not have come to pass
Had I not raised an offered glass

Oh those dinosaur boots, simply made from petroleum
A dino's cast amazed, when you hit the scene
So well protected another fad is crazed
You bring out another death of your own
A draggadon's breath steams away overblown
Blowing off some steam, some bad dreams that you've known

I hold on 'til reality stares me in the face
The mask so well covered and finely laced
I hear the lead so shall I now
Ye now see thy holy velvet
Why don't you wait, they'll come again
Oh the Valkyrie will surely send
Oh sail the sea, a second wave unto me
Do come with me, I'm lost in the breeze
Oh won't you tell, let's go, get away
Hold onto my hand Stop all of these lies, deceiving
Behind silent trees, how they go god only knows
I've got to be free, dyed in the sea, don't ever beseech me
Heaven please don't take away, I got to have a speed in the day
Oh be with me and help me to know, down the right path, the way to go
So far on earth, come with me so far away, today

It was you that hurt my arm, the sun is setting low
The witch is still here in my heaven
I know you meant me harm, the feeling's letting go
Burn the witches by eleven
Now raise your minds from the sky
For truly no one is going to die
She'll be the trade-off woman, and then she'll beg for more
In no hollowed action nor, in wretched replies I soon deplore

Broken glass pains my house, victims of my ways
The fragile force of the female psyche's ego
In disembodied untuned clamor, disharmonic metallic strains
My thrusting force must be wholly guarded
The weakness close to keep

'Tis he, he, he who calls the night
Until the sun will bring
Up and away well out of sight
????????????????????sing
Those noisy walks through la, la, limbo land
??????????????????????do

An echoed thought unarrested, on hallowed ground once contested
Growing stronger wills are tested, cloak my wretched nightly vision
And those far from sight, in??????????? shrouded toll's sole seclusion
With Swiss time winding in drowned delusion
Like black walls of sorrow, the inky deep while pities borrow
In ripple's wake treads on this time???????????????

A twist of fate, and gnarly branches curled
The latest sage by time, golden leaves unfurl too late
To stop the crime, a gothic mansion the pearl they ate
Tartened lemons and limes of fate, a friendly knowing fame to me
The possibilities are free, twirling gnarly branches
Curled in time, the stage is met it's surely mine
Golden leaves unfurl too late to stop this motion

472

Golden sunlight bathes the grass, leaves aglitter and painted glass
A wall of stone is crumbled now, a stairway rises thru futures time
Past a tattered table were once they dined
It'll take you down boy, I tell no lie
Pearly gates and golden flocks
To take in splendor, roses hollyhocks
With golden handles unlock the door
Don't wish to see just what's in store
Walk down a hallway of knotted pine
On a country estate past the grapened vine
Look up to the wall and what you see
A familiar face who could that be
Those wrought iron gates and stone fence wall
They'll drag you down to the dungeon halls
A gothic mansion arise so high
It'll take you down, though who knows why
If you hear it calling so deep in the night
Just stay down low and well out of sight
Wrought iron gate and stone fence wall
I believe they're calling, they call you now
Just don't go there, run to the hill
Get on your knees and pray for me
Pray as I call out, call out to thee
Don't step forth, just fade back
The spirit of yore in on the attack
Dinner's ready, pearls and lemon pie
With high class women, I tell no lie
They took me down, and my family too
That gothic mansion now comes for you
The gate's now open, open wide
So don't be drawn here, run to the hill
Hide 'neath the grasses so tall and still
Call out to the flowers that cover the ground
It's your only hope, as no one's around
A wrought iron gate and rock stone fence
Near that gothic mansion there's no defense

Kill my scream now before I wake
Acolytes vision another to take
Dreams go up in flamboyant desire
They need them all to feed the fire

Out of control she's spent two life savings
On a roll given in to beast like cravings
Sorry soul rubbing oiled engravings
Outer zone relenting with my?????
What does that sew, why she's all so easy
She never gave it up, so sticky sweet to me

Just a skip and a hop, past the resale shop
Run so fast past the candy store
As your grandpa beckons "no more, no more"
Rush out to lane just to see
Fresh bursting fruit from a ripened berry tree

The end a friend, in self-made prison
Built up from sad acts, stands a lonely person
Reaching out to hide facts, no logic can save him
No arithmetic chains as candlelight wanes
The breach of cocaine calls out from the darkness

Calculate advancement up the hilltop to reach
???????????????????????????????????
No signs of my enemy not here nor below

A tear from my heart reached the bottom of a well
A penny to wish for a favor to sell
A well flighted fancy held it all off
A penny to wish for a favor I'll find
In goodness well treasured, a kindness in kind
A burst and a spark, candied delight a fanciful lark
No alcohol will douse the burning embers of my mind
The real me is hiding too precious to find

In stolid repose virtues are captured now trapped in time
Intentions hyped in relevance, basking over bloated consequence
Breaking up with broken minded honeys
Meeting up with simple minded gals
No precept divisions, no coinage or monies
No hangout with fools or gallant fine pals
The tales of modern men, will shrivel in comparison
To what I've yet to tell about, courageous deeds unknown
Of this I'll leave no doubt, Ofherioic actions shown

A prince without a courtyard, no scepter to bequeath
No heaven rising skyward, no hell waits now beneath
As the subjects have all scattered, and the rule it seems by thumb
Royal garments torn and tattered, king's fool is warn and numb
But cocked upon the head, the royal boy wears thorns
Ruler's birthright leading men, whose hats are graced with horns
Not need anything like, as a brand-new spanking spat
To accent the avenue, I guess I wouldn't need a shoe
And truly wouldn't have a clue, but I'd know just what to do
As I'll be singing all day long, to put it in a catchy tune
Just like this oh so happy song, and when women all would swoon
And as they tried to catch their breath, I'd wink away all tragic death
Wouldn't such fancy cars, you wouldn't find me out in bars
Tho' as I wished upon the stars, for a woman just like you
'Cause you wouldn't need a name, where all the feeling are the same
And in my tropical desires, one wouldn't even need a fire

He pulled out an ace, 'cause he is in the hole
Running on a reckless pace, with the others on a roll
Morning's light into my head, alarming clock I'm still in bed
Paper says we've got to groove, purchased stock now on the move
Will this all stop if I remove, all concerns that do reprove

A friend's woman's revenge, a landlord's eviction
A troubled ex now intends, with a maiden's conviction
An old man's deranged, so muddled and blind

In a makeshift arranged, so messed up aligned
Tho' if he relents, then something's not right
As the fleeting new season has come down to this
So humbley with reason, hits not on a guess
That a woman's revenge, has an old man deranged
With exes and vengeance, so muddled and blind, white raged
Now makeshift arranged, so feral and wild now, so angry uncaged

I clung to life, and still made shade
Tho' still I couldn't make the grade
Little acorns growing within the scheme
Reaching growth and color with shady green
With saplings growing tall, reach for sunlight
Drought dried stems do stall, keeps the need, the flight
Then in the springtime life renewed, again will come to sing
Greenest branches leaves and weeds grew
Amongst the brown, now broken twigs
Leave until the light of day, as you know that I can't stay
The call of north's horizon, holds me in its gentle sway

Holding close and everything at ultra-dose
Bring me up to my peers, but with actors or careers
Hold now fast to your domain, I guard you all from feeling pain
Bring back the heights that I once felt, bring back that place I've found
Step by step, higher and higher, step by step, higher and higher

Was up one early morning, was greatly greeted by awesome hue
Such sweetness in the dawning, the open now inviting blue
Wrought and overturned, shifting into plot conspired
For sunny scenes tomorrow, attempt to break it off with you
My good times are borrowed, losing no matter what I do

As a sentenced phrase, turns to muddled malaise
Pictures dim and fade, a plan has now been laid
As those rejoice who've found their way

Sun shines in cheating on the din
Up and awake now it's time to make…the green
Oh god made it green, seems it ain't enough

Staying on the fringe of cordial conversation
Bow at the waist, an unneeded salutation
Politely replying about all my undying love for you
Hoping to be real, untried speculation
No complimentary deal, in daunting adulation
Took off the cuffs, messed up my hair
Venture seeking, in the village square
Let loose with a belly laugh
Guzzle down another quaff
Village square, so easy and so fair
All decked out in green, welcome to all sights unseen

Demonstrative speeches echo in the halls of Ivy
Awaken from a dream feeling rather lively
Take a note to jot it down, pencil in a funny clown

With executive hours they're building their towers
To hold another bench, clock watchers, coffee clutchers
Assembled at the gait, break into regiment
Staff sergeants, like standing in cement
Barking out commands, my psyche tells me how it stands
With unrelenting dilation, the world collapses in undulation
A blackened nightmare, foreign matter's decay
I know if I dare, to fend it off as here I lay
Here I stand, wait until the last song is over
Daffodils, don't you know I want to roll in clover
After all, it's not the seen but what goes unseen
Here I stand, come to me in darkest night bequeath me
Your gentle hand, to bring the orchestra to life
Shed these dreams, of imposition sung to cattle call in kind

Impressing with the grating of his verbal assault
Compressing all my sorrow into salt
Just like I said I thought I'd take a chance
Tell me really right now what's the deal

Don't build a brick house next to the woods
With sheet metal lining, or the arsonist will take his toll
Don't tell your nephews who their other uncle is
'Cause that will surely mean the end to your biz
'Cause that will surely spill those beans
Don't make love to your neighbor, even though she is sixteen
'Cause her father's rather mad, and all those cops will sure be mean

With misshapen heads they rise from their beds
To the call of misfortune's night
And now that I'm done, I leave this task up to you
When You partake of the devil's mistake
So badly you've got to fall
And now down to you, I'm telling it true
Dear brother you are going to fall

Your task now be true, so whatever you do
Beguiling the dreams of them all
And now that you're through, I've some pity on you
As life will begin once again
And through the dark ages, and now out of their cages
Is true justice still held within all men

I should have told them all the score
When I peaked back through that door
Wasn't taking chances, skipped the look of furtive glances
Well, I wasn't looking back

A young boy walked beneath a tree
Cherries quickly dropping gently just for me
Was a sweet squirrel truly thinking of thee

Oh the carefree life in a jungle song
Play the tunes and we'll all dance along
In line with a favored life, not to put off work or strife
A wooded valley, canary row, songs of virtue we will know
To a place of cane, and summer rain, up to the tree tops of Amy Lane
With trodden trails, and rabbit paths, the dear and gopher take their baths

Oh Karina play for me, ocarina play for me
My sweet and lovely creature do you see
Spinning twirling, dancing like a top
Ocarina play for me, oh Karina can you see
Such a twirly girl, she's all our heads in whirl
Oh surely girl, we love to watch that white flag unfurl

Straight shooter, goody booter, lean green shoot tall bean
Long dress tall walk, rootin' tootin' scooter
Sleek style with a captive smile, her hawking rooter
We're tied to all our things, like candy canes on Christmas trees
That decorate the fragrant wafting breeze
They stick from hearts of longing, elated chorus singing
Black glass burning fire, purple flame of my desire
Hot brass, a lot higher, those fated twists of warm desire
I see it's growing deep in the night
with you still teasing me into your sight
I hold up my end of the world
Atlas can dance yet I call the tune

I'm but an Old English poet, in a Shakespearian Play
Who recites his own lines, in greeting the day
To take note of the signs, and the role I must play

I ought naught speak of rope, and if offend a dope
Who's thinking of another type of vine
I shank recall days of yore, as they'll recall even more
That sinks now into sunken sands of time

In a place with no November, far off playthings that you remember
You long to touch, but trapped in time, while waiting idly you'll pay for your
crime
Dues, dues, Gentiles and Jews, dusty caves, and old moldy news
Unlock the doors and ye' shall find, those hidden corridors behind your mind
A gentle place where silence once slept, a hidden room with secrets well kept
A cunning game of our own mind's design, well structured thoughts our lives
are maligned
So quick and sudden now upon your tight door, fate's hand is knocking
completing the score
Traveling deep out of time, and right out of space, sorrow awaits in knowing
your face

To see that my bloodline, cast in mighty virtue
Until the end of time, seems like calling genius
To assist in another fiery birth, and children wearing beanies
May not be what it's worth, so I sit and ponder ways
To end this loneliness, as basking warmer days
A sun shimmers through her golden trees
So do it through those local teens
?????????????????????scenes
////////////////////////////mirth
?????????????????????????unearth

Sitting here waiting for the telephone to ring
Hey somebody out there, do you want to hear me sing
Although I sit here pondering the importance of it all, in an necessary call

Do I seem like a jock, cause I'm thinking like a dork
I'm feeling more like Spock, yet acting more like Mork
Now I don't know what to do, come across and journey unto me
It's one for the show, and then two more for me
When it finally becomes now three, upon a trip we'll go
Breach of all precepts, a passion in light
Stretching new depths deep into the night
Stand long now

Still twisting unfurling to seek upon the day
From a cavalier yearning to the brightest on display
???zone
??alone
The density of wood, the denseness of the tress
A propensity of good, in goodness and in these
Stuck between day, and 'tween night
Time is left to play, Neither timely nor devised
Refrain from the smoke you're now rolling
Something you say seems so right
Please just stop this equation, it's longer then you'll ever know
As long as you stop mild persuasion,???????????????
You're a good boy who can't resist a good tune
In thinking that parties all end, but too soon
Unto the place where they have couches, and hundred-dollar shoes
Or maybe just move away, in Bahama's hiding I'll stay
I won't call on mama to just to say I'm okay

Hot, hot heat so close in tight
Melt, melt melting into night
I felt it pelting me with fright
So warm so low, and out of sight
There is no want for pity's sake
I step in and march up to the door
My heartbeat's breakin' on the floor
Turn the knob unlock the key
As the sunlight showers over me
Take in a moment to compare
My own mood to the outside air
I stroll out to a grander view
A landscape evolving under dew
The stores are closed bit it's okay, I'm only window shopping anyway

Mindless microbes float along in protoplasmic disgrace
What's gone wrong or lost its place
So soon approaches my private inner space
Was it at the blood's first spill, that innocence forgotten
When taking chances on the kill, that ignorants turned rotten

You told a tale, you made your father sail
And as he spied upon a spouting whale
He chased it as the all went down, and all to no avail
The message that we sent, to tell another tale
As sinners now repent, as they sit around in jail

A passage traveled deeply, unmined but not unknown
Plains plummet oh so steeply, the trails been overgrown
With the warm and gentle breezes blown
Reap the seeds that you have sown
Sweet freedom's ever warm here, and eradiating glow
Accepting of my body, envelope all I've known
Enriched by gentle valleys, and reaping seeds I've sown

A storm cloud rolls in from the west, a lightening shot from the north
An old man buttons up his coat before casually venturing forth
A cold and cloudy day, that rains into the night
The moisture and the dampness covers all in
sight??????????????????????????????????????

I have all of the comforts of home, wherever I may roam
From old Rome and into Paris, your sweet face is always
fairest????????????????????????????

Invoking images unkind, poison visions in my mind
The situation will unwind, another nightmare you will find
To feed the basking rays, a lost soul, and I'm running late
As I recount upon my knees, I beg you everybody please
Impatiens and riotous flowers, come through in the darkest times

I

The ways that we dream to the light of the sea
They tell they hope, it will act upon all that I grow
As these kings of the sea, start to deal, rolling skyward
Uprights of the day, it seems they've found a new way
In the jungle they start in the night, yes it so old, chilly-dark in the night
As the sun rays shine upon my walls, my potted plant looks ten feet tall
Another dewy morning brings, the birds out on the wing
You want it, you want it, you want it from me
Well how can that be, I heard what you had to say
And watched you walk away, I heard what you had to say…go away
Well that sets me free, but wasn't it yesterday
You sighed, and watched me walk away
Well how can this be, yes I did know you

I held a pomegranate in my hand
It's stone containing the vital sands
So I expose them all to you, yes it's true
My sweet baby blue, we'll strike for a richer vein
Then a startled God's blackened sky
As the lightening cracked it open wide
No more candy, not one pose
Now open wide, I stepped into the day
A bitter brandy, nude silken hose
In shielded pride, held a scepter to the day

I love to plant in the springtime air
Dig in the ground in its lying bare
I swear upon this book and then
I'm running wide yet the testament
Is open, and I believe again
In springtime's hold, I release this dream
With no more cold, enriching running stream
As it wraps itself in the sun's delight
Well shown on the future reeds of light
And close my eyes to my plight, keep digging through the day

I bought a gun to caress my brow, in the midnight hours
When it's more than hours I'm losing
Not in the pale of looming morn, nor in the killer smoke that I devour
For a twilight world with you in mind, gassed up on sweet caffeine
Put your stocks into overdrive, and in loading up on greens
I've gotten past all your reamly dreaming
I've got to stop all of these lies, deceiving
And I've got to be able to see, how men lead
Through the silent trees, God only knows
That I've got to be free, while guiding I see
The way the world sits, bereaved
No don't ever beseech me
And fly away, today

Then appeared in a twinkling sphere of light
Growing in intensity, you were a good man
Yet light catches everything
Foisting your jewels, cast to the wicked crowd
You recite your wanting pleas aloud
They've got you once again
Fly past this scheming dream
Oh, hold onto life and then

Willy's lost his innocence,
Then shaved his head for the evidence
As he's sold his soul for just six pence
Yet all that he found were the remnants
Of days gone by, and childhood's past

Far away there's a town you'll pass by the river
It swiftly hooks around, more a taker than a giver
A whirring rushing sound springs forth from yonder meadow
What's on the other side can turn old women into widows
Oh bringing back, oh bringing back for another day
In bringing back, in bringing back to forge a better way
Oh bringing back, oh bringing back to find a brighter day

To know that fantasy me how could you walk away
And leave me in yesterday, where I'm just a fool
Once we were the same, just playing a children's game
The true hearted charmer with long flowing curls
He looks back and smiles upon me
Yes he knows, that just as the river flows

Don't show me your crystal ball, the wall's too tall
Reflected light and bent frustrations, lent refrains distinctions
Unknown to me yet at the ready, to groove the beat
To flow to heights I need to see, becoming more so the grander me
Magazines and tinseled teens, and baby knowing what it means
So dressed up in denim jeans, playing out such campy scenes
You're my heartache you're my dream, or just a nightmare I've once seen
I hold you closely but yet I know, in the end you'll only go
So stay with me tonight (woman) hold me closer hold me tight
Just to make me feel alright, make my load a little lighter, my days seem a
little brighter
This is just a movie I'd thought I'd cast myself
But the way that I've been losing, it must be something else
So lady let it glide, don't know of my mis-guider
I'll take you on a ride, 'til time is the divider
Hers:
You're so steely you're a screw, you're just a victim I once knew
You're so needy what do you do, just a victim I once blew (away)
Touch and feely yes I do, cause I'm still lickin', lickin' smooth
You were someone I once knew, just a needle in a groove
What I had yesterday came back up in the hands of fools
And now I have naught to give, swimming in tidal pools
I guess It's just let and live, in skirting by unwanted rules

So much living to do, but I can't go on without you
Oh ohoh Marina, I'm more of a man less of a fool
But now what comes next, is the bottomless pool
In the afterlife I'll pay for my mistakes and misconceptions
Holding court as a High King with servants and receptions

485

Lo' and behold, I'll be slapped right back down again
To fight the never ending battle against the other men
Oh Marina, I'm more of a man, less of a fool
Yet what comes next is the bottomless pool
If I can't recall who I truly am, I lose all that I have gained
I'll need to try and cram, all the years so well pained
Attributes in afterglow, is it better, best and beauty blessed
Rightful rondevous are super sensational and totally true
Vigorous and very vibrant, and so wonderfully wundebar
In exited youthful zest,

Elation is your middle name, and Joy is now your first
Amusement is my moniker, for your love I truly thirst
As jubilant as a honey bee, as gleeful as an elf
Stupendous is my frivolity, it's your to be dispersed
Monumental is your reach, your grasp is holy
In blessing all my verse, bells tolling for my loving nurse
Come a little closer let me feel your aural beat
I need some closer contact, and I'll remain discreet
Fill me with your childish laughter
Ode to your soul hand up to me
I'm getting warm and feel your heat

A thief steals away in the night, although his bag's not hidden from sight
Oh can we open up some more, let the beggar through the door
All undressed in tawdry sunshine, and exposed now to the dew
Each one of us must rise up, to do what we must do
I want to do so fast like lightening, or just go in my sleep
I want to see the end of my dream, the final draw on this endless stream
I wish to pull out my guns and stop this show
From damming up my sleep and haunting all I know

Halloween is on the way, so I had better right myself again
And though I'm haunted anyway, united once again, united with my men
As united we will stay, I've seen lovers and little men
With impish grins and fairies when, filled the aural glow

Color brightens, then fills my soul, fills me up when I'm feeling low

Hold still while maneuver, I guarantee long-term relief
Steady motion pin-pointed groover, electricity beyond belief
My heavy heart has tripped me, and now is filling with delight
It's a whole new old prescription, that I feel you ought to take
It comes so very freely, with sun's light shimmering on down
In freshened air with a new feeling, and both feet on the ground
All that's needed is to believe in your one true self
Then follow through the gates, to the watery lakebed shelf

Hibernia touch me and garden grow
Take me from this maddened dream
Lay me down near waters clean
Heaven's flowing, and endless stream
As hell's jaws open in an endless stream
Hibernia touch me, and garden grow

It's a flagpole's journey, and up I arise
For 12 short hours I'm up in the skies
Everlasting beauty, or merely ancient coal
I kiss the skies in a sweet lover's parade
Never chancing mercy, as time will take its toll

Is it not peculiar to have designs in one's beard
Though slim and taller for just five years
A hardened distinction displayed on your face
Well wrinkled patterns, a show of disgrace
Ladder climbing as a diplomat
The tattered changes all your wealth belies
So sharply focused in reddened eyes
Spiritually scripting all your last goodbyes
So they won't detect your impassioned cries

Sat smoking on a pipe to relieve some indignation
It sent me on a flight of astral visitation
Cold wind, a little bit older
Weighed down by a chip on my shoulder
Dragged down by some grain of alcohol
Ragged frame that once stood so tall
Tattered withered shoes, just like in cement
Battered ego bruised, cannot raise a cent
Chip in for a pint of Old Red Rose
Torn off buttons, an old coat will not close

Awoke today with a brandnew kind of feeling
A final kiss that your essence is still sealing
Well I finally have to realize, your goodness kissed my eyes
Now come along on this????????journey
Come and fill my cup, I am young, and I'm still learning
Wholly fill my glass, upon a wondrous globe we're turning

So I'll gladly sing tune, right now for you and you
And never looking back again, in confidence that grew and grew
I'll proudly wave this flag and then, offer up all my goods to you
If you need, come back again, please do, please do, please do
Indeed you'll come, indeed and when, Amen, Amen, Amen
Each cast in its own reflection, a folly filled and modern play
Each aspect of our purity, now perfect for today
When I was young I cried aloud for pompous fool who tried
I'm older now yet not so proud, through failings now denied
I'm failure to myself and others, I live vicariously through my older brothers
I'll just play the air instead, lone temporal rhythms so deep inside my head
So deep inside my head, so deep inside my head

Gotta' get her out, gotta' get her out of my mind
Twisting, turning, squeezing burning
Grip it hard and shake it out, taking hold, a snaky route
Oh I know I'll never learn, nor her love will I ever earn
Chiming, singing, flying, winging

Then moving into sight, so focused deeply in reflected light
I sit here and think sweetly of you
Songs in my head just make me blue
What I wouldn't do to have you back
But that's living in a dream, something of a miracle
Yes, it's part still part of my scheme
Though I know it isn't possible
Your love still blows my steam
I guess it's written indelible
To my knees to pray

Both bums from a hell world, with bitches and Saints
Up in the air tossed, and needlessly hurled
The clutching of Venus, her heart holding true
In virtuous honor, hold her shield to the light
Protecting with guidance, a watch through the night
No shepherd's entombing, can hold close to me now

Cover it all with a rose, and two fresh daffodils
Writing it down in prose, using nineteenth century quills
How am I to soothe, this thunder in my head
When outside it's still raining, now filling me with dread
Now the calmness enters and touches so close
A catalytic lightening, in effervescent green
Nothing is as frightening, as the visions that I've seen

The plant leaned with the sun, drawn by its magnetic waves
Into polaric conjunction, sprouting and spreading it reached out
Outward towards that life giving force, bathed in a breath of iridescence
Expellations for the living of the earth, to dwell on, live off, and return

A non-thieving coon now on the dole, you could surely say he was on a roll
And eating one too true with sweet, sweet sappy and sugary goo
In innocence blinding the truth of my soul
As chipmunks, and squirrels zip up the pole
In such regard I can't compete, the innocence of what they do

They planned this area well, that is something that you can tell
With two willow trees just out back,
And the dainty pinkish flowers out beside the road
Aspens oaks, and birches too

Your mother is an insane fluffed in the head bitch
She thought that she could be an evil dead witch
She prayed to be a devil queen bride
It was only her twisted self that lied
When you sinned now, you've died
Unresponsive your limbs, and your fingers they twitch
Which dark hall to fall down, which pathway, which, which
Oh women's work is hard to do
I can drive a truck about this big, anything under a semi rig
I can lift hard heavy weights, move them all around
I can ride a bicycle around the town, I can wear a red nose and act the clown
I can mow the graveyard, yes the lawn
I can work my ass off from dusk 'til dawn
But that women's work is hard to do

For now, I'll look forward to tomorrow, Sitting here in this rooted sorrow
It's alright 'cause I'm not so blue, It only hurts when I think of you
If you were with me what would you do?
I'd thank my God and you know that's true
Home rehabbing once more, you become the ultimate lover
It's all so clear when you discover
You give me everything I need, I'm your good time lover
A wretched hand reach out to take, with just one touch
A foreign land, unrighteous slake, So much

Happiest Man
I'm the happiest man in the world, and I just bought some shoes for $17.50
I seem to be the luckiest guy, take a look at my smooth
As I'm lookin' mighty nifty
All the mightiest weights that I've curled

One in each hand, they weigh a total fifty
And I'm the happiest man that could ever be
Even though I am known as drifty

Drunk On Love
I just got so drunk on love, yet I'm still drivin' my car
Yes I just got so drunk on love, I didn't even stop at the bar
It's pourin' from the heavens above, and I like to wink at that star
Because I got so drunk on love, and it's the highest high so far

Still Hangin'
I'm hanging onto the last strands of life
I've been here so long now, and without a wife
I reach out to the distance to pull back the strings
Enthralled with my failure and all that it brings
In hiding all virtue that clings to the truth
A trail of long shadows flows fast from my youth
I cling to a vestige of honor so true, to something I long for, I see it in you

Crabby The Winner
He was a crabby old man who gave a dirty look
He decided to pass, but when he got up to the light
There was only one thing to see, that light was red
So he sat there on his ass, maybe he had to take a pee
Then why look so sour at me, when that light finally changed
He so quickly hit the gas, he tore off down the hill
Because he always has to win, he sped out down that hill
Where all the men stand tall, and gorgeous women have a ball
Then I strut back down Avenues, yet some drivers need a clue
Dude almost hit me once again, the crosswalk counting down to ten

Be keen, don't fall, go ahead on your trip that's taken for one and all
Make a scene, hear the call shouting down the resounding echoed hall
Make the play, see it all, cut to the chase, be on that ball

With your boss, if you're into that hey, it's your loss
Yet you okayed the pay, hey check the cost
The bastard needs you, but in such a way bigger way
If he ever seems cross, then way he won't stay

Oh, you were funny 'til you got a job
So now you're working with a broom and mop
You say you'll work it, yeah it's no prob'
You're gonna scour so hard, 'til you're at the top
I say yes, and do even agree, it's all about your good attitude
So when you open your eyes, do really, really look
A tragedy of errors, yet one thing shines so bright
You've called off all darers, and stayed up to the darkness of night
No one thing will save you, it's all become a mess
Each and every facet of the maladies you once and again address
A teasing grayish overcast
Slung down around us from the sky
It threatened once again
I pray tonight that it won't last

Torn mind, tormented now with pain
As it falls upon us, we can't deny
The haunting daylight from the past den
Is it left to dark fate to now decide
Or our are we subject to affairs now so well forgotten
Now bathed and engrossed in dark facades
Through old songs we dance to abandon
Any thoughts of careless action, or misplaced wonton adulation

He's just a stoner, jonesin' for a toss lookin' for a smoke
Or tootin'bein', now just peein'
…gambles at a favored loss, chancing on a coin now tossed
Let it go, he's just a stoner, don't be afraid to
His only love is for dope, yes it's hard letting go of hope be alone
In his blindness he's seeking not, even though he thinks you're hot
It's only part, and not in the hair, although we all have some down there

I was under arrest by my bicycle, I was caught up in a button hole mess
When you live the life of Reilly
What will come to happen is anybody's guess
Oh well, it could have been a tricycle, was doing nothin' not on the dole
Dripping slowly like an icicle, building, growing as a big and empty hole
A thieving coon now on the dole, one may truly say he was on a sweeter roll
I've got a mom in Cincinatti, a wealthy uncle in Omaha
A brother in Kansas City, that's still running from the law
some trouble in South Detroit City, but I was faster on the draw
I've got a girl with a Masseratti, although it's paid for by her pa'
And an e-wife with a baby, although you'd never call her ma'

To patch up your broken life, to put it all once again in place
So to take it all away, and move on to another place
To start anew upon this day, to turn it all around with no disgrace
To open eyes to reveal truths, to start again anew
I vow today, and into night, that this is what I'll do

Highly relevant, duly prevelant, do you resent me, or rather present me
With such an obscure exclamation mark, or a Peter or a Paul
Shall we rise to the occasions or simply take the fall

When friends together shared, close moments, time was spared
For a graceful elegance, yet now love's touch slips through my fingers
Like so much of life's tortured lust, a vacant harshness still lingers
I am lost now so much out of alignment
In reaching for that gentle touch of refinement

Her pure and warmish heart made me a man I say
I struggle to maintain, with each and every gain
To the heights of premonition, in order to obtain
With the strength of many heroes, none of whom were slain
I call upon myself to perch atop the main

If you'd just knock on wood, and make those corn cakes like you should
In longing a newfound weakness, in true belonging toward the peak
For those tasty cornbread muffins I'll always search and seek

Oh where were you tonight
The kiss of your sweet scent still fills me with delight
Oh how you warmed inside my heart, with just a touch of your hot love
So swiftly folded, so deep into the night, so that you're never gone
As a milky dew bewets my cheeks, in the brisk and early dawn
In recalling your sweet face, I feel the close knit comfort
Of your gentle love's embrace
As I cling to the edge of my life's energy, I know I need you here with me
And in the silent scent of treasured memories
Bringing back a gentle spring breeze
I felt the world held something out for me
And as the tide goes rolling out to sea
Will you take my hand and carry on, and up to the hill to rest upon
A world of soft wonder that's turned around
A life of safe harbor is what I've found

A tragedy of errors, an incident of innocence
A teasing grayish overcast, slung down around us from the sky
I pray tonight that it won't last, as it falls upon us I can't deny

If you're in too tight, and not in with your boss
Who's to say what's right, or if to take a loss
Be keen don't fall, go ahead plan a trip for all

It seems so highly relevant, indeed so duly prevalent
Traumatic tragedies, tortoruos tensions, tearing at me, tear me free
From a rigid reliance on rhyming and reason
All for a fanciful strut through the seasons
And for fractured families with fortuitous factions

It was pissing out rain from a dead gray sky
In your darkest fantasies you'll stay so dry
It seems the world has more for me, it's turned around now I can see
Strewn like shells across the beach, so many things seem out of reach
I felt the sun would always shine, into my world to grace in kind

So deal it good in ones, while I'll be sitting in the sun
While I tip the girls as they go walking right on by, but just for fun
I'll modify my hairdo, and make it look so punk,
So that I cast dark shadows, though even when I'm drunk

In my crippled state of mind, all my tortured thoughts combine
As I reach for silver lined clouds, down from heaven they dimly shine
A wretched twisting not sublime, a faltering fate now lost to time
As I walk away from dread, I see the truthful twists instead

Thirteen nutty bitches sitting 'neath a tree,
you know you didn't want much innocence from me
look again look only sideways, it's in your family tree
Just don't come looking back here, looking back for me

Sitting on the edge of a low flat tub, I had decided to take a bit of rub-a-dub
Upon rising up to turn and dip, my crutch got caught causing me to trip
I lost my mind for a good nine days, I still feel uneasy with a misty haze
So if I ask you if we've ever met, well then I'm sure it's true
You surely know and you can bet, that I remember you

Delirium
Out to this frantic state of delirium, not that I intended at all to worry 'em
I marched so bold and into something, yet now I find (I'm way back in)
A frantic state of delirium, so now there's no need to hurry 'em
I brought it on with a fevered gusto, and now I'm spent in

I thought I had to go, yet it was just my heavy heart
Since things failed to come about, should I make another start
I feel strongly either way, and it's tearing at my mind

The perfume of sweetness still lingered on my lips
'Twas that of emotional longing, not for fingers nor for hips

I'll need one box for spices, and one just for nuts
And I'll need this other one here, just because I'm a klutz
When I drop things so often they fall on my feet
Steel toes are the fashion, I shan't be discreet

My Forefather
In 1662 my forefather sailed the ocean blue,
On to Barbados, oh yes it's true
In 50 years, and no less, they discovered that such poor terrain
Sucked so bad for that sugar cane, even though came across
From the coast of Spain, a resounding echo in the pouring rain
In five years time he had hit the main,
Working hard on a farm, yes once again
Pouring softly from above, a saturating liquid
A quickly zooming dove, the encompassing fluid
A runoff from a shove, a cold hard reaction
Received without love, in losing my traction and dropping my glove

Not merely a mystic fortune man, something more than this is what I am
There's often some darkness in what I see
Yet a bright tomorrow for you will see
Hold on dearly and not just to me, our sacred bonding does set us free
Cling to the fortune of bright yesterdays
Yet moving in motion in innocent ways

Oh, oh, oh he took me to heaven, but in a flat boat
And when I got off, I quickly started to float
To my surprise now what did I see, ten Holy Angels flying nearer unto me
I was off to the side and began to deep wade
When I started to fall deep into the sea
This is no mere dress rehearsal, there can be no return, reversal
The time is now don't strike in vain, it's now to lose to lose or gain
When I'm looking back to a time, so sad forlorn and forgotten

But then I feel you holding on, and I'm seeing a bright new day
It's your love that gets me through
But then I see it's so wrong, I can't take back my crime
It gets wrapped up in this song, lying so gently in rhyme
Yet there I feel you once again, your strength girl goes on and on
Too much nearer to the sun, time to land the journey's done
The deeper, farther that you got, the keenly clearer will know
That mortal man held gravity, bounds us to the ground
An ancient myth, a travesty, it seems like woes abound

Oh ooh ooh she was Little Miss Lou
A special girl to make an impression you
She just a country girl yet so refined, see her spin and twirl with grind
With her young look and cute smile, I'll make her mine then after awhile
We'll stroll around in such elegant style, just for her I'd go an extra mile
Yes, I finally know what love's all about
It's so intense and dramatic she's left no doubt
I'm a man today yes that's for sure
He sweetness flows and runs so pure
Such goodness now is in my heart
'Though that rockin' band sure did their part
Ooh, ooh, ooh, my very own sweet Little Miss Lou, she'd even do some
fishin' yes that's with you
Just like a city girl she's so refined
Before too long I'm gonna' make her mine
With her adultish look and that sassy smile
Oh she'll be just mine then in a while
For whatever ails me yes she's the cure
Whether old or young yes that's for sure
Her great, grand goodness is now in my heart
'Though that rockin' band sure did their part

The Id, The Ego
Don't look in the door, I don't want a witness any more
Of these abhorrent scenes, of a decadent's dreams
There'll be no more abhorrent dreams, filled with decadent scenes

'oh my pen' you'll say, well it's run away with your mind again
All dressed up like porcelain dolls
Daintily painted ladies hang from your hallway walls
Suspended laminations decorate your gaudy balls
Fall now the fragmented mask
Crash, crash, crass, it's only you who fall from grace
So hidden now the plaster scene's fade
From a culture shock and a cold embrace
Slithering gilded all dressed up in lace, tall white lights so patternly showed

I

I gather now to reap what's sown, bringing to a place I once called home
Pick up the day to find alone, I'm not lost but on the way
A manager a suffragette, good carpenter with nails to set

II

And as the frittered culture of America hides, what belies the grief beneath
The littered clutter's sheath, belies the lies and hides in time
What's just behind the teeth, the truth maligned in disbelief
It's all hiding underneath, a velvet robe of darkness
Masks the shiny steel of blades, and those enemies we've made
On bottom dollar dreams we trade, twinkled metal in the twilight's fade
A song a joyous jester's serenade, enlivens those who've made the grade
To gather 'round or contemplate, and bask beneath the silver moon
Resounding breaths of red hot sex, we'll drink julep tea 'til noon
As a velvet robe of darkness covers what we feel
In stealth to hide and lie behind
A lover's warm relief, a live presence transcends amends
Engrossed by how we've grown, a child rises up in falconed skies
To rear it's pretty head

III

Little ivy lambsydivey, so contrived and well conniving
Skipped another rock to sea to see, jarring jimmies jacked up jammies
So soaked in rain they came from Spain, then in an hour or a day or two
In Raena's tower are wilting flowers, so she'll throw some down for you

But the Cutie Katies can't be kept waiting, so lilting ladies and Lillian fradies
Cast their marks as they come now for you
Oh yes they'll come as they come for you
And you and you and you, with mettle Mongols mighty monsters
And neutral granny gangster's gazes, offered to only just a few

IV

As the fantastic frames of featureless dames
Dangle down to drop new famous names
Just furrows fastened forward, to find direction in their claims
To fortune and a dance divinely, while talking oh so kindly
As my pants are binding, my style is unwinding
Oh boy this girl is cute
Through fun delirious day games, to know a love that's without shame
We'll drink it in from a boot
Now up to candled catwalks, in contoured contrasted and well conjured night
With castles now calling to colored black coffins
Cambric creations for such close relations
A gallium gemmed and gargoyled gateway
Welcomes those that dare move through
To ring on through belfries those loud wailing reveilles
And pompous roasted toasts of ballyhoo
Brought on by beacons burning so brightly
That shine on towards deep in the night

V

Memories of warm and sleek surrender
So warm with charm so meek and tender
To let it go as fall is leaving, in twisted time the hands bereaved
With the barrister and the court deceived, a failed judgment I'll take my leave
In shadowed hour a darkened grief, so soon forgotten and now deceased
Such paled memories do soon fade, now forgotten and deceased

VI

When carbonless shadows come to life and take form

A swing from the gallows, a stray from the norm

A penny to wish for a favor to sell

A quick run for the gauntlet another to throw

An answer too swift for the asker to know

A kiss in the darkness now rends us apart

So that a poisonous love brings such death from the start

VII

'Tis the stature of man more than anything

And the glow of his altruistic eminence

That speaks to a woman evoking admiration

And respect lifting and embracing us all

And so the waist of a woman the same the distraction of the hips

The finer sheen the strands of hair

The fairer of the face all re-extend the dimensions of love

For a man trembles in his weakness

To take it all in as so he waits he listens then noticing

The nuance of speech of fluid grand mannerisms

In such a helpless state she is his to be absorbed into the psyche

To be finely wined and analyzed

With he of worthy character her intentions now are locked

He will search his own subconscious

For any red flags popping up, of any warning signals now shouting out

As none are present his protective mechanisms subside

They meet, they chat exchanging thoughts

They come together now as one

VIII

It's one hour 'til the drill, I'd better bite down on the pill

One hour 'til the drill fills with lightening, it's oh so very frightening

I've gotta' take it like a man, I always take it like I can

It's just one hour until I spill, then start oozing with a chill

Just one hour 'til the drill, better bite down on that pill

Well now I really know, 'cause my dentist told me so

"If you expect such brilliant whitening, no extractions crowns just whitening
You'd better give a bit of help, or let out a little yelp
So he'll ease up on the force, yet he'll be right back down of course
(of course, of course, of course)
He's just as fast as lightning, oh my it is so frightening
He'll extract my very root, and offer up a well-crowned tooth
Just ream a boat down my canal, yet I'll take it just like a good pal
Because I know that in the end, I'll have a pretty smile

IX

Now reunited at the table set, both for kin and those I've never met
Befitting knights shine on through all, as one from beyond the voices call
In being steadfastly free from all desire, a burning guidance to feed the fire
No failing fault nor lightening bright, shall hinder justice and what is right
From deep around where timbers reach
Near wooded edge where the shadows breach
Out now past a woodland scene, scampering out to meadow's green
Such high platitudes were seldom found
While seeking out the hallowed ground

X

Dove headlong from a rocky peak, to venture through strange worlds I seek
(May I be so bold, for I am of tradition)
Reaching out now swept away, clouds obscure an essence of today
Now that things show clearer, the game has seemed to change
Sleek enemies grow nearer, well past time to rearrange
Falling back now regaining sight, no other men can feel my plight
New strategies have come to me, played well off some far fantasy
In twists of time and turning fate, impassioned rhymes I need relate
A call to glory for gladdened arms, a fabled story with soothing charms
(But wait)
New smoke clouds obscure the essence of today
With people reaching out but from oh so faraway
It's so my life seems dearer, and yet the game is never won

A new strategy has come to me, still reeling from strange fantasy
As fastened chimes so true relate, the twist of time and burning fate
As new dust clouds obscure the essence of today

XI

As the raging defeats at my veins
Hide my feeling inside while taking great pains
To shut out such dark wild fright, so deeply concealed on this frigid of nights
This physical torment burns slow, in my knowledge of light does now show
With broken dreams and shattered limbs, I resign in my recliner
So near the edge of what it seems, 'twas tragic not so minor
I regain my grasp of elemental transformations
As I reach to clasp

Printed in the USA
CPSIA information can be obtained
at www.ICGtesting.com
LVHW010748310524
781341LV00001B/3